Colorblind Tools

Critical Insurgencies
A Book Series of the Critical Ethnic Studies Association

Series Editors: Jodi A. Byrd and Michelle M. Wright

Critical Insurgencies features activists and scholars, as well as artists and other media makers, who forge new theoretical and political practices that unsettle the nation-state, neoliberalism, carcerality, settler colonialism, Western hegemony, legacies of slavery, colonial racial formations, gender binaries, and ableism, and challenge all forms of oppression and state violence through generative future imaginings.

About CESA The Critical Ethnic Studies Association organizes projects and programs that engage ethnic studies while reimagining its futures. Grounded in multiple activist formations within and outside institutional spaces, CESA aims to develop an approach to intellectual and political projects animated by the spirit of decolonial, antiracist, antisexist, and other global liberationist movements. These movements enabled the creation of ethnic studies and continue to inform its political and intellectual projects.

www.criticalethnicstudies.org

Colorblind Tools

Global Technologies of Racial Power

Marzia Milazzo

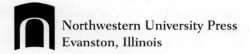
Northwestern University Press
Evanston, Illinois

Northwestern University Press
www.nupress.northwestern.edu

Copyright © 2022 by Northwestern University Press. Published 2022.
All rights reserved.

10   9   8   7   6   5   4   3   2   1

Library of Congress Cataloging-in-Publication Data

Names: Milazzo, Marzia, author.
Title: Colorblind tools : global technologies of racial power / Marzia Milazzo.
Other titles: Critical insurgencies.
Description: Evanston : Northwestern University Press, 2022. | Series:
    Critical insurgencies | Includes bibliographical references and index.
Identifiers: LCCN 2022027627 | ISBN 9780810145269 (paperback) |
    ISBN 9780810145276 (cloth) | ISBN 9780810145283 (ebook)
Subjects: LCSH: Post–racialism. | Racism—History. | Race in literature.
Classification: LCC HT1523 .M549 2022 | DDC 305.8—dc23/eng/20220613
LC record available at https://lccn.loc.gov/2022027627

per i miei genitori, Concetta e Francesco
e per i miei fratelli, Mattia e Mario

In liebevoller Erinnerung an
Katharina Czerwinski

If you stick a knife in my back nine inches and pull it out six inches, there's no progress. If you pull it all the way out, that's not progress. Progress is healing the wound that the blow made; and they haven't even begun to pull the knife out, much less heal the wound. They won't even admit the knife is there.

—Malcolm X

CONTENTS

Introduction. The Master's Colorblind Tools   1

Part 1. The Making of White Nations

1.   Colorblindness and Nation Building   57

2.   Mestizaje and Racial Genocide   81

Part 2. The Ongoing Race to Silence Race

3.   The White Mobilization against Desegregation
and Redistribution   129

4.   The Perils of White "Antiracism"   161

Part 3. Decolonial Imaginaries and Colorblind Logics

5.   Espousing Liberal Individualism in Cubena's Work   189

6.   Encountering the Other in Chicana Literature   221

Epilogue. An Undying Colonialism   261

Acknowledgments   269

Notes   275

Bibliography   325

Index   365

INTRODUCTION

The Master's Colorblind Tools

Europe has force-fed us with lies and bloated us with pestilence.
  —Aimé Césaire, *Notebook of a Return to the Native Land*

Racism bloats and disfigures the face of the culture that practices it.
Literature, the plastic arts, songs for shopgirls, proverbs, habits, patterns,
whether they set out to attack it or to vulgarize it, restore racism. This means
that a social group, a country, a civilization, cannot be unconsciously racist.
  —Frantz Fanon, "Racism and Culture"

"Race," therefore, travels: while we are confronted, from time to time, with
almost-evidence that the age of the postrace subject is upon us, we are just
as certain that its efficacies can, and do, move from one position to another
and back again.
  —Hortense J. Spillers, "'All the Things You Could Be by Now, If
    Sigmund Freud's Wife Was Your Mother': Psychoanalysis and Race"

Justo Jaén left the house to meet his friends on October 5, 1934, as he
had done many times before. A seventeen-year-old Black teenager, Jaén
that Friday headed to socialize on the beach in his hometown of Colón,
a city near the Panama Canal Zone that was home to a large West Indian
community.[1] He never returned home. While Jaén was playing cards in
a shack near the waterfront, the chief of police, a white man called José
Vicente Delgado, shot him in the head in a gratuitous act of anti-Black
violence and then continued to walk free and unpunished. The murder
sparked an uprising in the city as thousands of people demanded justice for Jaén. Mass mobilization eventually led to Delgado's arrest, but

1

he was soon acquitted in February 1935, despite the fact that, just two years earlier, Delgado had been indicted for abuse of authority and illegal arrests.[2] Crucial for the acquittal was the racist argument couched in colorblind language advanced by Delgado's defense, who criminalized Jaén, arguing that he was gambling and smoking marijuana, and depicted Colón as a city drowning in crime caused by "West Indian delinquents without work," the "damned heritage of the Canal construction."[3] That Justo Jaén was not West Indian did not come to matter in court. Criminalizing West Indian immigrants was a deliberate tactic that the defense deployed to deflect attention away from Delgado's racism and exploit the anti-Black sentiments of the jury, all without risking the accusation of racism against himself.

In using this strategy, Delgado's defense could rely on Panama's dominant racist discourse, which had established that the "antagonism against the West Indians was not racial but *cultural*."[4] The white disavowal of racism in early twentieth-century Panama, to which I will return in chapter 1, served crucial socioeconomic and political functions. With the aim to hinder alliances between local workers and West Indian immigrants, who represented the main workforce in the Canal Zone and were at the forefront of the labor movement, the white Panamanian elite branded West Indians as threats to national security, the interests of the working classes, and the Panamanian way of life. In the process, the Panamanian intelligentsia argued that their hostility against West Indians had nothing to do with racism. The white Panamanian ruling class could not openly admit to their racism and anti-Blackness, nor to their alliance with the USAmerican imperialists who controlled the Canal Zone, without alienating Black and mestizo Panamanians, who represented the majority of the working class and unemployed poor. The project to co-opt the local population and turn it against West Indian immigrants was thus accompanied by the white disavowal of racist intent and the packaging of racist propaganda in colorblind terms as a matter of culture, religion, and national security.

On August 9, 2014, another teenager left the house never to return. Michael Brown was coming back from the corner shop with a friend in his hometown of Ferguson, Missouri, when Darren Wilson, a white police officer, killed him in a gratuitous act of anti-Black violence and then continued to walk free and unpunished. Eighteen-year-old Michael Brown was merely walking, guilty of no crime, when Wilson executed him. When Brown collapsed after having been shot at least six times, Wilson did not even try to take a pulse or call for an ambulance. Michael

THE MASTER'S COLORBLIND TOOLS

Brown's body was left to lie on the street for four hours and was then removed in an SUV, not in an ambulance, and only after a protesting crowd prevented the police from putting the body in the trunk of a car.[5] The deliberate dehumanization of Michael Brown did not end the day of his murder. In his testimony, Wilson described him as a "demon" and "Hulk Hogan."[6] The media also quickly revealed that Michael Brown had THC in his body, indicating marijuana use. This irrelevant detail was exploited in court, where Wilson argued that Brown had attacked him, and the defense suggested that smoking marijuana caused Brown to have a violent psychotic episode. That smoking marijuana does not cause violent behavior, that Wilson was armed while Michael Brown was not, that Wilson had no bruises that could indicate an attack, and that he first refused to go to the hospital because, well, he was not injured, these facts were not made to count in court.[7] Michael Brown, the victim, was put on trial. Darren Wilson, the murderer, walked free.

Both Delgado and Wilson were chasing their victims when they murdered them. When asked why they did so, Delgado's lawyer and Wilson gave an eerily similar response. In chasing Justo Jaén, the defense argued, Delgado was "only performing his duty of protecting the 'interests of the honest people.'"[8] Asked why he ran after Michael Brown instead of staying in his car, Wilson contended, "that's what we were trained to do."[9] Mobilizing an epistemology of disavowal, Wilson insisted that racism had nothing to do with the murder. "You can't perform the duties of a police officer and have racism in you," he said. "I help people. That's my job."[10] In this way, both Delgado's defense and Wilson reproduced the persistent racist argument that, even when white cops murder innocent Black people, "they are simply people working a job."[11] In both cases, the outcome of the farce called trial was white impunity facilitated through the systematic disavowal of anti-Black racism and the demonization of the victims. Fred Moten and Stefano Harney denounce this reversal tactic as follows: "The prosecution of Michael Brown, which is the proper technical name for the grand jury investigation of Darren Wilson, the drone, is what our day in court looks like and always has."[12] This is nothing new, Moten and Harney remind us. Nothing new, the spirit of Justo Jaén echoes from the otherworld.

The striking parallels between the murders of Justo Jaén and Michael Brown, perpetrated eighty years and over five thousand kilometers apart, are not accidental. They exist because the white violence inflicted upon Black people is not localized and exceptional, but the enduring norm in the anti-Black world. In the wake of the brutal lynching of

George Floyd at the hands of white cop Derek Chauvin and his three police accomplices in Minneapolis on May 25, 2020, millions of people took to the streets to protest state-sanctioned racist violence not just in the United States, but also in Brazil, Mexico, France, Italy, the United Kingdom, South Africa, Australia, New Zealand, and many other places around the world.[13] While the localized modes of anti-Black violence may differ, the global fact of anti-Black violence remains constant. This is so because police terror against Black people exists within a global white supremacist system of which the police are only one symptom.

Anti-Black police violence in the United States is routinely followed by a pattern of mystifying explanations, including arguments that the police are not doing their job, need better training, or act out of fear. These arguments suggest that the police were created to protect and serve everyone. Yet the US police force was created specifically to protect and serve white people, white property, and, ultimately, white power.[14] When white US police kill Black people, they *are* doing the job that they were created to do. Black abolitionist activists and intellectuals have long argued that the police cannot be reformed but must be abolished. They also teach us that police abolition cannot be understood in isolation and outside the necessity to abolish prisons and the state.[15] Afropessimist thinkers push us to go even further, arguing that what is needed is nothing less than bringing forth "the End of the world" that Aimé Césaire invokes in *Notebook of a Return to the Native Land* and continuing to build, in Frank B. Wilderson's terms, "a movement toward something so blindingly new that it cannot be imagined."[16] They also invite us to think about anti-Black police violence outside the trope of fear. Discussions about white police killing Black people because of fear effectively disguise, as Wilderson writes, "the jouissance that constitutes the violence of anti-Blackness."[17] White police officers murder Black people because they *enjoy* doing so and because white supremacy—"the unnamed political system that has made the world what it is today"[18]—makes it possible for white people to live out our genocidal fantasies with impunity.

Such a formidable system structured in death does not sustain itself on brute violence alone. It requires an equally deadly, structural, and global discursive infrastructure. Time and geography thus dissolve in the face of the persistence of anti-Black violence *and* the arguments deployed to rationalize and uphold it. In other words, just as the murders of Justo Jaén and Michael Brown are not isolated cases, so are the parallels between the arguments used to absolve the white police officers who murdered them not accidental. These arguments belong to a global arsenal of strategies that white people have long systematically deployed to concurrently silence *and* reproduce structural racism and, literally, get away with murder. As shall become clear, the fact that some Black people and people of color also deploy some of these strategies does not make the arsenal any less white. Neither does it dislodge white people from being the principal deployers, chief protectors, and ultimate beneficiaries of the armory. This arsenal, its functions, its institutionalization, its intrinsic anti-Blackness, its continuity from the Americas to South Africa, and from the inception of colonial modernity to the present, is one subject of this book. The task is to demonstrate how racism reproduces itself through disavowal, disguise, and cosmetic change, while the substance of anti-Blackness remains constant.

The starting point for this study is the recognition that military power, biological warfare, and the control of the state and economy have not functioned alone in securing white people's long-standing global economic, political, and social dominance. Also indispensable have been the concurrent invention, deployment, and institutionalization of mechanisms that serve to hide white people's rapacious intentions and mask the modes of white domination. Whether in the form of an investment in its own invisibility or a chameleonic ability for adaptation, camouflage is a structural element of racism. Spectacular police violence itself operates as camouflage as it masks the everyday terror of racial profiling, police contempt, and the de facto occupation of Black neighborhoods.[19] In Huey P. Newton's words, "Black people desire to determine their own destiny. As a result, they are constantly inflicted with brutality from the occupying army, embodied by the police department."[20] This occupation is an enduring fact that the US state seeks to conceal.

Camouflage, of course, is a constituent of power at large. Michel Foucault contends that "power is tolerable only on condition that it masks a substantial part of itself. Its success is proportional to its ability to hide its own mechanisms."[21] As the foremost instantiation of power in the modern world (a fact that Foucault disavows), racial power is contingent on disguise for its reproduction.[22] Providing crucial insights into the workings of racism, Cedric J. Robinson writes in *Forgeries of Memory and Meaning*:

> Racial regimes are constructed social systems in which race
> is proposed as a justification for the relations of power. While

> necessarily articulated with accruals of power, the covering conceit of a racial regime is a makeshift patchwork masquerading as memory and the immutable. Nevertheless, racial regimes do possess history, that is, discernible origins and mechanisms of assembly. But racial regimes are unrelentingly hostile to their exhibition.[23]

Robinson calls attention to how racial regimes operate in a certain secrecy, how they are "unrelentingly hostile to their exhibition." In emphasizing the *unrelenting* character of this hostility, Robinson calls attention to its structural nature. The antipathy of racial regimes toward the exposure of their "origins and mechanisms of assembly" is not accidental, Robinson writes, but exists "because a discoverable history is incompatible with a racial regime and from the realization that, paradoxically, so are its social relations."[24] Through the deployment of "mythic discourses," racial regimes parade as natural and inevitable, while they are actually the constructed and mutable product of sociopolitical and cultural powers that work inexorably to maintain them.[25] Exposing the workings of racism poses a serious threat to global white interests and, for this reason, racism is constantly in hiding.

If, then, the murder of Black teenager Justo Jaén at the hands of white police officer José Vicente Delgado, the arguments that Delgado's defense deployed to win the case, and the racial disavowal and seeming "cultural racism" of the white elite in early twentieth-century Panama remind us of what scholars have described as a new era of colorblind racism or termed "the dominant form of racism today,"[26] it is because colorblindness is neither new, nor an era, nor a form of racism, but is constitutive of racism itself. Colorblindness is the engine of the white supremacist machine, a necessary weapon for the reproduction of racial power. Colorblindness is much more than a simple auxiliary of anti-Blackness and white supremacy: it is a tool that the master cannot do without.

Colorblind Tools: Global Technologies of Racial Power takes seriously Robinson's concern with the unrelenting hostility of racial regimes to the revelation of their historical contingency and modes of operation. Through the study of texts across genres and disciplines produced in Brazil, Cuba, Mexico, Panama, the United States, and South Africa, I examine colorblindness as a technology, a discourse, an epistemology, and a legal doctrine that serves to naturalize and render permanent what W. E. B. Du Bois in *The Souls of Black Folk* describes as "the

THE MASTER'S COLORBLIND TOOLS   7

color-line,—the relation of the darker races to the lighter races of men in Asia and Africa, in America and the islands of the sea."[27] Colorblindness is not a temporally circumscribed subtype of racism, I argue, but a constitutive technology of white supremacy that is global, structural, inherently anti-Black, and centrally indebted to colonial discourse and the liberal humanism of colonial modernity. It thus follows that it can only be understood by centering anti-Blackness and colonialism—and without subsuming the former under the latter.[28]

In understanding colorblindness as a tool that depends on other tools in turn, I am indebted to Audre Lorde, who in her well-known talk "The Master's Tools Will Never Dismantle the Master's House" critiqued white feminists for employing the same strategies as patriarchy. Observing that she was one of only two Black women invited to the 1979 Second Sex Conference, Lorde rejected claims of innocence that invoke ignorance ("We did not know who to ask") and instead held white women accountable for reproducing racist and sexist structures of domination.[29] Unavoidably informed by my lived experiences and positionality as a white European cisgender woman, this book recognizes that, far from being innocent bystanders, white women are central agents of white supremacy, perfectly capable of inhabiting the position of the master, a term that I employ to include white women so as to signal that "the mistress is not a subset of the master,"[30] but rather "the master's equivalent."[31] The claim of ignorance, I also recognize, is itself a colorblind tool that white people deploy to relieve ourselves from responsibility for upholding the racist status quo.

The *Oxford English Dictionary* defines a tool as "a device or implement, especially one held in the hand, used to carry out a particular function" and as "a thing used to help perform a job." The word tool derives from the Old English *tōl*, which means "instrument, implement used by a craftsman or laborer, weapon." A tool, then, is an object that is in use and serves a specific function. A tool is what is *at work*, for a tool that is not operative is not a tool, but a fossil. As an instrument or weapon, a tool is by definition a means to a larger end. It thus presupposes an agent, someone actively deploying the tool for their advantage. White people, I aim to demonstrate in this book, deliberately disavow racism and deploy colorblind language on a global scale to hide white power, demobilize Black resistance, halt intraracial organizing, and impede desegregation and redistribution measures. If we follow the commonsense understanding of the word colorblind as meaning "not seeing race," the term *colorblind tools* appears as an oxymoron. And this

8   INTRODUCTION

is precisely the point as I aim to dislodge the term colorblind(ness) from its popular usage to emphasize that not seeing race is impossible in a racialized world. The project of white supremacy, I contend, depends not on producing a blindness to color (which is a misnomer and impossibility), but on creating a system in which lies are institutionalized, made to appear unquestionable truths, and mobilized for the protection of whiteness.

Brazil, Cuba, Mexico, Panama, the United States, and South Africa are the main foci of this study because these locales allow me to illustrate the reaches of colorblindness across different histories, racial regimes, cultures, and languages. However, I do not intend to suggest that colorblindness, whether as a technology or discourse, is only operative in these locales. Scholars have identified the deployment of colorblind discourse on the part of white people in numerous other places around the world, including Australia, Canada, and New Zealand.[32] Here, I will also touch upon the workings of racism and colorblindness in Italy. I use the term *global* in the title of this book not to reproduce imperial logics, but to emphasize that colorblindness is structural, rather than localized, so that it transcends national borders and racial regimes. The specific contexts I engage are nonetheless particularly instructive. Considered to embody three archetypal racial systems, the United States (Jim Crow), South Africa (apartheid), and Brazil (racial democracy) have long been privileged sites for the comparative and relational study of racism, particularly in history and the social sciences.[33] While scholars have often approached these countries as embodying fundamental differences in how racism operates at the level of the state, the law, and ideology, I investigate connections and interactions between these sites—and others, such as Panama, that remain understudied—to demonstrate that white people share strategies across borders and racial regimes with the aim of maintaining power.

Instead of assuming that the nation-state is a self-contained entity that fully determines racial structures and ideologies at the local level, I privilege a relational approach to the study of racism that makes visible how local racial conditions, practices, and ideas are informed by those developed elsewhere and inform these in turn.[34] In the process, I challenge the argument that ideologies of racial mixture (which are dominant in Brazil, Colombia, Cuba, Mexico, Panama, and other Latin American countries) and ideologies of racial purity (which are generally associated with Europe, the United States, and South Africa) are incompatible or in competition with each other. Rather, white people work together

THE MASTER'S COLORBLIND TOOLS

across ideological and national boundaries to uphold white supremacy. In chapter 2, for example, I show how Mexican philosopher and politician José Vasconcelos offered mestizaje (racial mixture) as a eugenic solution to his US colleagues at the University of Chicago and how Brazilian anthropologist Gilberto Freyre similarly recommended that white people in South Africa and elsewhere should adopt mestiçagem to stymie Black resistance and maintain power in the African colonies. Looking across time and national borders demonstrates that colorblindness is modulated through national *and* transnational forces that reveal an enduring white investment in maintaining power—globally.

In this book, I historicize colorblindness as a technology, foreground its institutionalization, and examine the rhetorical strategies that structure it as a discourse. In doing so, I build on Robinson, who understands the history of racial regimes as encompassing *both* "discernible origins *and* mechanisms of assembly," and who emphasizes the crucial role that "mythic discourses" play in naturalizing and reproducing the racist infrastructure.[35] White power, I contend, relies on seemingly countless *colorblind tools*, which I describe as technologies, mechanisms, and strategies that, at once, dissimulate, naturalize, and reproduce white domination. The European invention of race can itself be understood as a primary colorblind tool given that race is a foundational technology of white supremacy grounded in an epistemology of disavowal that naturalizes and reproduces white dominance, a fact to which I will return in the second part of this introduction. But the reproduction of white supremacy also depends on seemingly more innocent, yet no less lethal, colorblind tools that manifest themselves as patterns of thought, "mythic discourses," and a vast number of rhetorical, argumentative, representational, and narrative strategies that always sustain racialized sociopolitical and economic systems of power.

Understanding the rhetorical moves and mechanisms that structure colorblindness as a discourse and revealing their transnational patterns is important for challenging racism. Critical race scholars have shown that the power of colorblind arguments is not dependent on their brilliance or originality. Neither are colorblind arguments effective because they are based on hard facts or logical reasoning. Rather, the power of most arguments that enforce colorblindness depends on the racialized positionality of the person or institution that reproduces them and on the capacity of these arguments to portray as progressive what is regressive, as discriminatory what is meant to challenge discrimination, and package colorblind logics under the disguise of common sense.

Certainly, colorblindness is not merely a discourse and much less a collection of rhetorical strategies. It is not a conglomeration of lies and misconceptions that, to cite Edward Said, "were the truth about them be told, would simply blow away."[36] Neither the lived realities of everyday racism that Black people and people of color experience, nor the large and unrefuted body of scholarship demonstrating the effects of racial inequality have managed to halt the power of colorblind arguments. There are structural reasons for this fact. Hortense J. Spillers's warning against understanding race merely as a metaphor is relevant here. Spillers writes that "'race' is not *simply* a metaphor and nothing more; it is the outcome of a politics. For one to mistake it is to be politically stupid and endangered."[37] Colorblindness, too, "is the outcome of a politics." It is, like race itself, a technology. To understand the implications of this argument, consider the explanation "I was afraid," which white police officers regularly deploy in US courts to justify murdering innocent Black people. White killer cops say that they are afraid of Black people not because they are actually afraid, but because *Graham v. Connor* (1989) has rendered fear a justifiable reason for killing someone, making it almost impossible for US police to be convicted of murder.[38] It thus makes sense that Darren Wilson argued that he killed Michael Brown because he was afraid, even though he followed Brown and shot him in the back.[39] The legal and political mechanisms that render the colorblind tool "I was afraid" an instrument of racial terror for Black people and an instrument of exoneration for white people are merely one example of how colorblindness is "the outcome of a politics." Many critical race scholars have demonstrated that colorblindness is institutionalized in the law, academia, and the media.[40] I build on this important work, which has mainly focused on the US context and the post–Civil Rights era, to reveal how colorblindness is institutionalized across time and national borders.

Colorblind Tools examines an eclectic body of texts, including academic scholarship across multiple disciplines in the humanities and socials sciences, political pamphlets, legal documents, speeches, journalism, novels, short stories, poetry, and drama. While the scholarly and legal production of knowledge is a main concern of this book, I recognize that imaginative literature is central to the social managing of racial difference.[41] As an analysis of everyday life, literature in a narrow sense is also a key site in which marginalized people have developed powerful critiques of the racist status quo. I closely examine individual texts rather than opting for distant modes of reading because, as Paula

THE MASTER'S COLORBLIND TOOLS   11

Moya writes, it is "via the individual text that literature is a sensitive indicator of the ideological underpinnings of human existence."[42] Literary works, of course, are not unmediated reflections of reality, but arbitrate an author's knowledges, desires, hopes, and dreams. In offering imagined resolutions to "real conditions of existence,"[43] literary works always exist in the realm of the ideological. Precisely because they may appear ideologically innocent, imaginative texts carry out ideological work especially effectively.

In the third part of this book, I examine literary works by West Indian Panamanian writer Cubena (chapter 5) and Chicana feminist writers Graciela Limón and Cherríe Moraga (chapter 6) to show that colorblindness can leave even some decolonial imaginaries riddled with contradictions.[44] The literary works I examine are crucial sites of theorization and depositories of knowledge not only about specific antiracist epistemologies and ontologies, but also about colorblindness itself and its far-reaching implications. These works provide a crucial lens into how colorblindness cannot be separated from colonial logics and liberal humanism. In the process, they demand that we pay attention to what Savannah Shange calls "the continuities between racism and antiracism, allowing us to disentangle intention from impact."[45] As they bring into stark relief how colorblindness and anti-Blackness are intertwined, the imaginative texts studied herein show that anti-Blackness can be reproduced even within radical decolonial works by non-Black writers of color (as well as by Black writers themselves through a commitment to liberal humanism). In this way, they support Afropessimist readings of anti-Blackness as configuring the social location and identity formation of all non-Black people, a fact encapsulated in Wilderson's statement that "the structure of the entire world's semantic field . . . is sutured by anti-Black solidarity."[46] Anti-Blackness is the constant that never fails to appear in the numerous works I examine in this book.

Radical artists and intellectuals committed to challenging the racist status quo constantly redeploy the master's tools and put them at the service of liberation. Lesego Rampolokeng points to this fact in "Rapmaster," where he writes, "i only shoot the british / with the bullets that are english,"[47] a reference to the imperative to use the colonial language against the colonizer. In examining how colorblindness can intrude in decolonial literary imaginaries by Black writers and writers of color I do not intend to share the blame. Neither do I pretend to answer the question of whether, to return to Lorde's metaphor, the master's tools can dismantle the master's house. In fact, I cannot do so. Much more

12   INTRODUCTION

modestly, I show that, when it comes specifically to colorblindness—a
tool that is *built into* the very foundations of the master's house—the
attempt to use it against the master threatens a work's antiracist politics.

Inspired by Césaire's query—"what, fundamentally, is colonization?"[48]—
this book, then, asks: What, fundamentally, is colorblindness? As it turns
out, these are not two separate questions as colonization and colorblindness are inextricably linked. And yet, scholars have often overlooked this
link. The dominant scholarly consensus is instead embodied by Naomi
Murakawa's statement that "the problem of the twenty-first century is
the problem of colorblindness."[49] Numerous other scholars across disciplinary boundaries have similarly argued that colorblindness is a recent
phenomenon. Postulating a fundamental shift in racial dynamics since
the post–World War II and post–Civil Rights formal demise of racial dictatorships, they have contended that racism today is radically different
from racism in the past, to the extent that it has been termed *the* new
racism, so that newness is turned into a constitutive element of racism
and the disavowal thereof into a trick of the last fifty years.[50]

A vast body of scholarship on racism produced since the 1950s, and
increasingly since the 1980s, is shaped by a paradox. Even as scholars argue that the official end of colonialism, World War II, the Civil
Rights Movement, or the formal dismantlement of apartheid did not
end institutional racism, they are routinely invested in theorizing
change over continuity. The obsession with change that especially pervades many social-scientific studies of racism can be situated within
the ongoing perception of historical temporality in Western modernity,
which remains anchored in ideologies of linear time and progress, and
in which shifts and crises must be imagined so that they can become
objects of policy intervention.

An unspoken emphasis on change underlies the very theory of racial
formation, which Michael Omi and Howard Winant in *Racial Formation in the United States* (1986) define as "the sociohistorical process
by which racial categories are created, inhabited, transformed, and
destroyed."[51] The theory of racial formation valuably emphasizes that
race is neither biological nor fixed, but a social construction that is
mutable. What concerns me about the theory is that it has established
change as the most important category through which scholars should
examine racism.[52] Omi and Winant argue that "theoretical work on race
has not successfully grasped the *shifting* nature of racial dynamics in
the postwar U.S., a failure which sparked important challenges as postwar racial events appeared to conflict with the predictions of theory."[53]

THE MASTER'S COLORBLIND TOOLS   13

According to Omi and Winant, racism in the United States has taken a dramatic turn since World War II and colorblindness is an expression of this turn. Implicit in the theory of racial formation, then, is a call for examining short-term changes in racial dynamics rather than considering the longue durée of slavery and colonialism.

This dominant theoretical commitment to change appears connected to a larger USAmerican academic tendency (prevalent among social scientists, but emblematic of the university more broadly) to develop the newest theory and speculate about the future, sometimes without adequately contending with the past or the complexities of racial dynamics outside the US context. These inclinations are visible, for example, in Eduardo Bonilla-Silva's Latin Americanization thesis, which argues that the US biracial order (whites versus the rest) is slowly transforming into a triracial system (with white people on top, a group of "honorary whites" in the middle, and Black people at the bottom) so that US race relations *will* soon resemble those of Latin American nations.[54] The practice of predicting the future without attending to the past is not confined to sociology. In *The Future of Whiteness* (2015), philosopher Linda Martín Alcoff also fails to consider the long fetch of history and the transnational workings of racism. Worryingly, Alcoff argues that the privileges of whiteness are eroding in the United States and that "the context of use for whiteness has changed to such an extent that white identity can be a disadvantage in some specific situations."[55] Both Bonilla-Silva's Latin Americanization thesis and Alcoff's future of whiteness thesis are grounded in the assumption that impending shifts in US racial demographics, particularly the fact that white people will soon be a numerical minority, will lead to significant changes in racial structure. The case of South Africa, a country in which white people have always been a small numerical minority of the population yet continue to own the vast majority of the country's land and wealth, throws these arguments into crisis and illustrates the ongoing need for scholarly approaches to racism that are historically grounded, genuinely transnational, and continue to make visible the unrelenting—rather than shifting—power of anti-Blackness and white supremacy.

Many European and US scholars have argued that, since World War II, racism has shifted from a so-called biological racism to a cultural racism, a term largely used interchangeably with colorblind racism and new racism.[56] These scholars rarely engage Frantz Fanon's seminal essay "Racism and Culture" (1956), a lecture that Fanon delivered in Paris at the First Congress of Negro Writers. This omission

14 INTRODUCTION

is striking since in this work Fanon already argued that, concomitant with a change in the means of production, there has been a shift from an "old-fashioned" racism grounded in biological arguments toward a modern "cultural racism."[57] Fanon conceives "old-fashioned" racism as a "vulgar, primitive, over-simple racism" that "purported to find in biology—the Scriptures having proved insufficient—the material basis of the doctrine."[58] This vulgar racism precedes "cultural racism," a form of racism in which white people no longer resort to arguments about biology to justify racial stratification, but rather attack "a certain form of existing."[59] Fanon argues that "vulgar racism in its biological form corresponds to the period of crude exploitation of man's arms and legs. The perfecting of the means of production inevitably brings about the camouflage of the techniques by which man is exploited, hence of the forms of racism."[60] However, as I show in the second part of this introduction, the camouflage of racism and the demonization of "a certain form of existing" are technologies of racial power that white people have deployed since the inception of colonialism and racial slavery. Conversely, the "crude exploitation of man's arms and legs" continues today, as colonized people still disproportionately perform manual labor in the neocolonies. Neither are the "old-fashioned positions" of so-called biological racism as rare today as Fanon argues.[61] Fanon, then, also centers change as he grapples with the workings of racism in his time. He, too, argues that since World War II racism has fundamentally changed.[62] However, to his credit Fanon never argues that he is living in a new racial era, while many European and USAmerican racial theorists do.

The focus on change as a privileged mode through which scholars should understand racism conceals important continuities between the past and the present. Black radical thinkers continue to remind us that slavery is not temporally circumscribed and that change is not the most productive category for understanding racism. Moreover, Karen E. Fields and Barbara J. Fields have shown that the racist theories and ideas developed in eugenics are still alive today, even as their present-day iterations are often described as being new.[63] Colin Wayne Leach has also pushed against the notion of a new racism, showing that covert racial discrimination existed before the 1970s, while overt racism in the form of arguments about genetics or intelligence has not disappeared today.[64] In addition, David Young has argued that "racial theory was never simply scientific or biologistic."[65] While racial categories certainly undergo transformation, racism has been a constant for over five hundred years. Emphasizing shifts in racial *order* rather than continuities

THE MASTER'S COLORBLIND TOOLS

in racial *structure* can lead scholars to confuse changes in appearance with changes in substance, developing theories that risk reproducing the colorblindness that they seek to challenge.

Certainly, racial meanings are not immutable in a given society, for as Malcolm X would say, "Racism is like a Cadillac; they bring out a new model every year."[66] Racism has always taken many forms and worn many masks with chameleonic dexterity. Confronted with relentless resistance and collective mobilization by Black people and people of color, racial regimes have had to constantly transform to ensure their reproduction. Indeed, as Fanon writes, racism "has had to renew itself, to adapt itself, to change its appearance."[67] Still, the anxiety to name a current racial "model" and differentiate it from the racism of the past should give us pause. Scholars have developed a massive number of terms to describe what they perceive to be the uniqueness of racism in the post–World War II and post–Civil Rights eras: cultural racism, culturalist racism, new racism/New Racism, symbolic racism, racial biologization, aversive racism, postmodern racism, differentialist racism, laissez-faire racism, neo-racism, racial hegemony, colorblind racism, racism without racists, racisms without racism, racism without races, post-racialism, post-racial racism, the New Racial Domain, racism 2.0, post-racial liberalism, colorblind white dominance, race after race, postrace, and the list continues.[68] These terms presume that there is something distinctive about "our" racism. Yet models are merely that: models. Noticeably, Malcolm X does not speak of a new brand in his analogy, but only of a "new model," and Fanon does not argue that racism has changed its substance, but merely "its appearance." Reform—that is, changes in appearance—is precisely how the racist infrastructure reproduces itself. Anthony Farley reminds us that "reform is a mode of repetition."[69] While racial forms mutate, the substance of state-sanctioned anti-Black and anti-Indigenous violence remains unchanged.

Our allegedly "new" racial order continues to rely upon "old" colonial methods, such as segregation, incarceration, violence, disenfranchisement, thingification (Césaire), pauperization, hunger, and death. While it has become routine to argue that racism today is less overt than in the past, white people continue to unleash an inordinate amount of violence onto Black people and people of color through the state apparatus. It thus remains essential to contend with Ruth Wilson Gilmore's definition of racism as "the state-sanctioned and/or extralegal production and exploitation of group-differentiated vulnerability to premature

16   INTRODUCTION

death."[70] In US inner cities, not unlike in Brazilian favelas or South African townships, Black youth have yet to learn "how to stop the police from murdering us and brutalizing us," as Dead Prez sing in "They Schools." White people, sometimes with the help of accomplices, have not stopped killing Black people through state-sanctioned guns, bombs, and lethal injections, nor through the more covert methods of white supremacist terror and genocide that are poverty, hunger, disease, environmental racism, posttraumatic stress disorder, and lack of adequate health care, schooling, and housing—racist methods that are not as loud as the gun, but "no less destructive of human life."[71] This is the *afterlife of slavery*, which Saidiya Hartman argues is manifested in "skewed life chances, limited access to health and education, premature death, incarceration, and impoverishment."[72] Rather than a new epoch, we are faced with a cosmetic alteration of the racist machine, cosmetic alteration itself being a central technology of white rule. The white supremacist machine has not changed. It is still a slaughterhouse.

While many white people in the United States insist that we live in a postracial era, white police and white members of civil society continue to execute Black people with impunity. In the words of Mumia Abu-Jamal, "it is not outrageous to the political and economic elite when Black and poor people are summarily executed by the state. This is exactly what is to be expected. It is nothing exceptional. It is their warped status quo."[73] To ensure perpetual white domination over Black people, the slave patrol morphed into the police, mass incarceration replaced literacy tests as a path to disenfranchisement and racial control, and racialized lynching continues unabated through the death penalty.[74] Far from abolishing slavery, the Thirteenth Amendment to the US Constitution reinscribed it through more sophisticated means by including an exception clause that allows for the enslavement of people who have committed a crime. During Reconstruction, the exception clause was immediately exploited in the convict lease system, and continues to be exploited today as Black and Brown people are criminalized, racially profiled, made to fill the prisons, and work virtually for free, while white individuals and white-owned corporations make billions exploiting the labor of incarcerated people.[75] Over 50 percent of the people on death row in the United States are Black and Latinx, while there are more Black people in prison today than there were slaves in 1850, as Michelle Alexander writes in *The New Jim Crow*.[76] While it denies holding political prisoners, the US government also continues to persecute Black and Indigenous revolutionaries, including Abu-Jamal, who has

THE MASTER'S COLORBLIND TOOLS   17

been on death row (now commuted to a life sentence without parole) since 1982, despite the lack of evidence against him.[77]

Though conspicuous in the United States, state-sanctioned anti-Black violence is clearly not a localized peculiarity. In an event that testifies to the ongoing killability of the Black person in neoapartheid South Africa, in August 2012 police opened fire on a group of striking Black miners who were demanding living wages at the Lonmin platinum mine in Marikana, killing at least thirty-four and injuring seventy-eight people.[78] That the police force executing Black workers is multiracial does not make this massacre and the protests that preceded it disconnected from white supremacy. The Marikana massacre starkly resembled the 1960 Sharpeville massacre, which also occurred in Gauteng after a protest that threatened the racist status quo. Illustrating salient continuities between the colonial past and neocolonial present, in 2012 the Lonmin Public Limited Company (founded in 1909 as the London and Rhodesian Mining and Land Company Limited) had its headquarters in London and counted executives from Anglo American Platinum and an Anglo-Swiss company among its shareholders. Shifting away blame, South African president Cyril Ramaphosa, who in 2012 was deputy president and a non-executive director and shareholder at Lonmin, told the Marikana Commission of Inquiry that responsibility for the massacre "has to be collective."[79] In a seemingly more compassionate gesture, Supra Mahumapelo, former North West premier, launched the Reconciliation, Healing, and Renewal program. This response is superficial as Marikana victims, just like the apartheid victims who testified in front of the Truth and Reconciliation Commission (TRC), continue to await reparations promised by the government. Noticeably, the TRC's promotion of "national unity and reconciliation"[80] was contingent on reinscribing nonracialism, the South African version of colorblindness, which is institutionalized in the Constitution.[81] Post-apartheid South Africa, a country where a Black majority holds political power while a white minority continues to control the economy, shows that anti-Blackness and white supremacy can also thrive under Black leadership. Rather than dismantling racist institutions, the Black elite that runs the South African government has seen fit to simply inherit them, perpetuating anti-Black violence and dispossession, while protecting the economic interests of white people.

If South Africa has long been viewed as the world's bastion of racism, Brazil exists in the global imaginary as the country of racial democracy and interracial conviviality. Yet the deadly effects of white supremacy and anti-Blackness are perhaps nowhere as evident as in Brazil, where military police killed 10,153 people between 1999 and 2014 in the state of São Paulo alone, according to the most conservative statistics.[82] While murders among the white population have fallen in the last decade, the violent death of Black Brazilians has steadily risen. The overwhelming majority of the victims of police murders in the country—79 percent—are Black boys and men.[83] Roberto Penha, Wilton Domingos Júnior, Wesley Rodrigues, Carlos de Souza, and Cleiton de Souza, inseparable friends since childhood, are among these victims. On Sunday, November 29, 2015, the five friends were driving around northern Rio de Janeiro to celebrate sixteen-year-old Penha's first paycheck when police officers fired more than fifty bullets into their car and then tampered with evidence to make the execution appear as self-defense. In an example of the structural disavowal of racism that defines white discourse in Brazil, former Rio state governor Luiz Pezão insisted that the murder of the five unarmed teenagers "não é racismo" (is not racism).[84] Black activists have long denounced such racial disavowal and called attention to anti-Black violence in Brazil. On August 22, 2014, over 50,000 people across Brazil joined the Second (Inter) National March Against the Genocide of Black People, organized by the Black grassroots movement Reaja ou Será Morto! (React or You Will Die!).[85] In Salvador da Bahia, the marches started with one person reading a long list of names of Black people murdered by police, in Brazil and around the world. Michael Brown was among the people named. Speaking to the global reaches of anti-Black police violence, these protests occurred at the same time as residents of Ferguson, Missouri, were marching to protest the murder of Michael Brown and assert that Black Lives Matter.[86]

The annihilating power of white violence has also consistently raised its deadly fist in Mexico, which has constructed itself as a country of mestizos to conceal the reality of white political and economic power. When members of the Ejército Zapatista de Liberación Nacional (Zapatista Army of National Liberation), mainly Tzotzil- and Tzeltal-speaking Maya, rose up in the state of Chiapas following the passing of the North American Free Trade Agreement (NAFTA) on January 1, 1994, the Mexican government responded to the uprising, in the words of former subcomandante Marcos, "with some 15,000 troops, torture, summary executions, and general repression."[87] The Zapatistas recognized that the neoliberal policies of free trade between Mexico, the United States, and Canada were not just an exploitation tactic on the part of Mexico's

THE MASTER'S COLORBLIND TOOLS   19

more powerful northern neighbors but represented a veritable death sentence for Indigenous people, who are dependent on subsistence farming, especially of corn, the production of which is heavily subsidized in the United States.[88] On December 22, 1997, paramilitary members of the Partido Revolucionario Institucional (PRI), which ruled Mexico uninterruptedly from 1929 until 2000, killed forty-five innocent Tzotzil people, including twenty-one women and fifteen children, while they were praying in a church in Acteal. Today, Indigenous people in Chiapas continue to be violently driven away from their homes and displaced in the ongoing attempt to appropriate their lands.[89] Racism is a daily reality also for the country's most invisible community: Mexico's 1.4 million Black people. Although the Mexican elite exploited the labor of enslaved Africans until the nineteenth century and Mexico has a rich history of slave uprisings such as the Yanga rebellion, Blackness has been relegated to the margins of national discourse, where it remains to this day.[90] Until 2015, Afro-Mexicans were not even counted in the census.

In Cuba, the revolutionary government has been subtler in manifesting its allegiance to white supremacy, but no less harmful to Black people, who face repression, police violence, and incarceration at levels unthinkable among the white population to the extent that Cuba's extremely large prison population is overwhelmingly Black.[91] Exiled Afro-Cuban scholar Carlos Moore, who was persecuted by the Cuban government in the 1960s for critiquing its anti-Black racism, encapsulates the dominant discourse around race in post-1959 Cuba as follows: "You people had it rough before the Revolution but you are living it up now. So what more do you want?"[92] While the Revolution eliminated racial segregation in public spaces and halted US colonialism on the island, it did not end structural racism, including within the white-dominated government. The state-sponsored commitment to colorblindness has instead led to the systematic silencing of anti-Black racism. The Cuban government symbolically celebrates Afro-Cuban culture, while Black Cubans are excluded from most positions of power and remain at the bottom of the socioeconomic ladder in what is allegedly a classless and nonracial society.[93]

Described as "the bridge of the world and the heart of the universe" because of its unique location and history, Panama also has a long tradition of romanticizing race relations in its territory. The local white elite, as we will see in chapter 1, has portrayed the United States as the sole harbinger of racism in Panama, removing local responsibility for

20   INTRODUCTION

racism against Black and Indigenous people. If racial harmony means merely the absence of widespread violent confrontation, Panamanian writer Justo Arroyo writes, then Panama could be considered a cradle of tolerance. However, racial harmony implies, in Arroyo's own words, "the forced and angry acceptance by one group, the Blacks, of the worst living, educational, and working conditions, the acceptance of their invisibility in 99 percent of the activities of daily life."[94] During the 1989 invasion of Panama, USAmericans killed thousands of people and left countless more injured and homeless. The overwhelming majority of the victims of US military operations were Black. Alberto Barrow writes, "I am quite sure that the U.S. military wouldn't have used a Stealth (fighter) bomber, such a destructive missile beast, in the neighborhoods where the non-Blacks reside."[95] Barrow's words conjure Christina Sharpe's assertion that "the perils are not now, and never have been, evenly distributed."[96] Conveniently named Operation Just Cause and presented as an attempt to safeguard democracy, the massacre of Black Panamanians at the hand of the US army was neither just nor genuinely "colorblind."

Cross the Atlantic, arrive in Europe, and racist violence remains firmly in place. The case of present-day Italy is instructive here. When three young white men from my dormant rural village of San Cono, Sicily, brutally attacked four Egyptian teenagers with a baseball bat in August 2016, leaving a sixteen-year-old boy in a coma, I was not surprised.[97] Neither was I surprised that many fellow Sanconesi sided with the attackers, to the extent that someone created T-shirts in support of Davide Severo, Giacomo Severo, and Antonino Spitale, the three assailants. The attack was not just a case of individual racism. Every non-Black person in San Cono profits from the exploitation of Black people, who perform backbreaking work picking fruits and vegetables on local farms for little pay. The reaction to the attack on the part of Salvatore "Nuccio" Barbera, the mayor of San Cono, and Gianluca Petta, the mayor of the neighboring village of San Michele di Ganzaria in which the four Egyptian boys were living in a reception center for unaccompanied minors, further demonstrates how the local investment in racism is structural. The two mayors exploited the violence against the Egyptian youth to request that the regional Sicilian government halt the creation of additional migrant centers in the two towns. That the Italian press provided only the perspective of the three Sicilian men, while the victims remained unnamed, also speaks volumes about how racialized refugees and migrants are rendered invisible in present-day Italy.

THE MASTER'S COLORBLIND TOOLS   21

The Egyptian teenagers violently attacked in San Cono are among the thousands of refugees and migrants who have arrived in Europe escaping wars, terrorism, and hunger that are the direct product of European and US imperialism in Africa and the Middle East. Violence against refugees, and the unwillingness of the Italian state to grant them the legal status of refugees, exists in a context where in 2015, as Sharpe writes, "the European Union (EU) voted to replace humanitarian patrols of the Mediterranean with military ones."[98] As a consequence, more than 23,000 people were left to die while attempting to cross the Mediterranean Sea between 2014 and 2021 alone.[99] The propaganda against Black refugees that is spouted unrelentingly in the Italian government, political rallies, and media sustains this structural violence. The school system, which is racist and forbids critical thinking, exacerbates the problem. Within the context of a lesson on Gabriele D'Annunzio, my Italian high school teacher once said that "Italians went to Libya because we needed space." If this was D'Annunzio's opinion, the teacher never challenged it. While teachers inculcated such colonial and imperialistic ideologies nonchalantly, the words colonialism and imperialism themselves were never uttered. Cristoforo Colombo (Christopher Columbus), when he was even mentioned, was a traveler and great explorer. To this day, the monument to Columbus stands undisturbed in his native Genova not simply because of inertia, but because most Italians would consider it a sacrilege to remove it. This makes sense as the values of Columbus are still those of present-day Italy, in which fascism is the state and the status quo, in which every party and every region is anti-Black, and in which institutional racism subjects Black people to harrowing living conditions, economic exploitation, police violence, and lack of access to adequate education and housing, as well as discrimination in the workplace, judicial system, and prison system.[100] Yet ask the average white Italian—the average white European, in fact—and you will hear without hesitation that we are not racist. There is no place in the world more democratic and egalitarian than Europe, my cousin texted me just a moment after he had expressed outrage at the murder of George Floyd. Statements such as these, of course, are themselves a manifestation of the superiority complex that structures white psychology, a product of the very white supremacy that we systematically disavow.

Colorblind Tools demonstrates that the white disavowal of racism is global. This disavowal is neither the product of ignorance nor coincidence, but a consequence of white people's active and collective

22   INTRODUCTION

investment in whiteness. In the hands and mouths of white people, colorblindness is underwritten not by an epistemology of ignorance, I argue, but by an epistemology of disavowal. Here, I part ways with Charles Mills, who argues that, on matters relative to race and racism, white people exhibit an "inverted epistemology, an epistemology of ignorance."[101] Mills views this epistemology, which he calls *white ignorance*, as a ubiquitous kind of ignorance produced through racial domination. Citing Woody Doane, Mills contends that white people "exhibit a general inability to perceive the persistence of discrimination and the effects of the more subtle forms of institutional discrimination."[102] This presumes that white people are generally ignorant about racial domination and therefore innocent.

Mills interprets Ralph Ellison's *Invisible Man* as an epistemological novel that explores the theme of white ignorance. Mills cites the famous prologue in which the unnamed narrator describes himself as an invisible man. He is invisible not because he is a ghost, but "simply because people refuse to see [him]."[103] It is important that the narrator frames his invisibility as the product of white people's *refusal* to see him, rather than their inability to do so. Refusal implies agency. White people do not want to see the invisible man as a human being with a complex interiority and individuality. The prologue's ending shows that the narrator in actuality challenges white ignorance. In an earlier passage, readers learn about a white man bumping into the narrator, who fights back and demands that the man apologize for his actions. The narrator returns to this incident at the end of the prologue, which makes an important argument about white knowledge and responsibility. The invisible man states: "He bumped me, he insulted me. Shouldn't he, for his own personal safety, have recognized my hysteria, my 'danger potential'? He, let us say, was lost in a dream world. But didn't he control that dream world—which, alas, is only too real!—and didn't he rule me out of it? And if he had yelled for a policeman, wouldn't I have been taken for the offending one? Yes, yes, and yes!"[104] The narrator argues that, while white people might be living in a "dream world," they themselves have fabricated and perpetuate this world and are thus responsible for it. Ellison's novel effectively illustrates the deficiency of arguments that portray white people as puppets at the mercy of ignorance or unconscious habits. White people refuse to see the invisible man because it benefits them.

As it demonstrates that white people are actively invested in maintaining white supremacy on a global scale, *Colorblind Tools* challenges

THE MASTER'S COLORBLIND TOOLS

the argument that white people do not understand the world that we have made. Instead, it supports Fanon's claim that "a social group, a country, a civilization, cannot be unconsciously racist."[105] As I show in chapter 4, the insistence on depicting racism as unconscious that especially pervades white philosophy on race is itself a tactic of racial disavowal. Whereas white ignorance, in Mills's understanding, implies both false belief (error) and lack of true belief (ignorance) and need not be based on bad faith, white people's ongoing global reliance on colorblind tools shows that racism, as Lewis R. Gordon would say, is a matter of bad faith.[106] The theory of white ignorance cannot explain the global white reproduction of colorblind logics across time, disciplines, languages, national contexts, and discourses that this book documents.

While ignorance has become the modus operandi for talking about white epistemology, I propose shifting the conceptual lens from ignorance to disavowal. In doing so, I recognize that, as Kimberlé Crenshaw writes, "race consciousness is central not only to the domination of blacks but also to whites' acceptance of the legitimacy of hierarchy and their identity with elite interests. Exposing the centrality of race consciousness is crucial to identifying and delegitimating beliefs that present hierarchy as inevitable and fair."[107] Foregrounding disavowal makes visible some of the workings of white racial consciousness in the making of racialized meaning. Here, I understand *disavowal* in Lacanian terms as a process that encompasses both denial and acceptance, which means that it depends on recognition. For Jacques Lacan, disavowal is antithetical to ignorance as it requires the simultaneous recognition of what is being disavowed.[108] The white disavowal of racism depends on the concurrent acceptance of racism and anti-Blackness as the baselines that should be maintained.

It is necessary to distinguish between white ignorance and the oral or textual white *performance* of ignorance aimed at occluding white people's knowledge of and global investment in racial domination. White people strategically feign ignorance as a tactic of domination. Alongside the concept of unconscious bias, the theory of white ignorance has gained much traction in US academia and beyond. It is my contention that scholars should rethink both. Afropessimist thinkers have argued that there is no such thing as a genuinely "colorblind" unconscious in the first place. Anti-Blackness structures the unconscious per se, to the extent that "Black people form a mass of indistinguishable flesh in the collective unconscious."[109] The global popularity of colorblind discourse among white people demonstrates the centrality of *white knowledge*—that is, the impact of white racial consciousness onto the production of white academic, legal, and popular knowledge itself. This book hopes to encourage further scholarly engagement with white knowledge.

White people silence racism not because we are ignorant, but because we understand that racism benefits us immensely. To protect these benefits, we disavow the differential value attributed to the lives of Black people and white people that is endemic in European settler neocolonies and Europe. Everywhere, white violence is accompanied by an unabated racial inequality as white people continue to own most of the world's resources and wealth, including through neocolonial organizations controlled by Europe and the United States that carry deceptive colorblind names such as the World Bank and the International Monetary Fund. In the United States, white people have concrete material advantages over Black people and people of color in every aspect of life, from wealth to income, housing, education, incarceration levels, and life expectancy.[110] The median white US household had $111,146 in wealth holdings in 2011, while the median Black household only had $7,113. This massive racial inequality is not a US peculiarity. In South Africa, Black majority rule has not brought improvements in living conditions for most people. White people, who are just 8.9 percent of the South African population according to the 2011 census, owned 87 percent of the land in 1994, and continue to own at least 72 percent of the land and the vast majority of the country's wealth today.[111] The racially differential life expectancy also powerfully reveals the enduring reality of anti-Blackness in South Africa, where life expectancy for Black people decreased from 60.7 years in 1985 to merely *49.2 years* in 2004, while for white people it is over 70 years.[112] Despite blatant racial inequality, the South African government no longer collects life expectancy statistics disaggregated by race, a move that speaks volumes about the institutionalization of colorblindness in the country. In Brazil, rampant racial inequality also affects Black people's very chance to reach adulthood. Infant mortality in the Southeast, one of the poorest regions of Brazil, is 52.7 per thousand Black children born alive, while it is 30.9 per thousand white children born alive.[113] Meanwhile, Black Brazilians on average earned 42 percent less than white Brazilians in 2015.[114] Activists and scholars have also called attention to the high rates of poverty and child mortality among Indigenous people in Brazil.[115] Racial inequality is also alive and well in Mexico, where scholars have found a strong correlation between skin tone and socioeconomic

THE MASTER'S COLORBLIND TOOLS   25

status, as people who are dark skinned are worse off economically and educationally than people who are light skinned.[116] In Cuba, Fidel Castro's declaration that Cuba is an African country and his support for the revolutionary war in Angola served to mask the fact that Black Cubans are the poorest among the poor and that government officials were, and continue to be, virtually all white.[117] Similar conditions are in place in Panama, where whites and mestizos control all institutions of power and the economy, while Black and Indigenous people inhabit the poorest sectors of society.[118]

These enduring global realities of racialized subjection and privilege defy notions of racial progress. Unwilling to dwell in the false comforts of racial optimism in the face of unrelenting white terror and racial inequality, *Colorblind Tools* follows Malcolm X's realist reading of the contemporary moment as one in which "the knife is [still] there."[119] The myth that time heals all racial wounds is itself a technology of racial domination that I call *colorblind time*. How many white people have I heard argue that racial inequality and anti-Black violence persist in South Africa because apartheid was abolished *recently*? We need to give it time, some argue. According to this logic, let's say, a German massacre of Jewish people almost two decades after the fall of the Nazi regime would have been a natural consequence of the regime's recent demise. Can we even imagine a state-ordered massacre of Jews occurring in democratic Germany? That we cannot, while a massacre of Black people *did* occur without international uproar in 2012 South Africa, reveals the anti-Blackness of colorblind time and speaks volumes about how slavery, to cite Calvin Warren, "exceeds the historical event that we are so eager to get over and indeed provides the condition of possibility for the liberal grammar of humanism that undergirds the compulsion to get over in the first place."[120] Only from the perspective of whiteness, time progresses in linear fashion, slavery leaves no traces, and it is time to "get over it." Black people cannot get over it because time has not fixed anti-Blackness. Instead, colorblind time—the invocation of time as racial healer—serves to conceal how time is itself a technology of racial subjection.

Colorblind time sells deceptive hope for the future while it makes the racially regressive operations of time and the global constancy of gratuitous anti-Black violence disappear. The discrepancy in life expectancy between Black and white people across national borders shows that time is itself racialized. It is the violent extraction of time from Black people that allows those of us who are white to enjoy wealth, leisure,

26 INTRODUCTION

and longevity itself.[121] Far from solving racism, time entrenches racial inequality. A character in Miriam Tlali's novel *Between Two Worlds* puts this reality succinctly: "The value of land never goes down, it always rises. . . . It always pays you in the end. In fact, the longer you wait, the more it pays you."[122] Since the assets that white people have acquired through slavery, genocide, and theft appreciate in value over time, the more time passes, the more the racial wealth gap in the United States keeps *widening*.[123] In South Africa, where anti-Blackness has been engraved in the democratic Constitution through a clause that protects private property, Black poverty has *worsened* since the 1994 democratic dispensation, while white people are even wealthier now than during apartheid.[124] The myth of time as progress does not allow us to make sense of these realities. The identifiable continuities between racial conditions in the past and the present—and the enduring logics of colorblindness at the service of ongoing racial oppression and racial privilege—demonstrate that we are still dealing with the master's tools of slavery and colonialism and have not entered a new racial era, despite claims to the contrary.

Time-Tested Tools

Dissimulation, disavowal, and denialism defined the colonial project from its inception. Colonialism was not advertised for the genocidal enterprise that it was. Rather, as Césaire writes in *Discourse on Colonialism*, Europeans disavowed their intent to kill and plunder, disguising imperial conquest as civilization and Christianization.[125] White people made enslavement, genocide, and theft disappear through rhetorical gestures which argued that colonization was "about progress, about 'achievements,' diseases cured, improved standards of living."[126] With no regard for fact or logic, lands populated by millions of people were declared "terra nullius" (no man's land), a continent that had been inhabited for at least 14,000 years was proclaimed "discovered" and named the "New World," and millions of people belonging to different ethnic groups unilaterally became "Indians," people literally born in death as, without genocide, in Wilderson's words, "Indians would not, paradoxically, 'exist.'"[127]

Backed by the European principles of right of discovery and right of conquest, and with the full support of the pope, Italian colonizer Christopher Columbus and his men already during the second transatlantic

THE MASTER'S COLORBLIND TOOLS   27

voyage in 1493 captured, raped, enslaved, tortured, killed, and burned
alive thousands of Indigenous women, men, and children.[128] The
violence that Europeans unleashed upon Indigenous people in the
Americas was so savage that, within one century, sixty to eighty million
Indigenous people were killed.[129] This violence was replicated in what
would become the United States of America, where Europeans literally worked Indigenous people to death, slaughtered them with axes,
hunted them as game and fed them to dogs, scalped their heads for
bounty and displayed them as trophies, and infected them with diseases
in deliberate acts of biological warfare.[130] And this was just the beginning. California governor Peter H. Burnett exemplified the dominant
white US stance on Indigenous people when he announced in his 1851
message that "a war of extermination will continue to be waged between
the races until the Indian race becomes extinct."[131] The white extermination campaign against Indigenous people continues today, carried on
through land dispossession, the dumping of toxic waste on Indigenous
land, police death squads, mass incarceration, the poverty that reigns
supreme on US reservations, and the until-recently routine sterilization
of Indigenous women and their ongoing murder and disappearance.[132]

If the Indian was born through genocide, slavery marked the creation
of the Black. As early as in 1441, as Gomes Eanes de Zurara writes in
The Chronicle of the Discovery and Conquest of Guinea, the Portuguese
brought nine Africans together with "a little gold dust" to Portugal.[133]
Between 1492 and 1865, Europeans tore almost twelve million African
people from their families and homelands and forcibly brought them
to the Americas: approximately one-half million Africans to the United
States and over eleven million to countries south of the US border, with
most enslaved Africans being trafficked to Brazil, the last country to
formally abolish slavery in 1888.[134] Black people resisted the inhumanity of bondage from the inception. C. L. R. James writes in *The Black
Jacobins* that, to halt the constant revolts, hunger strikes, and suicides
on slave ships, Europeans chained enslaved African people to iron bars,
one hand shackled to the leg, with barely five feet (150 cm) in length
and three feet (90 cm) in height of space, so that they could neither
fully lay down, nor fully sit upright.[135] So atrocious were the conditions
that Europeans forced enslaved people to endure that slave mortality
in the Middle Passage was over 20 percent on a given journey and one-
fifth of all African people trafficked to the Americas died each year.[136]
The coordinated spreading of lies to cover up these conditions was an
integral element of enslavism as, in the words of James, "propagandists

of the time claimed that however cruel was the slave traffic, the African slave in America was happier than in his own African civilization."[137] In reality, conditions on plantations and mines across the Americas were no better than on slave ships. In the nineteenth century, the life expectancy for enslaved people averaged less than seven years from their time of arrival on many Cuban plantations.[138] Everywhere, enslaved Africans revolted against captivity and European barbarism. The first collective slave insurrection on American soil occurred in Santo Domingo as early as 1522.[139]

Prior to the rise of the British Empire, Holland had been the main colonial world power for over one century alongside Spain and Portugal.[140] In 1602, the Dutch, Flemish, and Germans together formed the Dutch East India Company (DEIC), a monopoly with the right to declare war and sign treaties.[141] In 1652, Johan van Riebeeck colonized the Cape of Good Hope for the Dutch and began to wage war against the Khoena and the San, the Indigenous people who had lived in the area since around 1,000 B.C.E. [142] Later, the Dutch also sought to subjugate other ethnic groups. By 1656, Holland had appropriated two million square kilometers of land and trafficked millions of enslaved people to the so-called East Indies as well as into the Cape Colony.[143] By 1773, whites had occupied Khoe-San and amaXhosa land and stolen at least 40,000 cattle and 30,000 sheep belonging to the Khoe-San, who were enslaved or forced to flee.[144] The Khoe-San resisted persecution and enslavement. The Dutch conceded in 1776 that "so many thousands of Bushmen [derog. for San people] have united their inward anger."[145] Despite their resistance, by the time the British seized the Cape in 1806, the Dutch had nearly exterminated the Khoe-San, decimating their population from an estimated two hundred thousand in 1652 to a mere twenty thousand in 1806.[146]

To legitimize the domination over non-European peoples, as well as Europeans whom they deemed Other such as Slavs and Jews, Europeans invented the idea of race.[147] This means that the idea of race is a foundational colorblind tool in its own right. David Marriott writes that "the philosophical concept of race is itself constituted by a form of racist disavowal."[148] Here, I contend that "a form of racist disavowal" structures the invention of race itself. Racialization, in fact, functions as a dissimulation mechanism that seeks to make hierarchies created through conquest and slavery appear natural, while it conceals its own workings by operating through categories other than race. Skin color, which held no meaning in antiquity and first became codified as a racial

THE MASTER'S COLORBLIND TOOLS   29

marker with the advancing of scientific racism in the early eighteenth
century, is one of these categories.[149] According to Anne Lafont, "Art,
natural history, nascent anthropology, aesthetics, and colonial law con-
verged around 1700 (1685–1745) to establish and then stabilize color
as the main racial marker in the inventory of human diversity."[150] European physicians such as Carolus Linnaeus in *Systema Naturae* (1735)
and Johann Friedrich Blumenbach in *De generis humani varietate
nativa* (*On the Natural Varieties of Mankind*, 1795) were instrumental in
attributing racial meaning to skin color. Blumenbach ranked skin color
hierarchically, starting, you guessed it, with white, which he attributed
to European peoples and linked to beauty, while he placed black at the
bottom of the hierarchy.[151]

Color was not the only category that was strategically made to carry
racial meaning through colonial conquest and slavery. So were labor
and class, alongside others. Europeans early on devised a systematic
division of labor in the American colonies that confined wage labor
exclusively to white people. Labor was racialized in order to make the
race-class association seem natural as a mechanism of white domination.[152] In the United States, as Cheryl Harris has shown, race and
property became conflated and whiteness became a property in itself
as the conquest of Indigenous people was ratified by conferring property rights over their lands to white people (and to white people alone)
while Black people (and Black people alone) were treated as property.[153]
Constitutive to these extractive processes is capitalism, which is intrinsically racist, a fact encapsulated in the term "racial capitalism."[154] Land
theft and spatial segregation further ensured that the vast majority of
the land, resources, and jobs in settler colonies would remain in white
hands to this day.

Not just the idea of race, but also the construct of "the Negro" is a
white fabrication grounded in disavowal. The European invention of
"the Negro" is entangled with the European invention of the Human,
which positions Black people as its constitutive outside.[155] Robinson
writes, "The construct of Negro, unlike the terms 'African,' 'Moor,' or
'Ethiope' suggested no situatedness in time, that is history, or space,
that is ethno- or politico-geography. The Negro had no civilization, no
cultures, no religions, no history, no place, and finally no humanity that
might command consideration."[156] This construct, Robinson makes
clear, was not the product of white ignorance. Europeans had known
for centuries that Africans lived in complex societies, but they deliberately silenced this fact: "It was known that Africans lived in neat and

30   INTRODUCTION

spacious villages which allowed privacy to the individual while preserving an intricate system of class and family distinctions. . . . Numerous
books told of the Negroes' polite manners, their well-established patterns of trade, their knowledge of the planets and constellations."[157]
Disavowal is central to the fabrication of "the Negro" as a being devoid
of history, culture, and being itself. Instead of admitting to the scandal
of kidnapping and selling human beings, and the hypocrisy of doing so
with the backing of the Roman Catholic Church,[158] Europeans appropriated for themselves the category Human. They argued that only white
people are fully Human and therefore capable of rational thought, historicity, and change, while they confined Black people to what Fanon
calls "a zone of nonbeing."[159] This twofold process is co-constitutive,
given that Humanness, as Rinaldo Walcott writes, is "defined against
Black being."[160] Violence is integral to this process. To assert itself as
Human, the Human resorts to anti-Black violence, which is gratuitous,
while the violence exercised upon non-Black people is generally contingent.[161] It is fundamental, then, to underline that white supremacy and
anti-Blackness are not synonymous—and neither are colonialism and
slavery.[162] In fact, as Jared Sexton writes, "colonization is not essential,
much less prerequisite, to enslavement."[163] This means that the condition of Black people cannot be understood outside of slavery, nor can it
be solved simply through a politics of decolonization. It requires a commitment to abolition, which transcends sovereignty.[164] Slavery is not a
temporally circumscribed event, after all, but a set of paradigmatic and
ontological relations that continue in the present.[165]

The law has been central to the formation and stabilization of these
paradigmatic and ontological relations. Seemingly neutral and equally
applicable to all, the law is a technology of white supremacy that produces the categories and subjects that it purports to merely regulate.
It is an instrument of ontologization that creates persons and subper-
sons while it masks its own world-making scheme under the disguise of
simply regulating what is already there. In *Ontological Terror*, Warren
shows that contract law camouflaged its ontological project, even as it
emerged to make the African into a thing (an object of property) and
the European into a subject (the self-owned owner of property). Warren
writes:

> Contract law (law of chattel) is perhaps the hallmark of modern
> legal development, given the need to regulate commerce and
> specify the rights and entitlement of property holders. But this

THE MASTER'S COLORBLIND TOOLS   31

> corpus of law emerges because one needs to integrate the slave
> into the world. In other words, contract law conceals an onto-
> logical project: it uses the discourse of property, chattel, rights,
> and trade to *divide* the world into human subjects [Dasein],
> those who are entitled to the protection and enforcement of
> their ontological (non)relation, and the world of *things*, those
> entities lacking such protection of any relation, but whose exis-
> tence is necessary for the human to operate within the world.[166]

Warren shows that, through the contract form, which deceptively
imagines consensual signatories, chattel law "is predicated upon an
ontological difference that it disavows."[167] This ontological enterprise,
Warren argues, informs the law beyond chattel law for it is constitutive
of law itself. It would therefore be misguided to consider how colorblindness is institutionalized *in* the law, without considering how the
law, as critical race scholars have demonstrated, is a colorblind tool
that disavows its own essence *as* tool—a tool that is used by those of us
who are white to serve our own sociopolitical and economic interests.[168]

In the United States, this dual attribute of the law, as both a colorblind tool in its own right and a central site of the institutionalization
of colorblindness, is visible already in the manner in which slavery was
inscribed in the US Constitution. Addressing the disavowal of slavery,
Du Bois writes: "The men who wrote the Constitution sought by every
evasion, and almost by subterfuge, to keep recognition of slavery out of
the basic form of the new government."[169] The Constitution supported
slavery through colorblind language as it never explicitly mentions
either slavery or race. Slaves are instead referred to as "three fifths
of all other Persons"[170] in the three-fifths clause (article I, section 2,
paragraph 3), which gave slaveholding states more seats in Congress
and thereby disproportionate influence on the House of Representatives, presidency, and Supreme Court by counting the total number of
enslaved Black people as three-fifths of the total number of whites. The
fugitive slave clause (article IV, section 2, paragraph 3), which mandated that slaves who had escaped to so-called free states must return
to bondage, equally referred to slaves using colorblind language, stip-
ulating that "No Person held to Service or Labour in one State, under
the Laws thereof, escaping into another, shall, in Consequence of any
Law or Regulation therein, be discharged from such Service or Labour,
but shall be delivered up in Claim of the Party to whom such Service
or Labour may be due."[171] The US Constitution sanctioned slavery,

camouflaging it as "Service or Labour," without revealing its ontological project. Although they are property by law, slaves are named "Persons," while their status as objects and the fact of slavery itself are concealed through colorblind rhetoric. This example does not intend to suggest that *all* law deploys colorblind language, for that is certainly not the case. It is rather meant to show that white US lawmakers recognized the legal utility of colorblindness long before the post–Civil Rights era and deployed it accordingly.

Why did white USAmericans resort to colorblind language to inscribe slavery in the US Constitution? Surely they did not need to do so at a time in which overt racism was permissible. This belief relies on a misunderstanding of white power, colorblindness, and their modes of operation. It overlooks the fact that racism has always relied on overt *and* covert means to ensure its reproduction. We cannot underestimate white people's desire to protect themselves (and future generations of whites) from criticism and scandal. Most importantly, institutionalizing coded language robs those who are enslaved of the grammar to critique their condition, revealing colorblindness to be not just a tool of capacitation for white people, but also a tool of incapacitation for Black people.

White freedom and Black bondage are inextricably yoked. Toni Morrison describes white freedom as "parasitical" because it depends on the control, exploitation, and denigration of a Black population that is not free.[172] This must not be understood merely in metaphorical terms given that, as Daniel Martinez HoSang writes, "the liberties of white people depend on the subordination of others."[173] The slave trade and the labor that Europeans extracted from enslaved African peoples were immensely profitable for European nations, almost all of which were involved in the slave trade at one time or another.[174] Du Bois writes:

> By 1750 there was hardly a manufacturing town in England, which was not connected with the colonial trade. The profits provided one of the main streams of that capital which financed the Industrial Revolution. The West Indian islands became the center of the British Empire and of immense importance to the grandeur of England. It was the Negro slaves who made these sugar colonies the most precious colonies ever recorded in the annals of imperialism.[175]

To mask their collective investment in slavery, Europeans exploited discourses about freedom and equality.[176] The major white thinkers of

THE MASTER'S COLORBLIND TOOLS   33

the Enlightenment proclaimed the ideals of freedom, equality, and fraternity at the same time as they supported the enslavement of Black people. Immanuel Kant, who taught courses in anthropology and geography twice a year for forty years until his retirement in 1797, argued that "Die Menschheit ist in ihrer größten Vollkommenheit in der Rasse der Weißen. Die gelben Inder haben schon geringeres talent. Die Neger sind tiefer, und am tiefsten steht ein Theil der amerikanischen Volkerschaften." (Humanity has its highest degree of perfection in the white race. The yellow Indians have a somewhat lesser talent. The Negroes are much lower, and lowest of all is part of the American races).[177] Voltaire saw no irony in proclaiming that "All mortals are equal," while arguing that Africans are "animals" with "little or hardly any intelligence."[178] Owning hundreds of slaves did not prevent Thomas Jefferson from pronouncing in the US Declaration of Independence "that all Men are created equal, that they are endowed by their Creator with certain unalienable Rights, that among these are Life, Liberty and the Pursuit of Happiness."[179] Comparably, the first Brazilian constitutional charter of 1824 defined freedom and equality as the inalienable rights of men even as millions of Black people continued to be enslaved.[180] This shows how the freedom that Europeans envisioned was, as Fanon writes, "always white liberty."[181] Freedom, equality, and fraternity became universal values only insofar as the European alone was made to embody universality through imperial conquest.

As Europeans enriched themselves by enslaving and exploiting African people, they treated them with the utmost inhumanity and then projected this inhumanity onto Africans themselves. Black people this way became the central locus of what Spillers calls "externally imposed meanings and uses."[182] This external imposition of meanings is evident in the words of a white planter who wrote in his 1798 diary: "The Negroes . . . are unjust, cruel, barbarous, half-human, treacherous, deceitful, thieves, drunkards, proud, lazy, unclean, shameless, jealous to fury, and cowards."[183] Commenting on these words, James writes that "it was by sentiments such as these that they [slave owners] strove to justify the abominable cruelties they practiced."[184] Projecting white character traits and behaviors onto Black people is not a strategy confined to the remote past. White South African writer Sarah Gertrude Millin in a volume titled, wait for it, *White Africans Are Also People* (1966) argues that the Khoe-San are "cattle thieves and somewhat dangerous to human life."[185] And yet, it was white people who massacred the Khoe-San and stole their cattle. The planter's and Millin's statements show that slavery

34   INTRODUCTION

and colonialism are underwritten by lies that become an epistemology in themselves. They also illustrate how the position of the slave, as Hartman writes, is defined by "fungibility," which refers not just to the interchangeability that characterizes the slave as commodity, but also to how Europeans rendered the enslaved Black body "an abstract and empty vessel vulnerable to the projection of others' feelings, ideas, desires, and values."[186] These racist projections are colorblind tools that white people have deliberately created and deployed to make the enslavement, dispossession, and dehumanization of Black people and our own sociopolitical power and wealth appear natural.

Offering an important analysis of racist stereotypes that is useful for understanding colorblindness, Albert Memmi writes in *The Colonizer and the Colonized*:

> Just as the bourgeoisie proposes an image of the proletariat, the existence of the colonizer requires that an image of the colonized be suggested. These images become excuses without which the presence and conduct of a colonizer, and that of a bourgeois, would seem shocking. But the favored image becomes a myth precisely because it suits them too well.
>
> Let us imagine, for the sake of this portrait and accusation, the often-cited trait of laziness. It seems to receive unanimous approval of colonizers from Liberia to Laos, via the Maghreb. It is easy to see to what extent this description is useful. It occupies an important place in the dialectics exalting the colonizer and humbling the colonized. Furthermore, it is economically fruitful.
>
> Nothing could better justify the colonizer's privileged position than his industry, and nothing could better justify the colonized's destitution than his indolence. The mythical portrait of the colonized therefore includes an unbelievable laziness, and that of the colonizer, a virtuous taste for action. At the same time the colonizer suggests that employing the colonized is not very profitable, thereby authorizing his unreasonable wages.[187]

Memmi shows that racist stereotypes are not mistakes of observation, but purposely crafted tools of social control.[188] The image of the colonized, Memmi argues, is always accompanied by a mirror image of the colonizer: if the colonized is lazy, the colonizer is industrious; if the colonized is immoral, the colonizer is the embodiment of morality, and so on. Each racist fantasy or myth, to cite Marriott, "is contiguous

THE MASTER'S COLORBLIND TOOLS

to the others in so far as they fuse a Manichean logic—of self and other—with stereotypical languages and images of racial difference."[189] Each of these pairs has a specific function, as racist stereotypes are not immutable, but are shaped by shifting political and economic motives. Europeans, for example, did not usually depict Africans as inferior before the triangular slave trade; only when slavery became established did Europeans begin to systematically portray Africans as barbaric and evil as a mechanism of social control.[190]

Noticing the stability of specific racist stereotypes across time and geographies is nonetheless important. For centuries, white people have branded as "lazy" precisely the people who have been doing all the labor in the colony/neocolony. It is easy to understand why this stereotype is useful, as Memmi writes. It is not by coincidence that white people have often deployed similar colorblind tools to describe the vastly different peoples they have subjugated. White people have fixed Black people and people of color into a collective "they" through a racist representational strategy that Memmi calls "the mark of the plural."[191] This enforced homogenization is a central technology of whiteness, which has appropriated not just the category of the Human, but also the categories of the Individual and the Universal.

Racist epistemology stipulates that only white people can inhabit the positionalities of the individual and the universal. This is so because there is much power in positioning oneself merely as an individual and currently claiming, to cite Moten, "the universality that the West has mistakenly called its own."[192] The dominant epistemological stance still presumes that white people are unbodied, neutral, and objective, while it argues that Black people and people of color are bodied, partial, biased—the mirror opposite of whites. Prior to the election of Barack Obama as president, none but white men had been presidents of the United States. Despite a clear racialized pattern of only white men having access to the US presidency, these white male presidents presented themselves as unraced, ungendered beings who had merely "the interests of the country" at heart. Obama was not granted the positional privileges of universality and individuality. Even when attempting to pass legislation that benefited the US majority, such as universal health care, Obama had to contend with white accusations that such measures mainly benefited Black people.

Centuries after the transatlantic slave trade and the inception of colonialism, white people still insist that white presidents are simply presidents, European Americans are simply Americans, white law is

36   INTRODUCTION

simply *the* law, European philosophy is simply *Philosophy*, white writers are simply writers... In sum, racist epistemology dictates that white people are people, and people of color are, well, people *of color*. And the theories that people of color produce, epistemic racism argues, cannot be universally applicable because knowledge is the domain of white people alone. European culture this way continues to present itself as rational and as containing subjects, while it declares that non-Europeans can only be objects of knowledge.[193] Heaven forbid that a philosophy student has not read Kant, no matter that Kant never left Königsberg and is the embodiment of provincialism. (If only the philosophy students who still have Kant forced down their throats at least learned the truth about his racist ideas, but that is precisely what they are *not* taught). Holding a PhD in philosophy and never having read Fanon, however, is considered acceptable by Euro-North American standards. This logic holds across traditional disciplines. A few years ago in Nashville at an English department party, a doctoral student hushed me and looked around worried that someone might have heard me when I said that I had never read *Romeo and Juliet*. That I am not a Briticist, and neither is he, was irrelevant.[194] Shame—or worse, being considered incompetent—is the punishment for refusing to capitulate to the Eurocentric standards of one's discipline.

But academic disciplines are not neutral sites of knowledge production. They have been instrumental in legitimizing European imperialism and white supremacy.[195] Bonilla-Silva and Tukufu Zuberi show in *White Logic, White Methods* that racism impacts how social science research is dominantly conducted, starting from what questions are asked (and not asked) to how data is analyzed. White methods, which the authors define as "the practical tools used to manufacture empirical data and analysis to support the racial stratification of society," cannot be disentangled from white logics; that is, ways of making sense of the world that are both informed by and reproduce white supremacy.[196] These academic practices were perfected in the nineteenth century, when the social sciences became institutionalized into distinct disciplines, primarily history, economics, sociology, political science, and anthropology. What made the social sciences "science" was their stated aim to produce "objective" knowledge, in contrast with "speculation," which was considered to be the realm of philosophy.[197] Social scientists emphasized empirical knowledge and the alleged neutrality of the scholar, yet the new social sciences emerged precisely to justify racial stratification. It is not by coincidence that the rise of modern academic

THE MASTER'S COLORBLIND TOOLS   37

disciplines, and the social sciences in particular, occurred at the height of European colonialism.[198]

Appeals to the colorblind tools of objectivity, neutrality, and science served as powerful justifications for racism. Notice how Italian eugenicist Cesare Lombroso immediately invokes science to legitimize his white supremacist doctrines in *L'uomo bianco e l'uomo di colore: Letture sull'origine e le varietà delle razze umane* (The White Man and the Man of Color: Lectures on the Origins and Varieties of the Human Races, 1871). The first lecture in the book, which has not been translated into English, opens with the following passage:

> A science hardly new, yet gigantic, has suddenly emerged, oh Lord, from the fecund seed of the modern colleges, on the ruins of old and new prejudices. It is the science of anthropology, which studies man with the means and methods of the physical sciences, which in place of the dreams of the theologians and the reveries of metaphysics substitutes a few dry facts . . . . . but facts.
>
> One of the most probing problems that were agitating unresolved before its appearance was that of the origin and plurality of the human stock: if, namely, among the human races there are profound differences that have manifested themselves from the beginning and have persisted unchanged despite variations in time and climate, leaving their eternal imprint on the history and destiny of populations.
>
> This is a serious problem.
>
> The question is one of knowing if there is, or not, a relationship between history and nature, between the primitive man and the entire series of living things from which our vanity would like to consider us miles apart.
>
> The question is one of knowing if we whites, who tower proudly at the top of civilization, will one day have to bow our foreheads before the prognathous snout of the Negro and the yellow and wan face of the Mongolian; if, finally, we owe our primacy to our organism or to the accidents of chance. And it is also a question of deciding once and for all if we can, without fear, and without brazen audacity, adhere, more than to traditions, to the sole authority of our times, Science.[199]

That Lombroso uses the phrase "noi bianchi" (we whites) should not surprise anyone but those who believe that white people do not have

38   INTRODUCTION

racial consciousness. It also makes sense that Lombroso argues that "noi bianchi . . . torreggiamo orgogliosi sulla vetta della civiltà" (we whites . . . tower proudly at the top of civilization). After all, he writes *L'uomo bianco e l'uomo di colore* precisely to convince his audience that white people are the supreme race. What we should not take for granted is that Lombroso is still venerated today, as we will see in chapter 2. I want to blame the nonexistence of an English translation of this book for the uncritical way that many scholars still approach Lombroso's work, but I cannot because his best-known work, *L'uomo delinquente studiato in rapporto alla antropologia, alla medicina legale ed alle discipline carcerarie* (*Criminal Man*, 1876), is no less racist. White supremacy simply motivates and structures Lombroso's opus. By appealing to the principles of science, empiricism, objectivity, and neutrality, white scholars like Lombroso managed to transform lies into "scientific facts." Without irony, Lombroso invokes "o Signore" (oh Lord), while he dismisses theology as being concerned with dreams and philosophy with reveries. Instead, Lombroso argues, anthropology is science, and science is "[la] sola autorità dei nostri tempi" (the sole authority of our times), an argument sealed by the capitalization of "Scienza" (Science) that concludes the paragraph, indicating its assumed power and absolute authority. Through the concepts of science and scientific knowledge—and through the institution of the university more broadly—white people like Lombroso fabricated and sanctioned the myths of whiteness and white superiority.[200] Where military power failed to annihilate enslaved and colonized people, Western science declared them subhuman and therefore disposable. Literature and philosophy then guaranteed that these racist theories would be popularized outside academia and become commonplace.

It is not possible to understand the workings of racism and colorblindness outside these standardized white practices of disavowing, projecting, stereotyping, masking, appropriating, suppressing, and outright *lying*. The modes of racial production and dissimulation matter. Colonial powers have always attempted to "suppress the history of their own violence"[201] and dissimulate the racist infrastructure. If we are to understand colorblindness, we need to look much further than 1945 or 1964. We need to return to the early days of colonial conquest and racialized slavery. This is how Columbus described the Taino, the Indigenous people who lived on the island he called Hispaniola, in his letter to Ferdinand of Spain, written during his first voyage in 1493:

> The people of this island, and of all the other islands which I have found and of which I have information, all go naked, men and women, as their mothers bore them. . . . They have no iron or steel or weapons, nor are they fitted to use them, not because they are not well built men and of handsome stature, but because they are very marvelously timorous. . . . It is true that, after they have been reassured and have lost their fear, they are so guileless and so generous with all they possess, that no one would believe it who has not seen it. They never refuse anything which they possess, if it be asked of them; on the contrary, they invite anyone to share it, and display as much love as if they would give their hearts, and whether the thing be of value or whether it be of small price, at once with whatever trifle of whatever kind it may be that is given to them, with that they are content.[202]

Columbus's description of the Taino is carefully crafted to support European interests. The nakedness, lack of weaponry, timorousness, and gullibility that Columbus attributes to the Taino are designed to represent them as "primitive" and non-threatening. Through these images, Columbus suggests that the Taino have neither the intention nor means to defend themselves. To conceal white theft and silence Indigenous resistance, Columbus represents the Taino as "artless and generous," insinuating that they willingly gave gold and land to Europeans. This passage illustrates how the depiction of Indigenous peoples as "savage," which served to justify their genocide, coexisted with the portrayal of Indigenous peoples as naive and childlike, which meant to suggest that they were unable to govern themselves and in need of white "protection."

Since it is a constitutive element of racism, colorblindness displays temporal and local particularities while it maintains its structural function as a technology of white rule. It is helpful in this regard to consider the parallels between Columbus's depiction of the Taino in the Caribbean and Rijno Johannes van der Riet's portrayal of the Khoena in the Cape Colony more than three centuries later, as this demonstrates that Europeans deployed colorblindness across borders to facilitate both the conquest of land and the enslavement of people. Van der Riet, the landdrost (steward) of Stellenbosch, a town that remains an epitome of racial inequality today, relied extensively on colorblind tools to argue in defense of the enslavement of Khoena children. While slavery in

40   INTRODUCTION

the Cape Colony (today's Western Cape region of South Africa) was
instituted already in 1653, Europeans after 1775 also required Khoena
children to be enslaved until the age of twenty-five, a process that they
deceptively called "apprenticeship."[203] On April 1, 1810, just a few days
after Sara Baartman, a Khoe woman, was forcibly brought to Europe
to be exhibited in London like an object for the entertainment of European viewers, van der Riet defended slavery for Khoena children in a
letter to J. A. Truter, the fiscal of the colony, who had objected to the
practice. Written in the aftermath of the Haitian Revolution, the letter
provides key insights into the workings of colorblindness and is worth
citing at length:

> It is Your Honour's opinion that the reasons I gave . . . for this
> nation [the Khoena] to serve the inhabitants in whose care they
> were born and brought up, were not sufficient to explain why
> they should work for the inhabitants until their twenty-fifth
> year as a compensation for the care and trouble taken in their
> upbringing. . . .
>
> These objections are very acceptable and would be very
> applicable, if one were dealing only with Christians. But in my
> opinion they cannot be applied without adaptation to heathens,
> and especially not to Hottentots [derog. for Khoena], who are
> generally accounted to be of the most stupid sort, and who
> therefore never think, nor can think, as Christians do. . . .
>
> Years of experience have taught me to see quite clearly the
> utility of such an institution, which is derived from the fact that
> a Hottentot who is freed from service, and who may therefore
> come and go as he pleases, is never inclined to work, much less
> to learning a trade; I have never known a Hottentot who learned
> a trade. The very prospect is difficult for them to envisage and
> when effort and time are required, this is a burden to them.
>
> Many Europeans and those who do not know the natives at
> first hand, or have never employed them, cannot understand
> how lazy and stubborn a nation they are. They are by nature
> untrustworthy, slothful and drowsy, with very few exceptions.
>
> And if the master can get no work from the children of Hot-
> tentots, by obligation, in return for the care and the trouble
> taken in their upbringing, or have no prospect of keeping such
> Hottentot children in service . . . then many masters will soon
> perish from concern and worry. They will not be able to make

THE MASTER'S COLORBLIND TOOLS

a living anywhere for a Hottentot with children cannot obtain employment. This I have seen so often in the course of my professional duties. The farmers of the interior assert, and do so with right, that the children of this nation are more of a liability than the service of their mothers can be an asset. . . . The trouble and expense is made tolerable by the prospect of the services yet to be received. Should these services be abolished, would not the obligation fall away which motivated the farmer in the interior to bring up the children of this nation? These services having been abolished, the prospect falls away and therefore, this nation, instead of being done a service, would be done a disservice by regarding them as free people who should enjoy real freedom, which in practice would make them unhappy. . . .

I have already dealt with the trades . . . and so I pass on to . . . the way in which the natural freedom which inspires useful conduct might be deadened by a period of 25 years' service. This would certainly be a valid argument, or appear to be, but experience has taught me that, for the greatest part, Hottentots who have grown up outside service, wander about and become thieves. As they have never been encouraged to work in their youth, they are completely incompetent and incapable of doing so in their more advanced years, and the idea that they are free is more a burden to them than a real sentiment.

That nobody has the right to force people into bondage, as you assert, . . . is correct but superficial, for that flower could bear bitter fruit. What would become of us and of the whole colony if the natives were to feel that they should be free, were to know their power, and then join together to regain their natural freedom as the original possessors of this country? In effect, nothing but a second St Domingo. Is a policy not therefore required which will ensure that, although this nation is not in effect a nation of slaves, they might still be instilled with a certain sense of service and that the dangerous and idealistic feeling of freedom might be weakened, or at least kept within certain limits?

In my position, it has often been my experience that there are female Hottentots who leave their children . . . and are never heard to ask after them. What is now to be done with such unfortunate creatures, who are without a father or mother? Should they beg for food along the road, or should they work? . . . And to prevent such miserable people from perishing from hunger and worry, it has become customary for Landdrosts and Heemraden to bestow such a Hottentot child or children until his twenty-fifth year on one of the inhabitants who takes pity on him. . . .

In my experience, it has also often happened that the father and mother of Hottentot children themselves come voluntarily to give their children to the inhabitants until their twenty-fifth year, as they do not think of themselves able to support their child or children.[204]

Van der Riet goes to great lengths to convince his interlocutor that it is right to enslave Khoena children. He immediately invokes religion, arguing that Truter's objections to slavery would make sense if the Khoena were "Christians," but do not apply to them because they are "heathens." In this way, van der Riet conceals the fact that Europeans shifted their approach to conversion when it suited their interests. When a 1770 law prohibited the sale of Christian slaves, slave owners in the Cape responded by simply stopping the conversion of slaves.[205] The British revoked this law in 1809, after the official 1808 abolition of the slave trade in the British Empire, allowing whites to sell any enslaved person, baptized or not.[206] Discourses about whether Indigenous people have souls and can be converted were used to condemn and eventually ban the enslavement of Indigenous people in the Americas. However, conversion to Christianity never saved Black people from slavery. Following the banning of slavery for Indigenous people in the Americas, Sylvia Wynter writes, "the category of the *Negro and Negra*, would come to be perceived by the Europeans within their culture-specific representational system as the only legitimately enslaveable category—outside the limits therefore of the real 'we.'"[207] The Khoena can never partake in the same "we" as Europeans. By invoking Christianity, van der Riet strategically defends slavery without explicitly mentioning race, yet the term "Christians" here cannot be separated from whiteness as it is an ontological marker connoting personhood (as in the Sicilian word christianu, which means both Christian and person). For van der Riet, the Khoena are not people: they are "the only legitimately enslaveable category." They exist outside the category of the Human, whether they are baptized or not. Invoking Christianity is merely a colorblind tool that van der Riet deploys to mask and support (the two categories, as has hopefully become clear, go hand in hand) his white supremacist agenda.

THE MASTER'S COLORBLIND TOOLS   43

In arguing that the Khoena are "lazy," "slothful and drowsy," and "never inclined to work," van der Riet reproduces a discourse that white people commonly deployed in the Cape. This discourse shows that, as Tiffany Lethabo King writes, "the slave is essential as an object of negation for the construction of the master's notion of self."[208] Although idleness was a white privilege, van der Riet implicitly intimates that white people's wealth, including his own, is due to a presumed work ethic rather than to the enslavement of Black people, including children, and the theft of their land and resources. Representing enslaved and colonized peoples as idle, as we saw, is a colorblind tool that Europeans have used to justify exploitation across national borders. The Khoena were not exempt from this characterization. J. M. Coetzee writes in *White Writing* that the Dutch colonists in the Cape, and the British afterward, frequently depicted the Khoena as idle. However, this discourse was virtually absent prior to 1652: "Surprisingly little mention of Hottentot idleness occurs in the approximately 150 accounts that R. Raven-Hart summarizes from travelers who touched the Cape before 1652. But as the Company begins to settle in . . . the theme becomes more prominent, idleness being described and denounced in the same breadth."[209] What surprises Coetzee is not at all surprising if one considers the function of racist stereotypes, which Coetzee fails to do. Before 1652, white people had no need to rationalize the enslavement and exploitation of the Khoena. With slavery and conquest, white people put colorblind tools into action and the Khoena became "lazier than the tortoises which they hunt and eat," as Dutch colonialist Johan Nieuhof wrote in 1654.[210]

Van der Riet transforms slavery into benevolence as he misrepresents the enslavement of Khoena children as a just "compensation for the *care and trouble* [that white people take] in their upbringing."[211] Khoena children, he writes, are better off living with whites, who "care" for them. White people here are depicted as even better parents to Khoena children than their actual parents as van der Riet turns slavers, to cite Abu-Jamal and Stephen Vittoria in a different context, into "munificent and caring paternal white father figures."[212] Just as Columbus mystifies the theft of Indigenous land by arguing that the Taino "never refuse anything which they possess," van der Riet disguises kidnapping and structural violence by contending that Khoena parents *voluntarily* give their children away to white people. In the process, van der Riet argues that freedom is a "burden" to the Khoena and that slavery is in *their* best interest. Freedom, van der Riet argues, "would make them unhappy."

Yet van der Riet soon contradicts himself, revealing that he does recognize that the Khoena, like all people, have a desire for freedom so that, far from being servile "by nature," they have to be "instilled with a certain sense of service" through a specific "policy." Van der Riet is clearly afraid that Black people may "join together to regain their natural freedom as the original possessors of this country." Their feelings of freedom are "dangerous," van der Riet writes, and must be kept under control. Sealing van der Riet's investment in keeping slavery in place is his reference to the Haitian Revolution ("a second St Domingo"), which demonstrates that white anxieties over slave uprisings and the potential loss of white power reverberated well beyond the American continent, all the way to the Cape Colony.

The letters of Columbus and van der Riet show that white supremacist discourse has always relied on "biologizing" the behaviors of Black people and people of color. In portraying Black people as "lazy," "thieves," in need of control, unwilling to work and learn, and having negligent families, van der Riet's rhetorical arsenal is uncannily similar to contemporary pathologizing discourses that depict Black people as being simply unfit for freedom. Van der Riet's letter shows that enduring racist myths about Black deviance, cultural deficiency, and dysfunctional families are rooted in the same rhetorical archive that white people deployed to justify slavery and colonialism.[213] There is nothing new about these white tactics. Columbus's and van der Riet's writings demonstrate that racism has, from its very inception, relied on discourses of culture and what JanMohamed describes as "the transformation of racial difference into moral and metaphysical difference."[214] It is telling how quickly Lombroso in *L'uomo bianco e l'uomo di colore* moves from speculating on "Anatomical Differences between the Various Human Races" (the title of chapter 2) to "Moral and Intellectual Analogies between the Human Races" (the title of chapter 3).[215] Lombroso was not ahead of his time in arguing that Black people and people of color lack morality and intelligence. Centuries before the birth of scientific racism, the rise of Darwinism, the eugenics movement, and the consolidation of the biological sciences, Europeans like Columbus and van der Riet deliberately fabricated behavioral traits and then treated these traits as the immutable "cultural" properties of the people they enslaved and conquered as a means of racial control. What scholars have identified as a new mode of racialization alternately termed cultural racism, colorblind racism, new racism, or the biologization of culture, in sum, precedes not just the birth of scientific racism, but modern biology itself.

Itinerary

Colorblind Tools is divided into three parts. Part 1, "The Making of White Nations," demonstrates that colorblindness is a white tool of nation building that crosses racial regimes and national borders. Focusing on early twentieth-century Panama, chapter 1, "Colorblindness and Nation Building," illustrates how white nationalism relies on colorblind language, the active disavowal of racism, and the scapegoating of racialized Others as nation-building tools that serve to control the masses and garner political consent. Opening with the 1915 National Conference on Race Betterment, which took place in San Francisco as part of the Panama-Pacific International Exposition, the chapter places anti-Blackness and white supremacy in Panama within a larger hemispheric history in which eugenics, US imperialism, and the construction of the Panama Canal take central stage. Through the study of Panamanian-Ecuadoran writer and military cadet Olmedo Alfaro's 1925 political pamphlet *El peligro antillano en la América Central: La defensa de la raza* (The West Indian Danger in Central America: The Defense of the Race), I examine how the white Panamanian elite of the time targeted West Indian immigrants and conspired with the white USAmericans who controlled the Canal Zone to advance their own economic and political interests. Rather than admitting to their racism and anti-Blackness, white Panamanians like Alfaro argued that their enmity toward West Indian workers was motivated by allegedly unsurmountable cultural, linguistic, and religious differences between West Indians (who were mainly Protestant and English speaking) and local Panamanians (who were mainly Catholic and Spanish speaking). In the process, they propelled a nation building process that symbolically incorporated Afro-Panamanians into the nation-state. As the chapter challenges theories that distinguish between a past epoch of racial dictatorship and a present epoch of racial liberalism, it also throws into crisis the belief that Panama and the United States embody vastly different racial regimes and racial ideologies. Instead, the chapter illustrates the existence and endurance of a transnational white supremacist discourse linking Latin America, the United States, and Europe, the pan-white political and economic interests that shape it, and a long history of deploying colorblindness to bolster white nationalism and control Black mobilization and interracial organizing.

Chapter 2, "Mestizaje and Racial Genocide," demonstrates that white intellectuals in Brazil, Cuba, and Mexico have not only understood mestizaje (racial mixture) as a technology of racial obliteration, but have also actively promoted and exported this technology on a global scale. Starting with a critique of the ongoing transnational romanticization of racial mixture as a presumed social equalizer, I return to an important period in Latin American racial history, the early twentieth century, in which eugenicists shifted from advocating European immigration towards theorizing racial mixture as a tool of "whitening" and racial obliteration. The chapter examines understudied works by José Vasconcelos (Mexico), Fernando Ortiz (Cuba), and Gilberto Freyre (Brazil), three well-known white Latin American intellectuals whose theories of racial mixture have been central to nation-building projects in their respective countries and beyond. Rather than only focusing on their most famous works, I examine Vasconcelos's 1926 lecture "The Race Problem in Latin America," Ortiz's 1942 speech "Por la integración cubana de blancos y negros" (For the Cuban Integration of Whites and Blacks, translated as "The Relations between Blacks and Whites in Cuba"), and Freyre's 1954 "Report on the Most Important and Most Effective Methods for Eliminating Racial Conflicts, Tensions, and Discriminatory Practices Employed with Positive Results in Countries in Different Geographical Regions, in Particular Countries Where Conditions Approximate Most Closely Those of the Union of South Africa," which Freyre wrote at the request of the United Nations Commission on the Racial Situation in the Union of South Africa (UNCORS) and in which he defends colonialism. Through the analysis of these politically crucial yet critically neglected works, I show how Vasconcelos, Ortiz, and Freyre tried to convince, respectively, white USAmericans, Black Cubans, and the apartheid regime in South Africa as well as the global white community that they should deploy racial mixture for their own benefit. These transnational exchanges show that white people have actively shared strategies across national borders, racial regimes, and ideologies to quell the relentless surge of Black and Indigenous liberation movements. Far from being incompatible, I show, ideologies of racial purity and ideologies of racial mixture, as well as theories of assimilation and Ortiz's theory of transculturation, are two sides of the same anti-Black and anti-Indigenous coin.

Part 2, "The Ongoing Race to Silence Race," demonstrates that white people today deploy colorblind rhetoric to halt desegregation measures and prevent the redistribution of resources to Black people and people of color across national and ideological boundaries. Chapter 3, "The White Mobilization against Desegregation and Redistribution," brings

THE MASTER'S COLORBLIND TOOLS   47

together struggles against racial inequality in Brazil, South Africa, and the United States. Leading with the student protests that shook South African universities in 2015, the chapter shows how white people—through control of the media, the law, and academia—collude in silencing structural racism and undercutting desegregation measures and affirmative action programs across three continents. With the aim of illustrating the transportability, malleability, and power of colorblind rhetorics, I examine a body of post-1994 South African scholarship on race produced in economics, education, literature, and sociology alongside Brazilian journalist Ali Kamel's 2006 book *Não somos racistas: uma reação aos que querem nos transformar numa nação bicolor* (We Are Not Racist: A Reaction to Those Who Want to Transform Us into a Bicolor Nation), which demonizes racial quotas for Black students at Brazilian universities, as well as the US Supreme Court case *Parents Involved in Community Schools v. Seattle School District No.1*, which in 2007 struck down an affirmative action program that aimed to desegregate public schools in Seattle, Washington, and Jefferson County, Kentucky. Albeit arising in very different national contexts and belonging to disparate genres, I show, these texts avail themselves of a shared rhetorical repertoire in their common efforts to silence white supremacy and stop measures that aim to redress racial inequality, revealing an ongoing collective white investment in maintaining the racist status quo.

Chapter 4, "The Perils of White 'Antiracism,'" contends with what Wilderson calls *"the unrelenting terror elaborated whenever Black people's so-called allies think out loud."*[216] Drawing centrally from the work of Steve Biko, the chapter shows how white liberals continue to be chief henchmen of white supremacy. Beginning with a critique of the anti-Black politics of Alan Paton, South Africa's most celebrated white liberal, I illustrate how white people tend to frame the question "What should white people do?" in ways that leave white supremacy intact. The chapter examines philosopher Samantha Vice's essay "How Do I Live in This Strange Place?" (2010), which sparked a storm of controversy in South Africa, as a starting point for interrogating understandings of whiteness and racism that pervade white scholarship produced within critical philosophy of race and critical whiteness studies, both in South Africa and the United States. I argue that notions of white guilt, white shame, white habits, and white privilege as they are theorized largely by white philosophers minimize white people's active interest in reproducing the racist status quo. Studies, such as Vice's, that advocate affective responses to racism while silencing its institutionalization and

48   INTRODUCTION

the central cause for its existence and longevity—namely, white people's investment in maintaining white supremacy—sustain the racist infrastructure. These studies parade as antiracist, yet serve as feel-good therapy for white people, while they seek to stymie Black mobilization against racism. In this way, they reveal not just the racism and anti-Blackness of "antiracist" work that is produced from the vantage points of whiteness, but the impossibility of "white antiracism" itself.

Part 3, "Decolonial Imaginaries and Colorblind Logics," illustrates how colorblindness can infiltrate even decolonial literary imaginaries. In this way, it further reveals how colorblindness is intrinsically anti-Black, fundamentally entangled with colonial discourse and liberal humanism, and works with—and *through*—categories other than race, particularly gender, sexuality, class, ethnicity, and nationality. Chapter 5, "Espousing Liberal Individualism in Cubena's Work," starts by asking why the literary and cultural movement of Negritud, which blossomed in Cuba and Puerto Rico in the early twentieth century, did not take root in Panama. Having provided an overview of the location of Blackness in Panamanian letters, I show that Panamanian literature finally makes a decisive turn toward a strong Black consciousness and explicitly antiracist agenda with the appearance of Cubena's fictional works in the 1980s. The grandchild of Jamaican immigrants who built the Panama Canal, Cubena, born Carlos Guillermo Wilson, has dedicated his opus to contesting anti-Black racism and asserting the rightful place of West Indian immigrants in the Panamanian national and literary imaginary. Yet as Cubena's works remain bound to a liberal framework, they also mirror the regressive gender, sexual, and racial politics of white nationalism. Examining Cubena's novels *Chombo* (1981) and *Los nietos de Felicidad Dolores* (The Grandchildren of Felicidad Dolores, 1990) alongside Cubena's short stories, I show how the works' endorsement of liberal individualism and conflation of Blackness with heterosexuality undermine their antiracist agenda. Probing the strategies that Cubena's works deploy to contest anti-Black racism and the symbolic solutions to racism that they propose, reveals the limits of decolonial projects that fall back onto advocating assimilation into the nation-state for Black people. Collective Black liberation, Cubena's works unwittingly show, cannot be achieved from within the frames of liberalism nor through a commitment to heteropatriarchy.

Chapter 6, "Encountering the Other in Chicana Literature," examines Chicana indigenism as an aesthetic and discursive formation through an analysis of Graciela Limón's neo-indigenista novel *Erased Faces*

THE MASTER'S COLORBLIND TOOLS   49

(2001) and Cherríe Moraga's experimental play *The Hungry Woman: A Mexican Medea* (2001). Placing Chicana indigenism within a longer history of Chicanx cultural production and antiracist mobilization with roots in the Chicano Movement, I contend that Chicana writers have created powerful decolonial imaginaries that contest colonialism, heteropatriarchy, and the myopic politics of white feminism, yet a reliance on indigenist aesthetics creates paradoxes in Chicana literature that are in conflict with the theoretical insights of Chicana feminism itself. These paradoxes point to the importance of using these same insights to more carefully attend to the intersectional and relational dimensions of racial subordination. I argue that, as they challenge white supremacy and heteropatriarchy, Chicana indigenist imaginaries that confound the Chicanx self and the Indigenous Other also reinscribe the colorblindness of the white feminism and hegemonic multiculturalism that they contest. In the process, they display a pernicious anti-Blackness and reproduce an epistemology of disavowal that constructs the Chicanx subject as fundamentally innocent.

A Note on Method

Colorblind Tools probes the globality and institutionalization of colorblindness through socially and historically situated readings of texts produced across historical periods, national borders, academic disciplines, literary genres, and languages. While this book is deeply interdisciplinary and transdisciplinary, I do not intend to suggest that thinking outside the rigidities of disciplinarity is the holy grail in the study of racism and anti-Blackness or an antidote to colorblindness per se. More important are the frameworks and lenses through which the problems of white supremacy and anti-Blackness are approached. Not all tools are created equal and Black radical scholars, thinkers, and activists have produced crucial knowledge without which this book could not have been written and to which it is indebted. Here, I draw upon works and theories produced within the Black Radical Tradition (Robinson), Afropessimism, critical race theory (CRT), women of color feminisms, postcolonial theory, and decolonial theory to show that the investment in colorblindness is reflected in long-standing practices that have as their objective the permanence of racism. From postcolonial theory, I take what is useful and leave the rest. I also acknowledge that some particularly famous decoloniality scholars are white men who write as if they were unraced and ungendered beings, barely cite anyone in their work, and especially fail to cite Black scholars. Not all decolonial theory, it seems to me, is genuinely decolonial.

This book challenges the traditional conventions of literary scholarship. Some critics treat literary texts (in a narrow sense) as if they were inherently primary and academic scholarship as if it was intrinsically secondary, mainly there to be "applied." Yet many works of fiction produce theory and many works of theory produce fiction. Most importantly, I question the colorblindness at the heart of dominant literary criticism, which continues to consider the study of racism as extraneous to the discipline or as an ideological endeavor, while it posits ignoring racism as neutral.[217] But there is nothing neutral about silencing racism. As Morrison writes, "The world does not become raceless or will not become unracialized by assertion. The act of enforcing racelessness in literary discourse is itself a racial act."[218] Morrison's insight informs this writing.

I deliberately center racism and anti-Blackness in this book with the aim to highlight their global dimensions. In doing so, I do not intend to simplify the complexities of individual life experiences. Neither is it my intention to portray white supremacy and anti-Blackness as invincible forces. It is obvious, though, that a certain pessimism pervades this work. During the writing process, I have often thought of the words of Derrick Bell, who in the preface of *Faces at the Bottom of the Well* writes: "The challenge throughout has been to tell what I view as the truth about racism without causing disabling despair."[219] This has also been one of my many challenges in the crafting of this book. What is more, as a white woman, I am conscious of the fact that I cannot disentangle this work from the racism that it describes. If anywhere, hope herein lies in the histories of Black, Brown, and Indigenous resistance that permeate it—from the cimarrón revolts (slave uprisings) in Latin America to the Panamanian labor movement to which West Indian workers were central, from the Chicano Movement in the United States to the Zapatista Movement in Mexico, from the Black Consciousness Movement to the Rhodes Must Fall Movement in South Africa, and beyond. These histories show that white power and anti-Blackness are not unassailable, but constantly under threat. Colorblindness has not been around for over five centuries by coincidence. Its existence speaks to the fact that white supremacy is, at its core, fundamentally weak. It cannot sustain itself either on truth or morality and, like a thief who knows well that she is stealing, it wears a mask, tries to hide, and disavows its own existence.

THE MASTER'S COLORBLIND TOOLS 51

While I have chosen to employ it in this book, the term *colorblindness* is problematic and requires clarification. First and foremost, it suggests that race and color are equivalent, yet to view race as being synonymous with skin color is reductionist. Zuberi and Bonilla-Silva explain that "racial identity is about shared social status, not shared individual characteristics. Race is not about an individual's skin color. Race is about an individual's relationship to other people within society."[220] Race is about the *meanings* attributed to skin color and the differential ways in which dark- and light-skinned people are treated in a white supremacist society. Reducing race merely to skin color is itself a colorblind move.[221] In this view, racial categories such as *Black* and *white* are treated as apolitical and neutral descriptions, rather than as products of historical and material conditions of domination and dispossession produced through slavery and colonialism. Understanding that race and skin color are not equivalent, however, does not mean denying that race is embodied. Providing important insights on this matter, Fanon's analysis of antisemitism vis-à-vis anti-Black racism points to the unique ways that Black people are oppressed. Unlike Jewish people, Fanon emphasizes, Black people are immediately and inescapably racialized through their appearance. In Fanon's words, "The Jew is disliked from the moment he is tracked down. But in my case everything takes on a *new* guise. I am given no chance. I am overdetermined from without. I am the slave not of the 'idea' that others have of me but of my own appearance."[222] While it is not equivalent to race, color, Fanon reminds us, does matter a huge deal.

Coining a new term to substitute colorblindness, such as *raceblindness*, leaves open the question of what to do about *blindness*, a term which suggests that race is something that can be primarily seen with the eyes, meaning that it presumes an ophthalmic understanding of race. The term also intimates a false equivalence between blindness and the inability to perceive racial difference, although people who have been blind since birth can "see race" in a white supremacist society, as the scholarship of Osagie K. Obasogie shows.[223] This is so because complex social interactions give race its meaning, as people are racialized also through language, nationality, culture, or the neighborhood in which they live. The terms colorblindness and raceblindness are both vexed because they evoke the idea of "not seeing race," in the sense of omitting or ignoring race. In speaking of colorblind *tools*, I contest commonsense understandings of colorblindness and emphasize that assertions such as "I am colorblind!" and "I don't see race!" are not statements of fact. They are themselves colorblind tools.

52   INTRODUCTION

Among its multiple shortcomings, the term colorblindness is also fundamentally tied to the English language, to the extent that I myself struggle to translate the title of this book into Italian, my native tongue. The Italian word *daltonico* does not capture the metaphorical meanings that have come to be associated with the English term *colorblind*. The term colorblindness, in sum, is admittedly a placeholder that necessarily fails to capture the complexity of the object of analysis.

I choose to employ the term colorblindness despite its shortcomings not only because it has become established in the scholarly conversations that *Colorblind Tools* enters and seeks to challenge, but also because I recognize that, in the fight for racial justice, merely changing names only takes us so far. Here, I agree with George Lipsitz, who argues that "we need to change the game, not just the names by which it is called."[224] In historicizing and theorizing colorblindness as both a technology (a world-making instrument) and an epistemology (a way of understanding and describing the world), I aim to show that colorblindness is instrumental to the functioning of white supremacy and anti-Blackness. My intention in this book is not to reify the term colorblindness, and much less to redeem it, but rather to expose the violence that subtends it. Ultimately, what I aim to demonstrate is that disavowal is constitutive to racism as white people have always tried to hide the fact that, as Césaire writes, "Europe is responsible before the human community for the highest heap of corpses in history."[225] We must never take for granted that what Europe has said and continues to say about itself does not match the historical record. Neither should we ignore continuities between racist and antiracist discourses as these speak volumes about the insidiousness of colorblindness and the coloniality of our time.

Given that the contours of colorblindness are not easily delimitated, and that a study of race across historical, national, and linguistic boundaries always involves conceptual difficulties, a project such as this presents significant challenges and limitations. Like an octopus with wide-ranging tentacles, colorblindness avails itself of a multiplicity of tools and principles that do not always appear to have anything to do with race. It is also for this reason that colorblindness is so effective in supporting the racist infrastructure. While one goal of this book is to examine and make visible the rhetorical and narrative elements that structure colorblindness as a discourse, I recognize that I cannot provide a complete repertoire. Neither can I clearly define the boundaries of colorblindness—whether as a technology, a discourse, or an epistemology. Instead of attempting to resolve these limitations, I aim to make them speak to the power and malleability of colorblindness itself. Hence, *Colorblind Tools* concurrently illustrates the transportability of colorblindness across time and space, its contextual and geographical situatedness, and its inextricability from deeply entrenched ontologies and epistemologies grounded in racialized slavery and colonialism. As none of the works that disavow racism examined herein manage to leave race behind, they show that enforcing colorblindness is an act of epistemic violence: not even at the textual level is racelessness achievable.

Part 1

The Making of White Nations

I

Colorblindness and Nation Building

They talk to me about progress, about "achievements," diseases cured, improved standards of living. . . . They throw facts at my head, statistics, mileages of roads, canals, and railroad tracks. *I* am talking about thousands of men sacrificed to the Congo-Ocean. I am talking about those who, as I write this, are digging the harbor of Abidjan by hand.
　　—Aimé Césaire, *Discourse on Colonialism*

Nuestro país . . . puede presentarse como uno de aquellos en los que la discriminación racial es casi inexistente. (Our country . . . can present itself as one of those in which racial discrimination is almost inexistent).
　　—Jorge E. Ritter, then Panama's minister of foreign affairs, in a 1980
　　　　letter to the organizers of the First Congress of the Black Panamanian

In August 1915, a group of white men who represented the most prominent US eugenicists of the time met in San Francisco to discuss methods and policies that should be adopted to improve the white "racial stock" and achieve greater "racial purity." Organized by Stanford University's founding president David Starr Jordan, the National Conference on Race Betterment was a highlight of the Panama-Pacific International Exposition, a world's fair that celebrated the completion of the Panama Canal, entertaining nearly nineteen million visitors in 288 days.[1] On the closing day of the conference, eugenicist Henry Smith Williams, in a *San Francisco Chronicle* column titled "The Greatest Migration in History," defined the increasing presence of immigrants in the United States as "probably the greatest problem that has been presented since

57

58   THE MAKING OF WHITE NATIONS

civilization began."[2] However, he added, this "would have no great significance from the standpoint of the eugenicist if the immigrants who
have come to us in such numbers in the recent years were of the same
stock as the original colonists."[3] Perhaps due to the racial perception
that the US organizers had of their southern neighbors, Latin American
delegates were not invited to the conference. Panama itself was present only symbolically at the fair, as the embodiment of technological
progress, the reaches of manifest destiny, and US imperial ascendancy.[4]

Yet, while foreign delegates can be excluded, racist ideologies travel
freely across national borders. Four years before *The Birth of a Nation*
director D. W. Griffith could praise the Panama-Pacific extravaganza
as "the grandest thing the world has known,"[5] Brazilian eugenicist
João Batista de Lacerda predicted the extinction of Black people in his
country. At the 1911 Universal Races Congress in London, Lacerda
announced that, thanks to racial "miscegenation,"[6] the Brazilian population would be "whitened" completely by 2012 (one hundred years
later).[7] In *La raza cósmica* (*The Cosmic Race*), Mexican philosopher
and politician José Vasconcelos described the Spanish and the English
as "los dos tipos humanos más fuertes y más disímiles" (the strongest
and most different human types).[8] In 1925, the same year in which Vasconcelos published *La raza cósmica*, Panamanian-Ecuadoran writer and
military cadet Olmedo Alfaro expressed trepidation about the presence
of West Indian immigrants in Central America. In a pamphlet titled *El
peligro antillano en la América Central: La defensa de la raza* (The West
Indian Danger in Central America: The Defense of the Race), citing the
Panamanian weekly newspaper *Gráfico*, Alfaro writes:

> Uno de los más serios problemas que el país debe resolver es
> el de los antillanos que infestan nuestras principales ciudades,
> que están rebajando el *standart* de nuestra vida con sus costum-
> bres exóticas y que han dado a Panamá, Colón y Bocas, amén de
> otros lugares, el aspecto de harcas africanas. . . . Por qué no se
> resuelve de una vez un problema tan grave como éste, cuyo apla-
> zamiento redunda en perjuicio de Panamá, de su estirpe racial
> y de su buen nombre en el extranjero? O será que nos agrada
> que todo forastero que nos visita salga diciendo que somos una
> "manada de negros," porque los antillanos, sumados a nuestros
> negros nativos, abruman al elemento panameño y extranjero
> blanco, y damos la impresión de que aquí sólo hay negros.[9]

COLORBLINDNESS AND NATION BUILDING

> One of the most serious problems that the country must resolve is that of the West Indians who infest our main cities, who are lowering our standard of living with their exotic customs, and who have given Panama City, Colón, and Bocas, apart from other places, the appearance of African enclaves. . . . Why not solve once and for all a problem as serious as this, the postponement of which is detrimental to Panama, its racial stock, and its good name abroad? Or do we perhaps like the fact that every foreigner who visits us ends up saying that we are a "herd of Negroes," because the West Indians, added to our native Negroes, overwhelm the Panamanian and foreign white element, and we give the impression that here there are only Negroes.[10]

While US eugenicists were developing theories for the advancement of "racial purity" that theoretically excluded some of their ostensibly mestizo Latin American colleagues from the white community they envisioned, the white Latin American intelligentsia to which Alfaro belonged, this passage makes amply clear, was equally preoccupied with "su estirpe racial" (its racial stock) and equally invested in the expulsion of racialized immigrants.

Rather than being relevant merely as a historical artifact testifying to an archaic epoch of racial dictatorship that has allegedly been overcome, there is much to be learned from re-reading *El peligro antilliano* today. As he directs himself to a transnational audience, Alfaro argues that West Indian immigrants pose a problem not just in Panama, but in Central America as a whole, and specifically a problem for white people. Even as his commitment to white supremacy and anti-Blackness is explicit in the text, Alfaro denies any racist intent. Instead, Alfaro mobilizes an array of colorblind tools to persuade the reader that he has the interests of both Black and white people at heart, and that his presumed battle to defend Panamanians and Central Americans at large from what he terms the "West Indian problem" has nothing to do with racism and anti-Blackness, but constitutes a national, economic, cultural, linguistic, and religious *necessity*.

Placed within its historical and transnational context, Alfaro's manifesto challenges time-bound distinctions between racial dictatorship and racial liberalism as well as throws into crisis geography-bound assumptions that Panama and the United States embody fundamentally different racial regimes and racial ideologies. Intervening in Howard Winant's theory of the racial break, Jodi Melamed argues in *Represent*

60   THE MAKING OF WHITE NATIONS

and Destroy: Rationalizing Violence in the New Racial Capitalism (2011) that post–World War II racial liberalism represents "an epochal shift—a sea change in racial orders."[11] She posits a transformation even more radical than what Winant's theorization of a post–World War II shift from racial dictatorship to racial hegemony allows for. While she takes Winant's racial break as a key premise of her study, Melamed argues that the break "instantiated a new worldwide racial project that completely supplemented and displaced its predecessor: a formally antiracist, liberal-capitalist modernity articulated under conditions of U.S. global ascendancy."[12] *El peligro antillano* and the transnational histories that brought it into being unsettle this argument as the "conditions of U.S. global ascendancy" were *already* present in Alfaro's Panama.

The second edition of a work written a decade earlier, *El peligro antillano* shows that the history of US imperialism in Latin America must be read as the history of the protection of white privilege in "America's backyard." Born in Panama in 1878 to a powerful family, Alfaro was the eldest son of José Eloy Alfaro, who was president of Ecuador from 1895 to 1901 and 1906 to 1911, and Ana Paredes Arosemena, a Panamanian woman.[13] A general trained at the United States Military Academy at West Point and the École spéciale militaire de Saint-Cyr in Paris (then the training school for the French army), Alfaro presents himself as the defender of Panamanian national sovereignty in his pamphlet. Yet he is actually complicit with US imperialism. Rather than being rivals, white USAmericans—whom Alfaro defines as "una raza sincera y democrática, siempre que se trata de la expresión del pensamiento hablado o escrito" (a race that is sincere and democratic at least as far as the expression of their spoken or written thought is concerned)[14]—and members of the local white elite such as Alfaro shared similar racialized interests in the Panamanian territory and worked together to uphold them.

El peligro antillano challenges the dominant Panamanian argument that white USAmericans "imported" racism into Panama and are solely responsible for it.[15] On this matter, Michael Conniff writes: "Some Panamanians insisted that the country did not know race prejudice until exposed to the U.S. system. In this view, Panamanians learned prejudice from the Americans but then rejected it as unnatural. . . . The record does not support this interpretation, however, because the white Panamanian elite had collaborated with the Zonians to keep the racially mixed masses in a subservient position."[16] To understand how the Panamanian intelligentsia acted together with USAmerican imperialists to safeguard their common racialized interests, it is necessary to recall

COLORBLINDNESS AND NATION BUILDING   61

that the history of Panama is intimately tied to the United States, which exercised colonial control over Panama for over seventy years. When Panama gained independence from Spain in 1821, it was incorporated into the federation of Gran Colombia. Its successive attempts to achieve independence from Colombia failed, until the United States supported Panama's independentistas in 1903, in exchange for the right to control the Canal Zone in perpetuity.[17] While this history is well known, it is less often acknowledged that white USAmericans did not act alone in their conquest of Panama, but could count on the full support of members of the local white elite such as Alfaro.

As white Panamanians collaborated with the white USAmerican imperialists that controlled the Canal Zone, they concealed their alliance with the United States, projecting instead this alliance onto West Indian immigrants, whom they branded as complicit with US imperialism. Admitting to their anti-Blackness, white supremacy, and collusion with US imperialism would have been in conflict with the white Panamanian elite's attempt to co-opt the racialized working classes, who represented the majority of the population, and turn them against West Indian immigrants. White Panamanians thus disavowed any racist intent. Their intention was to divide Afro-Panamanians (mainly descendants of enslaved African people who were brought to Panama during the colonial period and who are referred to as *negros nativos* or *negros coloniales*; henceforth Afro-Panamanians) and West Indians (Black people who first arrived in Panama in the early nineteenth century and who are referred to as *afro-antillianos*; henceforth Antilleans, West Indians, or West Indian Panamanians).[18]

This divide-and-conquer strategy had damaging consequences for Afro-Panamanians, who were often co-opted into viewing their interests as conflicting with those of West Indian immigrants. Reacting to the murder of Justo Jaén that I describe in the introduction, a West Indian newspaper argued that "colored Panamanians, no matter how dark their complexion, have always insisted that they have nothing in common with the colored West Indian."[19] After the murder of his son, Justo Jaén's father himself sided with the authorities in condemning West Indians who had led an uprising in protest of the teenager's murder.[20] To this day, Blackness in Panama remains associated mostly with West Indians, who are often viewed as the only Black people in the country, while Afro-Panamanians tend to refer to themselves euphemistically as *morenos*.[21] The white ruling class to which Alfaro belonged exploited linguistic, cultural, and religious differences between Panamanians,

62   THE MAKING OF WHITE NATIONS

who are Spanish speaking and predominantly Catholic, and West Indians, who are English speaking and mainly Protestant.[22] In the process, they propelled a nation-building process that symbolically incorporated Afro-Panamanians into the nation-state without providing any material improvements in their living conditions.

The disavowal of racist intent and the packaging of anti-Black racism as a matter of culture, religion, and national security structures the rhetorics of *El peligro antillano*. Neither new nor geographically circumscribed, colorblindness is always in vogue where white supremacy and anti-Blackness are at work. As a discourse, it coexists comfortably with overt white supremacy. This is already evident from the title—*El peligro antillano en la América Central: La defensa de la raza* (The West Indian Danger in Central America: The Defense of the Race)—in which Alfaro defines West Indians as a "danger" and "the race" as something that should be *defended*. In adopting the wording "la defensa de la raza" in the title, Alfaro's writing preceded by more than two decades *La difesa della razza* (The Defense of the Race), the homonymous Fascist magazine founded by Italian journalist and antisemite propagandist Telesio Interlandi in 1938 that was instrumental in disseminating white supremacist doctrines in Benito Mussolini's Italy.[23] It should not surprise us that Alfaro, who in 1936 became consul general of Ecuador in Prague and then in Panama, would become an admirer of Adolf Hitler, whom he praised in various writings.[24]

El peligro antillano shows that lies, mystifications, and disavowal are immanent to white supremacist discourse. The pamphlet opens as follows:

> Las Repúblicas Ibero-Americanas tal como ahora las vemos desaparecerán, para unirse en un solo Estado compacto, y entonces nos encontraremos probablemente con el problema Antillano, tal como tiene Norte-América su problema racial negro, que tanto los preocupa, que ya causó una terrible guerra civil y cuyas proyecciones para el futuro aún son desconocidas.[25]

> The Ibero-American Republics as we know them now will disappear, to unite in one single compact State, and then we will be probably faced with the West Indian problem, just like North-America has its Negro racial problem, which worries them much, which has already caused a terrible civil war, and whose projections for the future are still unknown.

COLORBLINDNESS AND NATION BUILDING 63

Not just in Panama, Alfaro contends, but everywhere in Central America, West Indians pose a "danger." As he envisions this danger as crossing national boundaries, Alfaro argues that Central American nations are on the verge of uniting "en un solo Estado compacto" (in one single compact State). This, of course, never occurred. According to Ecuadoran historian Rodolfo Pérez Pimentel, Alfaro wanted the unification of all Latin American countries liberated by Simón Bolívar. In the attempt to materialize what appear to be imperial ambitions, Alfaro in 1933 presented a memorandum to the Venezuelan president outlining the necessary steps for the integration of the army, merchant navy, and for a common citizenship in all Bolivarian countries.[26] When he writes *El peligro antillano*, Alfaro has not even petitioned for such a unification yet. Nonetheless in the work he confidently announces that Central American nations "desaparecerán" (will disappear) into a single state. If Alfaro is no stranger to mystification, neither is Pimentel, his biographer. When Alfaro died, on May 18, 1959, not just authorities came to his funeral in Colón, Pimentel insists, but also "amigos y pueblo en general, especialmente los jamaicanos, sus vecinos de barrio" (friends and people in general, especially the Jamaicans, his neighbors).[27] As it conjures the racist "friend of the natives" trope, Alfaro's portrayal suggests that Pimentel knows well that Alfaro had no interest in the welfare of Black people. This is obvious in *El peligro antillano*, where Alfaro immediately defines "the West Indian danger" as a racial question to which *Blackness* is central. Referring to white people in the United States, Alfaro writes that "the West Indian problem" is analogous to the "problema racial negro, que tanto los preocupa" (the Negro racial problem, which worries them much).[28] But while Alfaro's commitment to anti-Blackness and white supremacy is evident from the start, he will soon disavow any racist intent.

El peligro antillano shows that colorblindness functions as a technology of white nation building that has historically relied upon, and continues to rely upon, the scapegoating of racialized Others to manipulate poor and working people into supporting a social system that does not benefit them. Engaging in the long-standing populist deployment of racialized anti-immigrant propaganda to support white power, Alfaro immediately (in the third paragraph) represents West Indians as a menace for "las clases obreras del Istmo" (the working classes of the Isthmus).[29] He describes the presence of West Indian immigrants in Panama as an "invasión" (invasion)[30] and argues that West Indian workers are profiting from jobs that rightfully belong to Panamanians.

In this way, Alfaro deceptively presents himself as concerned about the welfare of Panamanian workers. Citing again an article from the local newspaper *Gráfico*, Alfaro writes, "al elemento nativo se les estrecha cada día más el horizonte del trabajo, se les esfuman las perspectivas de ganarse la vida, se les va sumiendo, por la preferencia al extranjero, en un abismo de desesperación y de miseria" (for the native element, the horizon of work is getting narrower each day, the prospects for making a living vanish, they are disappearing, due to the preference for the foreigner, in an abyss of despair and destitution).[31] The argument that immigrants "steal jobs" from locals, which Alfaro reproduces here, is an old colorblind tool aimed at hindering solidarity among working people while garnering their consent. It allows white elites to profit from the cheap labor of vulnerable racialized immigrants (who must have as few rights as possible so that they can be maximally exploited), co-opt local workers into understanding themselves in competition with a foreign labor force, and solidify a nation-building process grounded in a commitment to chauvinism across class and racial boundaries—all while shielding the elites themselves from accusations of racism.

Alfaro is neither original nor ahead of his time in invoking proletarian precariousness and exploiting working-class fears of racialized competition in the labor market. In the United States, the historical deployment of racist propaganda as a divide-and-conquer strategy is as old as the history of whiteness itself. While the Panamanian case helps us understand how white people have long deployed colorblind rhetoric to divide poor people of color, the solidification of whiteness on US plantations shows that racist ideology also serves to control poor white people.[32] Racism is the great white unifier, the thing that whiteness is built upon. Derrick Bell writes that "even when nonracist practices might bring a benefit, whites may rely on discrimination against blacks as a unifying factor and a safety valve for frustrations during economic hard times."[33] During plantation slavery, poor whites in the US South usually preferred to serve on the slave patrol and maintain a system that financially disadvantaged them, rather than join forces with Black people to overthrow slavery.

Alfaro's argument that West Indians take jobs from Panamanian workers is a tactic to which white economic interests are central. Alfaro both fostered and exploited the local animosity against West Indians, who represented the principal workforce in the Canal Zone.[34] The years of the Canal construction were romanticized in Panama as a "heroic era, one of vast accomplishments, sacrifices, great men, camaraderie,

COLORBLINDNESS AND NATION BUILDING

and history-in-the-making."[35] West Indians sacrificed the most in the process, working ten hours a day for six days a week, yet they received no recognition for their labor and sacrifices.[36] Although Black people built and ensured the functioning of the Canal, white USAmericans claimed the Canal as a success story for themselves, greeting its completion with lavish celebrations at the Panama-Pacific International Exposition.[37] West Indians, whom USAmericans preferred to hire over the local population because they spoke English, were paid much less than white Canal workers, but "still received wages almost double those paid to Panamanians outside of the Zone."[38] This shows that the white Panamanian elite exploited Black and mestizo workers *even more* than white USAmericans did in the Canal Zone. Clearly, white Panamanians did not care about the "desesperación y . . . miseria" (desperation and . . . destitution) that the masses suffered. They were, after all, chiefly responsible for this suffering. To uphold this exploitation, they conveniently pitted Black Panamanians against Black West Indians, who became the scapegoats in a system that benefitted white people, both local and foreign.

White people targeted West Indians also because, through their collective mobilization, they posed a serious threat to white power. West Indians were at the forefront of the Panamanian labor movement. In the words of historian Jacob Zumoff, "The mainly West Indian workforce in the Panama Canal had the power to paralyze the Panamanian economy—and international commerce."[39] During the Canal construction years (1904–14), and also after the completion of the Canal, West Indian workers went on strike repeatedly to protest abject working and living conditions in the Zone, while the Panamanian government and the Zonians (white USAmericans) worked together to halt the strikes through violent repression.[40] For example, in April 1905, Jamaican workers protested against the poor quality of the food they were served in the Zone and against delays in receiving their salary.[41] When a group of approximately 150 Jamaicans employed to lay water mains and sewers in Panama City refused to work, the Panamanian police reacted by savagely clubbing and beating twenty-one people, all of them Black.[42] This brutal repression speaks volumes about what Rinaldo Walcott calls *the long emancipation*, namely how "at every moment Black peoples have sought, for themselves, to assert what freedom might mean and look like, those desires and acts toward freedom have been violently interdicted."[43] Despite this violent interdiction, Black people have relentlessly fought back. In Panama, West Indian workers continued

66   THE MAKING OF WHITE NATIONS

to organize even after the Canal was completed. Rather than relenting, they became more militant. Beginning in 1919, the teachings of Marcus Garvey, disseminated through the Universal Negro Improvement Association (UNIA) and Garvey's widely read newspaper the *Negro World*, exercised a powerful influence on Black workers in the Canal Zone, to the extent that many West Indian labor leaders were active UNIA members.[44]

Published by the National Press of Panama, the official press of the Panamanian state, *El peligro antillano* demonstrates that the Panamanian government actively targeted West Indian immigrants through racist propaganda. In 1926, just one year after Alfaro's pamphlet was reissued, the Panamanian government would pass Law 13, which halted the immigration of non-Spanish speaking Black people to the republic, and Law 6, which required 75 percent of employees in any businesses to be Panamanian.[45] In 1941, President Arnulfo Arias went as far as stripping Panamanians of West Indian descent of citizenship, including those born in Panama.[46] Works such as Alfaro's pamphlet fueled the persecution of West Indians, which culminated in a fully fledged deportation campaign. Alfaro nonetheless insists that his anti-West Indian sentiments have nothing to do with racism. He writes:

> No existe en nuestros pueblos el ánimo de oponerse a la invasión antillana por causas puramente raciales[;] sabe el mundo que aquellos colonos africanos que nuestros progenitores importaron a Ibero-América, recibieron siempre el mejor trato dentro de las costumbres de la época. . . . Comparado nuestro criterio para con las gentes de color, con el de otros pueblos del mismo continente: Estados Unidos, por ejemplo, el antillano aceptará que sólo existe de nuestra parte un deseo de defensa cultural y económica, más bien que racial. Tres mil ciento cuarenta y seis negros fueron linchados en Norte-América, en los treinta y nueve años que terminaron en 1923; entre nosotros no han pasado esas cosas.[47]

> In our countries a desire to oppose the West Indian invasion for purely racial reasons does not exist[;] the world knows that those African settlers that our progenitors imported to Ibero-America always received the best treatment within the customs of the time. . . . Comparing our criteria toward people of color with that of other people of the same continent: the United

COLORBLINDNESS AND NATION BUILDING

> States, for example, the West Indian will accept that on our part there only is a desire for cultural and economic defense, rather than racial. Three thousand one hundred and forty-six Negroes were lynched in North America in the thirty-nine years ending in 1923; here, these things have not happened.

Even as he describes the West Indian presence in Panama as an "invasion," Alfaro argues that his motivations are not racial, but only cultural and economic. Obfuscating the fact of slavery, Alfaro transforms enslaved African people into "colonos" (settlers), thereby silencing the fact that, to this day, as Walcott writes, "for Black subjects . . . settlement is impossible; citizenship is a mirage; and the nation-state is the site of our deepest estrangement and our deaths."[48] Rather than being a racial paradise, as Alfaro contends, Panama and other Latin American nations have been precisely sites of death for Black people. Invoking racial democracy allows Alfaro to guard both individual and collective white interests, presenting himself as an embodiment of the alleged characteristics of his society. This both de-individualizes his endeavor and universalizes white supremacy. Alfaro never says, "I am not racist." Instead, he resorts to a much more powerful colorblind tool: he discursively removes racism from the landscape he inhabits. Hence, he argues that "no existe en nuestros pueblos el problema social entre individuos de la raza Indo-Americana. No hay 'mío ni tuyo'; todos somos hermanos dentro de una verdadera democracia, tanto en el Brasil, en donde existen muchos millones de negros como en el Istmo Centro-Americano, en donde sólo suman aún pocos miles" (among our people the social problem among individuals of the Indo-American race does not exist. There is no 'mine or yours'; we are all brothers within a true democracy, whether in Brazil, where there are many millions of Negroes, or in the Central American Isthmus, where there are still only a few thousand).[49] Having argued that West Indian immigrants "overwhelm the Panamanian and foreign white element," Alfaro now invents an inclusive "Indo-American race" to further hide the existence of racial hierarchies in Panama and Latin America more broadly. However, Alfaro contradicts himself. Despite his invocation of a single "Indo-American race" he cannot avoid referring to Black people, revealing again his racist agenda through their demonization. Moreover, although here he states that there are "only a few thousand" Black people in Central America, Alfaro concurrently depicts Black people as an engulfing presence.

68 THE MAKING OF WHITE NATIONS

Confining racism to the United States (and Europe), as Alfaro does, is a strategy commonly employed by white Latin Americans to deflect attention away from their own racism. Deploying this tactic, white Mexican historian Enrique Krauze writes in *La historia cuenta* (1998): "Se ha dicho que nuestro país es racista. Quienes esto afirman deberían preguntarle qué es el racismo a un judío sobreviviente del nazismo, a los huérfanos y viudas de Bosnia o a alguno del medio millón de negros que marcharon hasta el Capitolio en Washington." (It has been said that our country is racist. Those who affirm this should ask what racism is to a Jewish survivor of Nazism, to the orphans and widows of Bosnia or to one of the half million Blacks who marched to the Capitol in Washington).[50] As they insist that racism is the prerogative of Europe and the United States, arguments such as these silence the fact of racial genocide in Latin America, the subject of the next chapter. The ideology of racial democracy that Alfaro exploits provides him with an expedient arsenal of rhetorical weapons for the protection of whiteness not always available to his white US contemporaries to the same extent. During the nineteenth and early twentieth centuries, US minstrel shows, the plantation writings of which Thomas Nelson Page's works are representative, and novels such as Harriet Beecher Stowe's *Uncle Tom's Cabin* also provided romanticized depictions of Black life under plantation slavery. Still, white Latin American intellectuals such as Alfaro have even more systematically relied upon idealized versions of history that have stood the test of time.

Alongside fears about the economic welfare of the working classes, Alfaro exploits local anxieties about being engulfed by an Other whose customs, language, and religion are different from those of the local population. Again disavowing his own racism, Alfaro argues that he is opposed to West Indian immigration because of the "descomposición del carácter nacional de los habitantes de la República de Panamá" (decomposition of the national character of the inhabitants of the Republic of Panama), which he describes as a disfiguration of "sus costumbres, su lengua, sus instituciones, su situación industrial y agrícola y aun su religion" (its customs, its language, its institutions, its industrial and agricultural situation and even its religion).[51] In the process, he demonizes West Indians by describing their presence in Panama as nothing less than a "colonización" (colonization),[52] projecting the colonization to which West Indians were subjected in the Canal Zone onto West Indians themselves. In a later passage, again citing the Panamanian newspaper *Gráfico*, Alfaro returns to the argument that West Indian

COLORBLINDNESS AND NATION BUILDING   69

immigrants take jobs from Panamanians: "Nuestra situacíon económica empeora todos los días; el trabajo escasea a diario; las oportunidades de ocupación son menos y menos con el tiempo. Vámos a permitir que se beneficie de ellas . . . un elemento extraño inasimilable, inferior y perjudicial desde todo punto de vista sociológico?" (Our economic situation deteriorates every day; work dwindles daily; job opportunities shrink as time passes. Are we going to permit that a strange, unassimilable, inferior and prejudicial element under all sociological aspects . . . should benefit from them?).[53] It is striking that the author of the *Gráfico* column that Alfaro cites refrains from employing discourses of biological inferiority, describing West Indians instead as *sociologically* inferior to Panamanians. As we saw, Alfaro writes that "West Indians are lowering our standard of living with their exotic customs." In this way, *El peligro antillano* also illustrates how white people have long invoked discourses of cultural deficiency, which conflate behavior and culture,[54] to reinscribe anti-Black racism.

The denigration of the Black Other in *El peligro antillano* is inevitably accompanied by a valorization of the white self. However, instead of calling white Panamanians by their name, Alfaro disguises the racial nature of this white self through colorblind tools that reference language and culture as he describes white people as "los amigos del idioma castellano y de la cultura Latina" (the friends of the Spanish language and the Latin culture).[55] Shedding light onto the workings of colorblindness, Claire Jean Kim explains that language "can sustain racialized meanings, even when publicly such may appear to be declined or disavowed. Discourses on 'race,' then, might not necessarily reference 'race' at all."[56] Employing racially coded language allows Alfaro to reinscribe racial power through the rhetorical manipulation of linguistic signifiers that concurrently conceal and reinforce the normativity of whiteness.

El peligro antillano reveals a commitment to what Tukufu Zuberi and Eduardo Bonilla-Silva define as "white methods."[57] The supporting data reported in the pamphlet has been carefully selected with the goal of depicting white people as a small and vulnerable minority threatened by an "overwhelming" number of Black people. Alfaro's figures show that Black people in 1911 outnumbered whites in the provinces of Panama, Colón, and Bocas del Toro.[58] The majority of Black people in the three provinces listed, Alfaro argues, "en su mayoría son Antillanos, que fueron traídos para la excavación y operación del Canal de Panamá" (are mostly West Indians, who were brought for the excavation and

70   THE MAKING OF WHITE NATIONS

operation of the Panama Canal).[59] As he fabricates racial data, Alfaro deliberately *only* lists the three Panamanian provinces that have a numerous Black presence, providing no information on any other province. Darién, for example, a region with a large Indigenous population and few inhabitants of African descent, is never mentioned in the text.

Published in the same year as Vasconcelos's *La raza cósmica*, Alfaro's pamphlet represents West Indians as enemies of the Panamanian nation and enemies of the white race. Indebted to the Darwinism and scientific racism of their time, Vasconcelos and Alfaro both invoke mestizaje (racial mixture) as a tool of racial obliteration. Alfaro raises the question of racial mixture, yet rapidly rejects the possibility of assimilating West Indians either culturally or biologically (the myth that races are a biological reality was a cornerstone of the race science that Alfaro and Vasconcelos espoused). Neither is Alfaro invested in constructing Panama as a mestizo nation, which is at the center of Vasconcelos's articulation of a Mexican national identity. Nonetheless, Vasconcelos and Alfaro's starting point (the belief that white people are superior) and their end goal (the maintenance of white supremacy and erasure of Black people) are the same.

In the early twentieth century, white Latin American scientists, politicians, and intellectuals, as we will see in the next chapter, started to theorize racial mixture as an efficient method for the realization of racial genocide. Why, then, does Alfaro reject miscegenation, and even cultural assimilation, as viable strategies for eliminating West Indians in the Isthmus? Alfaro lists more than one reason for his opposition to assimilation for West Indians. Citing Thomas Nelson Page, Alfaro argues that, from a first contingent of only twenty slaves, the Black population in the United States increased to twenty million people. Alfaro presents this as alleged proof that people of African descent *in general* reproduce rapidly. He continues:

> Por qué no puede convertirse el Istmo Centro-Americano en el futuro, en un centro poderoso de la raza negra antillana si a tiempo no se atiende el problema? Sabido es que nuestras poblaciones Istmicas Centro-Americanas, no cuentan con elementos de raza puramente blanca, en cantidades aplastantes que puedan absorber al correr del tiempo el elemento Antillano.[60]

> Why can't the Central American Isthmus in the future become a powerful center of the Negro West Indian race if the problem is

COLORBLINDNESS AND NATION BUILDING

not promptly resolved? It is well known that there are not enough elements of a purely white race in overwhelming quantities that can sufficiently absorb the West Indian element over time.

Alfaro illustrates how the goal of mestizaje is the *absorption* of Black people in a process aimed at "overwhelming" them and propelling their disappearance, as I explore in detail in the next chapter. This eugenicist process presupposes a white population that acts as a kind of solvent meant to dilute, and ultimately eliminate, the Black element. Let us remember that Lacerda announced that miscegenation would lead to the disappearance of Black people in Brazil. As Alfaro's language makes clear that the investment in a "purely white race" is not extraneous to Latin American racist discourse, Alfaro casts West Indians as radical Others who should not be assimilated from any point of view. Yet as he rejects assimilation for West Indians, he ironically grants West Indians the agency to collectively *exclude themselves* in an act of choice. Alfaro writes, "Es un hecho comprobado que el negro antillano no absorbe nuestra civilización, sino que permanece perfectamente extraño a ella." (It is a proven fact that the West Indian Negro does not absorb our civilization, but remains perfectly foreign to it).[61] Herein lies the racist paradox of assimilation discourses: Alfaro actively excludes Black immigrants from the nation-state, yet argues that Black immigrants themselves do not *want* to integrate.

The central location of white British and USAmerican writers in Alfaro's text further challenges discourses that posit clear-cut distinctions between Latin American and Euro-American racist theories and ideologies. In the ultimate attempt to argue against the assimilation of West Indians, Alfaro misquotes British eugenicist James Bryce, who in *The Relations of the Advanced and the Backward Races of Mankind* (1902) writes that "the mixture of whites and negroes, or of whites and Hindus, or of the American aborigines and negroes, seldom shows good results."[62] Alfaro deliberately manipulates Bryce's text, attributing to him the phrase, "la mezcla de los *negros-antillanos* y blancos, o los hindús, o los aborígenes americanos raramente da buen resultado" (the mixture of *West Indian Negroes* and whites, or Hindus, or American aborigines, rarely shows good results).[63] Citing Bryce's text accurately would undermine Alfaro's conjecture that "hay gran diferencia entre el negro antillano y el hombre de color desarrollado dentro de la civilización Indo-Americana" (there are vast differences between the West Indian Negro and the man of color developed within the

72   THE MAKING OF WHITE NATIONS

Indo-American civilization).[64] To effectively reproduce and mystify his racist agenda, Alfaro must maintain a discursive separation between Afro-Panamanians and West Indians, even as he simultaneously disavows differences between the two groups. The white deployment of the Latin American racial technology of mestizaje, Alfaro's work shows, always hits an impasse in the face of anti-Blackness. Only *some* Black people are seen as viable subjects for racial mixture in the works of Latin American white supremacists such as Alfaro or Cuban anthropologist Fernando Ortiz, about whom I write in the next chapter.

Alfaro relies on numerous colorblind tools in the attempt to sell the lie that West Indians are anti-Panamanian, complicit with US imperialism, and pose a larger threat to white people in Central America. Among others, he relies on decontextualization, dehistoricization, the "mark of the plural" (Memmi), and the appropriation and deliberate misreading of antiracist thought. The following passage shall illustrate these strategies:

> Entre los pobladores de la Zona del Canal, encontramos sin distinguirlos, morenos de origen antillano y otros estadounidenses, su parecido es tal, que solamente aquéllos que tienen afinidad personal con ellos pueden determinar su origen como nacionalidad. Y es cosa tan particular la psicología de la raza, en cuanto a lo referente a su sincera lealtad para con sus dominadores, los elementos anglo-sajones, que bien merece detenerse en ello.
>
> . . . Ya hemos visto cómo los Ejércitos estadounidenses han contado siempre con los negros como sus más leales aliados para conducir las guerras. . . . Y es por esto que es motivo de intranquilidad para los Estados más grandes de Sud América, que en el Istmo Centro-Americano se formen colonias poderosas [de antillanos], que pudieran ser algún día utilizadas ya sea por Inglaterra o cualquier otro país de Europa; o por los mismos Estados Unidos . . .[65]

> Among the inhabitants of the Canal Zone we find, without distinguishing them, Negroes[66] of West Indian origin and others from the United States; their resemblance is such that only those who have a personal affinity with them can determine their national origin. And the psychology of the race, with regard to their sincere loyalty towards their dominators, the Anglo-Saxons, is something so peculiar that it's worth dwelling on.

COLORBLINDNESS AND NATION BUILDING

> . . . We already saw how the US armies always counted on Negroes as their most loyal allies to conduct wars. . . . And this is why it is a source of concern for the largest states in South America that powerful colonies [of West Indians] are formed in the Central American Isthmus that could one day be used by England or any other European country; or by the United States itself . . .

As he hides his own complicity with US imperialism, Alfaro goes to great lengths to persuade the reader that West Indians are complicit with US imperialism. Alfaro deliberately misinterprets the work of Booker T. Washington, who writes that African Americans have participated in all US wars since independence. Not unlike today's appropriation of Martin Luther King's words to reinforce colorblindness in the United States, Washington's work is co-opted, decontextualized, and put at the service of white supremacy in *El peligro antillano*. The historically specific African American experience that Washington describes is made to unwearyingly epitomize *all* Black people living in former British colonies. To demonize West Indian immigrants, Alfaro not only postulates the existence of an intrinsic Black loyalty to British and US colonizers, but also argues that this presumed uniformity in behavior is determined by an alleged similarity in appearance: among the Black workers in the Canal Zone, Alfaro asserts, it is impossible to distinguish "Negroes of West Indian origin and others from the United States." Only people who have "personal affinity" with them can determine their national origin.[67] Although he presents himself as an expert on West Indian affairs, Alfaro ironically concedes that he is unable to differentiate West Indians from African Americans. But instead of indicating lack of intellectual rigor on the part of Alfaro, his very inability to discern between these two groups of Afrodescendants is presented as alleged evidence of their sameness. As a white writer, Alfaro can rely on what Edward Said calls a "flexible *positional* superiority," which enables him to maintain a discursive advantage in any relationship with the racialized Other.[68] Alfaro's positionality is constructed as being so radically superior to Black people that the acknowledgment of ignorance does not threaten his credibility. On the contrary, Alfaro presents ignorance as additional "evidence" that West Indians and African Americans do not just allegedly look the same, but also *behave* identically. In theorizing the existence of a shared "psychology of the race," Alfaro employs an authoritative stance that is further legitimized through his textual display of ignorance, rather than being undermined by it.

74 THE MAKING OF WHITE NATIONS

If Alfaro's stance appears anachronistic, one only needs to read a work such as Alice Goffman's ethnography *On the Run: Fugitive Life in an American City* (2014), with its pathologizing descriptions of Black people, to realize that some white scholars have not come far from Alfaro's idea that Black people share a common "psychology of the race." Goffman subdivides the Black subjects of her ethnography into stock characters that she describes as *clean* people, "who have no pending legal entanglements or who can successfully get through a police stop," and *dirty* people, "likely to be arrested should the authorities stop them."[69] In the process, Goffman herself criminalizes Black people and falsely suggests that, for a Black person, making it through a police stop without getting arrested or killed is a matter of having no criminal record. The same racist logic that allows Alfaro to maintain what Said terms "the relative upper hand"[70] in his description of West Indians, allows Goffman's work to be celebrated by white ethnographers as a "classic" and as "science."[71] No different from the epochs of Lombroso or Alfaro, science today is what white people say it is.

In their portrayal of Black people, Alfaro and Goffman both rely on what Abdul R. JanMohamed describes as a *manichean allegory*. Providing valuable insights on the rhetorical mechanisms of colonial discourse, JanMohamed writes:

> Just as imperialists "administer" the resources of the conquered country, so colonialist discourse "commodifies" the native subject into a stereotyped object and uses him as a "resource" for colonialist fiction. The European writer commodifies the native by negating his individuality, his subjectivity, so that he is now perceived as a generic being that can be exchanged for any other native (they all look alike, act alike, and so on). Once reduced to his exchange-value in the colonialist signifying system, he is fed into the manichean allegory, which functions as the currency, the medium of exchange, for the entire colonialist discourse system. The exchange function of the allegory remains constant, while the generic attributes themselves can be substituted infinitely (and even contradictorily) for one another. . . . While the surface of each colonialist text purports to represent specific encounters with specific varieties of the racial Other, the subtext valorizes the superiority of European cultures.[72]

COLORBLINDNESS AND NATION BUILDING

Alfaro commodifies Black people precisely by negating their individuality and subjectivity. The fact that Alfaro manages to appropriate works about Black USAmericans to support his racist conjectures against West Indians has nothing to do with actual similarities between these two groups of Afro-descendants, and everything to do with the malleability of colonial discourse that colorblindness depends upon. In similar fashion, Goffman's simplistic partitioning of a heterogeneous Black community into a binary set of, literally, "clean" versus "dirty" stock characters has nothing to do with objectivity, but is an example of the all too common white ethnographic literature that, as Robin D. G. Kelley writes, "provides less as understanding of the complexity of people's lives and cultures than a bad blaxploitation film or Ernie Barnes painting."[73] Both Alfaro's and Goffman's works pathologize Black people, feeding them "into the manichean allegory" and fixing them into easily recognizable types that are figments of the white imagination.

For the sake of racist argument, it does not matter that Black people in the United States have a very different history from Black people in the Caribbean and Central America, even as both groups share a history of slavery and dispossession. It does not matter that the existence of a variety of cultures, nations, and languages challenges monolithic definitions of West Indianness. Racist discourse willingly accommodates contradictions if these serve whiteness. It is necessary here to clearly distinguish between Alfaro's racist gesture, which posits a commonality in *thought and behavior* among Black people, and the understanding that Black people globally share a structural positionality so that, as Frank B. Wilderson writes, "the Black is openly vulnerable to the whims of the world."[74] Far from being concerned with the welfare of Black people, Alfaro engages in epistemic violence as the Black subject in *El peligro antillano* embodies what Toni Morrison calls an *Africanist persona*, "an informing, stabilizing, and disturbing element."[75] In Alfaro's and his white readers' racist imaginaries, Black people are not people, but "una 'manada de negros'" (a 'herd of Negroes').[76] They are denied individuality, complexity, and humanity itself, attributes that white people have appropriated for ourselves alone. What Alfaro, and indeed also Goffman, produce is nothing less than "colonialist fiction."

As he tries to convince his audience that West Indians are allies of the United States, Alfaro reproduces the racist myth that Black people are docile and have passively accepted racist oppression, a racist discourse that depicts Black people as not human (for what is more human that

76   THE MAKING OF WHITE NATIONS

the desire to be free?) without explicitly saying so. Alfaro strategically argues that Black people in former English colonies are loyal to "sus dominadores" (their dominators). In the process, he omits the hundreds of documented slave rebellions that occurred in the United States and beyond as mentioning them would challenge the conjecture that Black people do not have a desire for freedom. The racist myth of Black loyalty toward white people is not Alfaro's alone. At work in *El peligro antillano* is what Neil Roberts calls "the disavowal of slave agency," through which white people have systematically attempted to silence the revolutionary actions of enslaved African people.[77] In an example that echoes Rijno Johannes van der Riet's argument that freedom for Khoena people "is more a burden to them than a real sentiment,"[78] a colonist named La Barre in 1790 wrote to his wife in France assuring her that everything was under control in the colony of Haiti: "The Negroes are very obedient and always will be. We sleep with doors and windows wide open. Freedom for Negroes is a chimera."[79] Merely a few months later, Black people in that same colony would free themselves from slavery and lead a historic revolution that culminated in the independence of Haiti in 1804.

Since accounting for Black resistance in Latin America challenges the myth of racial democracy, Alfaro also erases the rich history of cimarronaje (slave uprisings) in Panama. The Spanish army faced numerous slave uprisings already during the early colonial period: in Santo Domingo in the 1530s and 1540s; in Venezuela, Panama, and Ecuador in the 1550s; and in Colombia and Mexico in the early 1600s.[80] According to historian Ruth Pike, "None of the cimarrón revolts elsewhere in the Spanish Empire in the sixteenth century such as in Mexico, Colombia, or Venezuela equaled the movement in Panama in numbers, intensity, leadership and duration."[81] The first palenque (autonomous maroon community) in Panamanian territory was founded as early as 1530, after an insurrection in which enslaved miners killed their owners and took refuge in the abandoned settlement of Santa María la Antigua.[82] The leader Bayano, called el rey negro (the Black king), together with other 1,200 cimarrones (maroons or runaway slaves), carried out a series of successful campaigns against the Spaniards, establishing a palenque in a remote area of dense jungle near the Atlantic coast. Only in 1556 did the Spanish manage to capture Bayano, and only after poisoning him during a feast.[83] While all independent palenques in Panama by the end of the sixteenth century had been defeated or were small, enslaved Black people in the Isthmus continued to resist relentlessly until the formal abolition of slavery in 1821.[84]

COLORBLINDNESS AND NATION BUILDING   77

Alfaro's silencing of cimarronaje is emblematic of the erasure of
Black people's contributions to national history that defines hegemonic
racial discourse in Panama, where West Indians are often still portrayed
the only "real" Black people in the country. The disavowal of Blackness in Panama is ironic given that the African presence in the country
predates the arrival of Europeans. Peter Martyr D'Anghiera, an Italian
historian at the service of the Spanish colonists, writes in *De Orbe Novo*
(1511), the very first Spanish crónica:

> The Spaniards found negro slaves in this province. They only
> live in a region one day's march from Quarequa, and they are
> fierce and cruel. It is thought that negro pirates of Ethiopia
> established themselves after the wreck of their ships in these
> mountains. The natives of Quarequa carry on incessant war
> with these negroes. Massacre or slavery is the alternate fortune
> of the two peoples.[85]

While D'Anghiera's depiction of Black people as "fierce and cruel" is
the product of his racist imagination, that the Spanish encountered
Black people in the province of Darién is attested by numerous historical sources.[86] Europeans believed that the Africans they encountered
were pirates who had been shipwrecked on the coast of Panama long
before white people arrived on the Isthmus.[87]

Europeans instituted slavery in Panama as early as 1511 or 1512,
after the Spanish had claimed the lives of thousands of Indigenous
people.[88] Enslaved Africans sustained the entire economy of colonial
Panama, which was based principally on mining, agriculture, cattle
herding, artisanry, commerce, and domestic work, all fields in which
Black people represented the principal and often the sole labor force.[89]
At the end of the colonial period, Black people accounted for 60 percent
of the population in the area between Panama City and Portobelo.[90]
In the nineteenth century, European traveler Thomas Gage noticed
that a small number of Black people, particularly women, engaged in
commerce and were members of the affluent elite. White women considered Black women threatening rivals and prompted the passing of a
law (Ley XXVIII) that banned Black women from using gold, scarves,
silk, and pearls.[91]

The Black people who have been in Panama for centuries include West
Indians, whom Alfaro wrongly depicts as newcomers. After the abolition
of the slave trade the number of people of African descent diminished

78 · THE MAKING OF WHITE NATIONS

in several Latin American countries. However, the opposite occurred in Panama, which has received immigrants from the Caribbean since the 1820s, mainly as construction workers, diggers, or workers on banana plantations, especially those on the Pacific Coast owned by the United Fruit Company.[92] Approximately five thousand West Indians migrated to work on the Panama Railroad between 1850 and 1855, and at least fifty thousand more arrived between 1881 and 1894, during the failed French attempt to build the Canal.[93] By the time the railroad was completed in 1885, harrowing working conditions, yellow fever, malaria, and lack of adequate health care had claimed the lives of thousands of West Indian workers.[94] Their working and living conditions did not improve when the United States acquired the rights to dig the Canal in 1903.[95] An estimated hundred and fifty thousand to two hundred thousand West Indian workers mainly from Barbados, Guadalupe, and Martinique migrated to Panama during the Canal construction years.[96] According to official records, between 1904 and 1914, some 5,609 workers died on the job, the vast majority of whom were Black people.[97]

As he silences the long history of Barbadian, Jamaican, and other West Indian communities in Panama, Alfaro also mystifies racialized conditions in the present. West Indians faced harrowing living conditions in the Canal Zone, yet Alfaro argues that West Indian workers "prosperan bajo las mejores condiciones higiénicas" (prosper under the best hygienic conditions).[98] Neither does Alfaro reveal how racial segregation and inequality structured everyday life in the Zone. The white USAmericans who controlled the Canal Zone subjected West Indian laborers to racial segregation, horrific working conditions, and exploitative pay through differential salaries for white workers (who were all white USAmericans, labeled "skilled workers," with privileged access to higher salaries through the so-called Gold Roll) and Black workers (mainly West Indians, who were labeled as "unskilled workers" and paid based on the so-called Silver Roll).[99] In 1913, Harry Frank, a white USAmerican, said about the Canal Zone: "Caste lines are as sharply drawn as in India."[100] The Canal Zone was a copy of the US South. However, differently from the US South, racial segregation in the Zone was enforced in all spaces and institutions, from housing to schools, without using explicit racial categories. Rather than the categories Black and White, the Zonians used the terms Silver and Gold, which represented the currency in which workers were paid.[101] Since the US Constitution did not allow federally mandated segregation, USAmericans denied practicing racial segregation in Panama. Employing the

COLORBLINDNESS AND NATION BUILDING

colorblind terms *skilled* and *unskilled* to racially categorize workers was a deliberate tactic aimed at obfuscating and maintaining white supremacy in the Canal Zone.[102]

Subjected to exploitative working conditions and stigmatized as divisive enemies of the nation, West Indians in actuality have worked tirelessly to promote unity among Black people in Panama. In 1980, West Indian Panamanians organized the Primer Congreso del Negro Panameño (First Congress of the Black Panamanian), initiating a campaign "dirigida a eliminar la idea generalizada en la gran mayoría de la población panameña de que solamente son negros aquellas personas de origen antillano" (aimed at eliminating the idea common among the vast majority of the Panamanian population that only people of West Indian descent are Black).[103] Recognizing that the antagonism between different groups of Black Panamanians was fabricated by the state, the congress organizers proposed eliminating the usage of the differential terms *coloniales* vs. *antillanos* in the documents of the conference so as to foster unity between the two groups of Afro-descendants. In 2000, Carlos Smith, the representative of the Sociedad de Amigos del Museo Afroantillano de Panamá (Society of Friends of the Afro-Antillean Museum of Panama), reaffirmed the urgency for all Panamanians of African descent to recognize their shared history of slavery and exploitation.[104] While West Indians aimed to make racism visible, the letter written by then Panamanian minister of foreign affairs Jorge E. Ritter to the organizers of the congress, as is evident in the epigraph, disavows racism, reinscribing the same colorblindness that characterizes Alfaro's essay.

The racist and anti-Black arguments that Alfaro advances in *El peligro antillano* are a reminder that white police officer José Vicente Delgado's 1934 murder of Justo Jaén and the defense's deployment of colorblind rhetoric to win the case, which I describe in the introduction, did not occur in a vacuum. They were expected in a white supremacist system in which white people deployed anti-Blackness and colorblindness as entangled instruments of racial control and nation building. *El peligro antillano* unwittingly testifies to the obvious: that in the anti-Black world there is no such thing as a genuinely "colorblind" xenophobia. Wilderson points to this fact when he writes, "Certainly, immigrants all over the world leave one country (or one place) for another. But only Black folk migrate from one place to the next while remaining on the same plantation."[105] Anti-Blackness is global and Black people are not safe in the world. Citizenship does not change this fact. That Justo Jaén was Panamanian did not prevent him from being the victim of murder because Jaén's Blackness marked him as killable in the white eyes of Delgado. Alfaro's booklet bolstered anti-Black violence in Panama, legitimizing it while disavowing its existence.

In revealing overlaps and continuities between the anti-Black racism of the past and the present, *El peligro antillano* demonstrates that the disavowal of racism is a technology of racial power that white people have long systematically deployed to protect our racialized interests across national borders. The white nationalist stance articulated in the pamphlet gives rise to an anti-Black rhetoric that, owing to the disavowal of its racist scope and its transnational character, appears remarkably contemporary. The strategies that Alfaro employs to demonize West Indian immigrants resemble those that white right-wing politicians continue to use today, whether Matteo Salvini in Italy, Marie Le Pen in France, Nigel Farage in Britain, or Jair Bolsonaro in Brazil. Afrophobic rhetoric is increasingly also used by Black politicians in South Africa as a tactic to gain votes, as demonstrated by the 2021 electoral campaign of Herman Mashaba, mayor of Johannesburg from 2016 until 2019 and founder of the overtly xenophobic party ActionSA. Reading *El peligro antillano* in our neocolonial era demands that we pay attention to the transnational interests that inform nationalist rhetoric and confront the manipulative motivations of racist propaganda. It urges us to refrain from conceiving white supremacist discourse in Latin America, the United States, Europe, and beyond as being new, incompatible, or nonexistent, and demands that we come to terms with the significance of its transnational continuities and longevity.

2

Mestizaje and Racial Genocide

As recently as 1982, there was a proposal of collective sterilization of blacks in São Paulo . . . on the grounds that they were becoming a majority electoral force. . . . Explicit racism having become less fashionable, we have lately been treated to a series of euphemisms like *"mestizaje,"* "mulattization," "metarace," and the raceless society . . . to substitute the whitening ideal. Such phrase-turning does not alter the anti-African bias of the miscegenation ideology, nor does it modify race relations characterized by segregation, discrimination, and cultural repression.
  —Abdias Nascimento, "Pan-Africanism, Negritude, and the African
     Experience in Brazil"

[W]e must attend to the material histories of our categories, as they are given shape and vitality by way of, and inside of, organismic bodies, even if (or especially if) ultimately our aim is to be rid of received categories because of their world-wrecking capacity and death-dealing effects. Otherwise, we will most likely build on foundations we would be better off destroying.
  —Zakiyyah Iman Jackson, *Becoming Human: Matter and Meaning
     in an Antiblack World*

Anthropologist Angela Gilliam observed during her visit to Brazil in the 1970s that racial categories were so fluid in certain areas of the country that "one can change one's race by changing jobs."[1] In one of her travels, Gilliam learned of a "former mailboat operator along the Amazon river who became white upon being elected mayor of his town."[2] When Gilliam expressed puzzlement and asked how this was possible, one of the townspeople responded: "It's simple, we would never have a black mayor!"[3] This and other experiences of racism propelled Gilliam

81

to rethink her romanticized vision of the country as a racial paradise. As a young woman, like other African Americans before her,[4] Gilliam had hoped to one day emigrate to Brazil to escape racism in the United States. But when she finally visited the country, she was confronted with realities of discrimination that resembled what she had left behind in the United States.[5] Gilliam's excitement at discovering a small Brazilian town with a Black mayor quickly gave way to the realization that racial mixture, fluid racial categories, and white supremacy are not mutually exclusive. As Gilliam's anecdote suggests, rather than signaling the absence of racism, racial fluidity in Brazil reflects a rigid racial hierarchy, a hierarchy that is reinforced through its appearance of instability.[6] Many scholars today nonetheless continue to compare the fluidity of racial classifications in Brazil and the relatively widespread racial mixture of its population favorably to the one-drop rule and ideologies of racial purity that are operative in the United States, reinscribing the idealized vision of Brazil that Gilliam fell prey to in the Jim Crow era. The myth that racial mixture implies the absence of racism reverberates beyond the Brazilian context, as several US authors continue to extol Latin American nations as models worth imitating.

Exemplifying this phenomenon, Carlos Fernández, former president of the Association of Multiethnic Americans, argues in "La Raza and the Melting Pot: A Comparative Look at Multiethnicity" (1992) that USAmericans should look at Latin America for a model of race relations to imitate because, in countries such as Brazil and Mexico, the US ideal of the melting pot "has been a living reality for centuries."[7] Adopting mestizaje would greatly benefit the United States, Fernández writes. Thanks also to Latino immigrants, he argues, the number of interracial relationships and multiracial children is growing in the United States, paving the way toward a society in which race will no longer matter. As the "browning" of the United States accelerates, he continues, "the race question may be naturalized and energies redirected to other pressing socioeconomic issues."[8] Fernández concludes messianically: "The fulfillment of the melting pot and La Raza Cósmica—ideals and realities on the continents of the Western Hemisphere—these will form the real New World for all humankind."[9] Fernández thus romanticizes race relations in Latin America and silences the anti-Blackness and white supremacy at the heart of both mestizaje and the US melting pot ideology. In doing so, he is not alone. The celebration of mestizaje and "brownness" as solutions to racism characterizes a large body of work across genres produced especially by conservative Latino authors.[10] In positing brownness as emancipatory while erasing Blackness, these works already reveal what Abdias Nascimento in the epigraph calls "the anti-African bias of the miscegenation ideology."[11]

The idealization of mestizaje is part of a much larger phenomenon. In the United States, racial mixture is often depicted as an antidote to racism and the rise of multiracialism as the expression of a new progressive dawn in US race relations.[12] Idealizing racial mixture, of course, is nothing new. Frederick Douglass, who was the son of an enslaved Black woman and a white slaveowner, argued in 1884 that the increase in mixed-race people and interracial marriages (like his own marriage to Helen Pitts) was a positive development which signaled that "in time the varieties of races will be blended into one."[13] While this romanticization is not new, the belief in the presumed redemptive properties of racial mixture holds particular weight today as multiraciality has become increasingly politicized and institutionalized.

This has serious material implications. Under Fernández's leadership, the multiracial organization Interracial/Intercultural Pride (I-Pride) sought legal recognition of multiracial identity in the 1980s and demanded that Northern California schools include a multiracial category on school forms. In the 1990s, there were forty such multiracial organizations across the United States.[14] Their mobilization eventually led to the inclusion of the "check all that apply" option on the 2000 census. While they appear progressive, these developments are harmful for the purpose of monitoring and redressing racial inequality. As many scholars have argued, multiracial politics are anti-Black and benefit white people.[15] It makes sense, then, that many of the original leaders of multiracial organizations were affluent white women married to Black men who insisted that their children should be classified as multiracial.[16] At play in these politics of multiraciality is a contemporary version of what Hortense J. Spillers calls "the *appropriation* of the interracial child by the genocidal forces of dominance."[17] Spillers writes that the term "mulatto/a . . . tells us little or nothing about the subject buried beneath the epithets, but quite a great deal more concerning the psychic and cultural reflexes that invest and invoke them."[18] The present-day politicization of multiraciality, too, reveals little about actual people who identify as "mixed race," but it does say a lot about the anti-Blackness and racism that motivate the extolling of multiracial identity in the first place. It reveals how the very idea of a mixed-race subject "locates in the flesh a site of cultural and political maneuver."[19] Discourses around racial mixture remain the locus of politics, on a global scale, to this day.

84   THE MAKING OF WHITE NATIONS

The uncritical celebration of racial mixture is a transnational phenomenon. White people across national boundaries today invoke racial hybridity to undercut arguments for affirmative action and deny the legitimacy of social movements that attempt to make redistributive claims based on racial difference.[20] In South Africa, some Afrikaners have moved from an obsession with racial purity toward invoking racial hybridity as a means to disavow their white privilege and lay further claims to land through a purported indigeneity.[21] Much post-1994 scholarship on race also celebrates "blendings, interconnections, hybridities and ambiguities"[22] in ways that conceal and sustain white supremacy. As mestizaje and mixedness are increasingly romanticized on a global scale, this chapter insists that, as Zakiyyah Iman Jackson states in the epigraph, we must "attend to the material histories of our categories."[23] Otherwise, as Jackson warns, we risk replicating their devastating effects in the present. Today, it is imperative to redirect the gaze toward a key historical period in Latin America—the early twentieth century—in which the shift from a commitment to doctrines of racial purity toward the valorization of racial mixture also served to solidify, rather than challenge, white domination.

In the nineteenth century, white and mestizo elites in the newly independent Latin American nations linked whiteness and modernization, while they considered Black, Indigenous, and mixed-race people to be inherently inferior and an obstacle to progress.[24] In countries such as Argentina, Brazil, Cuba, Mexico, and Venezuela, these elites aggressively promoted the immigration of Europeans as a means to achieve the racist goal of "whitening" their populations. In Brazil, whitening policies were implemented already during the colonial era, with João IV of Portugal sponsoring German and Swiss immigrants, who in 1818 founded the town of Nova Friburgo, near Rio de Janeiro. After emancipation, which ensued in 1888, Black people were abandoned without land and forced to fend for themselves, while the government continued to finance the immigration of white Europeans, many of whom came to Brazil with the additional financial support of their own governments.[25] Historian Clovis Moura writes that "there entered more Italian immigrants in the 30 years after abolition than the number of slaves who were benefitted by emancipation. With the abolition law, the marginalization of the Black people was instituted."[26] In Mexico, Porfirio Díaz's presidency (1876–1911) was also marked by the sponsoring of European immigrants and the belief that Black and Indigenous people were impeding the country's modernization.[27] White Cubans, too, advocated for the immigration of Europeans. Cuban eugenicist and anthropologist Fernando Ortiz, to whom I will return, started his career with fervent calls for European immigration, arguing that race was the most important factor in the recruitment of immigrants.[28]

European immigration was only one step in the whitening process as this period in Latin American history concurrently witnessed the violent repression of Black and Indigenous communities and practices.[29] In Brazil, where after 1888 thousands of "free" Black people moved to the cities, the government embarked on violent campaigns they called projects of "urban renewal" in cities like Rio de Janeiro, destroying entire neighborhoods with the explicit aim to remove Black people from city centers and confine them to slums on the city outskirts.[30] Met with large protests by Black people, these forced removals were accompanied by mass arrests and incarceration following the banning of Afro-Brazilian religious and cultural practices, including candomblé and capoeira.[31] So brutal was this repression that Black people who practiced capoeira were tied to horses and dragged to police headquarters at full gallop.[32] White people also systematically suppressed Afrocentric practices in Cuba, where African religions, dances, and carnival celebrations were banned.[33] When Black Cubans formed the Partido Independiente de Color (PIC) in 1908 with the hope of gaining access to the government, an amendment quickly outlawed any political party that only had members of one racial group and over two hundred PIC members were arrested. In 1912, when remaining members of the PIC organized an armed demonstration to demand the overturn of the amendment, the Cuban government responded with an extermination campaign in which the leadership and many Black Cubans who had no ties to the party were executed.[34] The Mexican government, meanwhile, continued to wage a genocidal war on Indigenous peoples through the twentieth century, appropriating Indigenous lands, sterilizing Indigenous women, and forcing millions of people into starvation. After the Mexican Revolution (1910–20), the state concurrently began celebrating a mythical "Indian" of the past as a symbol of national unity, while it silenced the contributions of Black people to national culture altogether.[35]

By the 1920s, white and mestizo Latin American politicians and intellectuals realized that the sponsoring of European immigrants had not been effective in "whitening" the population. Not only did Europeans often prefer to migrate to countries such as Australia and the United States, but white and mestizo intellectuals and politicians considered the very *existence* of Black, Indigenous, and mixed-race people

86 THE MAKING OF WHITE NATIONS

as a problem requiring a new strategy of racial obliteration: mestizaje became that strategy.[36] While white and mestizo intellectuals in Brazil, Cuba, Mexico, and elsewhere had previously espoused ideologies of racial purity that were dominant in Europe and the United States and had argued that mixing leads to racial degeneration, in the 1920s and 1930s they began theorizing racial mixture as an effective method of whitening.[37] Denise Ferreira da Silva writes that "the whitening thesis could not but rewrite miscegenation as an eschatological signifier that would result not in the 'degeneration' of the European but in the obliteration of the Indian and the African from Brazilian bodies and minds."[38] This rewriting of miscegenation from a curse for Latin American whites to their means of salvation transcended borders. The intellectual trajectory of Ortiz, who promoted the immigration of white Europeans at the beginning of his career and moved to advocating racial mixture in his mature works, embodies this formal shift.[39] The invocation of mestizaje, in turn, provided the basis for colorblind discourses of racial democracy that served to mask the reality of racial dictatorship as white people in countries such as Brazil and Cuba exploited the existence of a mixed-race population and the presence of cultural hybridization to argue that racism did not exist in their countries.[40]

A colorblind tool of racial expunging, mestizaje seeks to eliminate Black and Indigenous people from the nation-state while simultaneously serving as a nation-building tool. Defined by Peruvian cultural critic Antonio Cornejo Polar as "the most powerful and widespread conceptual device with which Latin America has interpreted itself," mestizaje (Spanish) and mestiçagem (Portuguese) conventionally refer to the racial hybridity that has characterized Latin American societies since European colonization, specifically Spanish and Portuguese.[41] However, as has hopefully already become clear, mestizaje is not a neutral term indicating a factual condition. Rather, mestizaje is invoked precisely to *construct* Latin American nations as the embodiment of such a condition. While mestizaje is the product of colonial violence, white and mestizo oligarchies in Latin America have deployed it, and continue to deploy it, as a leveling equivalent of homogeneity and fusion.[42] Far from being egalitarian, ideologies and theories of mestizaje, as Jared Sexton writes in *Amalgamation Schemes*, are predicated upon "the black's disappearance,"[43] a fact that shall become amply evident in this chapter.

In recent years, Latin American countries have officially moved from mestizaje toward multiculturalism, a turn characterized by constitutional

MESTIZAJE AND RACIAL GENOCIDE

reforms that formally recognize the identities and, to some extent, the rights of Indigenous communities and people of African descent.[44] However, mestizaje has not disappeared but has acquired new legitimacy, to the extent that multiculturalism has been described as "a new form of mestizaje."[45] The formal acknowledgment of ethnoracial diversity in states such as Colombia and Mexico has been accompanied by neoliberal policies that preclude redistributive justice and push Black and Indigenous people further into poverty.[46]

This chapter shows that white Latin American intellectuals, in the early and mid-twentieth century, disseminated the racial technology of mestizaje across national boundaries, racial regimes, and racial demographics, presenting it as a tool that should be widely adopted to ensure the maintenance of the racist status quo. To illustrate the travels of mestizaje, I examine understudied works by José Vasconcelos, Fernando Ortiz, and Gilberto Freyre, three well-known white Latin American intellectuals who were instrumental in articulating and popularizing nationalist ideologies grounded in mestizaje/mestiçagem in Mexico, Cuba, and Brazil, respectively. Most scholarship has focused on their most famous works, namely, Vasconcelos's *La raza cósmica* (*The Cosmic Race*, 1925), Ortiz's *Contrapunteo cubano del tabaco y del azúcar* (*Cuban Counterpoint: Tobacco and Sugar*, 1940), and Freyre's *Casa-grande e senzala: formação da família brasileira sob o regime da economia patriarcal* (translated as *The Masters and the Slaves: A Study in the Development of Brazilian Civilization*, 1933). While I touch upon these texts, I turn the lens toward later works that have been critically neglected yet are fundamental for understanding how the white theorization and propagation of mestizaje was motivated by a desire to suppress Black and Indigenous resistance and specifically obliterate Black people.

I examine Vasconcelos's lecture "The Race Problem in Latin America" (1926), Ortiz's 1942 lecture "Por la integración cubana de blancos y negros" (For the Cuban Integration of Whites and Blacks, translated in 1944 as "The Relations between Blacks and Whites in Cuba"), and Freyre's "Report on the Most Important and Most Effective Methods for Eliminating Racial Conflicts, Tensions, and Discriminatory Practices Employed with Positive Results in Countries in Different Geographical Regions, in Particular Countries Where Conditions Approximate Most Closely Those in the Union of South Africa" (1954), which Freyre wrote at the request of the United Nations Commission on the Racial Situation in the Union of South Africa (UNCORS). Through the analysis

88   THE MAKING OF WHITE NATIONS

of these texts, I show how Vasconcelos, Ortiz, and Freyre attempted to persuade, respectively, white USAmericans, Black Cubans, and white South Africans as well as the global white community that they should adopt mestizaje for their own benefit. These transnational entanglements demonstrate that white people in the early and mid-twentieth century collaborated across racial regimes and national borders to maintain power. They also illustrate the adaptability of colorblindness and demonstrate that white thinkers across racial regimes did not categorically perceive racial mixture and racial purity to be incompatible. The authors and texts examined in this chapter paraded as racially progressive, while they are actually anti-Black. In this way, they conjure the politics of the US multiracial movement, which appears antiracist while it undermines the gains of the Black Power Movement.[47] In an earlier similar move, as I will show, Latin American eugenicists mobilized discourses of racial mixture with the goal of suppressing Black resistance and political mobilization.

I begin by examining Vasconcelos's "The Race Problem in Latin America," one of three lectures sponsored by the Norman Wait Harris Foundation that Vasconcelos delivered at the University of Chicago in 1926, one year after the publication of *La raza cósmica* endowed him with international fame.[48] In this lecture, Vasconcelos presents mestizaje to his white USAmerican audience as an effective method of racial control that whites should also adopt in the United States. My reading challenges enduring misinterpretations of Vasconcelos's work, which persist despite decades of criticism of Vasconcelos across disciplinary boundaries. In an example of this persistence, Juliet Hooker argues in *Theorizing Race in the Americas: Douglass, Sarmiento, Du Bois, and Vasconcelos* (2017) that "Du Bois and Vasconcelos formulated mestizo futurisms that refuted the dictates of scientific racism and provided alternative visions to racist white supremacist utopias."[49] Hooker reproduces the myth that Vasconcelos's work is counterhegemonic because he "challenged the dominant view, derived from scientific racism, that mixed-race people were inferior."[50] However, Vasconcelos's work does not provide alternatives to scientific racism and white supremacy. Vasconcelos instead viewed racial mixture as a eugenicist tool of racial obliteration that is *superior* to racial purity.

If Vasconcelos's work continues to be misread despite much criticism, the work of Ortiz has been the object of even greater misunderstanding. The theory of transculturation that Ortiz developed is usually interpreted as indicating a form of cultural hybridization based on a *mutual*

MESTIZAJE AND RACIAL GENOCIDE 89

exchange between colonizer and colonized or, in Renato Rosaldo's terms, a "two-way borrowing and lending between cultures."[51] Scholars have systematically misread transculturation in opposition to assimilation. In this chapter, I challenge established (mis)interpretations of transculturation by offering the first sustained reading of Ortiz's seminal 1942 lecture "Por la integración cubana de blancos y negros" (For the Cuban Integration of Whites and Blacks), in which Ortiz explains precisely the phases of the transculturation process. I argue that Ortiz's understanding of transculturation is not in conflict with assimilation. Far from describing a mutual exchange that includes the acquisition of African racial or cultural elements by white Cubans, the theory of transculturation advocates the *disappearance* of Black people through their absorption into a superior tertium quid, a eugenicist synthesis that de facto replicates a whitening process.

Finally, I examine a politically impactful yet little-known work by Freyre.[52] In March 1954, UNCORS asked Freyre to write what he called "a comparative study of racial situations . . . with particular attention [to] the case of [South Africa]."[53] The United Nations commission, through a letter by UN personnel officer George Palthey, asked Freyre to present "méthodes les plus importantes et efficaces pour éliminer conflit racial ou tensions raciales" (the most important and efficient methods to eliminate racial conflict or racial tensions).[54] In the report, Freyre interprets the racial conflict that must be eliminated from the vantage point of whiteness, and proposes solutions *not* to racial inequality, but to anticolonial insurgency. How can white people, Freyre asks, maintain power in the face of growing revolutions, especially in Africa? His answer: follow the Brazilian model. Freyre presents mestiçagem as an effective method of racial control and argues that white people should deploy it also in South Africa and other African colonies for their own benefit. The report suggests that, through the United Nations, white people sought out and shared strategies aimed at suppressing independence movements that were burgeoning everywhere in the colonies. A group of powerful white people, posturing as allies concerned about the welfare of Black South Africans, joined forces to protect their own global interests in the wake of increasingly powerful national liberation movements.

Written and delivered at the height of Vasconcelos's, Ortiz's, and Freyre's careers, the works I examine in this chapter are crucial for assessing their thought and opus as a whole. They show that these white men viewed mestizaje as a powerful tool for the maintenance of white supremacy and, consequently, exported it across national

90   THE MAKING OF WHITE NATIONS

and racial boundaries. It is not by coincidence, then, that these works remain understudied. The importance of genre cannot be underestimated here: these are not articles published in obscure journals, but lectures delivered in two prestigious institutions (the University of Chicago in the case of Vasconcelos, and Club Atenas in La Habana in the case of Ortiz) and an official report written for the United Nations. Taken together, these texts demonstrate an active and global white investment in anti-Blackness and white supremacy that most white people—including many scholars of Freyre, Ortiz, and Vasconcelos—would prefer remained unknown.

José Vasconcelos: Gifting Mestizaje to White USAmericans

José Vasconcelos's writings were central to shaping and institutionalizing mestizaje in Mexico. An influential philosopher, educator, and politician whose thought was grounded in social Darwinism and scientific racism, Vasconcelos in *La raza cósmica* (1925) envisaged the arrival of a new revolutionary era in the development of humanity, a Spiritual or Aesthetic Era, in which all races would come together to form a superior race through the natural selection of love. In an argument that resembles the ongoing hegemonic celebration of mestizaje as harbinger of racial harmony, Vasconcelos contends that, thanks to widespread miscegenation, Latin America will be a leader in the emergence of this new age. His theory of mestizaje might seem progressive when contrasted with ideologies of racial purity that were dominant in Europe and the United States. Vasconcelos, however, theorizes mestizaje as an effective way—indeed, *the* way—to elevate what he considered to be inferior people to higher standards of living. In Vasconcelos's words, "Los tipos bajos de la especie serán absorbidos por el tipo superior. . . . El indio, por medio del injerto en la raza afín, daría el salto de los millares de años que median de la Atlántida a nuestra época, y en unas cuantas décadas de eugenesia estética podría desaparecer el negro." (The lower types of the species will be absorbed by the superior type. . . . The Indian, by grafting onto the related race, would take the leap of millions of years that separate Atlantis from our epoch, and in a few decades of aesthetic eugenics, the Negro could disappear).[55] As this quote reveals, Vasconcelos's theory positions Black and Indigenous people differently. While Vasconcelos views mestizaje as a means to "modernize" the Indigenous, he considers Black people to be incapable of modernization.[56]

Vasconcelos's investment in "desaparecer el negro" (disappearing the Negro) challenges María Josefina Saldaña-Portillo's argument that Vasconcelos in *La raza cósmica* "had a difficult time dividing the races, determining where indigenous qualities ended and black ones began, where black qualities ended and white ones began."[57] The boundaries between Blackness, indigeneity, and whiteness are, in reality, sharply drawn in the work. Vasconcelos envisions the "absorption" of the Indigenous into a superior mestizo subject, who in Mexico was made to embody the material and symbolic privileges of whiteness. In his optic, Black people should not be incorporated, however, but preferably eliminated. Mestizaje, as we already saw in the work of Olmedo Alfaro, reaches a deadlock when it encounters Blackness, even as it appears to accommodate it. This is not to say, of course, that Indigenous people were "better off" as the ultimate goal of mestizaje is the preservation of whiteness and white power. In fact, as we will see, Vasconcelos also envisioned the disappearance of Indigenous people. This does mean, however, that eugenicists like Vasconcelos placed Black people at the absolute bottom and, in fact, outside the racial hierarchy. While they viewed mestizaje as able to grant Indigenous people a qualified access to humanity, they a priori excluded Black people from this access.

To understand the extent to which mestizaje is a tool of racial genocide and racial control that Vasconcelos exported across national borders we must turn to "The Race Problem in Latin America." After the publication of *La raza cósmica*, Vasconcelos was invited to speak in Central America and the United States as his international fame grew. He was already an influential intellectual and political figure in Mexico, having been named minister of public instruction during Eulalio Gutiérrez's presidency and first chancellor of the Universidad Nacional Autónoma de México in 1920.[58] Vasconcelos had been to the United States before 1926. His familiarity with the country and the English language goes back to his childhood, when Vasconcelos lived with his family in Piedras Negras, on the Mexico–US border, and attended an English-speaking primary school in Texas.[59] This familiarity serves Vasconcelos well in Chicago where, in a lecture delivered entirely in English, he tries to convince his audience that mestizaje represents a more effective method of racial control and racial expunging than US segregationism. In the 1920s, racial segregation and racist violence were the norm in Illinois, where housing conditions in segregated Black neighborhoods were appalling, Black people were systematically denied access to hospitals and hotels, and the Ku Klux Klan was on the rise.[60] Geographer

92   THE MAKING OF WHITE NATIONS

Rashad Shabazz shows in *Spatializing Blackness* that, between the World Wars, entire Black families who migrated to Chicago from the South were forced to live in cramped and overpriced apartments called kitchenettes, which were no bigger than a room and often rat infested, as covenants forbade Black people from living in most areas of the city.[61] With his advocacy of mestizaje, which he conceptualizes both as miscegenation and cultural assimilation, Vasconcelos might appear to unsettle this racist status quo. In reality, he does exactly the opposite.

Readers who might wonder how Vasconcelos's ideas were received at the University of Chicago should also consider that some US anthropologists had previously theorized racial mixture as a eugenicist method of whitening, specifically one that could serve to control Indigenous people in US colonies. Challenging popular beliefs which presume that US eugenicists were exclusively committed to doctrines of racial purity, Maile Arvin shows in *Possessing Polynesians* that Louis R. Sullivan (1892–1925), a student of Franz Boas, promoted racial amalgamation policies for Polynesian people in the colony of Hawai'i and elsewhere in the US Pacific.[62] According to Arvin, "Sullivan lauded the benefits of racial intermixture for assimilating Native Hawaiians into proper white Americans."[63] As is the case for Latin American eugenicists like Vasconcelos, Sullivan theorized racial mixture as a process that sustains racial hierarchies and makes possible the assimilation, and thus the vanishing, of Indigenous people into a superior mixed-race subject.[64] The assumption is that mixed-race people are more likely to sustain the interests of white people. It is the white element, and therefore the closer proximity to whiteness, that renders the mixed-race subject superior in the eyes of white eugenicists who promoted racial mixture— whether in Latin America or in the United States.

In "The Race Problem in Latin America," Vasconcelos endeavors to sell mestizaje to his audience, first, by trying to convince them that it has already proven to be an advantageous tool for Spanish colonizers. Comparisons with the United States, a strategy that we saw employed also by Alfaro, are central to Vasconcelos's argument. Vasconcelos contends that the Latin American "mixed-race standard" stands in opposition to "the one-race standard" that defines race relations in the United States.[65] He refers to these racial systems as "the Latin system of assimilation and intermarriage and mixture" and "the Anglo-Saxon method of matrimonial taboos and pure-race standards."[66] A commitment to racial purity and segregation would have been unsustainable in Latin America, Vasconcelos argues, because "we do not have that

MESTIZAJE AND RACIAL GENOCIDE 93

element of pure racial stock that could undertake in our land that supposed leadership that has been taken here by the New Englander."[67]
That Vasconcelos here speaks of an "element of pure racial stock" is
ironic given that in the same lecture he contends that "a pure race is a
myth because all nations are the result of numerous mixtures."[68] Such
is the nature of racist discourse: it always accommodates contradictions
when these serve white supremacy.

Assessing the differences between the Latin American and the Anglo-
Saxon models in light of their effectiveness in supporting European
imperialism, Vasconcelos argues that mestizaje is a method superior
to the British and US system of racial segregation for imposing both
the colonizer's culture and colonizer's "blood" onto colonized people: "I
believe that we shall be justified in declaring that the cultural results
of the Spanish method are superior. The Spanish have succeeded
in reproducing their blood in part and their culture in full in twenty
nations that are today about as Spanish as Spain itself can be, though
independent politically and socially."[69] Vasconcelos thus lauds mestizaje
for its ability to carry on Spanish interests. The British, Vasconcelos
argues, have instead been unable to turn places like India into English-
dominant places because they have rejected mixture: "The English, on
the other hand, with their system of not even maintaining social inter-
course with the natives of India are today as completely strangers in
India as on the day their ancestors first landed; and it does not seem
probable that they will ever succeed in eradicating the Indian, to substitute for him the Islander."[70] Vasconcelos here silences the very existence
of a mixed Anglo-Indian population and the hegemony of the English
language in India.[71] He also reproduces the myth that racial mixing
did not exist in British colonies as well as silences the deployment of
technologies of racialized spatial containment in Mexico.[72] Most importantly, his emphasis on "eradicating the Indian" makes explicit that the
ultimate goal of mestizaje is not the inclusion but the *eradication* of
non-European peoples.

The romanticization of Mexico's Indigenous people that becomes evident in Vasconcelos's work epitomizes the contradiction at the heart
of the state-sponsored ideology of mestizaje that Vasconcelos helped
consolidate. Vasconcelos argues that the Spanish intermixed with
Indigenous people, while USAmericans presumably did not, because
Indigenous people in Latin America are superior to those in North
America: "Our Indians . . . are not primitive as was the red Indian, but
old, century-tried souls who have known victory and defeat, life and

death, and all of the moods of history."[73] As Vasconcelos depicts Native Americans as both primitive and extinct, his understanding of "civilization" conforms to Eurocentric standards that rank the societies of colonized people hierarchically. Vasconcelos argues that the Indigenous in Latin America represents "a decaying stock."[74] Of course, Vasconcelos is lying about Indigenous people being on the verge of extinction. In 2015, there were more than twenty-five million Indigenous people in Mexico.[75] That they do not just exist, but are also far from having succumbed to Spanish culture, language, and religion "in full" undermines Vasconcelos's argument about the effectiveness of mestizaje as a vehicle of Europeanization and is therefore conveniently omitted in his lecture.

While Vasconcelos confines any notion of civilization to white people or Indigenous people *of the past*, represented by brave Aztecs and Inca at the height of empire, he encroaches upon Indigenous movements in the present. He contends that sometimes "you still hear in Mexico an echo of the Indian voice that clamors for the return to the past of the race as a means of obtaining strength and inspiration."[76] This past is a time prior to the conquest, *before mestizaje*. Vasconcelos mentions Indigenous revolutions, such as the 1847–1901 uprising of the Maya against the white and mestizo elite in Yucatán and the Zapata Movement, but declares both as failed attempts to recuperate land. Why did these movements fail? According to Vasconcelos, "the weakness of the pure Indian movement lies of course in the fact that the Indian has no civilized standards upon which to fall back."[77] Two minutes earlier, Vasconcelos had argued that Indigenous people in Mexico have achieved levels of civilization superior to those of Native Americans, and that the Indigenous cultures of Southern Mexico and Guatemala specifically represent "higher civilizations."[78] Now, he contends that Mexico's Indigenous people have "no civilized standards upon which to fall back." The past apparently has no bearing on Indigenous peoples and cultures of the present, or so Vasconcelos would like his audience to believe as he removes what he calls the "new Mexico Indian" from their own ancestors and history.[79] In this way, Vasconcelos's speech continues to provide ample examples of the contradictory nature of white supremacist discourse, which cannot sustain itself on truth and logic, but to which fabrication and disavowal are constitutive. Vasconcelos's arguments are constantly unravelling under the weight of his own lies.

If the Indigenous is perennially on the verge of extinction, the mestizo for Vasconcelos is the embodiment of progress and modernity.

MESTIZAJE AND RACIAL GENOCIDE

The mestizo "is always directed toward the future—is a bridge to the future."[80] Vasconcelos's conceptualization of the mestizo shows how the idealization of mixed-race people as embodying progress, as harmonious "bridges" between different racial groups, that informs contemporary multiracial politics is grounded in eugenicist logics. The myth that racial mixture signifies the overcoming of racial prejudice and neutralization of racial hierarchies is a colorblind tool developed within white supremacist discourse. In Vasconcelos's words, "I doubt whether there is a race with less prejudice, more ready to take up almost any mental adventure, more subtle, and more varied than the mestizo, or half-breed. I find in these traits the hope that the mestizo will produce a civilization more universal in its tendency than any other race of the past."[81] The idea that mixed-race people embody positive traits or that miscegenation can lead to a universalist and "race-free" civilization reproduces biologistic understandings of race that catapult us back to the era of scientific racism.

As Vasconcelos displays a clear commitment to anti-Blackness and white supremacy, he reproduces, as expected, an epistemology of disavowal. Vasconcelos argues that the presence of racial mixture demonstrates that the Spanish are not racist (and, by implication, neither is he). The Spaniards, he insists, "have always disregarded this purely white prejudice and have actually created the millions of the mestizo stock of America and of the Philippines."[82] The mestizo is here presented as "evidence" of alleged lack of racial prejudice on the part of the Spanish in a move that both erases the violence that subtends racial mixture under conditions of conquest and slavery and confines racism to prejudice. Silencing white sexual violence against Black and Indigenous children, women, and men, Vasconcelos romanticizes miscegenation as the product of intermarriage, while he conceals the existence of racial hierarchies in Mexico and the Philippines.[83]

Demonstrating how Black people represent the ultimate targets of the genocidal logics of mestizaje, Vasconcelos offers mestizaje to this white USAmerican audience as the most efficient method for eliminating Black people and maintaining power. Vasconcelos contends that what he considers to be the "Indian problem" has been resolved both in the United States and in Mexico, while Black people's very existence is *the* ongoing problem that has yet to find a resolution in the United States. In his words, "The founders of the United States were fortunate in not finding in this territory a very large Indian population, and so it was easy for them to push the Indian back; but the importation

96   THE MAKING OF WHITE NATIONS

of the Negro has brought to this nation, as we all know, a problem harder, no doubt, than any known before."[84] Vasconcelos presents the very existence of Black people as "a problem" for white people that is "harder . . . than any known before." The phrase "as we all know" makes clear that Vasconcelos expects his audience to share in his anti-Blackness. North Americans, Vasconcelos states, "have followed the English system in regard to the Negro, that is to say, the system of strict avoidance of matrimonial relations with the colored race."[85] This strategy is misguided, Vasconcelos suggests, as he presents miscegenation as a tool that white people should also adopt in the United States if they want to eliminate Black people. In the process, Vasconcelos disavows the genocide of Indigenous people on both sides of the US–Mexico border and silences the very existence of Afro-Mexicans, who are never mentioned in the talk.

The last part of the lecture makes especially evident how Vasconcelos understood mestizaje as an instrument of racial genocide:

> If the Spaniard had not mixed his blood with the Indian, there would not be today on the map a large area of countries where the Spanish soul is alive and progressive. When, on the contrary, the dominating race stands apart and takes no interest in the life of the inferior, the inferior tends instinctively to increase its numbers in order to compensate through members what the dominating race achieves through quality. . . . But the lower, opposed breed, having no control, no hope, goes on multiplying madly; and the weight and the curse of this overpopulation is just as harmful to the elect as it is to the less fortunate. If we are ever to stop this misery, it is necessary that the superior takes pains to educate the inferior and raise his standards. If we do not wish to be overwhelmed by the wave of the Negro, of the Indian, or of the Asiatic, we shall have to see that the Negro, the Indian, and the Asiatic are raised to higher standards of life, where reproduction becomes regulated and quality predominates over numbers. Instead of the competitive manner of life advocated by the defenders of pure-race civilization . . . we shall have to adopt then the cooperative, collaborative manner of interracial organization.[86]

Vasconcelos draws a clear line between what he terms "the dominating race," also described as "the elect" and "the superior," and "the

MESTIZAJE AND RACIAL GENOCIDE

Negro, the Indian, and the Asiatic," whom he names "the inferior," "the lower, opposed breed." Vasconcelos's identification with a collective "we" understood as white and superior becomes obvious in this passage as national and ideological boundaries dissolve in the face of the collective investment in whiteness that Vasconcelos shares with his USAmerican audience. Notice the portrayal of whiteness as civilizing force that Vasconcelos reproduces as he argues that "the superior takes pains to educate the inferior." This is the white man's burden in action. Reproducing racist discourses that portray people who are not European as being at the mercy of uncontrollable sexual instincts, Vasconcelos contends that Black, Indigenous, and Asian people multiply "madly," and that their reproduction must be stopped to prevent that white people "be overwhelmed" by numerically superior people of color. Black people are not mentioned first by chance in Vasconcelos's list of racialized peoples who must be suppressed. Rather, Black people are the primary object of Vasconcelos's genocidal agenda. The "defenders of pure-race civilization," Vasconcelos reasserts, are wrong in refusing to mix with Black people and people of color. Only through mestizaje, here euphemistically described as the "collaborative manner of interracial organization," Vasconcelos insists, will "the present-day danger of the overpowering of the superior few by the uncivilized many . . . disappear."[87] Mystified as selfless cooperation with Black people and people of color, mestizaje becomes the ultimate gift that Vasconcelos bestows upon his US audience as the talk culminates with an appeal to fellow whites that clearly reveals Vasconcelos's anxieties about the possibility of white people losing power.

Vasconcelos's ideas have had a tremendous impact on Mexican politics and culture. In 1940, when the first Congreso Indigenista took place, indigenismo became the official ideology of the Mexican nation.[88] This state-sponsored indigenismo glorified Indigenous cultures of the past, while it silenced living Indigenous people and was often directly responsible for their extreme poverty.[89] The Partido Revolucionario Institucional (PRI), which was involved in the creation of the Instituto Nacional Indigenista (INI), treated Indigenous people as exotic entities, fetishizing them as living museums, while exploiting their cultural practices to bolster tourism.[90] Even as Mexico has moved towards multiculturalism, Vasconcelos's racist ideas have not lost their impact as practices and policies of racial genocide and cultural erasure persist. Today, state-sponsored aid to Indigenous populations in Mexico remain a largely paternalistic enterprise used for personal gain by ever-so-white

98   THE MAKING OF WHITE NATIONS

candidates during election campaigns and are informed by an ongoing desire to forcibly assimilate Indigenous people, divesting them of their customs, languages, and beliefs. One of the most recent publications of the INI before it was substituted by the Comisión Nacional para el Desarrollo de los Pueblos Indígenas (National Commission for the Development of Indigenous Peoples) in 2003, shows that members of the Institute considered the very existence of Indigenous people in Mexico as a failure of their assimilation policies:

> Various investigators of the indigenous populations have wished for about 50 years . . . that the social and cultural integration of the Indigenous population and the improvement of their living conditions would finally take place. Five decades later the situation is very different from expected given that, first and foremost, the Indigenous population, far from integrating and melting with the rest of the national population, constitutes at least ten percent of the total population; the ethnic and linguistic differences still persist.[91]

This shows that the ongoing Zapatista Movement in Mexico must be understood not only as a movement for land and political self-determination, but also as a movement against historical, racial, linguistic, and cultural erasure—in other words, a movement *against mestizaje*. In autonomous Zapatista communities in Chiapas, diverse Maya people continue to assert their right to land, to employ communal farming techniques, to practice Indigenous religious beliefs or to carry on governmental affairs and education in Tzotzil, Tzeltal, and other Maya languages instead of Spanish.[92] Far from being "a decaying stock,"[93] as Vasconcelos argued almost a century ago, Indigenous people in Mexico continue to resist colonial domination and assert their right to *exist*.

Fernando Ortiz: Selling Transculturation to the Black Cuban Middle Class

Cuba's most famous intellectual alongside national hero José Martí, Fernando Ortiz today is largely remembered as the founding father of Afro-Cuban studies and for having developed what is arguably the most influential anthropological contribution to come out of

Cuba: the concept of transculturation, which Ortiz first theorized in *Contrapunteo cubano del tabaco y del azúcar* (1940). Scholars have constructed a narrative in which Ortiz progresses from the young author of the eugenicist ethnography *Hampa afro-cubana: Los negros brujos—Apuntes para un estudio de etnología criminal, con una carta prólogo de Lombroso* (Afro-Cuban Underworld: The Black Sorcerers—Notes for a Study of Criminal Ethnology, with a Prologue-Letter by Lombroso, 1906) to his allegedly antiracist masterpiece *Contrapunteo*. This linear narrative presumes that Ortiz's mature works are no longer beholden to the scientific racism that defined his early writings and reimagines transculturation as a counterhegemonic theory in the process. "Ortiz begins with much prejudicial judgment," Beatriz Rivera-Barnes writes in an article that exemplifies this critical trend, "only to end with the notion of transculturation in the 1940s."[94] In his study of early twentieth-century anthropology, Kevin Yelvington also contends that Ortiz completely changed trajectory in his mature years. Having begun his scholarly career deploying a "positivist and racialist approach," Yelvington writes, Ortiz was eventually "in many ways co-opted by Afro-cubanismo, a literary and artistic movement beginning in the 1920s, and in a *remarkable turnaround* he became the movement's patron and source of legitimacy."[95] The uncritical praise-singing extends to Ortiz's persona. Cuban anthropologist Rosa María de Lahaye Guerra argues that "Durante más de medio siglo Fernando Ortiz ejerció una amplia campaña de investigación, propaganda y acción a favor de la causa antirracista, cual un enérgico apostolado en pro de la ciencia y contra el terrible mito de las 'razas.'" (For more than half a century, Fernando Ortiz carried out an extensive campaign of research, propaganda, and action in favor of the antiracist cause, like an energetic apostolate in favor of science and against the terrible myth of the 'races').[96] This concerning celebration of Ortiz transcends borders. In *The Intimacies of Four Continents*, Lisa Lowe goes as far as labeling Ortiz an "anticolonial and antislavery" thinker, placing him alongside Frederick Douglass, W. E. B. Du Bois, C. L. R. James, Walter Rodney, Cedric Robinson, and Sylvia Wynter.[97] Colorblindness, then, informs not only the theory of transculturation, but also the reception of Ortiz's work, as racism is routinely purged from it and rendered de facto invisible.

Transculturation has become a ubiquitous term and framework deployed across numerous disciplines, especially in cultural and literary studies. Beginning with Ángel Rama's *Transculturación narrativa en*

América Latina (translated as *Writing Across Cultures: Narrative Transculturation in Latin America*, 1982), many scholars have employed the term transculturation in ways that misconstrue Ortiz's understanding of the theory. These studies interpret transculturation as an antiracist theory that better describes processes of cultural exchange in colonial and postcolonial societies than acculturation, a term in use since the early 1930s. In the process, scholars have neglected to adequately engage Ortiz's work and mostly fail to engage it all. The critical consensus today is that transculturation describes a mutual process in which colonizer and colonized are both affected by each other's culture. For example, Jerry Hoeg contends in *Science, Technology, and Latin American Narrative in the Twentieth Century and Beyond* that "for Ortiz, transculturation describes a process of mutual, plural, and reciprocal influences between various cultures."[98] Comparably, David Attwell writes in *Rewriting Modernity: Studies in Black South African Literary History* that Ortiz's theory of transculturation, which provides the theoretical framework for Attwell's study, represents a rejection of acculturation and "by contrast, suggests multiple processes, a dialogue in both directions."[99] In *Mestizaje: Critical Uses of Race in Chicano Culture*, Rafael Pérez-Torres similarly argues that for Ortiz "transculturation names the process by which a subjugated group simultaneously incorporates and transforms the culture of a dominant group."[100] Engaging in an even deeper misreading, Joshua Lund argues in *The Impure Imagination: Toward a Critical Hybridity in Latin American Writing* that transculturation refers to "turning the cultural energy of colonialism (that is, theories and practices of forced acculturation) back against itself and thereby destabilizing the culture of the colonizer."[101] Similarly, Mary Louise Pratt in *Imperial Eyes: Travel Writing and Transculturation* contends that "Ortiz proposed the term [transculturation] to replace the paired concepts of acculturation and deculturation that described the transference of culture in reductive fashion imagined from within the interests of the metropolis."[102] As they either misread Ortiz's work or fail to read it altogether, these scholars and many others have contributed to silencing the white supremacy and anti-Blackness that structure the theory of transculturation.

Pushing against this uncritical consensus, in what follows I place Ortiz's theory of transculturation back where it belongs—within the archive of eugenics—to show that transculturation, far from "destabilizing the culture of the colonizer," envisions the reproduction of white supremacy and nothing less than the disappearance of Black people.

MESTIZAJE AND RACIAL GENOCIDE

Rather than describing "a process of mutual, plural, and reciprocal influences between various cultures," the process of transculturation positions Black people as what da Silva calls "the affectable, always already vanishing others of Europe that the scientific cataloguing of minds institutes."[103] Blackness within transculturation is that which must be expelled. Frank B. Wilderson writes that "at the core of what it means to be Cuban is an anxiety over *where* the Black is."[104] This is precisely the anxiety that animates Ortiz's work, an anxiety that is genocidal, bent on erasing Black people.

Ortiz first introduces the neologism "transculturation" in *Contrapunteo*, where he describes it as follows:

> Entendemos que el vocablo *transculturación* expresa mejor las diferentes fases del proceso transitivo de una cultura a otra, porque éste no consiste solamente en adquirir una distinta cultura, que es lo que en rigor indica la voz angloamericana *acculturation*, sino que el proceso implica también necesariamente la pérdida o desarraigo de una cultura precedente, lo que pudiera decirse una parcial desculturación, y, además, significa la consiguiente creación de nuevos fenómenos culturales que pudieran denominarse de neoculturación.[105]

> I am of the opinion that the word *transculturation* better introduces the different phases of the process of transition from one culture to another because it does not consist merely in acquiring another culture, which is what the English word *acculturation* really implies, but the process also necessarily involves the loss or uprooting of a previous culture, which could be defined as deculturation. In addition, it carries the idea of the consequent creation of new cultural phenomena, which could be called neoculturation.[106]

Instead of defining transculturation as a reciprocal exchange between people of different ethnoracial backgrounds, Ortiz speaks of cultural loss and the acquisition of new cultural elements. While his definition of transculturation here is ambiguous, it is relevant to notice that Ortiz describes it as a *process*. Even so, scholars have yet to carefully examine "Por la integración cubana de blancos y negros" (For the Cuban Integration of Whites and Blacks), the lecture in which Ortiz describes precisely the five phases of the transculturation process, and

102   THE MAKING OF WHITE NATIONS

generally ignore this work altogether. Paying close attention to this lecture demonstrates that the theory of transculturation is fundamentally anti-Black and that Ortiz was an unrepentant eugenicist throughout his career.

It is on a podium at the Club Atenas, in the heart of La Habana, that Ortiz delivers "Por la integración cubana de blancos y negros." Founded five years after the 1912 massacre in which US and Cuban troops killed thousands of Black Cubans who rose up to put an end to their oppression, the Club Atenas (Athens Club) was the most prestigious Black society in Cuba when Ortiz gives his talk on December 12, 1942.[107] This is not the first time that Ortiz addresses the intellectuals, doctors, lawyers, engineers, and other members of the Black elite that patronize the exclusive club. In 1937, when he presided over the inauguration of the Sociedad de Estudios Afrocubanos (Society for Afro-Cuban Studies) that he founded, Ortiz spoke on the same podium.[108] But this is a truly special occasion for Ortiz and he lets his audience know: "Esta hora que está pasando será recordada por mí como una de las más llenas y felices. Ella me indica la culminación de la parábola de mi vida intellectual." (I will always remember this hour as one of the fullest and happiest. It indicates to me the culmination of the parable of my intellectual life).[109] Tonight, Ortiz is introduced as an honorary member of the Club Atenas and his excitement is palpable: "¡Gracias! Eso os digo: ¡Gracias! Y os lo habré de repetir mientras viva." (Thank you! This is what I tell you: Thank you! And I will have to repeat it to you as long as I'm alive).[110] Ortiz knows that towering Black intellectuals and leaders such as W. E. B. Du Bois and Marcus Garvey have stood on the same podium.[111] If there is such a thing as honorary Blackness, Ortiz must have thought that night, *I finally earned it*.

Given that this event represents the high point of Ortiz's career, perhaps we should forgive him for leaving modesty at home that night and arguing that his honorary membership in the Club Atenas is not just significant for his own career, but "marca un punto histórico en la evolución de nuestra patria" (marks a historic moment in the evolution of our country).[112] The event, Ortiz will go on to argue, represents a victory for progress, science, race relations, and the Cuban nation itself. However, instead of actually talking about Cuba, Ortiz first places the spotlight on himself and his own scholarship. This makes sense given that "Por la integración cubana de blancos y negros" is Ortiz's manifesto for his own life and work, a fully fledged apologia pro vita et opera sua. It is through the concept of transculturation that Ortiz brings together Cuba, racist

MESTIZAJE AND RACIAL GENOCIDE

science, ideas of progress, and his own intellectual trajectory. But let me proceed slowly as Ortiz takes his time to get to transculturation that evening. First, he launches into an intellectual autobiography:

> Desde hace cuarenta años me hallo en la labor exploradora, de clasificación y de analísis, por esa intrincadísima fronda de las culturas negras retoñadas en Cuba. . . . Mi primer libro, aún cuando escrito con serena objetividad y con criterio positivista, y pese al prólogo con que lo honró César Lombroso, fué recibido por lo general entre la gente blanca con benevolencia, pero siempre con esa sonrisa complaciente y a veces desdeñosa con que suelen oírse las anécdotas de Bertoldo, los cuentos baturros o los chistes de picardía; y entre la gente de color el libro no obtuvo sino silencio de disgusto, roto por algunos escritos de manifiesta aún cuando refrenada hostilidad.[113]

> For forty years, I have been engaged in exploratory work of classification and analysis among this intricate foliage of Negro cultures that have sprouted in Cuba. . . . My first book, although written with serene objectivity and guided by a positivist criterion, and although it was honored with a prologue by Cesare Lombroso, was generally received by white people with benevolence, but always with that condescending and sometimes disdainful smile with which one tends to react to Bertoldo's anecdotes, barroom stories and off-color jokes; and among people of color the book did not elicit anything but a silence of disgust, interrupted merely by some writings that expressed a clear, albeit restrained, hostility.

In his first book, *Hampa afro-cubana: Los negros brujos* (Afro-Cuban Underworld: The Black Sorcerers), Ortiz represents Black people as intrinsically criminal and lacking humanity itself. At Club Atenas, he does not problematize this perspective, but rather argues that *Los negros brujos* is "written with serene objectivity" and represents Afro-Cuban religions and practices "tales como eran en realidad" (as they really were).[114] The words that Ortiz uses to describe his academic endeavor meanwhile reproduce racist associations between Blackness and savagery: the word "fronda" (foliage) is not far removed from jungle, the word used in the English translation of the lecture, which appeared in the United States in 1944.[115]

104   THE MAKING OF WHITE NATIONS

In *Los negros brujos*, Ortiz argues that Black traditional healers, whom he describes as brujos (witches or sorcerers), should be incarcerated perpetually, kept isolated from other prisoners, and subjected to forced labor. African dances should also be banned, he contends, as they are breeding grounds for witchcraft.[116] Less than fifty years after the abolition of slavery, Ortiz thus advocated for the imprisonment of Black people and the exploitation of their labor. His arguments had serious consequences for people of African descent: a practicing lawyer and politician, Ortiz presided over the Department of Penal Legislation of the National Codification Commission for several years and played an important role in shaping Cuban legislation.[117]

While we should not take for granted that Ortiz defends his first book at the apex of his career, the central location of Lombroso in his lecture should not surprise anyone familiar with Ortiz's biography. The father of Cuban criminology, Ortiz was a disciple of Lombroso, the discipline's founder, with whom Ortiz studied when he was an ambassador in Italy.[118] Lombroso portrayed crime not as the product of societal conditions or as part of the human condition at large, but as innate and residing in specific individuals who can be identified through physical features such as skull shape and facial expression.[119] Lombroso might have developed his racist and classist theories about deviance over a century ago, but his ideas have not lost their impact. The Museo di Antropologia Criminale Cesare Lombroso (Cesare Lombroso Museum of Criminal Anthropology) at the University of Torino, which was renovated in 2009 to *honor* the centenary of Lombroso's death, remains filled with the death masks and over four hundred skulls of presumed delinquents and other people, mostly poor southern Italians, whom Lombroso deemed "social misfits." Founded by Lombroso himself in 1876, the museum has been the object of calls for closure by organizations such as No Museo Lombroso, yet continues to legitimize overtly racist science in the twenty-first century.[120] Celebrated as an antiracist thinker today, Ortiz defended the same racist science in his 1942 lecture.

To legitimize his white supremacist doctrines, Ortiz appeals to scientific knowledge, creating an analogy between science, objectivity, and truth. In the process, he constructs a racist narrative that represents Black people as progressing from irrational beings who reject his scholarship to people who accept positivist science and thereby rationality itself. The Club Atenas members, Ortiz argues, belong to a small group of enlightened Black Cubans who understand that "la única via de liberación contra todos los prejuicios está en el conocimiento de las realidades, sin pasiones ni

MESTIZAJE AND RACIAL GENOCIDE

recelos; basado en la investigación científica y en la apreciación positiva de los hechos y la circunstancias" (the only path toward freedom from all prejudices is to be found in knowing reality, without passion or mistrust; based on scientific investigation and the positive appreciation of facts and circumstances).[121] While he discursively elevates the audience to a higher stage of being, Ortiz positions himself as a white savior who has come to rescue Black people from backwardness, bringing them closer to science, progress, and rational thinking.

Having argued that white people met *Los negros brujos* with ambivalence while Black people reacted to the book with hostility, Ortiz provides a litany of examples of this hostility. Symbolically likening his condition to that of Black people, Ortiz becomes a victim in his own story, in which the scholarship that tonight is celebrated, was once ridiculed. Studying Black people, Ortiz argues, "era tarea harto trabajosa, propicia a las burlas y no daba dinero" (was a very hard job that was prone to derision and didn't bring any money).[122] Still, he kept publishing. Slowly, Ortiz argues, Black people stopped being hostile toward him. Some even began to approach him. Others would ask him for favors, for legal protection. Ortiz comes out as resilient and triumphant in his self-constructed narrative of white injury. Regardless of their criticism, Ortiz says, he kept writing about Black people. Eventually, many of his critics relented: "Entonces ya comprendieron algunos, así blancos como de color, que mi faena de entografía no era un simple pasatiempo o distracción . . . sino que era base para poder fundamentar mejor los criterios firmes de una mayor integración nacional." (By this time some people, both white and of color, understood that my ethnographic work was not simply a pastime or hobby . . . but represented the basis upon which a more complete national integration could be constructed).[123] Ortiz positions himself as superior to Black people, whom he represents as in need of salvation—a salvation that is contingent on their acceptance of Ortiz's racist theories about Black people. He insists that his work is important for the Cuban nation as a whole because it can serve to establish "national integration." But what kind of integration does Ortiz envision? Is it the kind of integration that Steve Biko calls "real integration"—one predicated upon mutual respect between Black and white people and upon Black people's self-determination? Or is it akin to what Biko defines as "artificial integration," one in which white people continue to see themselves as superior and freedom for Black people is unthinkable?[124] The five phases of the transculturation process show that real integration is far from what Ortiz has in mind.

106   THE MAKING OF WHITE NATIONS

Ortiz explicitly compares his scholarly trajectory to the process of transculturation. He argues that the shift from hostility to acceptance that allegedly marked the reception of his scholarship mirrors the stages of the transculturation process: "Esta graduación que he señalado en cuanto a las varias actitudes con que durante cuarenta años se ha respondido a mi tarea intelectual es exactamente la misma con que se expresan los impactos de dos razas o culturas a través de todas las fases de su recíproca transculturación." (The adjustment that I have mentioned with regard to the reaction to my intellectual work during the last forty years is exactly the same as that which characterizes the impacts of two races or cultures as they go through the phases of their reciprocal transculturation).[125] The analogy that Ortiz constructs between the transculturation process and his own intellectual trajectory is telling, as both envision Black people as moving closer towards whiteness and thereby toward progress. In Ortiz's autobiographical narrative, Black people stop critiquing his racist scholarship, embrace it, and endow him with acclaim. In the theory of transculturation, Black people stop resisting, adapt to white supremacy, and get absorbed by a superior third entity. Although Ortiz defines transculturation as *reciprocal* in the quote above, it will become evident that the goal of the transculturation process is not to bring white people closer to Blackness, but to bring Black people closer to whiteness and, ultimately, obliterate them.

The first phase of the transculturation process, Ortiz writes, is one of hostility: white people enslave Black people, who in turn rebel. During this phase, he argues, "Todo en él [el negro] es infrahumano y bestial" (everything about him [the Negro] is subhuman and bestial).[126] Ortiz here conceptualizes an original phase in which Black people are seen as subhuman, a phase that he locates in the era of slavery. However, a closer look at Ortiz's work shows that he considered Black people to be stuck in an inferior stage of development that can be partially mitigated—but never fully surmounted—only by mixing with white people. To understand the significance of this argument we must return to *Los negros brujos*, in which Ortiz not only contends that criminality is the exclusive domain of Black Cubans, but also that Black people are inherently criminal:

> En Cuba toda una raza entró en la mala vida. Al llegar los negros
> entraban todos en la mala vida cubana. . . . En sus amores eran
> los negros sumamente lascivos, sus matrimonios llegaban hasta
> la poligamia, la prostitución no merecía su repugnancia, sus

MESTIZAJE AND RACIAL GENOCIDE

> familias carecían de cohesión, su religión los llevaba a los sacrificios humanos, a la violación de sepulturas, a la antropofagia y a las más brutales supersticiones; la vida del ser humano les inspiraba escaso respeto. . . . Pero la inferioridad del negro, la que le sujetaba al mal vivir era debida a falta de civilización integral, pues tan primitiva era su moralidad, como su intelectualidad, como sus voliciones, etc. Este carácter es lo que más lo diferencia de los individuos de la mala vida de las sociedades formadas exclusivamente por blancos.[127]

> In Cuba an entire race entered a life of crime. When the Negroes arrived they all entered the Cuban underworld. . . . In their love-affairs, Negroes were extremely lewd, their marriages would go as far as polygamy, prostitution did not deserve their repugnance, their families lacked cohesiveness, their religion led them to human sacrifice, to violating graves, to anthropophagy and the most brutal superstitions; human life inspired little respect in them. . . . But the inferiority of the Negro, which would subject him to criminality, was due to his integral lack of civilization, given that his morality was as primitive as his intellect, his desires, etc. This character is what differentiates him the most from the individuals involved in crime of societies formed exclusively by whites.

This passage shows that Ortiz viewed Black people as "savage," inherently criminal, and devoid of any sense of morality. In a move that brings the paradoxes of racist science to light, both Lombroso in *L'uomo bianco e l'uomo di colore* (The White Man and the Man of Color, 1871) and Ortiz in *Los negros brujos* represent Black people as intrinsically criminal, while they acknowledge that context shapes criminality for white people. Lombroso devotes an entire chapter to arguing that people of color *in general* have no sense of morality, which he tries to demonstrate through imaginative anecdotes that he presents as facts: "Un selvaggio australiano richiesto da un Europeo che cosa fosse il bene e il male: 'Bene, rispose, é mangiare il proprio nemico, male é esserne mangiato.'" (Asked by a European what good and evil are, an Australian savage answered: "Good is to eat your enemy, bad is being eaten.")[128] Anthropophagy, incest, and rape are only some of the negative characteristics that Lombroso indiscriminately ascribes to Black people and people of color. Ortiz is no different as he dehumanizes and criminalizes Black

108   THE MAKING OF WHITE NATIONS

people, resorting to every stereotype in the racist repertoire, from las-
civiousness to cannibalism. While many scholars praise Ortiz for having
initiated the study of Afro-Cuban culture, Ortiz makes clear in *Los negros
brujos* that he considers Black people worth studying only insofar as they
embody what he saw as a primitive and inferior stage of existence. Contrary to what scholars have assumed, Ortiz never repudiated *Los negros
brujos*. At the Club Atenas, he instead argues that the book was written
with "objectivity and guided by a positivist criterion." It is crucial to keep
this in mind when assessing the theory of transculturation.

Ortiz describes the second phase of the transculturation process as
one in which white people "give in" to miscegenation while Black people adjust and begin to feel love for their country. He calls this stage
"*transigente*," one of compromise. Mestizaje now enters the theory,
functioning as a colorblind tool that serves to erase violence and pos-
tulate a harmonious coming together across racial boundaries through
"sensual love." Ortiz writes that in this phase, "El amor sensual va hil-
vanando las razas con el mestizaje. El blanco va cediendo ya con sus
amorenados hijos; y el negro . . . se va reajustando a la nueva vida, a
la nueva tierra y sintiendo el amor de una nueva patria" (sensual love
intertwines the races through mestizaje. The white begins to relent with
his brown children; and the Negro . . . begins adjusting to the new
life, the new land, and feeling the love of a new homeland).[129] Ortiz,
like Freyre, romanticizes miscegenation as the product of "sensual love"
rather than what it was: rape under conditions of slavery. Reproducing
an epistemology of disavowal, Ortiz insinuates that the very existence
of racially mixed people signals white people's tolerance, a colorblind
move also deployed in Vasconcelos's and Freyre's works. Contrary to
what Ortiz argues, the existence of a mixed-race population did not
destabilize slavery in Cuba. The mixed-race children of a white master
and enslaved Black woman were not automatically granted freedom.

While Ortiz portrays the second phase as one in which harmony is
easily achieved, he describes the third phase as "acaso la fase más difi-
cil" (perhaps the most difficult).[130] But difficult for whom? Ortiz begins
describing this phase, which he calls "*adaptiva*" (adaptive) as follows: "El
individuo de color ya en la segunda generación criolla, trata de superarse
imitando al blanco, a veces con ceguera y así en lo bueno como en lo
malo." (The individual of color, already in the second Creole generation,
tries to overcome himself by imitating the white, sometimes blindly and
so in the good as in the bad).[131] The subjects of this transculturation
stage, once again, are Black people, who are imagined as being ashamed

MESTIZAJE AND RACIAL GENOCIDE

of their Blackness and aspiring to whiteness. This phase, like all others, centrally envisions changes *for Black people*. What is posited as difficult here for Black people is self-acceptance. The white subject enters this phase only briefly, as the "dominador" (dominator) who now begins to approach Black people more closely, which is contradictory given that previously Ortiz had posited an "intertwining" between the races through mestizaje. This adaptive phase, Ortiz writes, is in the past, although "aún ocurre todavía donde se vive con el ritmo pasado" (it still happens where people live in the rhythm of the past).[132] In this way, Ortiz presents white domination as a localized exception that has mainly been overcome.

Although the fourth phase of the transculturation process is called *"reivindicadora"* (one of revindication), it does not represent a real shift away from adaptation. Self-determination for Black people is not what Ortiz has in mind. Neither is this phase, which Ortiz locates in the present, about Black people attaining concrete material benefits and access to power. Instead, in this phase, "El hombre de color va dignamente recuperando su dominio y el aprecio de sí mismo." (The man of color begins to worthily regain control of himself and self-esteem).[133] The Spanish word *reivindicar* can be translated as to revindicate or to claim something to which you have a right. However, Ortiz locates progress for Black people strictly outside of materiality. For Ortiz, Black people can achieve self-confidence, but socioeconomic and political power must remain firmly in white hands. Ortiz in this way replicates the logics that also inform Alan Paton's liberal politics. As we will see in chapter 4, confronted with the rise of the Black Consciousness Movement in South Africa, Paton asserted that he could "understand the spiritual and psychological necessity for black people to be proud of black skin."[134] However, he had a problem with Black Consciousness getting "mixed up with black power."[135] Both Ortiz and Paton confine Black empowerment strictly to the psychological domain. Revindication for Ortiz does not mean that Black people demand what is rightfully theirs and gain access to power, but merely that they acquire "self-esteem."

Self-determination for Black people is unthinkable in Ortiz's theory of transculturation. Instead, the final phase conceives a fusion between cultures in which Blackness is swallowed up by a superior entity. Ortiz calls the fifth and last phase *"integrativa"* (integrative). In this phase, he writes, "Las culturas se han fundido, y el conflicto ha cesado, dando paso a un *tertium quid*, a una tercera entidad y cultura, a una comunidad nueva y culturalmente integrada, donde los factores meramente raciales han perdido su malicia disociadora." (Cultures have fused, and

110

conflict has ceased, giving way to a *tertium quid*, a third entity and culture, a new and culturally integrated community in which racial factors have lost their disassociating malice).[136] This is the phase of *tomorrow*, Ortiz argues, but it also exists in the present under some circumstances. The coming together of Black and white Cubans at the Club Atenas to celebrate his achievements, according to Ortiz, embodies a concrete example of this final phase. Ortiz argues that his own relationship with Black Cubans over his forty-year career mirrors the phases of the transculturation process: "desde la hostilidad y la desconfianza hasta la transigencia y, al fin, la cooperación" (from hostility and mistrust to compromise and, finally, cooperation).[137] Black people are here posited, once again, as changing and moving from hostility to cooperation. The transculturation process, then, is considered completed when Black people accept their own subjection and passively succumb to racism, including Ortiz's own. The cooperation embodied by the interracial encounter in Club Atenas, Ortiz argues, represents the consecration of mutual understanding "sobre la base objetiva de la verdad para ir logrando la integridad definitiva de la nación" (on the objective basis of truth in order to gradually achieve the definitive integrity of the nation).[138] Once more, Ortiz invokes objectivity and truth to sanction the legitimacy of his own academic work, which he insists serves to advance national unity. Ortiz appropriates truth for himself, presenting it as now mercifully bestowed upon a once critical and skeptical Black audience, who can finally partake in Ortiz's gift of science and contribute to national cohesion. This is the racist, paternalistic logic that structures Ortiz's speech in all its self-indulgence. Clearly, the kind of national integration that Ortiz envisions is grounded in white supremacy, embodying what Biko describes as *artificial integration*. Biko argues that true integration, understood as "the genuine fusion of the life-styles of the various groups" living in South Africa, presupposes "complete freedom of self-determination" and "mutual respect for each other."[139] Far from being based on self-determination and mutual respect, the process of national integration and fusion that Ortiz envisages is one in which Black people capitulate to white supremacy and are erased in the process.

Entrenched in the one-directional movement that defines the transculturation process is a hierarchy of values as Black people are envisioned as "blending in" and ultimately disappearing into a superior tertium quid, while whiteness maintains a diluting function. This process confines Black people to the status of non-human, while it

MESTIZAJE AND RACIAL GENOCIDE

makes whiteness the sole embodiment of humanity: only by mixing with white people can Black people achieve a higher state of being, one closer—albeit never identical to—the Human. In the theory of transculturation, it is Black people who have to transform, or rather have to be transformed, so that Cuba may remain as white as possible. Like other theories of mestizaje, transculturation is not a genuinely mutual process. Rather, it is meant to centrally affect Black people, who are positioned as objects that can be changed and molded to whites' liking, "subjected to outer determination, that is, affectable things."[140] The final stage of the transculturation process is a colorblind fusion in which white people retain the power to affect and rule. The fusion that Ortiz advocates operates in the same manner as invocations of postracialism, which aspire "to a raceless future while ultimately advocating the elimination not of racist domination per se, but rather of what it creates—*race*—or, more to the point, black people."[141] What must be eliminated in the logic of transculturation is not structural racism, but Black people.

As he defends the interests of white people like himself, Ortiz predictably reproduces an epistemology of disavowal that mystifies the reality of structural racism, its causes, and the actual ways to combat it. In a typical colorblind move, Ortiz reverses the cause and consequences of racism, arguing that "el complejo de inferioridad . . . [es], sin duda, el más grave obstáculo contra la dignificación y el ascenso social de las razas supeditadas a los niveles superiores de la indiscriminación" (the inferiority complex . . . [is], without doubt, the most important obstacle to the achievement of dignity and social ascension for the races most subjected to discrimination).[142] Ortiz here provides a misleading "solution" to racism that places the onus for white supremacy squarely onto the backs of Black people. Let us remember that the theory of transculturation describes progress for Black people strictly in psychological terms (Black people begin to love and accept themselves). Since Ortiz's project is about strengthening white power in Cuba, it can never envision concrete, material change. Instead, it conceals "the most important obstacle" to the achievement of economic and social equality for Black people: white people's active investment in reproducing the racist status quo, the same investment that motivates Ortiz's lecture.

That anthropologist Bronislaw Malinowski endorsed the term transculturation in the original introduction to *Contrapunteo*, where he portrays it as progressive vis-à-vis acculturation, might have contributed to the popularity of Ortiz's neologism. But this does not explain why today the term is especially popular in literary and cultural studies. Neither does it explain why transculturation has been embraced by postcolonial scholars in particular. Whether Ortiz is celebrated as an antiracist thinker or is merely an invisible residue in contemporary scholarship that invokes transculturation, what remains constant is the erasure of the white supremacy and anti-Blackness that motivated its theorization. The scarcity of scholarship on "Por la integración cubana de blancos y negros" might be due to the fact that Ortiz's anti-Black and white supremacist agenda is more explicit in this lecture than in *Contrapunteo*. And yet, scholars have also largely overlooked the anti-Blackness that animates Ortiz's most famous work. Ortiz argues in *Contrapunteo* that Jamaican and Haitian immigration to Cuba lowers "the living standard of Cuban society and upsets its racial balance, thus retarding the fusion of its component elements into a national whole."[143] For Ortiz, just as for Alfaro, Jamaicans and Haitians are racial undesirables. They lower "the living standard," Ortiz argues, insinuating that his attack is not racially motivated while he reproduces, verbatim, the same racist argument that Alfaro makes about Jamaicans and other West Indian immigrants in Panama. They "upset" the "racial balance," Ortiz continues, his racist agenda now becoming explicit. They delay the transculturation process, "the fusion" at the core of Cuba's white national project. For Ortiz, Jamaicans and Haitians are *too* Black. They must be expelled. Ortiz, who conflates Blackness and criminality, can envision Cuba as mixed, but never as Black. He thus demonizes Black people in what he considers to be *his* country, a country where white people, Ortiz insists, maintain the sole domain over knowledge, rationality, and ultimately humanity itself.

Gilberto Freyre: Bringing Mestiçagem to the United Nations and the Apartheid Regime

A popular idiom says that all Brazilians have *um pé na cozinha* (a foot in the kitchen), implying that everybody has African ancestors. Just as in the common description of the Afrikaans language as "kitchen Dutch" in South Africa, the kitchen here evokes servitude and domestic labor, specifically the unpaid labor of enslaved Black people. Racial and cultural mixture are certainly present in Brazil, yet white people remain at the top of the social ladder while most Black Brazilians continue to climb only the strenuous steps that lead to many favelas in cities

MESTIZAJE AND RACIAL GENOCIDE

like Rio de Janeiro, where the entanglement between race and place is everywhere visible.[144] The present-day idealization of race relations in Brazil finds its predecessor in ahistorical literary representations of Brazilian slavery as an allegedly humane process punctuated by romantic encounters between Portuguese colonizers and enslaved people of African descent.[145] With regard to this matter, Lamonte Aidoo writes in *Slavery Unseen* that "the perpetuation of white dominance depended greatly on concealing its existence and how it operated. This was achieved by constructing a myth of Brazil's more benign slavery and the gentleness of the master and mistress while devaluing slaves and shifting blame for white violence to them."[146] Although nearly five million enslaved Africans were brought to Brazil, which in 1888 was the last country to formally abolish slavery, white Brazilian intellectuals have a long tradition of portraying slavery as a mild form of servitude and presenting racial mixture as alleged proof of racial harmony.

The mystification of Brazil as a benevolent civilization, dubbed Lusotropicalism, is associated in particular with Gilberto Freyre's most famous work *Casa-grande e senzala* (1933), in which he constructed a prominent discourse of Brazilian exceptionalism founded upon mestiçagem and comparisons with the United States and other former British colonies. Colorblindness is systematically at work throughout *Casa-grande e senzala*, which is obsessed with disavowing racism to the extent that it readily gives away its obsession. Freyre makes three interconnected arguments that reappear throughout the book: miscegenation is at the core of Brazilian society; the existence of miscegenation demonstrates that the Portuguese are not racist; and the colonization of Brazil had nothing to do with race and everything to do with religion. Romanticizing slavery, Freyre describes the Portuguese as "o colonizador europeo que melhor confraternizou com as raças chamadas inferiores" (the colonizer who best fraternized with the so-called inferior races) and "o menos cruel" (the least cruel) because "sempre pendeu . . . para o cruzamento e miscegenação" (he was always inclined . . . toward mixture and miscegenation).[147] Freyre trivializes the sexual violence that Portuguese men exercised upon Black women, reducing rape to a game between children, while he presents racial mixture as evidence of racial tolerance.[148] In the process, he erases racism from Brazilian society, reproducing this racism in turn. In Freyre's words, "My paternal grandfather—a sugar planter—was a violin virtuoso. The keen taste for music was perhaps what made Brazilian slaveholders kind and gentle."[149] The grandson of a slaveowner, Freyre also had a personal interest in misrepresenting slavery.

114   THE MAKING OF WHITE NATIONS

Radical Black Brazilian intellectuals and activists have long challenged the racist lies about Brazilian society that Freyre propagated in his work. Nascimento writes in the book aptly titled *Brazil: Mixture or Massacre?* that there was nothing mild about Brazilian slavery:

> The truth is that the Portuguese colonial aristocracy in Brazil was utterly racist, cruel and inhuman in its treatment of Africans as any other white slaveholding elite of the Americas. Slaves were continually and systematically tortured, murdered, abused and maltreated. Since trade routes to Africa from Brazil and back were shorter and more direct, prices were lower than in North America. Slaves were so cheap in Brazil that it was more economical to buy new replacements than to care for them—especially old or sick people, children, or the many who were deformed or crippled from torture and overwork. The concentration of slaves on a single plantation was greater. Thus for purely economic reasons, living conditions for slaves in Brazil were far worse in general than in other colonies, where replacements were more expensive.[150]

Nascimento challenges the myth of Brazilian slavery as a benevolent enterprise, making visible the atrocious conditions in which enslaved people were forced to live. As he reproduces an epistemology of disavowal, Freyre instead necessarily relies on multiple omissions to reproduce the myth of racial democracy, such as the fact that racial mixture was not widespread in Portuguese colonies such as Angola and Mozambique. Freyre also silences the historical reasons for the relatively high degree of racial mixture that occurred in Brazil, which are to be found in the circumstances of its colonization. Most Portuguese colonizers who arrived in Brazil, in fact, were young men unaccompanied by white women.[151] Nascimento makes clear that sexual relations between white slaveowners and enslaved Black women were defined by violence: "The use of African women to satisfy slaveowners in the absence of white women was outright rape. It had nothing to do with 'respect' for the victims as human beings."[152] In his compelling study of Brazilian slavery, Aidoo shows that white women were not passive bystanders in this violence, but rather denigrated and raped both enslaved women and men, while Black men were also subjected to sexual violence on the part of male slaveowners.[153] To this day, far from being a racial democracy, Brazil remains a very segregated society, especially among

MESTIZAJE AND RACIAL GENOCIDE

the white elite and middle class. White Brazilians often live in neighborhoods and move in social circles that are as white as those of their USAmerican counterparts. Many white Brazilians hardly have any Black friends, much less partners. To this day, interracial marriages involving members of the white Brazilian middle and upper class remain a rare exception rather than the rule in Brazil.[154]

While his most famous book romanticized slavery and established him internationally as Brazil's best-known anthropologist, Freyre's racism did not subside, but rather consolidated in an aggressive defense of colonialism at the apex of his career. In 1954, almost exactly twenty years after the publication of *Casa-grande e senzala*, the United Nations Commission on the Racial Situation in the Union of South Africa (UNCORS), in the midst of growing decolonial movements in Africa and around the globe, asked Freyre to write a report providing, as the title states, "the most effective methods for eliminating racial conflicts, tensions, and discriminatory practices" that have already been implemented in "countries where conditions approximate most closely those of the Union of South Africa." This report followed a 1949 General Conference in which UNESCO announced a tripartite commitment to studying and collecting "scientific materials concerning questions of race," assuring the "wide diffusion" of these materials, and starting "an educational campaign based on this information."[155] UNESCO offered Freyre $1000 to write the report, selecting him as an "expert 'spécialiste des questions raciales'" (an expert "specialist in racial questions") over other proposed candidates such as Ernest Beaglehole (New Zealand), Claude Levi-Strauss (France), L. A. Costa Pinto (Brazil), Juan Comas (Mexico), and Morris Ginsberg (United Kingdom), all anthropologists, with the exception of sociologist Ginsberg, who had been invited to the 1949 conference.[156] Originally written in English and successively translated into French, the official language of the UN, Freyre's report supports colonialism, presenting to a global audience of fellow white people not "the most effective methods for eliminating racial conflicts, tensions, and discriminatory practices," but what Freyre deemed to be the most effective methods through which white people could *strengthen* power in the colonies. If white people want to remain in power in South Africa and elsewhere, Freyre argues in the report, they should adopt mestiçagem.

Freyre takes advantage of the report, and the international audience it granted him, to present an image of Brazil as a country free of racism. Given that the report idealizes Portuguese colonization, it makes sense that the Portuguese government advocated for its wide dissemination.[157] Freyre immediately defines slavery in Brazil as "very suave" and argues that the Portuguese accepted baptized Black people as equals. In Freyre's words: "It is true that a very suave form of slavery was then followed by the Portuguese with slaves who, after baptized, were taken as sociological members of Portuguese families and not put to work as if they were simply animals."[158] Freyre insists that the Portuguese displayed "an attitude [of] tolerance . . . towards Negroes, as soon as the Negroes became Christian and, as a result of this, potentially Portuguese."[159] Contrary to what Freyre argues, becoming Christian did not change the political and ontological status of Black people in Brazil. By the 1530s, Indigenous people in Spanish and Portuguese colonies had been declared free de jure, while Black people remained enslaved and, as Sylvia Wynter writes, "consigned to the pre-Darwinian last link in the Chain of Being—to the 'missing link' position, therefore, between rational humans and irrational animals."[160] Conversion to Christianity did not propel the abolition of slavery, nor did it grant Black people inclusion into the category of the Human. In the report, Freyre's invocation of Black humanity reveals itself as a colorblind tool deployed to give the text an antiracist veneer. Freyre's description of the Black as a "human being" coexists with his branding of Black people as "savage or primitive stocks."[161] The rhetorical attribution of humanity to Black people facilitates, rather than disrupts, the articulation and transmission of Freyre's anti-Black agenda.

Freyre depicts racial discrimination as the product of outside forces that are alien to Mozambican and Brazilian societies. Instead of outright omitting examples of racial discrimination in former and current Portuguese colonies, Freyre addresses specific cases of discrimination in order to disavow local responsibility for racism. He concedes that in Mozambique there are hotels that only admit white people, but contends that this is due to the influence that South Africa has exercised on some parts of the country and is "in conflict with some of its most characteristic Portuguese traditions."[162] Racial segregation in Mozambique, Freyre insists, is "a South-Africanism or an Anglo-Saxonism."[163] Racial disavowal is at work also in Freyre's reference to the discrimination case against African American dancer Katherine Dunham who, together with her troupe, was refused accommodation in a São Paulo hotel in 1950. A hotel refusing entrance to a Black person, Freyre argues, is a "very un-Brazilian happening," a localized peculiarity.[164] If discrimination against racialized foreigners exists in Mozambique and Brazil, Freyre insists, it is because foreigners themselves have introduced it.

MESTIZAJE AND RACIAL GENOCIDE   117

The racism that Freyre displaces elsewhere becomes visible in his own text, which reveals a clear ideological alliance with the South African apartheid regime that Freyre is supposed to be critiquing. Freyre noticeably argues *against* outlawing racial discrimination even as apartheid was a system of legalized racial discrimination. In 1951, following the racist incident in the São Paulo hotel, the Brazilian government passed a law against racial discrimination (commonly referred to as the Lei Arinos), which Freyre fervently condemns. Not only does Freyre argue that outlawing racial discrimination is a "problem," but he also likens the Lei Arinos to "dictatorial" and "police-flavored" methods used in the Soviet Union.[165] Invoking the Soviet Union to discredit antidiscrimination law is a powerful move in the context of the Cold War, in which Western Europe and the United States attempted to consolidate their global image as defenders of liberal democracy in opposition to communist Russia. Illustrating how the report served the interests of white power, Freyre brands the banning of racism as antidemocratic, as "coercion from the State."[166] Apartheid was inscribed in South African law through hundreds of racist acts that ensured white control over Black people's land, labor, and lives. Legal changes were therefore one necessary step in its formal undoing. Not so for Freyre, who argues that apartheid should remain in place.

The "solutions" to racism that Freyre proposes demonstrate that endorsing individual responses to structural problems is a calculated white strategy of domination. In the effort to uphold material conditions of Black dispossession and white privilege, Freyre argues that "education, information, enlightenment, rather than legislation, are the socially and psychologically most profitable ways of dealing with the problem of race prejudice."[167] While he rejects legislative changes, Freyre defines racism as a series of irrational behaviors that psychologists and teachers can "cure" through education. Of course, the fact that Freyre condemns using the law as a means of racial redress shows that he knows well that racism is institutionalized and not simply a matter of psychology. Freyre's confinement of racism to individual prejudice is not random: it is part of a global white campaign of silencing the structural dimensions of racism. Between 1949 and 1955, UNESCO sponsored several activities and publications aimed *not* at dismantling institutional racism but at "combating racial prejudice and the discrimination to which it gives rise."[168] Positing prejudice as the cause (rather than consequence) of racism—and postulating the mere overcoming of individual prejudice as the ultimate remedy to racism—bolsters white supremacy. Casting light onto this racist strategy, Khalil Saucier and

Tryon Woods write that proponents of colorblindness first construct racism as prejudice and then represent integration itself as the antidote to racism. This racist logic, which is visible in Freyre's report, goes as follows: "integrate the prejudicial mind through education and raising awareness; eradicating prejudicial thoughts will lead to equal treatment; equal treatment leads to integrated social spaces."[169] This logic silences the fact that racism is institutionalized. It is not by coincidence that UNESCO and Freyre called for the eradication of prejudice, rather than the dismantlement of structural racism.

Contrary to what Freyre and UNESCO assert, racism is not equivalent to individual prejudice. Kwame Ture and Charles Hamilton, who coined the term *institutional racism* in *Black Power: The Politics of Liberation* (1967), distinguish between overt acts of racial violence and intolerance (individual racism) and the collective, covert, and structural domination of Black people and people of color (institutional racism). In Ture and Hamilton's words:

> When a black family moves into a home in a white neighborhood and is stoned, burned or routed out, they are victims of an overt act of individual racism which many people will condemn—at least in words. But it is institutional racism that keeps black people locked in dilapidated slum tenements, subject to the daily prey of exploitative slumlords, merchants, loan sharks and discriminatory real estate agents. The society either pretends it does not know of this latter situation, or is in fact incapable of doing anything meaningful about it.[170]

Institutional racism, Ture and Hamilton show, is the normalization of white supremacy in institutions, laws, policies, and practices that produce racially differential access to jobs, organizations, services, spaces, wealth, and so forth. Every major institution in Brazil and in the United States is under white control. This is racism. Ture denounces the futility of appeals to the sympathy of whites such as those that Freyre advocates.[171] Appeals to the conscience of white people presume that Black people are granted the privilege of recognition. However, Blackness, as Wilderson writes, "destabiliz[es] civil society's ontological structure of empathy."[172] Black people are a priori excluded from the conceptual framework of empathy because they are barred from the community of Humans/Masters. Freyre knows that attempting to persuade white people to change their attitudes does not challenge institutional racism.

MESTIZAJE AND RACIAL GENOCIDE   119

This is precisely why he advocates educating white people while he demonizes legislative changes.

A pervasive white anxiety about losing economic and political power in the face of mounting organized Black resistance emanates unequivocally from Freyre's document. It would be, in fact, a mistake to argue that Freyre is concerned only about the preservation of European *culture* in the colonies. Rather, the report aims to secure the European preservation of the colonies themselves. Freyre opens the report arguing that there are vast differences between the Catholic/Portuguese and the Protestant/Anglo racial systems and that racism only exists in British colonies. However, Freyre quickly reframes these presumed differences as being irrelevant in the face of a collective white interest in safeguarding power across national borders. Freyre argues that (white) Brazilians and South Africans find themselves in

> similar conditions of danger or risk to "European civilization" and its almost sacred notion of "progress" due to the fact that in Brazil, as in South Africa, Europeans and descendants of Europeans have found themselves, as carriers of that civilization and promoters of that progress, as minorities under the menace of being defeated by non-European groups and non-European cultures.[173]

As he portrays progress and civilization as the sole prerogative of Europeans, whom he represents as a vulnerable minority in the colonies, Freyre worries that white people will be "defeated" by Black people and people of color, whom he describes in a denigrating manner as "non-progressive, non-civilized, and non-European."[174] Clearly, Freyre considers Black and colonized people as a "menace" to white power that must be suppressed.

Freyre presents mestiçagem as an efficient method of racial control that white people should adopt in South Africa and other African colonies to ensure that they maintain power. Mirroring Vasconcelos's strategic binary partitioning of racial regimes into "the Latin system of assimilation" and "the Anglo-Saxon method of . . . pure-race standards,"[175] Freyre describes the Portuguese as following an "assimilative policy," while Europeans in British colonies or the Belgian Congo follow "the non-assimilative policy."[176] Despite the deceptive title of the report that posits the two countries as being similar, Freyre presents Brazil and South Africa as "the two most important opposite extremes in regard to racial attitudes."[177] However, in the common goal of

120 THE MAKING OF WHITE NATIONS

preserving whiteness, Freyre contends, white South Africans need not fear miscegenation and cultural mixture as the Brazilian case shows that "'white culture' . . . may be preserved without 'white race purity' being made a condition for the preservation of cultural values."[178] Just as Vasconcelos argued that Spanish culture is alive and well in Latin America despite (and, in fact, thanks to) mestizaje, Freyre contends that racial mixture does not destabilize, but rather protects white interests. Following the Portuguese example, he argues, would allow white South Africans to continue to control Black people and exploit their labor without losing either political or cultural dominance. According to Freyre, this assimilative model has already proven fruitful in Brazil and Venezuela, countries that he describes in clearly anti-Black terms as having "been invaded by 'oceans of blackness' without having to become lost for civilization and Christianity."[179] Thanks to a policy of mestiçagem, Freyre contends, the Portuguese "were not defeated by the non-European groups who now consider themselves 'Brazilian.'"[180] Mestiçagem does not threaten whiteness, but rather assists in its perpetuation, Freyre argues, so that white South Africans are foolish in their obsession with racial purity.

Freyre, like Vasconcelos and Ortiz, thus views Black people as an invading element that should be eliminated—were it not for the fact that white people's wealth depends on exploiting the labor of Black people. Freyre writes:

> [In South Africa] the subordinated group is too numerous, too vital and too resourceful, in comparison with the white one, to be eliminated in the same way that the more scarce group of Amerindians, when not absorbed in the social systems of the white settlers of America, were eliminated by these same settlers, overwhelmed by them in numbers or kept, in small groups, either isolated or almost enslaved, as in a few of the Spanish-American Republics and in the United States. . . . [I]t is when the invading settlers are unable to control the native population with certainty, owing to their relative numerical weakness, that "a struggle for land, status, and the possession of a social order develops into a race conflict if [sic] the most intense kind" (43). For this kind of inter-racial tension, that is also an inter-cultural conflict, no solution is seen by social scientists outside of the one that is being traditionally followed by such countries like Brazil and Venezuela, and also by USSR in a very systematic

and energetic way, without any risk, at least immediate, of their national cultures, that are predominantly European, becoming "barbaric" or "inferior."[181]

As becomes clear in this passage, Freyre offers mestiçagem to white South Africans as a tool that may allow them "to control the native population with certainty" and uphold power. Given that Black people in South Africa are too numerous and too useful to be downright exterminated, Freyre argues, white South Africans should assimilate Black people like the Portuguese have allegedly done in their colonies. Freyre writes that Black people are "too vital and too resourceful," meaning that their cheap labor is essential for the functioning of the South African colony and the wealth of the colonists, so that Europeans cannot annihilate them as they have done with Indigenous people in the Americas. Given that white people profit from the extraction of Black people's labor, assimilation is the only way to continue to exploit Black people while preventing them from making gains in the "struggle for land, status, and the possession of a social order." There is one solution to the looming loss of European power in the African colonies, Freyre insists: white people must follow the Brazilian path and adopt mestiçagem.

Freyre is alarmed by Black anticolonial mobilization. Targeting specifically Black consciousness and Pan-Africanism as forces that threaten white interests, Freyre writes:

A situation has developed there [in Africa] similar, in some respects, to that of the Negro in the United States, where group consciousness has developed. . . . The result is that, as there is today a highly unified "American Negro," there seem to begin to rise in Africa an "African Negro" who adds to his sub-group consciousness a super-national pride as an "African Negro" to who Africa should naturally belong, outsiders having to adapt themselves to a mere condition of "ethnic minorities." Such a consciousness is already evident in some of the African Negro leaders, whose Pan-African consciousness is rather invigorated than weakened by their activities as national agitators or guides, among certain specific African groups.

I was interested in finding out that in Portuguese Africa such a Pan-African consciousness among Negroes and quase-Negroes is evidently weaker, in its development, than in other African areas or regions.[182]

Freyre fears that the divide-and-conquer strategy of enforcing ethnic differentiation among Black and colonized people—a central white strategy of domination in the African continent and beyond—is faltering as Africans have developed a unified racial consciousness and no longer see themselves "as members of very particular etnico-cultural groups."[183] Freyre suggests that, to counter Black unity and revolution, whites everywhere should follow the Portuguese model of assimilation. Mestiçagem, he believes, has a "sociological advantage" as it has been allegedly successful in stymieing Black resistance in Portuguese colonies and ensuring that Black people identify with their colonial masters.[184] Freyre's line of argument here resembles Vasconcelos's contention that "the cultural results of the Spanish method are superior."[185] In the process, Freyre erases Black and Indigenous resistance.

The Quilombo dos Palmares, in what is today the Brazilian state of Alagoas, in which maroons resisted Dutch and Portuguese armed attacks for nearly one century from 1605 until 1694, Nascimento's own commitment to Pan-Africanism, or the Angolan, Mozambican, and Guinean independence wars that would erupt in the 1960s and lead to the unraveling of the Portuguese empire, show that Freyre was, of course, lying by arguing that Black people in Portuguese colonies are loyal to the colonizers. This makes sense as lies are precisely what white supremacist discourse is about so that Freyre, disavowing the historical evidence of unrelenting Black resistance in Portuguese colonies and elsewhere, concludes by arguing that, "The so-called 'Brazilian' or 'Venezuelan' or 'Fusionist' solution should be made widely known today in Africa."[186] The report requested by the United Nations Commission on the Racial Situation in the Union of South Africa thus reveals itself as a colorblind tool in its own right. Packaged as a benevolent document meant to deliver the "most effective methods for eliminating racial conflicts," the report interprets the pursuit of solutions to "racial conflicts" from the vantage point of whiteness, envisioning independence movements as that which must be eradicated. As it formulates collective Black resistance as the problem it needs to solve, the report proposes methods not for eliminating racism, but for eliminating Black insurgency.

Freyre, then, not only mystified the reality of violence that defines slavery, but also explicitly defended and supported colonialism at the zenith of his career. Despite these facts, or precisely because of them, Freyre today continues to be praised by white politicians, academics, and journalists in Brazil and the United States alike. In a pamphlet of

MESTIZAJE AND RACIAL GENOCIDE

the Brazilian House of Representatives issued in 2000 to commemorate the centenary of Freyre's birth, political scientist Luis Fernandes denies that Freyre romanticized slavery and describes him as "o gênio . . . da nossa formação social" (the genius . . . of our social formation),[187] a glorification that informs the pamphlet as a whole. In *Gilberto Freyre e os estudos latino-americanos* (Gilberto Freyre and Latin American Studies, 2006), which includes essays in Portuguese and Spanish, US scholars Joshua Lund and Malcolm McNee also provide a celebratory reading of Freyre's work. The book is emblematic of a larger body of work that has begun "once again to evoke Freyre's name with respect."[188] As we shall see in the next chapter, Freyre's work today is invoked to delegitimize racial quotas in Brazilian universities. Lund and McNee nonetheless dismiss criticism of Freyre, arguing that his work "tem mantido muito do seu lustre e continua a inspirar epifanias e novas revelações" (has maintained much of its luster and continues to inspire epiphanies and new revelations).[189] The project to redeem Freyre's work and silence the racism that defines it, clearly, is a transnational white project.

As a colorblind tool, mestizaje is infinitely productive because it is infinitely deceptive. By virtue of strategic comparisons with Europe and the United States, white people in Latin America and beyond continue to present mestizaje as inspirational and counterhegemonic. Like Freyre, Ortiz, and Vasconcelos before them, white Latin American intellectuals routinely continue to perpetrate the myth that social conditions for Black people and people of color are better in Latin America than in the United States. Embodying this attitude, Enrique Krauze writes in a *New York Times* article titled "Latin America's Talent for Tolerance" (2014):

> European-style racism—which not only mistreats and discriminates but also persecutes and, in the very worst cases, tries to exterminate others because of their ethnicity—has been the exception and not the rule in modern Latin America. . . . In places where the mixing of ethnicities (mestizaje) and cultures prevailed under the Spanish and Portuguese empires—countries like Mexico, Colombia and Brazil—racist attitudes and practices have been far less pronounced.[190]

Already from the title, Krauze puts colorblindness to work as he silences the reality of racism not just in Mexico, but in Latin America

124   THE MAKING OF WHITE NATIONS

as a whole. In the piece, Krauze erases white supremacy from Latin American nations by positing ethnicity, and not racism, as the causal factor for discrimination. Like Freyre in the UNESCO report, Krauze disavows structural racism, invoking merely "racist attitudes and practices." In the process, like Alfaro, Freyre, Ortiz, and Vasconcelos, he presents mestizaje as evidence of racial harmony. As the archive from which Krauze draws is obvious, his statement signals not the absence of anti-Blackness and racism in Latin America, but the persistent effort on the part of white people to hide it.

This same anti-Blackness and idealization of racial mixture defines *Brown: The Last Discovery of America* (2002), a memoir by Mexican American author Richard Rodriguez, who argues that the race problem will be resolved once USAmericans—and especially Black people—complete a process of fusion through miscegenation. In Rodriguez's words: "Most American blacks are not black. . . . What I want for African Americans is white freedom. The same as I wanted for myself. The last white freedom in America will be the freedom of the African American to admit brown. Miscegenation."[191] As Rodriguez silences the obvious fact that racialization for Black people and people of color is not a matter of choice, he portrays miscegenation as a novelty and as emancipatory for Black people. Revealing again the anti-Blackness that structures the extolment of racial mixture, in his call for Black people to "admit brown" Rodriguez posits Blackness as that which must be erased. While he purports to envision a raceless future, Rodriguez clearly wants one that is, and shall remain, white.

These dominant valorizations of racial mixture depend on an unspoken biologism that reverts us right back to the era of eugenics. As Karen E. Fields and Barbara J. Fields write, "restoring notions of race mixture to center stage recommits us, willy-nilly, to the discredited idea of racial purity, the basic premise of bio-racism."[192] The same race science that Freyre, Ortiz, and Vasconcelos propagated in the twentieth century is at work in a large body of scholarship that centers mestizaje today. Many scholars, especially social scientists, still posit "mixing" as a biological process and mixed-race people as either superior beings embodying progress or troubled people embodying confusion. In both cases, racial mixture is viewed as an essential, biological reality. The late Catalan anthropologist Claudio Esteva-Fabregat, for example, argues in *Mestizaje in Ibero-America* (1995) that race is a genetic reality, just as US political scientist Rex Wirth in a more recent essay argues that "melting and mixing are not confined to genetics, but the genetic aspect is of

MESTIZAJE AND RACIAL GENOCIDE

particular importance."[193] Genetic understandings of race are also perpetrated in biomedical research, which still misrepresents racial mixing as a biological reality and searches for supposed racial differences in manifestations of disease.[194] If we believe that biological understandings of race are a thing of the past, we are deluding ourselves.

A seemingly opposite impulse animates cultural studies, which has detached analyses of hybridity from a concern with so-called miscegenation, thereby moving, metaphorically speaking, from blood to culture. While seemingly progressive, this move is not free from contradictions as many works concerned with cultural hybridity, such as Néstor García Canclini's *Culturas híbridas: Estrategias para entrar y salir de la modernidad* (*Hybrid Cultures: Strategies for Entering and Leaving Modernity* 1995 [1990]), Paul Gilroy's *The Black Atlantic: Modernity and Double Consciousness* (1993), Homi Bhabha's *The Location of Culture* (1994), and Sarah Nuttall's *Entanglement: Literary and Cultural Reflections on Post-Apartheid* (2009), the latter to which I return in the next chapter, present hybridity as an intrinsically counterhegemonic category, while they erase the centrality of violence to hybridization and silence the fact that notions of hybridity remain structured in anti-Indigeneity and anti-Blackness. Since the 1990s, these works and numerous others have established hybridity as a privileged category for social and cultural analysis. Discourses of hybridity have even taken center stage in much scholarship produced in Black diaspora studies.[195] This is no cause for celebration.

Consider how in *The Black Atlantic*, Gilroy posits the "theorisation of creolisation, métissage, mestizaje, and hybridity" or what he calls "a litany of pollution and impurity" as central to the cultural processes of exchange that, he argues, define the Black Atlantic, which he also describes as a "transcultural, international formation."[196] In the process, Gilroy reproduces some of the racist logics that define eugenicist theories of mestizaje and transculturation. This makes sense, given that, to cite Jackson in a different context, Gilroy "build[s] on foundations we would be better off destroying."[197] *The Black Atlantic* valorizes Black cultural productions to the extent that they are hybrid, reinscribing an understanding of mixedness as inherently valuable. Gilroy promises to illustrate "the complicity and syncretic interdependency of black and white thinkers."[198] However, except for chapter 3, which focuses on Black music, Gilroy mainly traces the influence of white European thinkers onto African American intellectuals. As Black people in the work are not just centrally positioned as receptors of white thought but even as subjects that are *improved* through contact with Europe,

The Black Atlantic replicates the one-directional and anti-Black logic of Ortiz's transculturation theory.[199]

Today, as in the past, much academic discourse in the United States and beyond continues to posit hybridity, mixture, and impurity as sites of intrinsic value in ways that, albeit often unwittingly, reinscribe eugenicist values. It is ironic that the theory of transculturation continues to be employed especially by scholars who, as Pérez-Torres writes, are "interested in the dissemination of and resistance to dominant power."[200] This is also the case for many scholars who specifically turn to hybridity, mixture, or impurity, although certainly not all. While US scholars who aim to challenge racism agree that there is little to celebrate in the category *purity*, they often ignore that white people have deployed both discourses of purity and impurity as technologies of racial genocide—and centrally as methods to eliminate Black people. The extolment of mixedness and brownness, we must remember, is predicated upon the erasure of Blackness. The rejection of racism, though, cannot occur, to cite Lewis R. Gordon, "without a dialectic in which humanity experiences a *blackened* world."[201] As the romanticization of hybridity, mestizaje, transculturation, browning, and impurity itself shows no signs of abating, critically examining the writings that Vasconcelos, Ortiz, and Freyre produced at the height of their careers is more crucial today than ever, lest we forget the genocidal agenda that motivated their celebration of racial mixture. As this chapter has hopefully shown, mestizaje is neither an alternative to ideologies of racial purity, nor does it stand in opposition to the racial technology of whitening, but is an insidious instantiation thereof that masks its ontological scheme of racial genocide under the deceptive appearance of "including" Black and Indigenous people by way of miscegenation and acculturation. As mestizaje is a colorblind tool, Vasconcelos, Ortiz, and Freyre inevitably reproduce an epistemology of disavowal. They disavow the existence of racism in Latin America, even as their own racism becomes more than evident. Today, it is imperative to return with a critical eye to these understudied eugenicist texts as they repackage racial genocide as racial democracy in ways that resonate deeply with the ongoing global circulation of myths about racial mixture. In the next chapter, I show that, just as the eugenicists studied in this chapter deployed mestizaje to demobilize Black and Indigenous resistance, white people continue to invoke discourses of mestizaje and hybridity alongside many other colorblind tools to halt the demands of Black movements, across national borders, in our time.

Part 2

The Ongoing Race to Silence Race

3

The White Mobilization against Desegregation and Redistribution

They tell us that the situation is a class struggle rather than a racial one. Let them go to van Tonder in the Free State and tell him this. We believe we know what the problem is, and we will stick by our findings.
　　—Steve Biko, "Black Consciousness and the Quest for a
　　　True Humanity"

Well this is not 76
I insist this is not 76
But in the streets
I am still rioting, boycotting prejudice
And skin colour bribery
Police brutality
Human rights violation
Public harassment callousness
Where is black consciousness?
When we are susceptible to reliance
Poor domestic servants and peasants
　　—Unathi Slasha, "Black Paint"

On June 16, 1976, pupils in the South African township of Soweto revolted against the apartheid government's imposition of the Afrikaans language as a medium of instruction. Protests soon spread across the country, with students from urban centers and rural areas alike mobilizing in solidarity with the youth of Soweto. The white government responded with utmost brutality as police and military squads killed at

129

least 575 children.[1] Four decades later, Black South African students again mobilized en masse against racism in the largest student protests since the Soweto uprising. This time, students demanded the genuine decolonization of South African universities, which remain white-dominated, Eurocentric, and unaffordable for most students. Students at historically Black institutions had been protesting routinely since 1994, but the media ignored them until the protests also shook historically white institutions with the Rhodes Must Fall Movement. Even after the removal of the Cecil John Rhodes statue from the University of Cape Town campus on April 9, 2015, students continued to protest and call for change under the banner of Fees Must Fall. During these protests, the democratic government and university administrators reacted to students' demands with renewed ruthless repression. On October 26, 2016, with the aim of hunting down and arresting student leaders, police on the Rhodes University campus in Makhanda went as far as shooting rubber bullets and firing stun grenades *inside* the Jan Smuts student residence, forcing terrified students to flee and seek shelter at friends' homes.[2]

Thabo, a resident of Jan Smuts, was luckily not in his room during the shooting.[3] He was on his way to the library. But Thabo's attempt to study for a test was disrupted before he could enter the building as police started firing stun grenades at the students who had gathered in front of the library. Police also proceeded to arrest students at random. Thabo went to sleep at a friend's house that night since he no longer felt safe in his residence. He only moved back into his room when the protests died down, days later. As soon as the academic year ended, he moved off campus altogether. When I spoke with Thabo eight months after the incident, he still looked shaken while recounting the events of that day: "The res is old and made of wood," he said. "A fire could have easily started. We are not even allowed to bring spirits into the res because they are highly flammable." Thabo's experiences were not unique. On other campuses across the country and during off-campus protests, police responded with ferocious violence that left countless students physically and psychologically scarred.

South African universities, as universities elsewhere in settler neo-colonies, are breeding grounds for white supremacist violence, a fact that led the South African Human Rights Commission to hold a hearing on racism in South Africa's universities in 2014. They also remain deeply racially unequal. Since the formal end of apartheid, affirmative action programs have led to an increase of Black students at universities. The overall proportion of enrolled Black students has grown from 32 percent in 1990 to 60 percent in 2000 and 76.7 percent in 2020.[4] Still, racial inequality in higher education persists. At Rhodes University, which protesting students renamed the University Currently Known as Rhodes (UCKAR), 41 percent of students were white in 2013, in a country in which white people are less than 9 percent of the population.[5] In 2016, I myself witnessed and participated in this inequality. That year, I was to my knowledge one of twelve Mellon postdoctoral fellows at Rhodes University alongside two other white women, both South African, and nine Black men, only one of whom was South African. The absence of Black women, whose place I and the other white women were clearly occupying, was conspicuous. When I attended a braai (barbecue) with other postdocs at the university, it became obvious that the overrepresentation of white men and women, severe underrepresentation of Black men, and absence of Black women were a structural issue not confined to a particular postdoctoral fellowship. When I raised this issue with white senior faculty at the university, I was told that "Black students do not apply," an argument that can only be false and for which, in fact, they had no evidence. The sheer frequency with which I have heard this argument suggests that it is itself a colorblind tool. Due to the exclusion that Black students and scholars continue to experience, the marginalization of Black people in South African universities extends to faculty positions. In 2020, only 27.9 percent of staff at the University of Stellenbosch and 32.8 percent of staff at the University of Pretoria was Black.[6] That same year, white students had the highest graduation rate among all racial groups, while Black students had the lowest.[7] In the meantime, even as the implementation of race-based redress measures in South Africa (unlike in the United States) is protected by the Constitution, affirmative action policies at universities are under attack.[8]

Since the formal fall of apartheid, countless white South African academics, and a few academics of color, have increasingly devoted their scholarship to vilifying race-based affirmative action policies, minimizing or outright denying racial discrimination, and disavowing the fact of white privilege. The declining significance of race myth that pervades US sociology thus has its equivalent miles across the Atlantic.[9] While disciplines with a significant impact on public policy—such as sociology, education, and economics—have become leading venues for the dissemination of racist doctrines in South African academia, no traditional discipline is immune from the phenomenon as colorblindness, as I will demonstrate, informs the logics, arguments, and findings of a conspicuous body of South African scholarship on race produced since the democratic dispensation, both in the social sciences and in the humanities.

The South African case is emblematic of a larger global reality in which white people continue to maintain control of the most prestigious institutions of higher learning. This is also the case in Brazil and the United States. White people achieve this, among other things, by limiting the access of Black people and people of color to academia, restricting and policing the production of antiracist scholarship, and rewarding scholars who reproduce colorblindness in their work.[10] The systematic silencing and bolstering of white supremacy that dominantly structures academia beyond national boundaries speaks to how the university continues to be, as Fred Moten and Stefano Harney write in *The Undercommons*, "the site of the social reproduction of conquest denial."[11] While the university appears to exceed the state, Harney and Moten show, it mirrors the totalitarian ambitions and modes of knowledge production of the state: the university portrays itself as a place of enlightenment, yet participates in the conquest, theft, and exploitation of those who exist within it and at its margins, people whom the university continues to depend upon but whose exploitation and key roles as producers of knowledge it disavows. The university today has not abandoned its role as handmaid of colonial power; it merely conceals its racist operations by presenting itself as a place that, as Moten and Harney put it, "makes thought possible."[12] Among multiple strategies, the university uses the colorblind discourse of academic freedom to protect itself from scrutiny, masking the fact that the institution and its history cannot be disentangled from its infringement upon the freedoms of enslaved and colonized people, whom the Western university has produced as unreasonable, while it has constructed reason as its own property and the property of whiteness.

In Brazil, the United States, South Africa, and across numerous other "former" European settler colonies, white people control the economy, the university, and the media, and have left in place a powerful tool for the reproduction of white power: the law. This chapter illustrates how many white people, and some people of color, use their position within these institutions to delegitimize ongoing demands for racial redress and redistribution in Brazil, the United States, and South Africa. Colorblind rhetoric is their weapon of choice. To demonstrate how white people continue to disavow racism to maintain power on a global scale,

THE WHITE MOBILIZATION   133

I examine a body of post-1994 South African scholarship on race produced in economics, education, literature, and sociology alongside Brazilian journalist and sociologist Ali Kamel's 2006 book, *Não somos racistas: uma reação aos que querem nos transformar numa nação bicolor* (We Are Not Racist: A Reaction to Those Who Want to Transform Us into a Bicolor Nation), which attacks affirmative action policies in Brazilian universities, and the US Supreme Court case *Parents Involved in Community Schools v. Seattle School District No.1* (2007), which struck down an affirmative action program that aimed to desegregate public schools in Seattle, Washington, and Jefferson County, Kentucky. Albeit arising in very different contexts and belonging to disparate genres, these texts avail themselves of a shared rhetorical repertoire in their parallel efforts to halt policy measures that attempt to redress racial inequality.

As the white investment in racism is not a South African peculiarity, neither are the struggles that Black students face. In Brazil, Black students who resist structural exclusion have also been met with the violent hand of the state. In October 2016, while protests were shaking South African universities, Brazilian students occupied thousands of schools and universities, giving rise to the largest student occupations in Brazil's history, in response to the government's attempt to implement drastic budget cuts to public education that would disproportionally affect Black children and youth. Military police reacted by arresting students and cutting off water, food, and electricity in many occupied schools, while right-wing groups went as far as organizing militias to disrupt student occupations.[13] Brazilian schools and universities, like their South African counterparts, remain deeply racially unequal. Decades of Afro-Brazilian mobilization led the government to adopt a range of affirmative action policies in the mid-1990s and early 2000s, such as admission quotas for Black and Indigenous students in public universities. While these policies have had a positive effect, racial inequality persists. In a country where no less than 50 percent of the population is Black, only 8.3 percent of Black people between the ages of 18 and 24 were enrolled in institutions of tertiary education in 2009, compared to 21.6 percent of white people.[14] Moreover, 68 percent of those attending the prestigious and tuition-free state universities are white.[15] Affirmative action policies, nonetheless, are also under fire in Brazil.

Kamel's *Não somos racistas* (We Are Not Racist) epitomizes the widespread deployment of anti-affirmative action arguments among white Brazilians and the centrality of colorblind rhetoric to these arguments.

As the title already reveals, Kamel denies that Brazil is a racist society. But he also has a more specific goal: halting the implementation of racial quotas for Black and Indigenous people in Brazilian universities. To this end, he deploys a litany of colorblind tools that resemble those used by white authors who demonize race-based affirmative action elsewhere. At the same time, as we shall see, Brazil's dominant ideology of mestiçagem (racial mixture) provides Kamel with racist strategies that are not always available to South African and US authors to the same extent.

Não somos racistas also illustrates the migration of colorblindness across journalism and academia. To demonstrate his arguments, Kamel invokes an array of Brazilian scholars who also support racism and demonize race-based policies in their work. Academics in turn have provided Kamel with additional platforms from which to spread his anti-affirmative action propaganda. For example, he was invited to speak alongside rector Aloísio Teixeira and other academics at a 2004 debate on university reform held at the Institute of Philosophy and Social Sciences at the Federal University of Rio de Janeiro. Delivering the first talk of the event, Kamel tellingly devoted it to attacking university admission quotas for Black students.[16]

The executive director of journalism for Brazil's most powerful media network, TV Globo, Kamel has the power to shape public opinion and policy within and beyond Brazil's borders. But *Não somos racistas* does not warrant critical attention merely because of Kamel's individual influence. Far from being the exceptional product of an isolated individual, the book is representative of a larger phenomenon. Kamel reproduces the same hegemonic discourse that defines what is said and left unsaid about racism in the Brazilian public sphere and the media, which are controlled by a white and conservative elite. *O Globo* and TV Globo actively pushed for the impeachment of Brazil's democratically elected president Dilma Rousseff, leader of the leftist Partido dos Trabalhadores (Workers' Party). Following Rousseff's impeachment in May 2016, interim president Michel Temer tellingly unveiled an all-white-male cabinet and eliminated the Ministry of Women, Racial Equality, and Human Rights, paving the way for the election of far-right candidate Jair Bolsonaro as Brazil's president in 2018. As Rousseff has not been found guilty of any crime, the impeachment de facto represented a coup, an attempt by the white conservative elite to regain full control of the government and cut back on social programs for poor Brazilians, who are mainly Black.

THE WHITE MOBILIZATION   135

In the United States, youth of color remain similarly underrepresented in institutions of higher education. In 2013, the college enrollment rate for white people was 42 percent, compared to 34 percent for Black people and 34 percent for Latinxs.[17] In 2015, in US universities across the nation, Black students and students of color led protests paralleling those in South Africa, with students demanding, among other things, greater access to higher education, more faculty of color, and an end to systemic racism on university campuses. As part of these efforts, the Black Liberation Collective, a collective of Black students who aim to transform higher education, organized a National Day of Action against Racism and Student Debt in April 2015, calling for tuition-free public college for Black and Indigenous students, the cancellation of all student debt, a living minimum wage of $15 for campus workers, and universities' divestment from private prisons.[18] These demands have yet to be met.

Affirmative action programs have a longer history in the United States than in Brazil and South Africa. The term itself is a US coinage. Feeling the pressure of the demands that Black people and people of color were making as part of the Civil Rights Movement, Lyndon B. Johnson in 1965 signed an executive order that required government contractors to "take affirmative action" in hiring and employing people of color. Many colleges and universities subsequently began taking race into consideration for admission criteria. This led to an increase of students of color in predominantly white universities. Soon, white backlash followed. Beginning with *Regents of University of California v. Bakke* (1978), the first Supreme Court case that called into question the constitutionality of race-based affirmative action programs in higher education, these policies have been increasingly curtailed.[19] Instrumental for their curtailing is the legal doctrine of colorblindness, an interpretation of the law favoring formal symmetry over racial justice that critical race scholars have called *colorblind jurisprudence* and to which I will return.

The lack of access to higher education for most Black students and students of color in the United States, Brazil, and South Africa reflects the deep racial inequality in the school system, as Black students predominantly attend underfunded public schools, while white students usually attend well-resourced public schools and private institutions. In the United States, some school districts have taken the matter of school desegregation into their own hands only to find their efforts branded as unconstitutional by the Supreme Court. In an exemplary case, the

Seattle School District adopted a voluntary integration program that included considering a pupil's race as one of several tiebreakers in the admission process. In doing so, the district recognized that discriminatory housing practices in Seattle had led to a racially segregated and unequal school system. However, in *Parents Involved in Community Schools v. Seattle School District No. 1*, the first US Supreme Court case that addressed race-based redress measures in schools rather than universities, the court struck down affirmative action programs that aimed to desegregate public schools in Seattle and in Jefferson County. Drawing from the same arsenal of colorblind tools used in three previous cases that curtailed affirmative action policies in higher education, the court in *Parents Involved* held that the plans implemented to desegregate public schools in Seattle and Jefferson County violated the equal protection clause of the Fourteenth Amendment.[20] In *Parents Involved*, the commitment to colorblindness reveals itself already in the case title. Who are, in fact, these racially unidentified "parents" who filed suits arguing that "allocating children to different public schools based solely on their race violates the Fourteenth Amendment's equal protection guarantee"?[21] These white parents organizing to protect their children's white privileges insisted that they should be perceived merely as a group of "involved parents" who are concerned about their children's wellbeing. Yet their collective action as white people infringing upon the well-being of Black children tells a racialized story. Especially powerful when white women position themselves as mothers, the white invocation of parenthood for the defense of white supremacy is also an old story.[22]

The petitioners and the court in *Parents Involved* present equal protection rhetoric as neutral and just, yet the equal protection doctrine silences the normativity of whiteness in order to protect white domination.[23] The equal protection doctrine requires that white USAmericans be considered *racial* subjects in ways that transcend the traditional legal standing of whiteness as tacit norm. In arguing that everybody should be treated equally regardless of race, the law treats whiteness as just one racial category among others, although whiteness is the norm against which all other racial categories are constructed. The strict scrutiny (equal protection) doctrine that considers race as an intrinsically suspect category empowers specifically white USAmericans as racial subjects to challenge affirmative action and brand it as a form of racial discrimination against white people.[24]

The systematic white deployment of similar colorblind tools to stop desegregation and redistribution measures and maintain power across

THE WHITE MOBILIZATION   137

three continents speaks to how white people work together to keep control over the land, wealth, and resources we have stolen and continue to actively extract from Black and Brown people. The works examined herein show that white knowledge—white people's consciousness of white privilege and desire to protect it—is the central frame through which we are to understand white epistemology. As these works testify to a global white investment in maintaining the racist status quo, they show that the disavowal of white knowledge is itself the expression of white knowledge. In the pages that follow, I aim to show that the investment in silencing race within works that are chiefly *about* race, especially racial inequality, is a paradox of no little significance.

Reading Racial Power

In October 2010, a number of leading South African academics gathered at the University of the Witwatersrand in Johannesburg for a colloquium titled "Revisiting Apartheid's Race Categories." Inspired by a debate about admission criteria and affirmative action that had taken place at the University of Cape Town in 2007 and cohosted by the School of Human and Community Development, the Transformation Office, the Faculty of Humanities at Wits University, and the Centre for Critical Research on Race and Identity at the University of KwaZulu-Natal, the colloquium featured many papers that critiqued the employment of racial categories in general and in university admissions in particular.[25] Ongoing academic efforts to revise and silence apartheid categories beg the question that Harry Garuba posed in the closing remarks of the colloquium: "What are the conditions of possibility for the emergence of a particular problematic concerned with bureaucratic and administrative classification and not another, say, one concerned with the material and discursive production of race?"[26] Even as more empirical research on institutional racism in South Africa is sorely needed, racial categories themselves, and not structural racism, have been the object of extensive scholarship since the formal end of apartheid. This focus is not accidental.

The obsession with racial classification that pervades much post-apartheid scholarship on race is part of a systemic agenda aimed at curtailing measures that attempt to redress racial inequality. This becomes evident once we consider that the theoretical deconstruction of racial categories often goes hand in hand with the demonization of

138 THE ONGOING RACE TO SILENCE RACE

race-based affirmative action policies. Numerous white South African scholars, with the complicity of some scholars of color, brand race-based affirmative action policies as "discriminatory practices,"[27] as "pro-African racial discrimination,"[28] or as "forms of racialized book-keeping,"[29] while they vilify the racial categories necessary to implement these policies as having "negative effects,"[30] causing "separation,"[31] "entrenching racial prejudice,"[32] yielding "disharmony, distrust and dis-integration,"[33] and even bearing the potential for "racism and group violence."[34] Jonathan Jansen goes as far as attacking affirmative action policies as follows: "Black nationalists are doing after apartheid exactly what Afrikaner nationalists did under apartheid: promoting people on the crude basis of colour, this time to meet employment equity pres-sures and through a misguided sense of parity with white academics."[35] This statement equates white supremacist policies with measures that are intended to compensate for them. It also suggests that white aca-demics are superior to Black scholars. In a noteworthy body of South African scholarship on race—especially scholarship produced in dis-ciplines with a direct impact on public policy such as sociology and education—racial categories, and not structural racism, are routinely endowed with the power of maintaining apartheid logics, reproducing colonial violence, and creating racial conflict.

Attacking racial categories themselves is a global white strategy. Given that collecting racial data is necessary in order to implement affirmative action measures, racial classifiers are a common target in attempts to delegitimize state-sponsored redress measures. Consider how the con-curring justices in *Parents Involved* halted desegregation measures in the Seattle and Jefferson County school districts by treating racial clas-sification as "inherently suspect."[36] In a typical colorblind move, the court did not distinguish between racial classification for the purpose of *remedying* racial inequality and classification that serves to *maintain* racial hierarchies. Although the court did not find any evidence of white pupils having been injured by the voluntary desegregation measures at hand, it placed the potential injury that white pupils *might* suffer over the real injury that Black pupils experience every day in the racist school system.

To appreciate the ramifications of this argument, it is necessary to grapple with colorblindness as a legal doctrine, as this will illustrate continuities between the past of de jure and present of de facto segre-gation and the centrality of colorblindness to maintaining white power in both periods. The application of the term *colorblindness* within US

THE WHITE MOBILIZATION   139

legal scholarship derives from its appearance in the Supreme Court
case *Plessy v. Ferguson* (1896), specifically in the dissenting opinion
of justice John Marshall Harlan, who declared: "Our Constitution is
color-blind and neither knows nor tolerates class among citizens."[37] It
is important to pay attention to what Harlan said *prior* to declaring the
alleged colorblindness of the US Constitution: "The White race deems
itself to be the dominant race in this country. And so it is, in prestige,
in achievements, in education, in wealth, and in power. So, I doubt not,
it will continue to be for all time, if it remains true to its great heritage
and holds fast to the principles of constitutional liberty."[38] Clearly, neither the US Constitution nor Harlan are genuinely "colorblind."

In 1892, Homer Plessy, who had been racially classified as an "Octo-
roon" in Louisiana (which means that he was considered Black under
state law), refused to sit in a segregated train reserved for Black pas-
sengers. Plessy challenged the constitutionality of racial segregation
in his home state by arguing that: (1) legal racial classification was
irrational and prevented him from being granted equal protection of
the law; and therefore (2) the racial segregation statute that separated
those classified as white from those classified as Black was unconstitutional.[39] The Supreme Court rebutted that the segregation statute
was constitutional. And yet trains in Louisiana were not just racially
segregated but deeply unequal, so that Black people were forced to
travel in crowded, hot, and noisy trains, while white people could enjoy
safe and comfortable rides. The court upheld the constitutionality of
segregation through a specific colorblind tool: it distinguished between
a (protected) civil sphere and an (unprotected) private sphere, reducing
the meaning of equality to formal symmetry in treatment. The court
did not concern itself with the material context of racial discrimination, but rather aimed at rendering this context invisible and thereby
permanent. As civil equality only came to mean equality in form rather
than content, it was fulfilled through the argument that equality was
embodied in the formal symmetrical treatment that prevented Black
people from accessing trains for white people just as it prevented white
people from riding in trains reserved for Black people. The court deliberately silenced the historical, material context that would explain that
the trains reserved for Black people were inferior.[40]

The same appeal to colorblind formalism invoked to maintain racial
segregation in *Plessy* is still upheld to curtail desegregation and affirmative action measures today. The court in *Parents Involved* proceeded
to halt desegregation measures in Seattle and Jefferson County by

prioritizing formal symmetry in treatment over redistributive justice and by interpreting race as being merely equivalent to skin color. "Having determined, then, that everyone was equal in the sense that everybody has a skin color," Kimberlé Crenshaw writes in a different context, "symmetrical treatment was satisfied by a general rule that nobody's skin color should be taken into account in governmental decision-making."[41] In this way, the court disconnected race from history and placed it beyond the social, economic, and political values that give race concrete meaning in society. History itself is made to disappear in the ruling of *Parents Involved*. It is telling that the dissenting justices are the only ones who provide an account of the long history of legalized racial segregation that led to racially unequal school systems in Seattle and Jefferson County. That these hard facts did not manage to challenge the ruling speaks to the institutionalized power of colorblindness and its ongoing function as a technology of white rule.

Racial classification is an easy target. Since it has been an instrument that governments have used to oppress Black people and people of color, critics of racial classification seem to float on a higher ground to the extent that their critique may appear legitimate and even antiracist. Yet getting rid of racial classifiers in censuses or university applications further entrenches structural inequality. The question must be about the purposes that racial classification serves, not about classification per se. A cornerstone of US colorblind jurisprudence, the critique of racial classification relies on a problematic understanding of race that equates it merely with skin color, a depoliticized interpretation of race that legal scholar Neil Gotanda has defined as *formal-race unconnectedness*. This interpretation views racism as being simply synonymous with individual prejudice. "Society's racism," Gotanda explains, "is then viewed as merely the collection, or extension, of personal prejudices."[42] Such individualized understandings of racism serve to occlude the fact that racism is a structural feature of society.

It is revealing that governments use racial classification for a range of purposes beyond remedial policies, but it is only when racial categorization is put at the service of racial redress and redistribution that white people have a problem with it. Preference measures for people with disabilities and for women are rarely contested. In the United States, white women have profited the most from affirmative action programs, but one rarely if ever hears men argue that affirmative action policies constitute "reverse sexism," yet white people do routinely brand affirmative action policies as "reverse racism."

THE WHITE MOBILIZATION   141

While they have become associated with the white attempt to delegitimize affirmative action, white accusations of reverse racism are an enduring, and global, colorblind tool. The Black Panthers in the United States, the Black Consciousness Movement in South Africa, the Black section of the Communist Party in Cuba, and the Movimento Negro (Black Movement) in Brazil have all been accused of being racist. As Elisa Larkin Nascimento writes, these imputations "rob those excluded of the legitimacy of their protest against discrimination, placing on their shoulders the onus of the very racism that operates their exclusion."[43] The term "*reverse* racism" meanwhile lays bare the disavowal that informs its deployment: it shows that white people know well that *we* are the perpetrators of racism and violence, and that racism against white people does not exist. Unmasking this white tactic, Kwame Ture and Charles Hamilton write in *Black Power*:

> Some observers have labeled those who advocate Black Power as racists; they have said that the call for self-identification and self-determination is "racism in reverse" or "black supremacy." This is a deliberate and absurd lie. There is no analogy—by any stretch of definition or imagination—between the advocates of Black Power and white racists. Racism is not merely exclusion on the basis of race but exclusion for the purpose of subjugating or maintaining subjugation.[44]

Ture and Hamilton make visible how accusations of reverse racism are a strategy that white people have long leveraged against Black people who have asserted the right to organize against white supremacy. Racism, they emphasize, refers to actions or policies that have as their aim "subjugating or maintaining subjugation." A few years later in South Africa, responding to similar charges that attempted to delegitimize the Black Consciousness Movement, Steve Biko would echo Ture and Hamilton's definition of racism. In Biko's words, "Those who know, define racism as discrimination by a group against another for the purposes of subjugation or maintaining subjugation. In other words one cannot be a racist unless he has the power to subjugate. What blacks are doing is merely to respond to a situation in which they find themselves the objects of white racism."[45] Like Ture and Hamilton before him, Biko rejected the racist logic that analogizes white terror and Black people's resistance to that terror.

Malcolm X also denounced accusations of racism and violence leveraged against Black people and Black liberation movements as white

142 THE ONGOING RACE TO SILENCE RACE

tactics of racial control. On February 14, 1965, just after his house had been bombed while his wife and his four young children were sleeping, Malcolm X delivered a talk in Detroit in which he indicted the press for delegitimizing Black people's right to self-defense, a right sanctioned in the US Constitution:

> The press calls us racist and people who are 'violent in reverse.' This is how they psycho you. They make you think that if you try to stop the Klan from lynching you, you are practicing violence in reverse. . . . I say it is time for black people to put together the type of action, the unity, that is necessary to pull the sheet off of them so they won't be frightening black people any longer. That's all. And when we say this, the press calls us 'racist in reverse.'[46]

Malcolm X shows how accusations of racism in reverse and violence in reverse are attempts to brainwash and control Black people by projecting onto them the racism and violence that white people perpetuate. Reproduced at the highest echelons of white society, and with the complicity of the media, these accusations aim to control public opinion through the perennial construction of Black individuals and collective movements as violent.

White accusations of racism continue to have tangible consequences for antiracist organizing across national borders in our time. In an event that testifies to the institutionalization of colorblindness in post-apartheid South Africa, white journalist Katy Katopodis in 2008 lodged a complaint to the South African Human Rights Commission accusing the Forum of Black Journalists of discriminating against white people and being racist for having prevented white journalists from attending their assembly. As a consequence of this public performance of white injury the South African government banned Black-only organizations.[47] Ironically, Biko managed to form a Black-only organization under racial dictatorship, while today racial privacy for Black people has become a punishable offense by a mere stroke of the democratic law. In the meantime, Franz Jooste, former member of the South African Defence Force and current leader of the far-right organization Kommandokorps, is allowed to indoctrinate young Afrikaner boys into white supremacy and train them in the use of weapons at white-only paramilitary camps.[48]

While white supremacist organizations thrive undisturbed, the mere deployment of racial categories is routinely branded as racist in South

THE WHITE MOBILIZATION 143

Africa and beyond. Rather than treating racial classification as inherently suspect, it is necessary to differentiate between classification for the purpose of redress and for purposes other than redress, precisely the kind of contextualization that proponents of colorblindness fail to provide. In order to understand the importance of racial classification for both ideological and redress purposes, it is useful to consider how the Movimento Negro in Brazil has responded to the collection of racial data in the national census. In 1976, researchers from the Pesquisa Nacional por Amostra de Domicílios (National Household Sample Survey) noticed that 136 different categories were used in response to an open question about racial identification, including numerous euphemisms for Blackness denoting a dark skin tone such as *bronzeado* (tanned), *queimado de sol* (sunburned), *tostado* (toasted), and *moreno* (dark-skinned or brown), a term that we already saw deployed in Panama in the same manner. The Movimento Negro interpreted this as a sign of the perniciousness of Brazilian racism, which has aimed to prevent the development of racial consciousness and solidarity among the Black majority. Recognizing the importance of the census in the country with the largest population of African descent outside the African continent, Black activists proceeded to create an awareness campaign to incentivize Black people to declare themselves as such in the 1991 census. Their campaign slogan "Não deixe sua cor passar em branco" relies on a double-entendre: it means both "Don't leave your color blank" and "Don't let your color go white." Through campaign posters, activists exhorted Black people to do the following: "Confirme a sua descendência africana seja lá que for a cor da sua pele." (Confirm your African descent whatever your skin color).[49] The call to identify as a person of African descent *regardless* of skin color acknowledged the common experience of racism among all Black people as light-skinned people of African descent are also subjected to structural racism and discrimination in Brazil (and beyond).[50]

The attack on racial classification takes on an especially insidious form in the persistent white attack on racial binarism, which refers to the employment of only two racial categories (such as *Black* and *white* or *non-white* and *white*) for the purpose of implementing racial redress policies. Proponents of racial quotas in Brazilian universities have largely adopted a binary classification system that rejects the category mixed (*pardo* or *mestiço*) and instead categorizes students as either Black or white, or non-white and white. In this way, they acknowledge that race supersedes color as students of African descent continue to be excluded from higher education regardless of whether they are light skinned or dark skinned, while white students are structurally advantaged. This antiracist strategy also rejects the terms pardo or mestiço, recognizing them as ideological tools of the state.

Opening *Não somos racistas* with an explicit critique of affirmative action, Kamel argues against the Brazilian deployment of the category "negro" (Black).[51] This category, according to Kamel, not only denies miscegenation but also represents Brazil as "uma nação de brancos e negros onde os brancos oprimem os negros" (a nation of whites and Blacks in which whites oppress Blacks).[52] Kamel denies that this is the case. Moreover, Kamel defines racial binarism as "a construção racista americana segundo a qual todo mundo que não é branco é negro" (the racist American construction according to which everyone who is not white is Black).[53] Kamel here conveniently silences the fact that the Movimento Negro and Afro-Brazilian publications such as the journal *Quilombo*, which Abdias Nascimento edited from 1948 until 1950, have historically employed the term *negro* to refer to Brazilians of African descent.[54] The term is far from being a US importation. Kamel also misses the mark on the US context as the attack on racial binarism might be prevalent in Brazil, but is not a white Brazilian strategy alone. The concurring justices in *Parents Involved* also rejected the classification of students into *Black* and *white* that the Seattle School District had used in order to remedy school segregation, contending that "classifying and assigning children according to a binary conception of race is an extreme approach."[55] The Supreme Court in this way chose to follow the extreme route of upholding racial discrimination in the Seattle and Jefferson County school districts.

The demonization of racial classification leads to paradoxes that reveal its intrinsic anti-Blackness. Kamel argues that racial categories "são em si racistas. Porque não devemos falar em negros, pardos, ou brancos, mas apenas em brasileiros" (are in themselves racist. Because we must not speak about Blacks, browns, or whites, but merely about Brazilians).[56] The racially homogenizing category *brasileiros* here functions as a colorblind tool that disavows racial hierarchies and thereby protects them. Since enforcing colorblindness is an act of epistemic violence, Kamel necessarily contradicts himself as he cannot avoid using racial classifiers. Strikingly, as Kamel contends that racial terminology should not be used, he argues *for* employing the racial category *pardo* (brown or racially mixed) to denote all Brazilians. The differential way that Kamel treats the category pardo—which is never questioned

THE WHITE MOBILIZATION   145

but remains fixed in the text, in contrast with branco (white) and negro
(Black), which are disputed—further reveals how the racial category
pardo is not an objective descriptor, but an instrument of white power.

The colorblind argument that everyone is of the *same* race, which
Kamel deploys here, functions similarly to the colorblind argument that
there is *no* race. To say that everybody is pardo (brown) in Brazil accom-
plishes a dual goal: it supports the racist status quo while appearing
antiracist (for a white person who argues that they are brown or racially
mixed surely cannot be racist, or so Kamel would like us to believe).
What white people like Kamel who argue that everybody in Brazil is
Black, brown, or mixed are actually saying is: in our country, white
people do not exist. At play in this colorblind move is the disavowal of
whiteness. If nobody is white, then nobody can be held accountable for
racism. And if everybody is considered to be mixed, mobilizing on the
basis of race becomes even more difficult for Black people and people
of color, racial inequality cannot be monitored, racial quotas cannot be
implemented, land cannot be redistributed, reparations are out of the
question.

Kamel's choice of pardo as a term that can seemingly encompass
Brazil's "racial essence" reveals his anti-Blackness. Arguing that Brazil is different from the rest of the world because most people in the
country allegedly are racially mixed, Kamel replicates the colorblind
argument advanced in Gilberto Freyre's *Casa-grande e senzala*,[57] which
I discussed in the previous chapter. According to Kamel, the existence
of racial mixture demonstrates that racial prejudice is not a feature of
Brazilian society. In his own words: "ainda somos uma nação que acred-
ita nas virtudes da nossa miscegenação, na convivência harmoniosa
entre todas as cores" (we are still a nation that believes in the virtues
of our miscegenation, in the harmonious coexistence of all colors).[58]
Kamel obfuscates the fact that, rather than indicating racial harmony,
miscegenation has historically largely been the product of white men's
sexual violence against Black women. Illustrating how racial hybridity
is invoked to curtail affirmative action programs and protect white privilege, Kamel portrays the category pardo as a self-evident signifier rather
than as what it is: a colorblind tool.

The prominent place that Freyre occupies in Kamel's book shows
that Freyre's thought and the myth of racial democracy that he helped
to consolidate are still deployed to undercut the demands of the Brazilian Black Movement today. Already on the second page, Kamel defends
Freyre with the aim to delegitimize affirmative action. Misrepresenting

Freyre as an antiracist advocate, Kamel argues that Freyre challenged ideologies of whitening that were dominant in the social sciences in early twentieth-century Brazil and advocated for mestiçagem (racial mixture) instead. Kamel thus mystifies the fact that mestiçagem is a technology of racial obliteration and whitening. Further revealing his investment in white supremacy, Kamel continues his defense of Freyre with an explicit attack on the Black Movement, writing: "Hoje, quando vejo o Movimento Negro depreciar Gilberto Freyre, detratando-o como a um inimigo, fico tonto. Os ataques só podem ser decorrentes de uma leitura apressada, se é que decorrem mesmo de uma leitura." (Today, when I see the Black Movement despise Gilberto Freyre, treating him as if he were an enemy, I am shocked. The attacks can only be the result of a rushed reading, if they are based in a reading at all).[59] As he disavows Freyre's racism, Kamel presents knowledge as the sole property of white people and white academics in particular. Members of the Black Movement, he suggests with arrogance, have not read Freyre's work and are misinformed. Freyre's work and the racist ideologies it perpetrated clearly have not lost their power in present-day Brazil.

While Freyre figures centrally in Kamel's book, he is not the only Brazilian scholar whom Kamel invokes to delegitimize affirmative action. In a move that illustrates how colorblind tools not only migrate across journalism and academia, but are also reciprocally validated in these realms, on the very first page of *Não somos racistas*, Kamel names several Brazilian anthropologists, historians, and sociologists that also disparage race-based affirmative action policies in their work. English-Brazilian anthropologist Peter Fry, whose work Kamel invokes as authoritative, reproduces arguments similar to those that Freyre and Kamel advance. In *A persistência da raça: ensaios antropológicos sobre o Brasil e a África austral* (The Persistence of Race: Anthropological Essays on Brazil and Southern Africa, 2005), Fry argues that, in relying on three main racial categories (negros, brancos, indios), affirmative action strengthens the "idea of race" and negates the miscegenation that characterizes the Brazilian population. Fry explicitly denies that racism is institutionalized in Brazil, which he argues is radically different from the United States and South Africa. Like Kamel, who states that "acreditar que raças existem é a base de todo racismo" (believing in the existence of races is the basis of all racism),[60] Fry reiterates the popular colorblind argument that merely recognizing that race exists is itself racist. These arguments are not confined to Brazil. South African sociologist Gerhard Maré does the same in *Declassified*,

THE WHITE MOBILIZATION   147

where he argues that "race thinking" causes "the dehumanization and mass extermination of fellow human beings."[61] These white men portray thought as something disembodied that exists outside of history and materiality, a colorblind move that allows them to deflect attention away from white people's collective role as central agents of white supremacy. They direct the reader's attention toward race as an abstract concept, rather than toward racism as an ingrained dimension of economic and political systems that allow white people to benefit handsomely from the oppression and exploitation of Black people and people of color.

The project of silencing and reproducing racism is further enabled by arguments that question the legibility of race. As we saw, Kamel argues that in Brazil it is impossible to know who is white and who is Black because most people, according to him, are pardos (mixed). To support his contention, he cites former Brazilian president Fernando Henrique Cardoso who, during the visit of then South African president Thabo Mbeki to Brazil, argued that "branco no Brasil é um conceito relativo" (white is a relative concept in Brazil).[62] What neither Cardoso nor Kamel say is that white people in Brazil control the economy, the government, and the media. Just as Kamel asks, "Quem é branco no Brasil?" (Who is white in Brazil?),[63] Kennedy in this opinion to the court in Parents Involved queries, "Who exactly is white and who is nonwhite?"[64] Questioning the legibility of race is a colorblind tool that white people also deploy in South Africa. In Declassified, Maré recounts the story of a teacher who was required to record the race of her pupils for the sake of monitoring inequality. Seemingly unable to do so, the teacher appealed to the Department of Education asking: "How black is black? And when is a pupil coloured?"[65] Maré cites this example to argue that it is impossible to identify someone's race just by looking at the person and therefore race-based remedial measures cannot be implemented effectively. The argument that racial classification and racial remediation policies are not perfect and therefore should be abandoned altogether is a colorblind tool. Kamel and Kennedy know very well that they are white and precisely for this reason deny that white people exist.

While invoking racial mixture has been central to the disavowal of racism in Brazil, white people also invoke discourses of hybridity to uphold racism in South Africa, a country that has enforced a rigid racial classification system. In Entanglement: Literary and Cultural Reflections on Post-Apartheid (2009), literary scholar Sarah Nuttall critiques

148   THE ONGOING RACE TO SILENCE RACE

racial binarism while she portrays hybridity as an essentially emancipatory category. She writes:

> South African studies have, for a long time, been overdetermined by the reality of apartheid. . . . A theory of entanglement can be linked in important ways to a notion of desegregation. One could argue that the system of racial segregation in the political, social and cultural structure of the country paradoxically led to . . . a form of segregated theory. Segregated theory is theory premised on categories of race difference, oppression versus resistance, and perpetrators versus victims.[66]

Nuttall argues that scholarship on hybridity and creolization produced elsewhere is useful to theorize post-apartheid social relations in South Africa. She conceptualizes the move away from an engagement with Black-white racial difference and toward hybridity, literally, as an example of "desegregation." As she views postcolonial theory's emphasis on difference as "a political resource in struggles against imperial drives to homogenize and universalize identity politics," she fallaciously constructs hybridity and entanglement as essentially progressive categories, erasing the violence that hybridity depends upon.[67] The very employment of "categories of race difference" is here once again framed, albeit implicitly, as being itself racist, even as Nuttall herself cannot avoid using racial categories.

Nuttall is one of several white South African scholars who portray the abandonment of "categories of race difference" in post-apartheid scholarship as progressive. Yet the eagerness to abandon notions of "oppression versus resistance" in favor of a colorblind heterogeneity is itself a racial move. Providing a valuable viewpoint on this issue, Vilashini Cooppan argues that "to imagine, as contemporary post-colonial studies sometimes seems to do, that we can simply choose one (hybrid) model of identity over another (particularist) one . . . is to forget precisely the ways in which these conceptual categories are collectively bound to one another."[68] Discursively detaching racial mixture from the white supremacist violence that produced it entrenches the structures of racial domination that the move alleges to challenge. We should not take it for granted that in *Entanglement* the valorization of hybridity and the critique of scholarship that makes racial power visible are accompanied by attempts to rescue white people from stigmatization, as Nuttall explicitly directs the reader's attention toward the growth of

THE WHITE MOBILIZATION 149

the Black middle class and the growth in *intraracial* inequality in post-1994 South Africa, but silences the persistence of white economic and social dominance.

Nuttall is not alone in arguing that celebrating difference in general is emancipatory, but acknowledging the reality of racial difference is reactionary. An earlier essay of post-apartheid criticism reproduces the same contradictory logic. In "Rehearsals of Liberation: Contemporary Postcolonial Discourse and the New South Africa" (1994), literary critic Rosemary Jolly takes on postcolonial criticism as it has been applied to the South African context. She argues that it is necessary to undertake "a critical evaluation of the terms used to phrase condemnations of racism" in post-apartheid South Africa.[69] Jolly envisions this task as a "massive critique" that should occur in several intersecting domains, including the economic and political spheres, both at home and abroad.[70] Examining primarily anti-apartheid theater and Jacques Derrida's essay "Racism's Last Word," Jolly argues that the strategies some postcolonial critics have employed to denounce South African racism are misguided and represent a "reactionary measure."[71] She contends that the effects of Derrida's essay are "neo-colonial rather than counterdiscursive."[72] This is so, she argues, because Derrida retains Manichean oppositions and depicts South Africa as "spectacularly other."[73] Jolly rejects any theoretical approach on post-apartheid South Africa that "requires maintenance of the binary colonizer/colonized as an essential racial opposition."[74] Jolly postulates that Derrida's understanding of colonizer and colonized as categories that are inherently racial is at odds with his intended goal of condemning racism. Just as Nuttall argues that silencing racial categories is a desegregationist move, Jolly insists that postcolonial scholarship should move away from viewing the categories colonizer and colonized as being intrinsically racialized.

As Jolly appropriates postcolonial discourse, she advocates for a colorblind multiculturalism that relies on the silencing of race through the strategic valorization of ethnic difference. She argues that to achieve a "post apartheid era" it is necessary to highlight the "multiple differences among and within racial groups."[75] Recreating yet another dichotomy, she stipulates that speaking of ethnic difference is progressive, but focusing on racial difference is reactionary. Jolly stresses that "there are marked differences within the black community in South Africa," and argues that eliding these differences would mean maintaining "the hegemony of apartheid."[76] Jolly here silences the embeddedness of ethnic

150   THE ONGOING RACE TO SILENCE RACE

categories within hierarchical structures of power that remain racialized. She omits the fact that racial domination in South Africa, as in the rest of the African continent, has relied precisely on fabricating ethnic identities and enforcing ethnic differentiation among African peoples as a central strategy of colonial rule. Mahmood Mamdani writes in *Citizen and Subject* that in South Africa, white domination was imposed by means of a "system of ethnic pluralism (institutional segregation), so that everyone, victims no less than beneficiaries, may appear as minorities."[77] This divide-and-conquer strategy reached an institutionalized apex through the government's creation of the so-called Bantustans, which segregated Black people into remote and impoverished "homelands." Recognizing the anti-Blackness of state-sponsored segregation and ethnic differentiation, Biko exhorted Black South Africans to reject tribalism and organize against white supremacy as a united front. In his own words, "We are oppressed not as individuals, not as Zulus, Xhosas, Vendas or Indians. We are oppressed because we are black. We must use that very concept to unite ourselves and to respond as a cohesive group. We must cling to each other with a tenacity that will shock the perpetrators of evil."[78] The deployment of ethnic differentiation as a technology of racial domination that Biko denounced during the apartheid era is still operative in Jolly's essay, which demonstrates that white people continue to highlight ethnic differences among Black people in order to make white people appear as a small and vulnerable minority, rather than as the group that still holds economic and social power.

Jolly's article exposes the racial anxieties of a white critic who fears to be "politically disabled" in democratic South Africa. Minimizing white privilege, Jolly asserts that it is "profoundly irresponsible" for white South African academics to "assume that their position of *relative privilege* renders them politically disabled" and that therefore "their work is futile, since it does not affect the 'masses.'"[79] This argument reveals how colorblindness relies on an epistemology of disavowal that accepts white supremacy as the political system that must endure, while it denies its very existence. In fact, who are the masses that Jolly mentions here? If these masses are not to be understood in racial terms, as Jolly insists, then why do they stand in opposition to *white* critics? Jolly demands that scholars do away with race, yet her own work cannot transcend it. Although she asserts that it is necessary to "avoid essentially racial oppositions in contemporary South African literature," Jolly writes of "black illiteracy," a "black majority," and a "generation of black Afrikaans writers."[80] In various instances, Jolly speaks of Black people

THE WHITE MOBILIZATION   151

by referring to *culture* instead of race, but employing racially coded language, as we have seen, does not mean transcending race. Deployed by white people to refer surreptitiously to Black people and people of color since the inception of colonialism, discourses of culture are still invoked today to silence racism.

The appropriation of deconstructionism and antiracist thought for the defense of white privilege that informs Jolly's essay is not the sole domain of literary critics. In "The Modern Construction of Race: Whither Social Constructionism?" (2012), education scholar Crain Soudien also cites Derrida with the aim to support structural racism. While Jolly accuses Derrida of reproducing colonial logics, Soudien appropriates Derrida's argument to argue that the employment of the category race itself constitutes a challenge much more serious "than its manifestations in apartheid."[81] Co-opting Derrida's definition of apartheid as "the most racist of racisms," Soudien contends that simply *mentioning* race is the "most racism [sic] of racisms."[82] While Derrida's work is critiqued in Jolly's essay and valued in Soudien's, its strategic location in these texts remains unchanged: in both cases, thought that is critical of racism is appropriated, repackaged, and put at the service of racial power.

Even the work of Biko is deliberately misread and appropriated in ways that demonstrate the fundamental anti-Blackness of colorblind logics. In "Apartheid Race Categories: Daring to Question Their Continued Use" (2012), Zimitri Erasmus states that in the 1970s the Black Consciousness Movement defined Blackness "*not* as a race category or classification, but rather a global political identification premised on resistance to oppression in contexts of white supremacy."[83] Erasmus here misinterprets the gesture. Biko's politicized understanding of Blackness was not a theoretical intervention in the abstract rethinking of apartheid racial categories per se. Biko's usage of the collective term *Black* was grounded in the concrete need to forge solidarities among Black people across ethnic differences and between Black people and other oppressed groups, such as Indian South Africans, with the aim to propel the dismantlement of apartheid. Erasmus silences the fact that Biko's definition of Blackness *only* includes people who are not white. Biko defines Black people as "those who are by law or tradition politically, economically and socially discriminated against as a group in the South African society and [identify] themselves as a unit in the struggle towards the realization of their aspirations."[84] Just as Biko had to contend with white disavowal, Black radical thinkers in South Africa continue to highlight the mechanisms through which white people still maintain power by rendering this power invisible. Critiquing the willful misreading of Biko's definition of Blackness that is common in present-day South Africa, Andile Mngxitama argues that "Biko's dictum of 'being black is not a matter of pigmentation,' has been abused by race denialists and coconut intellectuals."[85] The misreading of Biko's thought in South African scholarship reveals the ongoing currency of appropriation as a technology of silencing.

The scholarship of Edward Said is also depoliticized and manipulated to sustain a discourse of liberal humanism that aims to secure the reproduction of racial inequality. In "The Modern Seduction of Race," Soudien cites Said's *Culture and Imperialism* to argue that Said called for a historiography that was attentive to "human experience in all its diversity and particularity."[86] While Soudien considers this positive, the abstract valorization of human diversity is here accompanied by efforts to silence racialized particularity. Comparably, in "Confronting the Categories: Equitable Admissions without Apartheid Race Classification" (2010), Erasmus attacks affirmative action, opening with an epigraphic citation from Said's *Humanism and Democratic Criticism*.[87] As they appeal to humanity itself, these studies fail to recognize Black people as deserving of redress.

The liberal humanism that Soudien and Erasmus invoke is entwined with individualism, which claims that people are to be judged on the basis of their individual actions and hinges on an abstract individual who is free from societal constrains, entirely ruled by personal agency. A creation of the European Enlightenment, the abstract individual continues to be mobilized today to delegitimize Black people's demands for redistribution and redress, even as Black people continue to be excluded from subjecthood.[88] Contrary to what Soudien and Erasmus suggest, it is not a claim to universalism—the belief that "we are all just people"—that will make racism disappear. The dismantling of racial regimes requires the complete abolition of the racist infrastructure, not abstract arguments about the sanctity of the individual or the commonness of humanity that disavow the ontological collapse between being white and being Human. In Frank B. Wilderson's terms, "if Blacks were completely genocided, Humanity would find itself in the same quandary that would occur if Black people were recognized and incorporated as Human beings. Humanity would cease to exist; because it would lose its conceptual coherence, having lost its baseline other."[89] The argument that "we are human beings ultimately" disavows the fact

THE WHITE MOBILIZATION 153

that Black people do not inhabit the ontological position of the Human, which depends on anti-Blackness for its existence.

The discourse of liberal individualism is often mobilized alongside arguments that emphasize personal choice and individual merit to further delegitimize race-based affirmative action policies across national borders. In *Parents Involved*, justice Stevens, citing *Rice v. Cayetano*, argues that "one of the principal reasons race is treated as a forbidden classification is that it demeans the dignity and worth of a person to be judged by ancestry instead of by his or her own merit and essential qualities."[90] Kamel also invokes the liberal discourse of merit as he applauds the decision of the University of São Paulo not to implement racial quotas. According to Kamel, "O que a universidade faz é preservar o sistema de mérito: entram os melhores, independentemente da cor" (What the university does is preserve the merit system: the best ones are admitted, regardless of color).[91] In *Declassified*, Maré analogously relies on the colorblind tool of merit, arguing that there is a "tension between merit-based selection . . . and race-based selection."[92] These authors depict their countries as meritocracies and silence the fact that, in a white supremacist society, not everybody is given an equal start to begin with. In contrast with what they falsely suggest, there is no such a thing as a common baseline. The discourses of merit and equal opportunity are themselves technologies of white power as there is no racially neutral slate in the anti-Black world.

White people across national boundaries go as far as disavowing structural racism itself. Kamel argues that racial discrimination in Brazil "não é estrutural" (is not structural).[93] As he falsely argues that there have been no institutional barriers against Black Brazilians since the abolition of slavery, Kamel silences the fact that Black people were abandoned without land, education, or any kind of support from the state after emancipation, while Europeans were given land and money to emigrate to Brazil.[94] The only racism that Kamel acknowledges is not actually racism, but individual prejudice. As he renders institutional racism invisible, Kamel projects his own racism onto antiracist policies, which Kamel describes as "a adoção de medidas racistas para combater o racismo" (the adoption of racist measures to combat racism).[95] In the same text, Kamel denies the existence of racism, arguing that "discriminações não serão nunca 'efetivamente' raciais, porque razas não existem" (discriminations will never be "effectively" racial, because races do not exist).[96] With no consideration for logic or contradiction, racism is conveniently invoked in one instance and disavowed in another.

154 THE ONGOING RACE TO SILENCE RACE

In *Declassified*, Maré goes even further than Kamel by arguing that institutional racism itself is a myth. Race and racism, Maré writes, "can all serve as the basis for discrimination—but this is not systemic as the operation of capitalism is."[97] Maré, of course, does not support this statement with any evidence and also fails to include statistics on racial inequality as these would undermine his argument. In the process, Maré outright denies that he is enforcing colorblindness. In his own words, "it is in the notion of non-racialism that I believe the most helpful possibility of a future beyond 'race' continues to lie. Non-racialism is not to be seen as colourblindness—not in the least. Indeed, non-racialism relies on critical colour awareness."[98] The dichotomy between nonracialism and colorblindness that Maré postulates is false. During the anti-apartheid struggle, the nonracialism promoted by the African National Congress (ANC) represented a practical strategy that attempted to foster unity and collaboration across racial lines while advancing Black people's agenda.[99] Although it is rooted in an ANC history of resistance, nonracialism no longer serves an emancipatory function today (if it ever did). Nonracialism and colorblindness have become de facto synonymous in South Africa. They also function as one and the same thing within *Declassified*. Further revealing its global dimensions, the disavowal of structural racism is also at work in *Parents Involved*, in which the concurring justices argue that Seattle schools "were never segregated by law."[100] The justices make segregation disappear as they trivialize desegregation as "racial balance pure and simple" or demonize it as, in the words of Clarence Thomas, "forced racial mixing."[101] The terms structural racism and institutional racism are never mentioned in *Parents Involved* as the ruling upholds the racist status quo.

As white people collectively disavow racism, they also insist that whites are victims in the current racial order and thereby reproduce the transnational discourse of white injury.[102] The scholarship of South African sociologist Jeremy Seekings is a case in point. In a paper titled "The Continuing Salience of Race: Discrimination and Diversity in South Africa" (2008), presented at a UCLA conference on legal and political remedies to discrimination, Seekings argues that "racial discrimination in economic life against black people has been largely ended in South Africa."[103] In *Race, Discrimination, and Diversity in South Africa* (2007), Seekings even argues that white people are disadvantaged in South Africa. He writes that "racial discrimination is practiced in favour of black applicants through affirmative action and BEE [Black Economic

THE WHITE MOBILIZATION   155

Empowerment] policies."[104] White South African children, Seekings continues, are subjected to the "disadvantage of being white in an affirmative action environment."[105] According to statistics released by the South African government, from April to June 2017 the unemployment rate for Black people was a jarring 31.3 percent, while the unemployment rate for white people was only 5.7 percent. That year, the NEET (not in education, employment, or training) rate increased for all racial groups in South Africa *except* whites, for whom it actually declined 1.1 percent.[106] Yet Seekings argues that affirmative action forecloses working opportunities for white people and insists that white South Africans are increasingly migrating "to avoid unemployment."[107] In this way, he postulates a complete reversal in relations of power: white people, who continue to own the vast majority of the wealth in South Africa, are here depicted as the victims of racism.

Seekings's scholarship shows that the disavowal of white privilege relies on the manipulation of history. Seekings writes that the apartheid system required racial classification to maintain its three main objectives, which he argues are: first, ideological (maintaining "racial purity"); second, economic (protecting the economic privileges of whites); and third, political (maintaining the political dominance of whites).[108] Seekings denies the primacy of economics and political power in explaining the workings of racism and instead provides a revisionist history that literally whitewashes apartheid. Although Seekings admits that the 1950 Group Areas Act "led to the forced removal of almost one million people," he represents spatial segregation mainly as a way to preclude racial mixing and prevent "temptation."[109] Seekings depicts racist ideologies as independent from, and more important than, the sociopolitical and economic structures they sustain. This colorblind move portrays segregation as the consequence of white people's misguided ideas and fears about miscegenation, rather than as the deliberate attempt to manage difference so as to make white economic dominance and Black poverty permanent.

In the process, Seekings invokes the discourse of cultural deficiency to make white advantage and Black disadvantage appear unrelated to racism. Tukufu Zuberi and Eduardo Bonilla-Silva write that "another way to minimize the effects of racial stratification is by portraying the effects of poverty as the causes of poverty; specifically, by focusing on the 'culture of the natives' as the problem."[110] Reproducing this strategy, Seekings affirms that many Black workers in South Africa are unemployable because of a long series of hindrances that begin during childhood.

Black children, Seekings maintains, are raised in "home environments which are not conducive to educational success, and attend schools where the quality of education is very poor."[111] Seekings pathologizes the Black family and locates the causes of Black poverty in the home, while he refuses to acknowledge that poor schooling is the product of institutional racism.

One of the most popular colorblind tools that Seekings and many of his white South African colleagues and their accomplices deploy is the argument that inequality is the product of *class* rather than racial disparities. While this argument has particular salience today, it is by no means a new strategy. During apartheid, too, Biko had to fend off white South Africans' arguments about the alleged primacy of class over race, as the epigraph shows. This colorblind argument finds its present-day variant in the insistence that racism might have shaped inequality in the past, but in post-1994 South Africa there has been a "shift from race to class," as Seekings and Nicoli Nattrass argue in *Class, Race, and Inequality in South Africa* (2005).[112] The authors deny that the special advantages that whites receive depend on "collective, cumulative, and continuing forms of discrimination."[113] Since the value of assets appreciates over time, white people reap the benefits of past and present discrimination and pass wealth onto the next generation of whites.[114] Racial inequality is not merely residual, but contingent upon the ongoing exploitation of Black people and the past and present seizure of their land, labor, and being. The wealth that white South Africans possess is directly traceable to colonialism and apartheid and is protected through the property clause included in the South African Constitution, which ensures the permanence of white supremacy in the country.

Nattrass and Seekings also reproduce the free-market ideology, which deceptively portrays the market as neutral, fair, and genuinely "colorblind." Often operating in conjunction with the laissez-faire ideology (which demonizes state intervention, especially for the purpose of redress), the free-market myth obfuscates the fact that the market is not free, but rather reliant on racialized capitalist exploitation. These ideologies, as Robin D. G. Kelley writes, serve to camouflage "the critical role that the state has played in reproducing inequality and creating an *uneven* playing field."[115] Seekings and Nattrass tether their argument about the alleged class basis of South African inequality to the false premise that sustaining "privilege in the market" is *not* a racialized endeavor. And yet, the market during apartheid was open only to whites and continues to be virtually a white-only space. Only 2 percent of the

THE WHITE MOBILIZATION 157

companies listed on the Johannesburg Stock Exchange are fully under Black leadership.[116]

In the attempt to further convince readers that inequality is a matter of class rather than race, Seekings and Nattrass highlight what they argue is "the steadily declining importance of interracial inequality and rising importance of intraracial inequality" in post-apartheid South Africa.[117] They write that "by 2000, there were about as many African people as white people in the top income quintile."[118] In this way, the authors mystify a very simple fact: white people are less than 9 percent, and not 50 percent, of the South African population. For Seekings and Nattrass, that white people occupy circa 50 percent of the top earning quintile does not show that racial inequality remains rampant, but rather demonstrates that racism no longer determines life opportunities. But if class can autonomously explain inequality, why focus on the racialized phenomenon of intraracial inequality? By directing the reader's attention to the income gap that exists *among* Black South Africans, Seekings and Nattrass's work exhibits paradoxes inherent in scholarship that enforces colorblindness while producing knowledge about racial inequality. This also shows that colorblindness depends on deliberate omissions: *Class, Race, and Inequality in South Africa* does not provide detailed data about the racial composition of the lower class, which remains overwhelmingly Black, nor does it examine the significance of the striking difference in life expectancy for Black and white people. Rather than speaking to a "shift from race to class" or, as Maré argues in *Declassified*, a "deracialization of capitalism," these realities show that the South African class structure remains deeply racialized and that institutional racism impacts not only economic distribution, but also Black people's very chance to reach adulthood.[119]

As he insists that class can explain economic inequality in post-apartheid South Africa, Maré also strategically concentrates on the *upper* echelons of South African society, which are increasingly multiracial, while the poorest of the poor remain overwhelmingly Black. Illustrating how the deployment of colorblindness is modulated through the local dynamics of race, Kamel does exactly the opposite. Given that in Brazil there are also poor white people (they are a small minority compared to Black people, a fact that Kamel does not disclose), Kamel focuses on the racial composition of the *lower* classes in his attempt to render white supremacy invisible. To show that inequality in Brazil can allegedly be explained through class alone, Kamel presents statistics showing that in Brazil "negros e brancos pobres se parecem" (poor

Blacks and whites are similar).[120] Although Kamel previously stated that in Brazil it is impossible to tell who is Black and who is white, he now contends that racial quotas for Black people are illegitimate because a sector of the white Brazilian population is also poor. White people, then, do exist, but only when it is convenient for Kamel's argument. In the meantime, Kamel chooses to omit that there is hardly a Black middle class in Brazil and that the upper class is as white as snow in Antarctica. Conversely, Maré focuses only on the new Black elite, whom he stigmatizes as being "filthy rich" and prone to "conspicuous consumption."[121] This focus on Black consumption is a convenient way for white authors to mystify their own and collective white wealth. Sociologist Deborah Posel in particular has dedicated extensive scholarship to what she calls "the issue of newly acquired wealth within the black population and the conspicuous consumption associated with it."[122] This scholarship aims to direct attention away from the fact that it is white people who continue to be "filthy rich" thanks to wealth accumulated and passed on over centuries of slavery, colonialism, ongoing white ownership of land and resources, and the exploitation of cheap Black labor. Black people, including members of the small Black elite, do not have intergenerational wealth and are burdened by the so-called Black tax, as they financially support family members who continue to be poor. What are systematically made to disappear in these texts are white wealth, its intrinsic dependence on the theft of Black people's lives, land, and labor, and the white supremacist violence deployed to preserve it.

On June 6, 2014, the South African Institute of Race Relations (IRR) issued a press release titled "Affirmative Action is Killing Babies and must be Scrapped." Citing the death of three children after they drank contaminated water in the municipality of Bloemhof, the CEO of the IRR Frans Cronje argued that "the officials responsible for these deaths were appointed, at least in part, on grounds of race-based affirmative action and that a direct causal link therefore exists between the policy and the deaths."[123] The demonization of affirmative action detracts attention from white responsibility for the ongoing abject life conditions faced by most Black South Africans and speaks powerfully to white people's investment in reproducing white supremacy. As George Lipsitz writes in a different context, white attacks on affirmative action "guarantee that whites will be rewarded for their historical advantage in the labor market rather than their individual abilities or efforts."[124] Despite (or, rather, precisely because of) the stark differential life expectancy

THE WHITE MOBILIZATION   159

for Black people and white people in South Africa, the IRR, like the
South African government itself, publishes colorblind life expectancy
statistics that do not once mention the word race and funds scholarship
that enforces colorblindness.[125] The IRR is not an exception. Strikingly,
South African scholars who embrace colorblind doctrines are appointed
to administrative positions created to rectify racialized imbalances in
the student and faculty body. Soudien, for example, condemns affirmative action policies in his scholarship,[126] yet he formerly chaired the
Ministerial Review Committee on Transformation in Higher Education
and was deputy vice-chancellor in the area of transformation and social
responsiveness at the University of Cape Town. The term "transformation" in the post-apartheid context has come to indicate official and
unofficial attempts to redress racial inequality, especially in educational
institutions and the workplace. That the scholarship of an official who
should guarantee desegregation demonizes measures needed to make
desegregation possible speaks volumes about the institutionalization of
colorblindness in South African academia.

Since colorblind doctrines dominate South African academia, too
few courses today give adequate attention to apartheid and even fewer
engage Steve Biko's writings. Revealingly, during the first semester of
2010 the Department of Historical Studies at the University of Cape
Town offered three graduate courses on the Jewish experience, one of
them specifically on antisemitism, but *none* on anti-Black racism in
South Africa or explicitly on apartheid. In the meantime, not unlike
ethnic studies programs in Arizona and the United States at large, the
UCT Centre for African Studies has to battle to ensure its continuing
existence. As white domination persists, the South African case reveals
itself as symptomatic of an ongoing global assault on the knowledges
and lives of Black people and people of color. Millions of students of all
backgrounds are being indoctrinated into naturalizing and reproducing
racial inequality.

The presence of strikingly similar rhetorical and institutional moves
that disavow racial inequality and seek to impede redistribution and
desegregation measures for Black people and people of color documented in this chapter cannot be considered fortuitous and much less
the product of ignorance. White ignorance cannot explain the systematic promotion of colorblindness across legal, scholarly, and journalistic
works produced in countries as diverse as Brazil, the United States,
and South Africa. This is the consequence of racialized knowledge and
testifies to an ongoing collective white commitment to upholding racial

160 THE ONGOING RACE TO SILENCE RACE

inequality beyond national boundaries. The recurrence of racial disavowal and the rhetorical contradictions it textually produces need to be adequately accounted for in any assessment of white scholarship and beyond. In societies in which racial inequality is rampant, this chapter has hopefully shown, the desire to suppress race as a category of analysis *always* creates textual paradoxes. It also produces metadiscursive contradictions. It is indeed ironic that Maré should direct a Center for Critical Research on Race and Identity while insisting that we should no longer talk about race. If "race thinking," as Maré argues, is not "appropriate in a democratic 'non racial' South Africa,"[127] then why study race? If race does not matter, then what is the value of engaging it academically? The fact that Maré has devoted most of his recent scholarship to examining race implies that, at least to the scholar himself, race *does* matter a great deal. The global disavowal of racism illustrated in this chapter speaks volumes about the shared white investment in whiteness that underlies the deployment of colorblind rhetoric. It also testifies to the differential way in which structural racism is treated in society. While the denial of the Jewish Holocaust is a crime in at least sixteen countries and can rightfully cost you your career, the denial of anti-Black racism is not just common practice, but is actively encouraged and rewarded, *especially* in academia, beyond national boundaries.

4

The Perils of White "Antiracism"

A game at which the liberals have become masters is that of deliberate evasiveness. The question often comes up "what can I do?" If you ask him to do something like stopping to use segregated facilities or dropping out of varsity to work at menial jobs like all blacks or defying and denouncing all provisions that make him privileged, you always get the answer—"but that's unrealistic!" While this may be true, it only serves to illustrate the fact that no matter what a white man does, the colour of his skin—his passport to privilege—will always put him miles ahead of the black man. Thus in the ultimate analysis no white person can escape being part of the oppressor camp.
  —Steve Biko, "Black Souls in White Skins?"

First, there is the terrorism of what Gramsci referred to as "political society": the police, the army, the prison-industrial complex.

Second, there is the terror of civil society's hegemonic blocs and its clusters of affilial formations: like the mainstream media, the university, or the megachurch.

But there is also a third tier of terror with which Black thought must contend. . . . *The unrelenting terror elaborated whenever Black people's so-called allies think out loud.*
  —Frank B. Wilderson III, *Afropessimism*

Arguably South Africa's most celebrated white liberal, Alan Paton continues to be widely praised as an antiracist activist who fought for the abolition of apartheid. Paton's own work and actions, however, show that nothing could be further from his actual racial politics. "Black Consciousness," a short essay that Paton published in 1972, is revealing

162   THE ONGOING RACE TO SILENCE RACE

in this regard. Resenting the critique that the South African Students'
Organisation (SASO) had leveraged at white liberals like himself, Paton
writes:

> It is not surprising that SASO and the Black Consciousness
> Symposium held in Durban in December of last year, have so
> far directed their specific fire at white liberals. If they were to
> direct their fire at the Government and Boss and the Security
> Police they would not find it so easy to hold conferences. . . .
> Indeed, as I asked Miss Masekela of the December symposium,
> who said that white liberals are a major stumbling block in the
> way of black liberation, what should white liberals do? Should
> they leave the country? Should they keep silent for ever more?
> Should they go north to be trained as guerilla fighters? Or
> should they just lie down and die?[1]

Paton questions the legitimacy of the "fire" that Black Consciousness
discursively set on white liberal politics. As he attacks SASO, which
Steve Biko cofounded, Paton depicts Black Consciousness as a dangerous movement and the potentiality of Black rule as a threat that
white people should prevent at all cost. Paton makes explicit that he is
"concerned with the needs of white people in South Africa" and that he
considers "black people in power" a threat to white people.[2] Paton can
accept that Black people are "proud of black skin," but not that Black
Consciousness gets "mixed up with black power."[3] Of course, this should
not surprise anyone who has carefully read Paton's famous 1948 novel
Cry, the Beloved Country, which defends racial segregation, criminalizes
Black people, and delegitimizes calls for Black political empowerment.
For Paton, as his later work also makes clear, power must remain firmly
in white hands. With the paternalism that is the signature of white liberals, Paton thus insists on speaking for Black people, demonstrating
how white people, as Biko puts it, "see nothing anomalous in the fact
that they alone are arguing about the future of 17 million blacks—in a
land which is the natural backyard of the black people. Any proposals
for change emanating from the black world are viewed with great indignation."[4] Adamant about keeping the racist status quo in place, Paton
tries to maintain control of the terms of liberation.

It makes sense, then, that in the same article Paton defends the racist
statement that he had made during an interview in London, namely,
that "'perhaps apartheid is worth a try.'"[5] Reproducing an epistemology

THE PERILS OF WHITE "ANTIRACISM" 163

of disavowal, Paton argues that in making this statement, he was not "speaking about apartheid at all," but about "those instruments of power which the Government has created, namely, the territorial authorities."[6] Also called Bantustans, homelands, or tribal reserves, the territorial authorities that Paton endorses were reservations for Black people, veritable extermination camps, that the South African government created as a means to keep the vast majority of the land and resources in white hands. Through the creation of the Bantustans, whites forced Black people into the most inhospitable regions, created a vast pool of exploitable Black labor, divided the Black population to stifle resistance, and manipulated international opinion by making it appear as if Black people had achieved some kind of independence. Biko fervently opposed the Bantustans, arguing that "the whole idea is made to appear as if for us, while working against our very existence."[7] Paton disavows his support for apartheid, yet the Bantustans *are* apartheid. They represented one key implementation of the separate development policy, which aimed to keep Black people in perpetual poverty and powerlessness, while locking wealth and power in the hands of white people, where they remain today.[8]

Paton's defense of apartheid shows that white liberals worked alongside white nationalists to uphold white power in South Africa. In "Biko and the Problematic of Presence," Frank B. Wilderson argues that the radicalization of white South African liberals in the late 1960s and early 1970s, which was a direct consequence of Black Consciousness's critique of their hypocrisy, was succeeded in the 1980s by white liberals' resentment of Black Consciousness and their unwillingness to let Black people decide the terms of the struggle.[9] In reality, already before the 1980s, white liberals mobilized against their own potential loss of power. Paton's attempt to delegitimize the Black Consciousness Movement illustrates this fact. In doing so, it testifies to what Biko calls "the totality of the white power structure,"[10] namely how white people work together across ideological affiliations to ensure the maintenance of the racist status quo.

Rather than subdividing the white community into good and bad individuals, Biko argues that white supremacy is endorsed by the entire white community. In Biko's terms, "whites in general reinforce each other even though they allow some moderate disagreements on the details of subjugation schemes."[11] Within the totality of white power, Biko argues, white liberals represent an especially pernicious problem for Black people. Biko describes white liberals as "that curious bunch of nonconformists who explain their participation in negative terms: that bunch of do-gooders that goes under all sorts of names—liberals, leftists, etc. These are the people who argue that they are not responsible for white racism and the country's 'inhumanity to the black man.'"[12] Biko indicts white liberals not simply for being uncommitted to racial justice, but for actively preventing change through a variety of tactics aimed at perpetuating the racist status quo.

In refusing to treat liberalism as an abstraction and disentangle liberal ideology from white people (its main adherents), Biko left a blueprint for understanding how structural and individual racism work together to ensure the maintenance of white supremacy. Biko was not alone in viewing the actions of white liberals as antithetical to Black people's quest for freedom. Black radical thinkers and activists from Assata Shakur to Kwame Ture have highlighted the dangers of white liberalism. Ture denounces the futility of appeals to the conscience of white people as follows: "We have repeatedly seen that political alliances based on appeals to conscience and decency are chancy things, simply because institutions and political organizations have no consciences outside their own special interests. The political and social rights of Negroes have been and always will be negotiable and expendable the moment they conflict with the interest of our 'allies.'"[13] Biko's position on white liberals, then, must be understood within a larger framework of global Black resistance against white power and the centrality of the Black Radical Tradition to this resistance.

This chapter shows that white liberals remain central agents of anti-Blackness and white supremacy today. Paton's question—"What should white liberals do?"—epitomizes the treacherous discursive practices of the white liberal. What looks like a question is not actually a question, but a colorblind tool through which Paton tries to delegitimize the demands of the Black Consciousness Movement. As the epigraph shows, Biko himself exposed this question as a white tactic of racial control.[14] Today, this question continues to be posed almost obsessively in a body of scholarship produced mainly by white philosophers, both in South Africa and in the United States. In this scholarship, too, the question "What should white people do?" is asked in bad faith. The insistence with which this question continues to be asked shows that white people know what we need to do to dismantle white supremacy. We just do not *want* to do it because it has a cost. Hence, we keep asking the same question over and over so that we can appear antiracist while providing answers that keep racism firmly in place.

THE PERILS OF WHITE "ANTIRACISM"   165

With the goal of illustrating how white racism and white "antiracism" are intertwined, this chapter examines Samantha Vice's article "How Do I Live in This Strange Place?" (2010), which sparked a storm of controversy in South Africa, as a starting point to critique white scholarship on whiteness that presents itself as concerned with racial justice while it is actually anti-Black. Deploying Biko's work as framework, I pay attention especially to white South African and US scholarship situated within critical philosophy of race and critical whiteness studies because in these fields the question "What should white people do?" has been asked particularly insistently. Theorizations of racism and whiteness produced at the intersection of these fields, especially by white scholars, are often problematic and deserve critical attention. In interrogating how hegemonic understandings of racism and whiteness can be reproduced even within seemingly counterhegemonic scholarship, I recognize that the production of knowledge plays a key role in protecting white privilege. Scholars such as Linda Martín Alcoff, Robert Bernasconi, Tommy Curry, Emmanuel Eze, Lewis R. Gordon, María Lugones, Charles Mills, and Lucius Outlaw have shown that examining the location of whiteness within the discipline of philosophy is a generative task. Offering valuable insights into the limitations of US philosophy of race, Curry argues that "the sophistication of American philosophy's conceptualizations of American racism continues to lag behind other liberal arts fields committed to similar endeavors."[15] Curry shows that white US philosophers largely marginalize or misrepresent the theoretical contributions made by Black scholars, including the important knowledge about racism produced in critical race theory (CRT). These problems are widespread in the discipline of philosophy, which often relies on an individualistic and moralistic framework that does not readily allow us to grasp the complex workings of structural racism. However, I do not intend to suggest that the problem simply lies with philosophy as a discipline (as if disciplines did not have practitioners), but rather aim to call attention to how many white philosophers in particular, both the United States and South Africa, theorize whiteness and racism in ways that sustain the racist status quo even as they appear to unsettle it.

A significant body of philosophical scholarship on whiteness written largely by white academics obfuscates the structural dimension of racism, provides individualistic explanations for structural problems, and thereby sustains white dominance. I argue that notions of white guilt, white shame, white habits, and white privilege as they are theorized in a noteworthy body of critical philosophy of race and critical whiteness studies share a crucial limitation: they minimize white people's active interest in reproducing the racist status quo. Studies, such as Vice's, that frame racism as a moral dilemma while silencing its institutionalization and the central cause for its existence and longevity—that is, white people's investment in maintaining economic, political, and symbolic power—sustain anti-Blackness and white supremacy. While Vice's essay does not provide us with adequate tools for understanding and tackling racism, it does offer insights into the reproduction of whiteness itself as it reveals how hegemony works.

White liberals are not just centrally responsible for white supremacy. They also reproduce racism in ways that are especially insidious, appropriating the language of antiracism for racist ends. These liberal tactics, as James Baldwin writes, are "really much worse" as they consist of a "system of lies, evasions, and naked oppression designed to pretend that it isn't so."[16] Racist scholarship packaged as antiracist work travels between the United States and South Africa in ways that reveal the centrality of white racial consciousness to the production of white academic knowledge. In reading Vice's essay through Biko's work and through a critical race lens, and in situating it within a larger material and discursive context, I aim to show that it is symptomatic of the pitfalls—indeed, the perils—of white "antiracism" more broadly. What this chapter does not do is tell white readers how they should *feel*. Doing so would reinscribe the problematic critical preeminence of affect in white scholarship on whiteness that I aim to critique. Analogously, my purpose is not to provide a neat package of easy solutions, but to call attention to how white people tend to frame the question "What should white people do?" so as to leave white supremacy intact.

Rehabilitating Whiteness

It seems bizarre that an article written for an academic audience and published in the *Journal of Social Philosophy* should become cause for public outrage, enduring debates in the media, and even exhortations for its author to commit suicide. Yet Samantha Vice's essay "How Do I Live in This Strange Place?" elicited precisely such responses after Eusebius McKaiser engaged it sympathetically in the South African press.[17] Vice's arguments that white people should feel shame and guilt, and should refrain from expressing their political views in the public

THE PERILS OF WHITE "ANTIRACISM"

arena, especially angered many of her fellow white South Africans. In a *Mail & Guardian* column titled "Why My Opinions on Whiteness Touched a Nerve," Vice responded to the disparaging criticism that her article elicited as follows: "I have been characterised as a self-hating attention-seeker and directed to commit suicide. . . . These responses are extreme. . . . I may be wrong in my conclusions, but the debate they have generated indicates that this is a conversation we urgently need to have in this country and that my critics lack the good faith, empathy and calm heads it would require. It has certainly brought to the surface the intense and personal nature of race and identity in this country."[18] The hostile reactions to Vice's essay speak volumes about white mobilization in the face of an apparent threat to white privilege and represent an interesting and sobering object of analysis in their own right. Still, not all responses to Vice's essay have been negative. On the contrary, the article has received an extraordinary amount of attention, including the South African weekly newspaper *Mail & Guardian* launching a special report on whiteness, the Centre for Ethics at Wits University hosting a seminar on the topic, the *South African Journal of Philosophy* publishing a special issue with responses to Vice's article by US and South African philosophers including Alison Bailey, Ward Jones, Lawrence Bloom, Eusebius McKaiser, and Charles Mills, and a 2015 seminar at the University of Oxford specifically on the article. Catapulting Vice to academic stardom, the article can be credited for Vice's quick climbing of the academic ladder from lecturer to distinguished professor, demonstrating how white people are actively rewarded for merely raising the issue of racism, as long as we do so in ways that do not threaten the racist status quo.

Vice writes in the opening sentence of "How Do I Live in This Strange Place?" that the essay represents "an attempt to critically reflect upon what it is to be white in a country like South Africa."[19] Contending that South African philosophers have a moral duty to address race and oppression, Vice asks how white South Africans can *live well* with the knowledge that they are privileged. She interrogates the implications of racial privilege from both a personal and representative position, asking: "What is it like to live here as a white person? What is the morally appropriate reaction to one's situation of privilege? Is it possible to live well?"[20] Having established that "to live well" is one of Vice's chief concerns, the article subsequently embarks on the problematic mission to rehabilitate white people. Vice argues that white people should realize that we have been morally damaged by racism, acknowledge that we are a problem, and ultimately "concentrate on recovering and rehabilitating our selves."[21] Her project is a narcissistic one that postulates "a morally damaged white self,"[22] a white self in need of saving, one that has been injured by racism and needs to be refashioned. Vice's goal is not to work toward abolishing the racist infrastructure. She instead aims to cleanse the white self of a blemish that causes white people feelings of discomfort and, through this cleansing exercise (based on "direct work on the self"[23] and the cultivation of shame), ensure that white South Africans continue to "live well." In proposing affective solutions to structural problems, Vice's essay is emblematic of the pitfalls that define seemingly antiracist white efforts to address racism.

Vice answers in the South African context the question that Linda Martín Alcoff poses in "What Should White People Do?" (1998). However, Alcoff, unlike Vice, transcends the query itself and instead critically interrogates white US authors' attempts to confront racism. Reviewing popular works such as Judith Katz's *White Awareness: Handbook for Anti-Racism Training* or Noel Ignatiev and John Garvey's journal *Race Traitor*, Alcoff demonstrates that white antiracism is often flawed. For example, she critiques Katz for treating racism "as a psychosocial pathology that can be solved through behavior modification,"[24] a conceptualization of racism that also informs Vice's article. Amid abundant shortcomings, *White Awareness* gets one thing right, Alcoff suggests: "Katz is highly critical of white guilt fixations, because these are self-indulgent."[25] Even as Vice cites Alcoff's article, she replicates this indulgence on the white self that, guilty and shamed, craves attention and care.

Vice explicitly places her article within a tradition of white South African antiracist advocacy. The title "How Do I Live in This Strange Place?" refers to a line in "Reggae Vibes is Cool" by Afrikaner rock star Bernoldus Niemand, whose anti-apartheid songs were in part inspired by Bob Dylan's protest music. "Reggae Vibes is Cool" came out in 1984, during a period in which revolts against the apartheid regime were gaining momentum despite brutal repression. Niemand and Dylan have more in common than an apparent commitment to antiracism: both made a fortune appropriating Black music, yet are heralded as quintessential white antiestablishment musicians. Their anti-Black theft masked as antiracism speaks to the structural ways that whiteness creeps through when whites speak on behalf of Black people, evoking what Eric Lott in the homonymous book calls a dialectic of *love and theft*.[26]

THE PERILS OF WHITE "ANTIRACISM"

The line "How do I live in this strange place?" is also the epigraph in *My Traitor's Heart* (1990), the autobiography in which Afrikaner journalist and songwriter Rian Malan previously asked the question of how to live a happy and moral life as a white South African.[27] What stands in the way of Malan leading a fulfilled life are feelings of guilt that drive his writing. Beyond sharing a concern with guilt and white South Africans' wellbeing, Vice and Malan both incorporate aspects of confessional writing. However, neither author provides a perspective that is merely personal. Vice and Malan's preoccupation with whiteness is motivated by their experiences and structural positionality as white people. In "Reflections on 'How Do I Live in This Strange Place?'" (2011) Vice concedes: "Certainly, the paper is an exploration of a deeply felt personal issue—being white in South Africa—and some of my background philosophical concerns will not be shared by other philosophers. However, I hoped that my position as a white South African was representative and some of my views reasonably public."[28] On the one hand, Vice advocates a "moral progress or rehabilitation" for white people through an individual "inward-directed, nonpolitical moral process."[29] On the other, she attempts to manage white people's collective location within post-apartheid society and politics, and thus indirectly the position of Black people as well. Vice advances arguments about how white people *should* feel and what sociopolitical role they *should* play in a democratic South Africa. Vice's essay is not simply a personal reflection on the self, in other words, but a work of normative ethics with serious political implications.

Vice immediately constructs a moral equivalence between colonizer and colonized, a colorblind move that serves to conceal hierarchies of power and disavow white culpability for racism. Vice concurrently argues that moral damage is a white attribute and universalizes this moral damage, arguing that "under conditions of oppression, both the oppressed and the oppressors are morally damaged, although of course in different ways, and even if this damage is not their responsibility."[30] Vice postulates a shared grammar of injury between oppressor and oppressed, who are positioned as being equally "damaged," bound by a presumed common moral taint. Of course, Vice never demonstrates the argument that the oppressed are "morally damaged" because she cannot do so, but this does not prevent her from making this problematic statement as it is a useful colorblind tool.

The enforced symmetry between oppressor and oppressed soon gives way to a *reversal* of power as Vice's central preoccupation with "the moral damage done to the oppressors' character by habitual white privilege"[31] reproduces the discourse of white injury, which represents white people as harmed by racism. This is worrisome because white people's victimization plays a fundamental role in preserving white power. In the previous chapter, I showed how the US Supreme Court in the *Parents Involved in Community Schools v. Seattle School District No. 1* case constructed an equivalence of harm between Black and white children in ways that privilege white people. The court valued the *presumed* harm that white children might encounter by being bused to schools in which Black students are a majority over the *actual* harm that Black students suffer by being placed in structurally underfunded schools. This shows how colorblindness relies on reproducing what Carl Gutiérrez-Jones calls a "'moral equivalence' between injured and injuring parties," a model that is "at the core of [the US] legal system."[32] Deployed also by Vice, this model advantages white people by positioning us as also injured by racism, while it disappears white culpability for racism and the actual injuries that Black people incur as a consequence of racial discrimination.

In creating a moral equivalence between Black and white people, Vice's essay reproposes the fallacy of other works in whiteness studies which, as Robyn Wiegman writes, "construct a mutuality of harm hypothesis that powerfully appends whites to the harmed position of people of color."[33] This colorblind move is popular among white scholars who parade as antiracist while they support the racist status quo. In "The Oppressor's Pathology" (2010), Chilean-South African philosopher Pedro Tabensky also constructs "a mutuality of harm hypothesis" between Black and white people as he argues that "the dynamic of oppressor and oppressed creates widespread psychological damage on both sides of the oppressive divide, typically making both oppressor and oppressed into psychological cripples."[34] The moral damage that Vice postulates as affecting both oppressor and oppressed is here reproposed as a "psychological damage" that turns both perpetrators and victims "into psychological cripples." The thin line between creating an equivalence between Black and white people and portraying white people as victims of racism is, once again, quickly crossed. Racism, according to Tabensky, is something that white people "suffer from," as they are "best described as the victims of bad habits, relatively thinly conceived, instilled in them by the air of their times."[35] The portrayal of white people as *suffering from* racism relinquishes white responsibility for racism and silences its institutionalization. Racism here is portrayed as a question of "bad habits," as an individual behavioral trait that is neither structural nor actively reproduced, but merely passively "instilled" in white people "by the air of their times." The air itself, it seems, is responsible for racism. White people are literally reduced to puppets without agency in this white liberal scholarship. They are not just constructed as innocent, but as people who are *subjected to* racism, in a perverse reversal of power. Tabensky argues that "white oppressors, not solely those who are militantly committed to oppressing others, are alienated from the world and from themselves, making their behavior seem like that of soulless dolls."[36] Representing white people as "alienated," as "soulless dolls," takes away agency from white people, reducing them to beings who do not know what they are doing even when they actively oppress Black people.

Tabensky's colorblind moves are not original. US philosopher Shannon Sullivan also conceives white people as being "constituted by" something unconscious or preconscious (habits), something outside of their control (affects), or something external to them, as in "the (white-privileged) world."[37] Vice similarly writes: "Because of the brute facts of birth, few white people, however well-meaning and morally conscientious, will escape the habits of white privilege; their characters and modes of interaction with the world will just be constituted in ways that are morally damaging."[38] In these analyses, white people do not co-constitute the world. Rather, they are portrayed as being at its mercy. Yet what continues to perpetuate whiteness is white people's active investment in maintaining power—an investment that is also visible in this scholarship through the disavowal of white people's responsibility for racism.

Vice calls attention to the persistence of injustice in South Africa in her essay, yet she does not explicitly racialize this injustice. Instead, she turns it into an occasion to obscure the intrinsic relationality between Black poverty and white wealth, even as she appears to make this relationship visible. Creating a bridge between the past and the present, Vice states that South Africa's "famous history of stupefying injustice and inhumanity feels still with us."[39] The consequences of apartheid, she continues, are palpable "in the visible poverty, the crime that has affected everyone, the child beggars on the pavements, the *de facto* racial segregation of living spaces, in who is serving whom in restaurants and shops and in homes."[40] It is not necessary to more explicitly racialize this narrative; the reader knows, or so the passage suggests, who the servant is. While framing crime as having "affected everyone" reveals a possible anxiety about political correctness, here the condition of the Other is the primary measure of apartheid's effects. The reader is invited to locate the material outcomes of apartheid *there*: in the destitution and labor of the serving, rather than in the wealth and comfort of the served. This should give us pause. In an essay that asks how white people can live well in contemporary South Africa, why is the condition of the Other, rather than the self, presented as the primary measure of apartheid's effects? If "Whites in South Africa ought to see themselves as a problem,"[41] then why is the white theft of Black people's land, resources, labor, and lives *not* at the center of Vice's writing? This omission is not accidental.

White advantage in Vice's article is depicted as something simply inherited from the past. Yet racial domination is actively reproduced in the present and manifests itself most strikingly in white people's economic, political, social, and symbolic privileges. White wealth is a direct consequence of Black poverty. Racism must thus be examined through a relational lens. By locating the effects of apartheid in the poverty of the Other, rather than also in the wealth of the self, Vice makes white economic power and the inherent interdependence of white privilege and Black dispossession disappear. George Lipsitz explains that "focusing on Black disadvantages deflects attention away from the unearned advantages that whites possess. It is not so much that Blacks are disadvantaged, but rather that they are *taken advantage of* by discrimination in employment, education, and housing, by the ways in which the health care system, the criminal justice system, and the banking system skew opportunities and life chances along racial lines."[42] While Lipsitz focuses on the United States, these insights also apply to the South African context. Many white South Africans, as many white people elsewhere, nevertheless deny that they are privileged.

David Benatar is a case in point. In "Why Samantha Vice Is Wrong on Whiteness" (2011), Benatar avails himself of a familiar rhetorical arsenal. He contests Vice's attribution of moral indecency to white people and enforces colorblindness by co-opting Martin Luther King's statement that one "should judge people by the 'content of their character' rather than by the colour of their skin."[43] Good and bad people come in all colors, Benatar states, and Vice is on the wrong side of the argument because she engages in harmful "stereotyping." In this colorblind move, Benatar conceives *Black* and *white* as apolitical categories that are synonymous with skin color. Denying that white South Africans have profited, and continue to profit, from racial discrimination,

THE PERILS OF WHITE "ANTIRACISM"   173

Benatar argues that "while it is clearly true that some 'whites' were benefited by discrimination against 'blacks,' other 'whites' are no better off than they would have been if 'blacks' had never been the victims of discrimination. Indeed, I think that in general 'whites' are better off now that apartheid has ended and I think that many of them would have been still better off if it had never been implemented."[44] The irony of affirming that whites "are better off now that apartheid has ended" in order to prove that white privilege is nonexistent must have escaped Benatar. When he argues that Vice "overstates" the power that white people hold in South African politics, Benatar resorts to another colorblind tool: the discursive minoritization of white people. He argues that whites, who are "a minority of the population" in South Africa, are "hardly capable of managing and shaping" the political landscape.[45] Contrary to what Benatar affirms, being a numerical minority has never prevented white South Africans from controlling the economy or the political landscape. For these colorblind arguments to be effective, any reference to economics and history must be omitted.

While they disagree on various fronts, Benatar and Vice share an individualistic understanding of racism and a concern with the welfare of white people. In Vice's article, it is not just the relational nature of racism that is rendered invisible. As Vice conveniently turns white privilege into a set of individual behaviors, she also silences the material advantages of whiteness. Masking the fact that white privilege is underwritten by concrete material and psychological payoffs for white people, she conceptualizes white privilege as a set of *habits*. In this logic, racism is made to acquire a disembodied life of its own. Racism does not give white people structural material and psychological advantages, Vice suggests, but it merely "infuses" us with a particular set of behaviors. In a citational practice that illustrates how white people continue to exchange colorblind strategies across national borders, Vice relies heavily on Sullivan's *Revealing Whiteness: The Unconscious Habits of Racial Privilege* (2006) for her theorization of white privilege. Sullivan argues that white privilege "is best understood as a constellation of psychical and somatic habits formed through transaction with a racist world."[46] The equation of white privilege with a set of psychic behaviors depicts racism as a pathology and obscures the fact that whiteness has concrete material value. Sullivan, like Tabensky and Vice, treats racism as if it was an illness from which white people suffer and from which we can be cured, rather than a structure that we have deliberately created and continue to actively reproduce through violence and disavowal.

174 THE ONGOING RACE TO SILENCE RACE

If the representation of white privilege as a series of habits that Sullivan theorizes and Vice adopts was not troubling enough, a closer look at how Sullivan conceptualizes the development or acquisition of these habits reveals an even greater problem. White people's habits, in Sullivan's view, are "formed through transaction with a racist world."[47] In this understanding of white privilege, white people are not agents, but merely inhabit "a racist world" that is already there and for which we are not responsible. This description shifts the blame for racism away from white people and toward a larger entity that operates outside of our control. Sullivan portrays white people as both passive and innocent, while the world itself becomes a scapegoat. This formulation is not Sullivan's alone. Vice comparably writes: "When white privilege is unwanted but inescapable, it is the world that is not how it should be."[48] White people do not cocreate this world, Sullivan and Vice suggest, but there is a racist world *out there* that overdetermines white people's behaviors. For Sullivan and Vice, it is the world that is wrong; white people were just born into it and are passive inheritors of privileges and behaviors that are out of their control. Racism in this scholarship is like nitrogen in the atmosphere. It is simply *there*. White people, Vice and Sullivan suggest, are not responsible for racism, in the same way that a person walking outside without an umbrella will get wet on a rainy day but is not responsible for the fact that it is raining. Fully disentangled from white people, racism here becomes a natural attribute. In the process, these works reproduce what Tyrone Palmer calls "the *givenness* of the World" that permeates affect theory and disavow Black affect, which is non-relational and positioned both outside and against the world.[49] Clearly anti-Black, these theorizations of white privilege fail to name white responsibility for the ongoing exploitation of Black people and provide no space for envisioning a possible *end* to whiteness and, indeed, the world.

Sullivan, Tabensky, and Vice are silent about the fact that white people want, enjoy, and police our white privilege. Vice goes as far as insinuating that white people do not *want* to have privilege. She describes white privilege as "nonvoluntary in its origins," having "unwilled and unwanted effects," "unavoidable," "unwanted, nonvoluntary," and "unwanted but inescapable."[50] This suggests that unwantedness is a common sentiment among white people when it comes to our privilege. Sure, Vice has a point when she argues that white privilege is "nonvoluntary in its origins" (in the sense that white people are structurally advantaged from birth). However, this does not mean that white

THE PERILS OF WHITE "ANTIRACISM" 175

privilege is "unwanted." The repeated framing of white privilege as unwanted that informs Vice's essay is itself the expression of a desire to protect white privilege.

To corroborate her contentions about white privilege, Vice appropriates Biko, even as Biko's views on whiteness conflict with Vice's. To make Biko agree with her, Vice extrapolates his words, conveniently omitting Biko's critique of white liberals' active investment in white supremacy. Vice writes:

> It is important to see that [white] privilege in this sense is non-voluntary in its origins, although of course later on it may be more or less consciously embraced or rejected. In an essay written decades earlier, the South African activist and black consciousness leader, Steve Biko, emphasized this when assessing the role of well-meaning white liberals in Apartheid South Africa: "It is not as if whites are allowed to enjoy privilege only when they declare their solidarity with the ruling party. They are born into privilege and are nourished by and nurtured in the system of ruthless exploitation of black energy."[51]

Vice here cites a passage from Biko's "White Racism and Black Consciousness," yet she omits Biko's preceding sentence, which makes clear that Biko condemns white people for collectively creating and maintaining the racist status quo that gives birth to the symptom of white privilege in the first place. "White society," Biko writes in the preceding sentence, "collectively owes the blacks so huge a debt that no one member should automatically expect to escape from the blanket condemnation that needs [sic] must come from the black world."[52] Vice also omits the sentence that follows, in which Biko states: "For the 20-year-old white liberal to expect to be accepted with open arms is surely to overestimate the powers of forgiveness of the black people. No matter how genuine a liberal's motivations might be, he has to accept that, though he did not choose to be born into privilege, the blacks cannot but be suspicious of his motives."[53] While Vice misappropriates Biko to exculpate whites from responsibility, Biko does exactly the opposite as he asserts that white people—as a group and not as mere individuals—cannot be trusted and cannot expect to escape collective condemnation.

That white people have a *collective* responsibility for racism is clear from the very first section of "White Racism and Black Consciousness,"

176   THE ONGOING RACE TO SILENCE RACE

importantly titled "THE TOTALITY OF WHITE POWER IN SOUTH AFRICA." Here, Biko writes, "So blatantly exploitative in terms of the mind and body is the practice of white racism that one wonders if the interests of blacks and whites in this country have not become so mutually exclusive as to exclude the possibility of there being 'room for all of us at the rendezvous of victory.'"[54] Biko makes clear that white supremacy is a totalitarian system that operates through a multiplicity of mechanisms of social control, including the deliberate stratification of marginalized peoples into subgroups that are given differential treatment, the exploitation of Black people and creation of an economic system in which Black people's money unidirectionally flows into white people's pockets, or the creation of so-called homelands for Black people.[55] As Vice obscures the structural dimensions of racism that Biko instead places at center of his analysis, she omits this passage.

Contrary to what Vice argues, it is not the prelapsarian innocence of white people that Biko theorizes, but rather white people's collective responsibility for creating and perpetuating institutional racism. White "antiracism" itself, Biko contends, is merely a performance, a selfish façade that white people adopt to appease our own conscience and control Black people's reactions to racism. In Biko's words,

> Instead of involving themselves in an all-out attempt to stamp out racism from their white society, liberals waste lots of time trying to prove to as many blacks as they can find that they are liberal. This arises out of the false belief that we are faced with a black problem. There is nothing the matter with blacks. The problem is WHITE RACISM and it rests squarely on the laps of the white society. The sooner the liberals realise this the better for us blacks. Their presence among us is irksome and of nuisance value. It removes the focus of attention from essentials and shifts it to ill-defined philosophical concepts that are both irrelevant to the black man and merely a red herring across the track. White liberals must leave blacks to take care of their own business while they concern themselves with the real evil in our society—white racism.[56]

As this passage shows, Biko recognized that white people bring their paternalism and superiority complex to bear on Black spaces and insisted on the importance of Black self-determination and racial privacy. Before Biko cofounded SASO in 1968, most Black student

THE PERILS OF WHITE "ANTIRACISM"   177

organizations in the country were under white direction, a fact that
Biko exposed as emblematic of white liberals' arrogance, paternalism,
and desire to control Black people's responses to racism.[57] As Biko
exhorts white people to focus on white racism and abandon the racist
urge to be leaders of Black organizations or to formulate "solutions" to
racism that inevitably entrench the racist status quo (tendencies, these,
grounded in our superiority complex), he outright rejects the possibility that any genuine liberation can come from white people. This is so
not because white people are born with some kind of moral deficiency
in the same way that one is born with an immutable eye color, as Vice
suggests, but because by virtue of being white in a white supremacist
society, we have advantages that place us in positions of power, "miles
ahead" of Black people. Even when we ask the question "What can I
do?" we are merely protecting our own interests.

The scholarship examined in this chapter offers precisely "ill-defined
philosophical concepts that are both irrelevant to the black man and
merely a red herring across the track." These concepts serve to obscure
white supremacy. The "deliberate evasiveness" that Biko addresses in
the epigraph is at the heart of the white knowledge produced in Vice's
essay, in which the question "What can I do?" is a maneuver for actually
evading the question, all while being patted on the back by other white
scholars and journalists for asking the question at all and doing the
good white liberal work of seemingly agonizing over the answer. Think
about it: in a country in which white people continue to own virtually
the entirety of the land and economy, it does not take long philosophical arguments to figure out what white people ought to do. That white
debates about what white people should do nevertheless persist, yet
the question of land and wealth redistribution is rarely raised in these
debates, shows that these discussions are not meant to demolish but to
entrench racism as a system.

Not surprisingly, Vice silences the fundamental issue of land redistribution. The word *land*, understood as the earth's surface, shines
through its absence in her essay. The word land does appear, and it
appears more than once, but merely as a synonym of the word *country*.
Land is a ghost, repressed yet haunting the text, as we learn in the very
first paragraph that "South Africa is still a visibly divided and suspicious
land."[58] On the next page, Vice again asks "how white people can *be*
and live well in such a land, with such a legacy."[59] Land soon turns into
landscape, the locus of white attachments, with Vice arguing that some
white South Africans feel "an intense love of the physical landscape."[60]

178   THE ONGOING RACE TO SILENCE RACE

However, white people's relation to this landscape, Vice suggests, is no longer bucolic as whites must now "recognize just how brutely defined one is by the human and natural landscape of one's country."[61] The landscape here appears as a source of doubt, even discomfort, for white people, who are again depicted as being passively affected by the environment. One is almost made to feel sorry for South African whites, their selves so "brutely defined" by the human and natural landscape. One wonders who has actually brutalized whom and whose country South Africa fundamentally is, as the "landscape" acquires an agency of its own and white people's violent dispossession of land from Black people vanishes from the text. Neither does the reader learn that white people are *still* in possession of the vast majority of South Africa's land as Vice silences the near-complete European monopoly on land that persists today in the southernmost country of the African continent.

If Vice silences the land question, the textual presence of reparations differs only on the surface from the textual absence of land (understood in material terms). Vice raises the question of reparations merely to ensure that no reparations are made, and that white people can continue to "live well." Vice mentions reparations more than once only to dismiss reparations as a viable political project and, later, argue against white involvement in politics altogether. She writes:

> One could of course become politically or socially active, financially supporting worthy causes, joining or working for a relevant organization to make reparations for the harm one's whiteness expresses and maintains. Perhaps in this way the self can be refashioned through work. This approach accepts the political and public aspects of one's identity and works to change the situation that brought about our whitely habits. This seems the best response to guilt, but perhaps it does not fully take on board the logic of shame, which has *metanoia* as a proper end. It is surely true that our selves can be changed through our actions, but I do not think this can be enough if the theses of moral damage and white habit are correct—direct work on the self is also required, and it is this I want to focus on.[62]

As the quote illustrates, Vice mentions economic changes and specifically reparations, yet swiftly returns to a call for affective change for white people. Vice's focus is not on social justice. It is not on attempting to level the playing field between Black and white people in concrete,

THE PERILS OF WHITE "ANTIRACISM" 179

material ways. In fact, Vice is not concerned with the wellbeing of Black people at all. Her preoccupations lie with reinscribing the comforts of the white self. Reparations are useless, Vice suggests, implying that they are useless for white people. Her goal is redeeming white people, saving them from their feelings of shame, and reparations are unable to do that. Reparations might be good for Black people, but those are not the people whose welfare Vice is concerned with.

Vice asks how white South Africans can live well, but she fails to ask how Black people are to live *at all* under neocolonial conditions. Vice argues that in post-1994 South Africa "materially nothing much has changed for anyone, black or white."[63] In reality, material conditions have *worsened* for most Black South Africans since the democratic dispensation, while white people collectively are wealthier now than ever. Vice does not argue that one morally appropriate reaction to white privilege would be to attempt to relinquish some of the material benefits of whiteness. Even as Vice invites readers to witness in the destitution of the Other, she remains chiefly concerned with rehabilitating the self. This gesture presumes that white moral regeneration can occur prior to and *irrespective of* land and wealth redistribution. The task of "lessening" whiteness that Vice advocates need not cost white people anything. White souls can be saved and whiteness can be redeemed at the same time as most Black people continue to live in poverty.

The response to white privilege that Vice proposes is *affective*. Advancing a thesis that infuriated many of her fellow white nationals, Vice argues that white South Africans should cultivate feelings of guilt and shame as these are appropriate responses to white privilege. Shame is even more fitting than guilt, Vice writes, because the latter "is a reaction to what one has *done*, not primarily to who one *is*."[64] Guilt is about one's actions, while shame is about the self. Shame, according to Vice, is preferable over feeling guilt because shame does not presuppose active participation. Rather than calling for collective responsibility, Vice thus essentializes whiteness. She argues that it is not white people's actions and choices but whiteness itself that should be a cause for shame.

In contrast with Vice, Biko emphasizes the primacy of economics in understanding and combating racial domination. He writes, "There is no doubt that the colour question in South African politics was originally introduced for economic reasons. The leaders of the white community had to create some kind of barrier between black and whites so that the whites could enjoy privileges at the expense of blacks and still feel free to give a moral justification for the obvious exploitation that pricked

180 THE ONGOING RACE TO SILENCE RACE

even the hardest of white consciences."[65] While Biko addresses the psychological effects of white supremacy for white people (as when he critiques white people's superiority complex in "Black Souls in White Skins?"), he approaches psychological conditions as symptoms, as the outcome of colonial structures of domination that need to be radically dismantled. For Biko, mental liberation for Black people represents a means to a larger end, which is complete freedom through the liberation of Black people's land and being. In much white philosophical scholarship, affective and psychological changes for white people instead become ultimate goals. In saying this, I don't mean to suggest that Biko's insights on Black and white psychology are equivalent, for they are certainly not. Rather, I aim to highlight the anti-Blackness of white calls for affective change that leave material conditions untouched.

In "The Uses of Anger: Women Responding to Racism," a keynote lecture delivered at the 1981 National Women's Studies Association conference, Audre Lorde argues that anger is an appropriate and productive response to racism, while she criticizes guilt as being a detrimental force in the fight against racism. Unlike many white scholars featured in this chapter, Lorde does not posit affective change per se as a solution to racism. She instead argues that to be a catalyst for progress anger must be "focussed with precision."[66] Anger must be *put to use* in concrete and targeted ways. As Lorde views anger as a generative force that can be channeled towards the abolition of racism, she counterposes anger to guilt, which she considers "a device to protect ignorance and the continuation of things the way they are, the ultimate protection of changelessness."[67] Lorde presents guilt as a tool of stasis and disavowal, as "another way of avoiding informed action."[68] This is precisely how guilt functions in much white scholarship.

The flawed guilt-versus-shame debate that animates Vice's essay sidesteps discussions about justice and concrete ways to achieve it. Vice is not alone in recommending that white people should feel shame, which has become *the* privileged emotion advocated by and for white people in numerous philosophical studies.[69] For instance, in "White Shame: Responsibility and Moral Emotions" (2009), Daniel Haggerty argues that white USAmericans, too, should feel more shame and less guilt because shame presumes moral taint, which exists outside white people's actions and choices. Many white scholars do not just posit shame as a valuable emotion, then, but prescribe shame to white people. However, not only is there no proven relationship between feelings of either guilt or shame and white people's antiracist action, but demands

THE PERILS OF WHITE "ANTIRACISM" 181

for affective modification misconstrue racism as a matter of individual bias, as a pathology, rather than as a sociopolitical system that white people have created and continue to actively maintain in place.[70] What is more, feeling ashamed for one's whiteness can actually be beneficial for white people as it can lift a psychological burden and help us become more comfortable with our privileges.[71]

The problematic centrality of affective responses to racism for white people informs white scholarship that advocates white shame and white guilt as well as scholarship that critiques notions of white shame and white guilt. Sullivan, for example, criticizes shame and guilt in *Good White People: The Problem with Middle-Class White Anti-Racism* (2014) only to default to another affective mode through which, she argues, white people can more effectively respond to racism. Sullivan describes shame and guilt as narcissistic feelings that cater to white middle-class subjects. White people should relinquish their obsession with shame and guilt altogether, she writes, and instead work toward a transformative self-love. I agree that shame and guilt re-center the white subject. Like Sullivan, I also believe that guilt and shame share negative traits with hatred and fear, emotions that continue to structure white actions toward Black people and people of color. White people's attempts to frantically escape our own selves can exacerbate aggression toward Black people and phenomena such as cultural theft. While, following Lorde, I consider anger a more suitable affect for antiracist action than either shame or guilt (not anger addressed at the self or the Other, but directed at racial injustice), I recognize that approaching racism by centering white feelings, as Sullivan does, is especially damaging without a structural analysis.

White scholars who understand that white people are the problem cannot in good faith be invested in managing or soothing white feelings. If whites are the problem, the solution clearly cannot be to help white people become more comfortable with our whiteness. Importantly, Sara Ahmed has critiqued any antiracism that reinstitutes a positive white identity or makes white people feel better about themselves. She writes: "The white response to the Black critique of shame and guilt has enabled here a 'turn' towards pride, which is not then a turn away from the white subject and towards something else, but another way of 're-turning' to the white subject."[72] According to Ahmed, declarations of white shame, especially in academic settings, are part of "a politics of declaration," a process whereby white individuals or institutions admit that they have engaged in bad practices and this admission itself then

182   THE ONGOING RACE TO SILENCE RACE

becomes a good practice.[73] While Sullivan does not overtly advocate white pride, she does invite white people to love themselves and reenvisions whiteness as a positive identity. Even as she critiques shame and guilt, Sullivan remains trapped in a behavioral, individualistic framework: rather than feel guilt, shame, or fear, white people ought to love themselves. How and whether self-love can affect structural change is not clear. Love, then, becomes enough.

Framing racism as a moral dilemma and asking white people to *feel* a certain way, common responses to racism in white philosophical scholarship on whiteness, gives the impression that mere shifts in individual behavior can combat racial inequality. Not only is institutional racism primary, but individual and institutional racism also operate semi-independently from one another.[74] Whiteness is not centrally a question of feelings. Whiteness is, first and foremost, about power. As Cheryl Harris has argued, whiteness is a *property*.[75] Given that racist ideology is a pretext for economic exploitation, Biko made clear that, at the very least, the entire economic system has to be changed for racial equality to be achieved. When asked whether he believed that an egalitarian society was a socialist one, Biko answered:

> Yes, I think there is no running away from the fact that now in South Africa there is such an ill distribution of wealth that any form of political freedom which does not touch on the proper distribution of wealth will be meaningless. The whites have locked up within a small minority of themselves the greater portion of the country's wealth. If we have a mere change of face of those in governing positions what is likely to happen is that black people will continue to be poor, and you will see a few blacks filtering through into the so-called bourgeoisie. Our society will be run almost as of yesterday. So for meaningful change to appear there needs to be an attempt at reorganizing the whole economic pattern and economic policies within that particular country.[76]

Biko's words have been prophetic as South Africa today is indeed "run almost as of yesterday." Central to the ongoing inequality is the fact that most wealth is still locked in the hands of a white minority. Within this context, calling merely for affective changes for white people and asking whites to refrain from engaging in politics, as Vice does, reveal themselves as tactics geared toward keeping resources in white hands.

THE PERILS OF WHITE "ANTIRACISM"

183

Even as Vice makes a public intervention herself, she ironically argues that white people should withdraw from publicly offering their opinions about "the political situation." In her own words, white South Africans should

> live as quietly and decently as possible, refraining from airing one's view on the political situation in the public realm, realizing that it is not one's place to offer diagnoses and analyses, that blacks must be left to remake the country in their own way. Whites have too long had influence and a public voice; now they should in humility step back from expressing their thoughts or managing others.[77]

Ironically, Vice's views on the role that white people should play in the fight against racism might have been influenced by (a misreading of) Biko, who contends, as we saw, that "white liberals must leave blacks to take care of their own business while they concern themselves with the real evil in our society—white racism."[78] Rather than managing Black organizations, Biko argues, white people should tackle racism within their own communities. However, Vice advocates "silence in the political realm," arguing that whites should turn "attention to the self."[79] In this way, she ignores Biko's call for white antiracist work in white spaces. All that white people need to do, in Vice's view, is to feel ashamed while sitting quietly in our comfortable homes. And we need to feel ashamed *not* because we are responsible for racism, but simply because we are white. Since being white is something that white people did not choose, this logic reveals itself as tautological: white people should be ashamed for being white; being white is something that white people did not choose; hence, white people have nothing to be ashamed about.

Changing individual attitude, reflecting upon what it feels to be a problem, and feeling ashamed of being white do not automatically challenges whiteness. Vice's essay suggests that the opposite is the case. "For white South Africans," Vice writes in the closing paragraph, "work on the self . . . might also be one way of saying that I am not merely a product of what is worst about me and a refusal, finally, to be fully defined by it."[80] Vice thus posits "work on the self" as a means through which white people can free themselves from the overdetermination of racial identity. A critical engagement with one's whiteness may not allow the burdened white self to feel utterly content, Vice suggests, but it may allow it to feel better than if white privilege had not been addressed at all. Even critical self-analysis reveals itself as empowering for white people.

In a column suggestively titled "End to Whiteness a Black Issue" (2010), Andile Mngxitama argues that projects such as Vice's, which rescue whiteness without relinquishing the material conditions that sustain it, contribute to demobilizing Black demands for land and wealth redistribution. These projects, Mngxitama writes, "reduce whiteness and white racism to a mere misunderstanding among friends."[81] Black South African activists and intellectuals continue to be at the forefront of the struggle against anti-Black racism, but their assessments of whiteness are unlikely to elicit seminars among scholars and largely continue to be silenced in academia altogether. While the views of Black radical thinkers are often ignored, Vice was praised for having revealed the proverbial elephant in the room when she issued her critique of whiteness. In whose room was the elephant not standing before Vice brought it to public attention? The privilege of ignoring racism is never granted to Black people, who face its consequences on a daily basis. Only for those of us who are white can white privilege become a topic that deserves attention *suddenly*.

This chapter has aimed to show that white liberals remain a problem for Black liberation today as they propose misguided "solutions" that further naturalize and sustain white supremacy. It should not surprise anyone, then, that in more recent publications Vice and Tabensky demonize Black South African students who have protested to decolonize the university, portraying them as angry, irrational, and anti-white. According to Tabensky, the Black students who demanded the removal of the Cecil John Rhodes statue from the University of Cape Town campus in 2015 were "venting their obsessive vengeful hatred towards inanimate sculptures."[82] These students, he continues, display "warning signals of an unhealthy relationship to whiteness, indeed of an obsessive concern for whiteness, which cannot explicitly be endorsed."[83] Clearly, Tabensky does not want Black people to be concerned with whiteness. He would rather that Black people left us alone, basking in our privileges and colonial attachments. In a 2016 article, Vice similarly charges: "The current debates about transformation in higher education are often explicitly racialized and polarized with white teachers and students being told that they have no place in South Africa and the university, and radical black students rejecting any white 'western' philosophy. If such heightened circumstances and such angry demands

THE PERILS OF WHITE "ANTIRACISM" 185

do not warrant introspection, then nothing does."[84] As they pathologize Black people and seek to delegitimize Black liberation movements,
these arguments are unquestionably anti-Black. Revealing ongoing
white anxieties about Black empowerment, these arguments bring us
back to Paton's racist condemnation of the Black Consciousness Movement which opens this chapter. At work in these responses to students'
calls for decolonization is what Baldwin describes as white people's
"profound desire not to be judged by those who are not white."[85] What
happened, in fact, to Vice's call for white people to be humble and
ashamed of their whiteness or her claim that "blacks must be left to
remake the country in their own way"?[86] White people clearly still cannot accept criticism on the part of Black people, nor that Black people
free themselves on their own terms. When Black people set the terms of
liberation, they are attacked with the same viciousness that Paton displayed against the Black Consciousness Movement during apartheid.

Today, as in the past, white people continue to work together as a
collective across ideological affiliations and national borders to protect
white interests. Biko's analysis of the central role that white liberals
play in maintaining the racist status quo and his emphasis on how white
people act in unison to stall Black liberation is more relevant today than
ever. In Biko's terms, "Basically the South African white community is a
homogeneous community. It is a community of people who sit to enjoy
a privileged position that they do not deserve, are aware of this, and
therefore spend their time trying to justify why they are doing so. Where
differences in political opinion exist, they are in the process of trying
to justify their position of privilege and their usurpation of power."[87]
Biko's insights about the totality of white power hold across national
borders. Far from being motivated by good faith or ignorance, white
"antiracism" remains an anti-Black technology of racial power today. It
is indeed ironic that Vice argues that white people should work quietly
on the self and not share their political views publicly, while she herself
does something very different: publish scholarship that is invested in
maintaining white supremacy and is therefore chiefly political.

The white "antiracism" that Vice's work represents brings us right
back to the nineteenth century, when white abolitionists aimed to
convert one white heart at a time. The connection to the antislavery
movement does not end here. Let us remember that Vice's goal is to
rehabilitate white people. White abolitionists, too, were often concerned with saving white souls, while Black abolitionists were fighting
to save Black lives. This makes sense as even white people who think

of themselves as liberal, Biko reminds us, tend to shun real change. Baldwin similarly argues that "the very notion of change, *real* change, throws Americans into a panic and they look for any label to get rid of any dissenter."[88] While institutional racism remains intact, white "antiracism" routinely recycles maneuvers that did not help Black people in the past and do not help antiracist movements today. As it produces false controversies over what kind of white supremacy will exist, it aims to render unthinkable the concrete dismantling of the structured advantages of whiteness.

Part 3

Decolonial Imaginaries and Colorblind Logics

5

Espousing Liberal Individualism in Cubena's Work

The experience, besides my personal experiences, that moved me to write is my deep concern for the suffering of people of African descent in South Africa, Haiti, Latin America, and, in particular, Panamá. . . . My mission as a Latino writer of African descent is first to present a positive self-image of the Latinos of African descent. It is also to make public, or known, the many contributions that people of African descent have made in Latin America in the last five hundred years (1492–1992) in the development of what is considered the Latin American culture, e.g. art, music, language, culture, history, folklore, religion, and literature. Also, several very important aspects, and I consider these to be my personal mission as a writer, are to denounce racial injustice in Latin America, to attack the dehumanization brought about by these practices and, above all, to expose the insincerity, the hypocrisy and the complacence of all those who deny the existence of racial discrimination in Latin America.
    —Cubena, "Interview with Dr. Carlos Guillermo Wilson"

Our attitude here is that you cannot in pursuing the aspirations of black people achieve them from a platform which is meant for the oppression of black people.
    —Steve Biko, "Our Strategy for Liberation"

In the early twentieth century, Negritud became an important literary movement and aesthetic mode of representation in Spanish-speaking countries of the extended Caribbean. While various Cuban and Puerto Rican poets were following in the footsteps of the francophone

189

190 DECOLONIAL IMAGINARIES AND COLORBLIND LOGICS

Negritude writers Aimé Césaire, Léopold Sédar Senghor, and Léon Damas by symbolically celebrating the African roots of national culture, Black and white Panamanian writers alike shunned any notion of Negritud. As a valorization of the African elements of national culture did not occur systematically in Panamanian letters, scholars seeking Panama's equivalent of Nicolás Guillén, the Cuban master of Negritud poetry, or Luis Palés Matos, Puerto Rico's best-known negrista poet, will be confronted with vacuums that reveal the racial repression and exclusionary nature of literary practice in the country.[1] It is not until Cubena, born Carlos Guillermo Wilson,[2] publishes the novel *Chombo* in 1981 that we encounter Panamanian literature that is unapologetically Black and antiracist. One of Panama's most prominent writers and the grandson of Jamaican immigrants who built the Panama Canal, Cubena has dedicated virtually the entirety of his oeuvre to combating anti-Black racism and asserting the rightful place of West Indian immigrants in the Panamanian national and literary imaginary. Cubena's works cut through the lies and mystifications of the racial democracy myth, making visible how social relations in Panama and elsewhere in Latin America are defined by anti-Blackness and white supremacy. Yet the works also fall prey to the allures of liberalism and heteropatriarchy in ways that make apparent how both are fundamentally at odds with the goal of challenging racism.

Cubena's works, as the epigraph shows, are a privileged site for the confluence of multiple agendas that are potentially in conflict with one another. On the one hand, they contest racial discrimination in Latin America and critique Panamanian nationalism for being grounded in whiteness and anti-Blackness. On the other, they are essentially nationalistic as they portray West Indians as a patriotic "model minority" invested in building the nation. The tension between Cubena's critique of Panamanian nationalism and his articulation of a West Indian Panamanian identity supports Paul Gilroy's contention that the tasks of "opposing racism on the one hand, and of elaborating the symbolic forms of black identity on the other . . . are not synonymous or even coextensive though they can be rendered compatible."[3] As we saw in chapter 1, in the attempt to conceal their own complicity with US imperialism in the Canal Zone and divide the racialized working classes, white Panamanian elites in the early twentieth century promoted the myth that West Indian immigrants were enemies of the state aligned with US imperialism. West Indians were cast as dangerous and unassimilable Others whose religion, language, and customs are radically different from those

ESPOUSING LIBERAL INDIVIDUALISM IN CUBENA'S WORK   191

of the local population. People of African descent who had been in Panama for centuries (whom I call Afro-Panamanians to distinguish them from West Indian Panamanians) were co-opted and pitted against West Indian immigrants in a divide-and-conquer maneuver that stifled solidarity between the two groups while serving as a nation-building tool. Cubena's works, I argue, contest the racist representation of West Indians as threats to national unity, yet they also reproduce the exclusionary logics of white nationalism. In doing so, they reveal how colorblindness works with, and through, nationality, ethnicity, gender, and sexuality in ways that make especially evident its insidiousness.

This chapter examines Cubena's most famous novels, *Chombo* (1981) and *Los nietos de Felicidad Dolores* (The Grandchildren of Felicidad Dolores) (1990), alongside Cubena's short stories. These works provide incisive critiques of the racist propaganda that white Panamanians unleashed onto West Indian Panamanians, a propaganda epitomized by Olmedo Alfaro's *El peligro antillano en la América Central: La defensa de la raza* (The West Indian Danger in Central America: The Defense of the Race), which I examined in chapter 1. Set against the backdrop of the 1977 Torrijos-Carter Treaties, which stipulated that Panama would regain control of the Panama Canal in 1999 after almost a century of US occupation, *Chombo* narrates the life stories of two generations of West Indian Panamanians. In the novel, James Douglin (Papá James) migrates to Panama from Barbados and Jamaica to work as a digger in the Canal Zone. Papá James and his wife Nenén are the grandparents of the protagonist Litó, who returns to Panama City from the United States to study in the renowned Instituto Nacional. The title refers to a racist slur that Panamanians use against West Indian immigrants. Like the title of Carlos Moore's autobiography *Pichón*, which references a racial slur used in Cuba against people of West Indian descent like Moore himself, the term "chombo" in the title centers the oppression that West Indians face at the hands of white Panamanians and, according to the novel, Afro-Panamanians as well.

Cubena further engages the experiences of West Indian Panamanians in *Los nietos de Felicidad Dolores*, which opens in a New York airport in 1999, an imagined future in which a group of West Indian expats return to Panama to witness the handing over of the Canal. *Los nietos* fictionalizes two key events in Panamanian history: the construction of the Panama Railroad, which began in 1850, and the imposition of Arnulfo Arias's constitution, which in 1941 institutionalized racism against West Indians by forbidding the immigration of Black people whose first language was not Spanish. The entanglement between racial conditions in the colonial past and neocolonial present is everywhere visible in *Chombo* and *Los nietos*. The works, as we will see, are shaped both by nationalist and diasporic impulses, reflected in their concurrent emphasis on the specifics of Panamanian racism alongside the inclusion of a proud African and Afrodiasporic history that strives to achieve epic proportions.

Probing the narrative strategies that Cubena's works deploy to contest racism and the symbolic solutions to racism that they propose, as I do in this chapter, shows that the attempt to fold Black people into the logics of liberalism upholds the racism and anti-Blackness that liberalism depends upon. Following Lisa Lowe, I understand modern liberalism as "the branches of European political philosophy that include the narration of political emancipation through citizenship in the state, the promise of economic freedom in the development of wage labor and exchange markets, and the conferring of civilization to human persons educated in aesthetic and national culture."[4] Charles Mills argues in *Black Rights/White Wrongs* that liberalism must be understood as *racial liberalism* given that it is an instrument of white rule. Far from simply being a political ideology, liberal individualism is intimately tied to the novel and its historical production. In *How Novels Think*, Nancy Armstrong contends that the history of the modern subject and the history of the novel are coextensive. This is not simply because the British novel came into being at the same time as the modern individual was on the rise in Europe, Armstrong contends, but because the novel itself was instrumental to the birth of the individual. Only after it was formulated in fiction did the individual as a basic unit enter the realms of medicine, law, history, political philosophy, and other fields. In the process of turning the white bourgeois subject into the individual through fictionalization and repetition, the cultural, class, and racial specificities of this subject, Armstrong argues, were rendered opaque: the (white) individual became constructed as universal.[5] While she confines her analysis to British novels, Armstrong suspects that this process also holds true for novels in other contexts and calls on critics to interrogate whether postcolonial fiction in particular challenges or perpetuates the liberal assumptions of the British novel.[6] I do not pretend to be able to answer Armstrong's call in this chapter, nor is it my desire to do so. The very category "postcolonial fiction" is not particularly useful because it collapses a plethora of different works under one slippery, colorblind, umbrella term. Many critics even label the works of a white writer such

ESPOUSING LIBERAL INDIVIDUALISM IN CUBENA'S WORK   193

as J. M. Coetzee as postcolonial, further revealing how the term often functions as a colorblind tool.

What this chapter does aim to illustrate is how a commitment to the self-regulating subject compromises Cubena's attempt to challenge racism. My thinking on this matter is informed by Saidiya Hartman's analysis of the relationship between anti-Black racism and the individuation strategies of the liberal individual.[7] Hartman writes in *Scenes of Subjection* that "liberalism, in general, and rights discourse, in particular, assure entitlements and privileges as they enable and efface elemental forms of domination primarily because of the atomistic portrayal of social relations, the inability to address collective interests and needs, and the sanctioning of subordination and the free reign of prejudice in the construction of the social or the private."[8] Hartman shows that, after emancipation, formally endowing Black people with the responsibilities of the liberal individual was a means through which white USAmericans abdicated responsibility for enforcing the rights stipulated in the Reconstruction Amendments, plunging Black people into "a travestied emancipation and an illusory freedom."[9] As it fails to envision liberation for Black people as a collective, the liberal individual of Cubena's novels is also bound to "an illusory freedom."

Chombo and *Los nietos* both advocate unity and education as the principal symbolic solutions to Black people's concrete conditions of existence. Yet as the novels posit a strictly heteronormative West Indianness as synonymous with "authentic" Blackness, they undermine their own goal of fostering intraracial unity. Instead, they reproduce hierarchies between different groups of Afrodescendants and exclude LGBTQ people from the Black community that Cubena envisions altogether. Michelle M. Wright argues in *Becoming Black* that "like their white counterparts, many Blacks in the diaspora prefer formations that, whether explicitly enunciating 'nation' or 'diaspora,' implicitly embrace nationalist discourse's call for an enforced heteropatriarchal homogeneity through which 'authentic' Blackness comes into being."[10] Cubena's works are committed precisely to an enforced "heteropatriarchal homogeneity" that clashes with the works' aim of advancing liberation for Black people. Offering important insights into how heteropatriarchy inevitably colludes with white supremacy, Roderick Ferguson argues in *Aberrations in Black* that a commitment to dominant gender and sexual norms creates "odd bedfellows" in literary imaginaries and critical discourse, so that formations which generally are in conflict with liberalism, such as Marxism, end up mirroring liberalism.[11] Ferguson writes

194   DECOLONIAL IMAGINARIES AND COLORBLIND LOGICS

that, in being "aggressively heteropatriarchal," Richard Wright's masculinist nationalism exhibits an affinity with white supremacist logics
even as Wright was dedicated to challenging racism.[12] A commitment
to heteropatriarchy also undercuts the antiracist agenda that Cubena's
works seek to put forth. To understand the significance of these arguments and the importance of Cubena's works themselves, however, it
is necessary to take a detour and place the works within Panamanian
literary history, to which I will now turn.

The Location of Blackness in Panamanian Literature

In the late nineteenth and early twentieth centuries, as we saw at the
beginning of this chapter, Negritud and negrismo were burgeoning
literary movements in the extended Hispanophone Caribbean. Yet in
Panama, Black, white, and mestizo writers alike largely ignored Panama's African heritage.[13] While white and mestizo writers did so because
of their rampant racism, Panamanian poets of African descent avoided
referencing Blackness as a mechanism of self-defense against racial discrimination.[14] When white and mestizo writers did engage the African
elements of national culture, they generally provided negative representations of Black people. Cubena addresses this issue in the essay "La
poesía afro-panameña" (Afro-Panamanian Poetry) as follows:

> Por lo general en la poesía panameña se presenta una imagen
> negativa del negro, y sobre todo del negro antillano. . . . Los más
> ilustros poetas panameños como Ricardo Miró (1883–1940)
> y Rogelio Sinán (1904) hacen caso omiso de la rica temática
> negroide que se presenta en Panamá. Es más, los mismos poetas
> negros de principios del siglo XX no llegaron a ser paladinos de
> la 'negritude.'[15]

> In general, Panamanian poetry provides a negative image of
> the Black, and especially of the Black West Indian. . . . The
> most illustrious Panamanian poets such as Ricardo Miró
> (1883–1940) and Rogelio Sinán (1904) disregard the wealth of
> Black themes that exist in Panama. What is more, not even the
> Black poets of the early twentieth century became paladins of
> 'negritude.'[16]

As Cubena denounces the anti-Blackness of white Panamanian literature, he laments that Black Panamanian writers did not "become paladins of 'negritude'" either. This is not merely a Panamanian phenomenon. Juan Francisco Manzano's *Autobiografía de un esclavo* (*Autobiography of a Slave*, 1840), the first slave narrative published in Latin America, the "cult of whiteness" of the Parnassian poetry of João Cruz e Sousa, who introduced symbolism into Brazilian letters in his poetry collections *Missal* and *Broquéis* (1893), or the modernist poems of Panamanian writer Gaspar Octavio Hernández attest to the pressure to conform to Eurocentric literary forms and modes of representation that Afro-Latin American writers experienced in the nineteenth and early twentieth centuries.[17] The disavowal of Blackness, Frantz Fanon argues in "West Indians and Africans," also shaped literary production in the West Indian context. Fanon writes: "Until 1939 the West Indian lived, thought, dreamed (we have shown this in *Black Skin, White Masks*), composed poems, wrote novels exactly as a white man would have done. . . . Before Césaire, West Indian literature was a literature of Europeans. The West Indian identified himself with the white man, adopted a white man's attitude, 'was a white man.'"[18] Fanon's words remind us that the seeming racelessness of much early Afro-Latin American and Afro-Caribbean literature is not a sign of racial harmony, but a symptom of racialized repression and the racially exclusionary dimensions of literary practice.[19]

Despite these assimilationist pressures, some nineteenth-century Afro-Panamanian poets did make explicit mention of Blackness in their works. Federico Escobar (1861–1912), also known as el bardo negro (the Black bard), infused some of his writings with references to his racial heritage.[20] One of the most important poets of his time and a carpenter working on the French canal project, which earned him the nickname el carpintero poeta (the carpenter poet), Escobar wrote Romantic poetry and later became one of Panama's greatest modernist writers.[21] The following excerpt from the poem "Nieblas" (Mists) illustrates the contours that Blackness assumes in Escobar's work:

> *¡Negro nací! La noche aterradora*
> *trasmitió su dolor sobre mi cara;*
> *pero al teñir mi desgraciado cuerpo*
> *¡dejó una luz en el cristal del alma!*
>   C. Obeso

196 DECOLONIAL IMAGINARIES AND COLORBLIND LOGICS

También negro nací; no es culpa mía...
El tinte de la piel no me desdora,
pues cuando el alma pura se conserva
el color de azabache no deshonra.
Hay en el mundo necios que blasonan
de nobles por lo blanco de su cara;
que ignoran que en la tierra sólo existe
una sola nobleza: la del alma . . .

I was born Black! The dreadful night
transmitted its pain onto my face;[22]
but as it colored my disgraced body
it left a light in the crystal of the soul!
    C. Obeso

I was also born Black; it is not my fault...
The color of my skin does not tarnish me,
for when the purity of the soul is preserved
the color of jet does not dishonor.
There are fools in the world who boast
that they are noble because of their white appearance;
who ignore that on earth only
one nobility exists: that of the soul . . .[23]

Escobar challenges anti-Black racism within the parameters available to him as a Black poet writing in the nineteenth century under a system of white supremacy. It is not his fault, Escobar writes in an apologetic tone, that he was born with a dark complexion. Skin color is no cause for shame and dishonor, he contends, because he is virtuous *despite* his Blackness, which in the poem does not presume the articulation of an oppositional racial consciousness. Blackness is not depicted as a source of pride, but as an impediment to Escobar's desire for equality and inclusion, a marker that should rather be overlooked, and which Escobar chooses not to acknowledge in most of his works.

While Escobar's poetry grappled marginally with Blackness, the work of Gaspar Octavio Hernández (1893–1918), a great admirer of Escobar, displays a cult of whiteness that further reveals the constraints that early Black writers faced in Panama. Hernández, whose formal education did not reach beyond the third grade and who died of hemoptysis at the young age of twenty-five, was a journalist who pioneered modernist

ESPOUSING LIBERAL INDIVIDUALISM IN CUBENA'S WORK

poetry in Panama.[24] Hernández's poems are filled with patriotic tones and references to "heroínas rubias, con ojos azules" (blonde heroines, with blue eyes),[25] while only one of his poems, "Ergo Sum," explicitly references his racial heritage.[26] Hernández also participated in the nationalist discourse that cast West Indians as Others. In "El culto del idioma" (The Cult of Language, 1916), he scorned West Indians for not speaking Spanish and accused them of expressing themselves "en incomprensible y tosco *patois* anglo-yankee" (in an incomprehensible and rough Anglo-Yankee patois).[27] That Hernández was posthumously canonized as a national poet likely would not have occurred without the silencing of Blackness, appraisal of whiteness, and anti-West Indian stance that inform his work.[28]

During the second half of the twentieth century, US colonial domination over Panama and the demographic shift produced by the immigration of West Indian workers influenced cultural production. The humiliating experience of being subjected to US imperialism inspired a number of Panamanian writers to denounce discriminatory practices in the Canal Zone and provided a generative terrain for the inclusion of Black characters in works of fiction. Afro-Panamanian writer Joaquín Beleño, a former Canal worker and one of Panama's most popular authors, writes about the abject working conditions in the Zone from the perspective of the exploited silver men in the novels *Luna verde* (1941), *Gamboa Road Gang/Los forzados de Gamboa* (1960), and *Curundú* (1963). His best-known novel, *Gamboa Road Gang/Los forzados de Gamboa*, attempts to reaffirm a sense of national pride in defiance of US imperialism. The novel is inspired by the true story of Lester León Greaves, a Canal Zone worker of West Indian descent who, having been falsely accused of raping Annabelle Rodney, a white US citizen, was condemned to spend fifty years in the Gamboa penitentiary. Although USAmericans revoked Greaves's sentence in 1962, the events stand as a reminder of the reaches of structural racism in the Canal Zone.[29] In Beleño's fictionalization of the event, the protagonist Arthur Ryams, nicknamed Atá, serves a fifty-year sentence for the alleged rape of Annabelle. Throughout his imprisonment, Atá believes that Annabelle will return to him, testify to his innocence, and they will finally marry. But his hopes for freedom are forsaken when she marries a white US officer. While he is incarcerated, Atá's feelings of racial superiority (he is "half white") cause conflicts with other prisoners, particularly with those of West Indian descent, whom Atá constantly subjects to racial slurs.

198   DECOLONIAL IMAGINARIES AND COLORBLIND LOGICS

In the novel, Beleño attempts to portray the plight of Black Canal workers and to reaffirm a sense of national pride in defiance to North American imperialism. For instance, the West Indian character Perla Watson affirms in the novel: "No soy nadie. Nada me pertenece. Mis padres vinieron de lejos a morir aquí para construir el canal. Pero aquí solo el gringo es el amo." (I am nobody. Nothing belongs to me. My parents came from afar to die here to build the canal. But here only the USAmerican is the master).[30] One the one hand, Beleño manages to give voice to the predicaments of afflicted neocolonized Panamanians, denounce racism and segregation in the Canal Zone, and construct a j'accuse narrative against US colonialism in Panama. Yet in casting West Indians as intrinsically foreign and complicit with US imperialism, Beleño's work capitulates to anti-West Indian propaganda, colluding with the white supremacy that it seeks to contest. His portrayal of West Indian characters remains infused with stereotypical notions of Blackness and a paternalistic tone that renders their representation disquieting.

Cubena's works hence arise in a context in which local writers either largely ignored Panama's African heritage or provided denigrating images of Black people and West Indians in particular. The reception of Cubena's novels demonstrates that the repression and marginalization of Black writers has not stopped in contemporary Panama.[31] Cubena's works have been mostly published in the United States, where Cubena has lived since 1959, when he was 18 years old, and have not received much critical attention in Panama. In fact, they continue to be omitted from the canon and most Panamanian literary anthologies precisely because they critique anti-Black racism.[32] While Cubena's novels have received more attention in the United States, Afro-Panamanian literature remains understudied in both countries. Sonja Stephenson Watson's *The Politics of Race in Panama: Afro-Hispanic and West Indian Discourses of Contention* (2014) is currently the only book-length study published in the United States that focuses centrally on Afro-Panamanian literature.

While Cubena's works have been silenced in Panama, they have largely been praised in the United States. Literary scholar Elba Birmingham-Pokorny has lauded Cubena's works for providing "scholars of Afro-Hispanic literature with a thorough appreciation of what, in essence, constitutes the black experience in Latin America."[33] Not only must analyses that invoke a racial essence be taken with a grain of salt, but Cubena's works themselves defy the conjecture that there is one singular "Black experience" in Latin America. It is also

ESPOUSING LIBERAL INDIVIDUALISM IN CUBENA'S WORK 199

true that works of fiction are not unmediated reflections of reality, as Birmingham-Pokorny suggests, but have a complex relationship with the world, displaying their own internal tensions and contradictions. While scholars have largely chosen to ignore the contradictions at the heart of Cubena's novels and short stories, in the pages that follow I hope to show that engaging them not only acknowledges the complexity that defines them as works of fiction, but also deepens our understanding of the insidious workings of colorblindness.

Entering Cubena's Novels

Cubena's novels grapple with the centrality that slavery holds in understanding the struggles that Black people in the diaspora (and beyond) continue to face. In the process, they confront readers with the fact that, as Africans were enslaved and trafficked to the Americas, they were subjected to the constant threat of death that was the condition of their bondage and the forcible suppression of their languages, customs, and histories. Addressing these harrowing realities, bell hooks writes:

> The traumatic experiences of African women and men aboard slave ships were only the initial stages of an indoctrination process that would transform the African human being into a slave. An important part of the slaver's job was to effectively transform the African personality aboard the ships so that it would be marketable as a "docile" slave in the American colonies. The prideful, arrogant, and independent spirit of the African people had to be broken so that they would conform to the white colonizer's notion of a proper slave demeanor. Crucial in the preparation of African people for the slave market was the destruction of human dignity, the removal of names and status, the dispersement of groups so that there would exist no common language, and the removal of any overt sign of an African heritage.[34]

As they enslaved African people, hooks reminds us, Europeans were cognizant that Africans are human beings and had to be indoctrinated into their new roles. White people, hooks writes, used violence, terror, and deprivation to "transform the African personality" and subjugate the people they enslaved, including the deprivation of their own names.

200   DECOLONIAL IMAGINARIES AND COLORBLIND LOGICS

Cubena's own life and work display a commitment to recovering the histories of Black people in the Americas that have been erased through slavery, a fact visible in the central place that African and Afrodiasporic history and mythology assume in Cubena's novels as well as in his own decision to adopt an African name.

This centrality is immediately evident in *Los nietos* and *Chombo*, which both open with the image of a shield described as "ESCUDO CUBENA" (Cubena Shield). Concurrently shield and gate, the Escudo Cubena stands as entry point between the reader and the story, giving us interpretive keys. Under the shield, a legend explains that the word "Cubena" is the Hispanicized version of the Twi word Kwabena, meaning Tuesday, the day of the week in which Cubena was born. Born Carlos Guillermo Wilson in Panama City in 1941, the author in the 1970s changed his name to Cubena, becoming one of the first Black Latin American writers to take an African name.[35] If the name Cubena symbolically retraces a West African lineage lost through slavery, so does the first image represented on the shield: a chain with seven rings. In *Los nietos*, the legend states that the chain represents "los pueblos y culturas africanos que fueron esclavizados en las Américas: Ashanti, Bantu, Congo, Dahomey, Efik, Fanti y Yoruba" (the African peoples and cultures that were enslaved in the Americas: Ashanti, Bantu, Congo, Dahomey, Efik, Fanti, and Yoruba).[36] The naming of specific ethnic groups places Afrodescendants in the Americas within specific West African cultures in a gesture that seeks to counter the violent erasures of slavery.

The shield centers Black people's resilience and survival. Placed under the chains, a group of stars symbolizes "las regiones donde más africanos fueron esclavizados: Brasil, Cuba-Puerto Rico, Jamaica-Martinita, Panamá, Perú-Ecuador, República Dominicana-Haití y Venezuela-Colombia" (the regions in which the majority of Africans were enslaved: Brazil, Cuba-Puerto Rico, Jamaica-Martinique, Panama, Peru-Ecuador, Dominican Republic-Haiti, and Venezuela-Colombia).[37] The image of a turtle with a bee on its shell occupies the bottom part of the shield, with the bee symbolizing "cadenas, latigazos, injusticias e insultos que desde 1492 han sufrido los esclavos africanos y sus descendientes antillanos y latinoamericanos en las Américas" (chains, whiplashes, injustices and insults that since 1492 African slaves and their West Indian and Latin American descendants have suffered in the Americas).[38] Finally, the turtle represents "el tipo de carácter que han desarrollado los de ascendencia africana durante su odisea por las Américas" (the type of character that Afrodescendants have developed throughout their

ESPOUSING LIBERAL INDIVIDUALISM IN CUBENA'S WORK 201

odyssey in the Americas), which in *Chombo* is described as being patient and strong.[39] Girdled by a ribbon with the words "EYE YIYE" ("the future will be better" in Twi), the shield looks at the past, grapples with the present, and forebodes hope for the future.

What does it take to change the course of history and create a better future for Black people in the diaspora? Through the next image on the shield, Cubena provides an answer to this question. The image of a wide-open book is placed next to images that evoke slavery and racial discrimination. Prominently placed on the upper right side of the shield, next to the stars and the chains, the book is described as "el símbolo de la principal fuente para combatir la esclavización de la mente" (the symbol of the principal source to combat mental slavery). Through the metonymic image of the book, education is posited as a key solution to combat the contemporary legacies of slavery. This suggests that the problem that Black people must overcome is not structural racism per se, but "mental slavery," which is a consequence of racism. The image of the book foreshadows how the solution to racism that the novels advocate is not the dismantlement of the racist infrastructure, but the eradication of ignorance. In the process, they place the onus for racism upon the backs of (*some*) Black people who, Cubena's works suggest, need to be reformed through education. This starting point elicits additional questions: What kind of education do Cubena's works advocate? What kind of knowledge do they produce? The answers to these questions, as we shall see, reveal the treacherous workings of colorblindness that Cubena aims to challenge.

Recovering the Past

Having included the Escudo Cubena, *Chombo* provides the following note to the reader:

Panamá, 1 de octubre de 1979

Estimado Lector:

Esta novela, *Chombo*, la primera de una trilogía, está preñada de datos históricos y anécdotas de los negros antillanos— *chombos*—los que tanto sudor y sangre dieron en la construcción del ferrocarril transístmico y el Canal de Panamá.

202   DECOLONIAL IMAGINARIES AND COLORBLIND LOGICS

> En la lectura que usted está a punto de iniciar, encontrará las razones por las cuales es menester y, sobre todo, URGENTE combatir la perniciosa discriminación racial y las otras injusticias.[40]

Panama City, October 1, 1979

Dear Reader:

> This novel, *Chombo*, the first of a trilogy, is filled with historical data and anecdotes about Black West Indians—*chombos*—who gave much sweat and blood in the construction of the transisthmian railroad and the Panama Canal.

> In the reading that you are about to begin, you will find the reasons why it is necessary and, above all, URGENT to combat pernicious racial discrimination and other injustices.

The note makes explicit Cubena's desire to give voice to the struggles of West Indian immigrants in Panama through the inclusion of "historical data and anecdotes" that challenge the marginalization to which West Indians have been subjected in the country. The epigraph by Marcus Garvey that precedes the note speaks to the importance that history plays in the novel and points to its pedagogical agenda: "*A people without knowledge of their past history, origin and culture is like a tree without roots.*" As *Chombo* recovers and reimagines the histories of West Indians and other Afrodescendants in the Americas, it strives to teach readers these histories. Like other novels by Cubena, *Chombo* is didactic in the truest sense of the term.[41] This didacticism is not a shortcoming, but an integral element of the works' antiracist politics. Offering more than simple entertainment, Cubena's novels document the contributions that Black people have made to American societies and contest the racism at the heart of Panamanian nationalism. Cubena makes clear that in *Chombo* we will find nothing less than the "reasons why it is necessary and, above all, URGENT to combat pernicious racial discrimination and other injustices." Cubena's works attempt to correct the fabrications, lies, and silences of white supremacy. They are not written to amuse. They strive to be both testimony and insurgent critique.

Cubena, who published *Chombo* five years after the 1976 Soweto uprising and denounces apartheid in the novel, views challenging racism as a central goal of his art.[42] In their unequivocal denunciation of racism, impulse to document racial oppression, and propensity for didacticism, Cubena's novels display interesting parallels with an important body of fiction in English written during apartheid by Black South African authors, who considered it crucial to denounce racial oppression in their work, an impulse epitomized by Mothobi Mutloatse's famous statement made in a 1981 interview that "any writing which ignores the urgency of political events will be irrelevant."[43] The same sense of urgency animates Cubena's works. At the same time, his novels transcend the stark realism that characterized much apartheid fiction by incorporating African and Afrodiasporic mythology and rejecting a linear narrative.

Cubena's works unsettle dominant versions of Panamanian history and national identity. *Chombo* immediately situates Blackness within the Panamanian national and racial imaginary. The novel opens with an exclamation that conveys indignation: "¡Carajo! Me ca..." (Damn! I sh...).[44] The speaker is Litó, who is described as "un furioso joven negro . . . de ascendencia afro-antillana" (a furious young Black man . . . of West Indian descent).[45] Litó cannot finish his sentence. He is interrupted by Don Justo, a blind Panamanian elder. Don Justo's blindness symbolizes his refusal to acknowledge both the African within himself and the reality of white supremacy in Panama. Despite the fact that Don Justo has dark skin and curly hair, he argues that he has "sangre castellana pura" (pure Castillian blood).[46] Litó challenges Don Justo by asserting that there is no such thing as "pure Castillian blood" given that "los iberos, antiguos pobladores de la Península Ibérica, eran del Africa" (the Iberians, ancient inhabitants of the Iberian Peninsula, were from Africa).[47] In this way, the novel both counters the white disavowal of a historical African presence in Europe and shows that Black people have influenced Panama's racial and cultural makeup from the inception. Including Africa in the racial heritage of the Panamanian elite allows Cubena to represent Blackness as fundamentally Panamanian, countering racist discourses that portray West Indian immigrants as the only Black people in Panama.

Valorizing the contributions that Black people have made to national culture is not a strategy unique to Cubena's works. Excluded and marginalized in their countries of birth, many Black writers in the diaspora have proclaimed the Blackness and hybridity of the nation to counter the lies and erasures of white nationalism. Nicolás Guillén insisted that all Cubans are "un poco níspero" (a little brown),[48] while Ralph Ellison argued that US culture is not white, but rather owes much to Black

204   DECOLONIAL IMAGINARIES AND COLORBLIND LOGICS

people, as in the United States "even the most homogeneous gatherings of people are mixed and pluralistic."[49] Affirming the Blackness or mixedness of the nation-state belies white supremacist discourses that deny the extent to which American societies and their cultures are indebted to African people.

In Cubena's novels, particular importance is placed on affirming the historicity of the African continent, a historicity called into question by colonial representations of Africa as the "dark continent," as a place without history.[50] The novels are replete with references to African empires, such as those of Ghana, Mali, and Songhai (which are mentioned, in this very order, more than ten times in *Los nietos*). Through this retrospective gaze directed at grand African empires, Cubena's novels attempt to instill a sense of pride for their African roots among Black people in the diaspora as well as foster unity and insurrection among Black Panamanians in particular. This echoes Steve Biko's emphasis, following Frantz Fanon, on the importance of turning to the past as a means to advance the political project of Black Consciousness. Biko writes:

> In an effort to destroy completely the structures that had been built up in the African Society and to impose their imperialism with an unnerving totality the colonialists were not satisfied merely with holding a people in their grip and emptying the Native's brain of all form and content, they turned to the past of the oppressed people and distorted, disfigured and destroyed it. No longer was reference made to African culture, it became barbarism. . . . No doubt, therefore, part of the approach envisaged in bringing about "black consciousness" has to be directed to the past, to seek to rewrite the history of the black man and to produce in it the heroes who form the core of the African background.[51]

The frequent reiteration of the historical importance of ancient African civilizations and African leaders enables Cubena precisely to "rewrite the history of the black man and to produce in it the heroes who form the core of the African background." Cubena turns the lens toward the past and toward African history and mythology not for its own sake, but in the hope that the gesture may further inspire collective mobilization against racism.

The inclusion of African histories and tales also allows Cubena to create a distinct Black Panamanian literary voice rooted in a decolonial

ESPOUSING LIBERAL INDIVIDUALISM IN CUBENA'S WORK   205

sensibility. Cubena's strategies are reminiscent of those employed by Chicanx writers who, during the Chicano Movement of the 1960s, envisioned a proud Aztec lineage and relied on Mesoamerican mythology for artistic and political inspiration, as we will see in the next chapter. Just as Chicanx writers turned to Aztec and Maya civilizations of the past in their recovery of an Indigenous consciousness, Cubena's novels invite Black readers, as Hartman writes in a different context, to "marvel at the wonders of African civilization or to be . . . proud [of] the royal court of Asante."[52] The return to Indigenous history and mythology represented a way for Chicano Movement writers to forge a resistant collective identity and emerge from the distortions and silences produced by dominant versions of history. Cubena's novels, too, turn to the past to counter the violent lies and erasures of white supremacy. Fanon compellingly articulates the significance of such a restorative gesture in *The Wretched of the Earth*:

> I am ready to concede that on the plane of factual being the past existence of an Aztec civilization does not change anything very much in the diet of the Mexican peasant of today. I admit that all the proofs of a wonderful Songhai civilization will not change the fact that today the Songhais are underfed and illiterate, thrown between sky and water with empty heads and empty eyes. But it has been remarked several times that this passionate search for a national culture which existed before the colonial era finds its legitimate reason in the anxiety shared by native intellectuals to shrink away from that Western culture in which they all risk being swamped.[53]

Fanon shows that the impulse to recover a historical moment untainted by colonialism is a tool through which colonized intellectuals have resisted white supremacist ideologies and narratives that aim to "swamp" them, drowning their voices under the pressures of assimilation. However, in Cubena's novels, the turn to the past is not without contradictions.

Both *Chombo* and *Los nietos* make visible how Black people have played central roles in the building of American nations as well as in the history of Europe, facts that are silenced in Eurocentric historiographies. In the process, the novels construct a rich Afro-Latin American genealogy that reaches back to the Olmecs, one of the earliest known Mesoamerican civilizations. In the novels, Black people in the Americas, and West Indians in particular, are described as descendants of ancient Mesoamerican civilizations, African emperors, Africans who resisted and escaped slavery in the Americas, Black founders of USAmerican cities such as Luis Quintero, the cofounder of Los Angeles and Santa Barbara, as well as the small number of Africans who arrived in the Americas alongside the Spanish and aided colonization. Cubena frequently reminds us that enslaved Africans collectively resisted and posed a serious threat to the institution of slavery in the Americas. For example, in *Los nietos* Yanga is described as Mexico's most famous African and "el valiente cacique cimarrón que fundó el pueblo San Lorenzo de los Negros de Córdoba, en Veracruz" (the brave maroon chief who founded the town of San Lorenzo de los Negros in Cordoba, Veracruz).[54] In this way, the novels resist the white silencing of the central role that Black people, Black culture, and Black labor have played in the making of Latin American societies and Europe.

As it challenges racist logics, however, the retrospective gaze creates tensions in Cubena's works which reveal that the line between challenging and reproducing racist ideologies is sometimes tenuous. This becomes apparent if we consider that *Chombo* and *Los nietos* glorify Africans who participated in the conquest of Latin America. Juan Cortés, for example, is described as "uno de los africanos que acompañó al gran conquistador de los aztecas" (one of the Africans that accompanied the great conqueror of the Aztecs).[55] Maroons and African conquistadores will both take center stage in Cubena's third novel, *La misión secreta* (The Secret Mission, 2005), which also suggests that Africans played a significant role in the conquest of Latin America.[56] The inclusion of a rich Afrodiasporic genealogy for West Indian characters in all of Cubena's novels serves to reaffirm that Black people have a long history in Panama that precedes West Indian immigration. At the same time, the condemnation of slavery and critique of imperialism that the novels articulate are at odds with their simultaneous appraisal of empires as pinnacles of civilization and their valorization of colonialism itself, evident in the description of the Spanish colonizer Hernán Cortés as "the great conqueror of the Aztecs." The repeated references to "la gloriosa época de los imperios de Ghana, Mali y Songhay" (the glorious epoch of the empires of Ghana, Mali, and Songhai)[57] or "el gran imperio africano en Zimbabwe" (the great African empire in Zimbabwe)[58] further create tensions in Cubena's novels that attest to how restorative projects grounded in nationalism can reinscribe Eurocentric values. The paradoxes are immediately evident: How to reconcile the critique of imperialism, colonization, and slavery with the idealization

ESPOUSING LIBERAL INDIVIDUALISM IN CUBENA'S WORK

of African empires and representation of Africans who participated in colonial conquest as models of heroism that contemporary Black Panamanians should be proud of?

Contesting Racial Disavowal

Chombo and *Los nietos* forcefully oppose colorblind discourses that depict Latin American countries as racial El Dorados. With the aim to silence racism in their own nations, white people in Latin America often depict the United States as the sole cradle of racism in the Americas, arguing that US racism, as Peter Wade writes, is "'deep'—deeply rooted in the social fabric," while in Latin America "racism is said to be superficial—subordinate to class and based on mere phenotype, only 'skin deep.'"[59] Cubena's novels turn this dominant argument on its head and draw comparisons with the United States to argue the opposite: that racism is worse in Latin America than in the United States. In *Chombo*, the following dialogue between Litó and his mother illustrates this strategy:

> "Aquí nunca se va a permitir una organización racista como el Ku Klux Klan; aquí nunca habrá ahorcamiento de negros como en Mississippi; aquí nunca estallará una bomba dinamita asesina en una iglesia atestada de niñitas negras como un domingo en Alabama" [dijo la madre de Litó].
>
> "A decir la verdad–dijo el hijo–yo no sé cuál es peor: la bomba de dinamita o el mestizaje. Por todas partes dicen que hay que mejorar la raza, o sea, hay que blanquearse. Opino que este tipo de racismo es peor que la dinamita asesina porque el mestizaje es una muerte lenta, lentísima."[60]

> "Here they will never allow a racist organization like the Ku Klux Klan; here there will never be lynchings of Black people like in Mississippi; here an assassin dynamite bomb will never explode in a church full of little Black girls as [it happened during] a Sunday in Alabama" [Litó's mother said].
>
> "To be honest—the son said—I don't know what is worse: the dynamite bomb or mestizaje. Everywhere people say that one has to better the race, that is, one has to whiten. I believe that this type of racism is worse than the assassin dynamite because mestizaje is a slow, very slow, death."

208 DECOLONIAL IMAGINARIES AND COLORBLIND LOGICS

The argument that Litó's mother utters conjures the disavowal of racism at the heart of *El peligro antillano,* in which Alfaro insisted that racism does not exist in Latin American societies but is confined to the United States and other former British colonies. Through the opposition between "the dynamite bomb or mestizaje," Litó hints at how mestizaje is a tool of racial genocide. He also suggests that racism in Latin America is especially insidious because it hides its workings effectively. The opposition that Litó sets up highlights the specific challenges that come with confronting racism in Latin American societies.

In this regard, Cubena's works are aligned with those of Abdias Nascimento, who criticized how the demonization of the United States has bestowed upon Latin American nations a complacent sense of moral superiority that has contributed to entrenching the racist status quo. These positions contrast, for instance, with the stance held by Guillén, who wrote many poems that condemn racism against Black people in the United States (as in "Crecen altas las flores," "Escolares," "Está bien," or "Little Rock"), while his postrevolutionary oeuvre celebrated the alleged end of racial discrimination in his native Cuba (as in "Tengo," "Vine en un barco negrero," or "Se acabó").[61] In focusing only on the horrors of US racism, Guillén participated in the consolidation of a nationalistic discourse of racial democracy that situated racial oppression outside of Cuban borders. Cubena's works, by contrast, denounce racism *both* in his country and in the United States.

Critiquing racism in Latin America through comparisons with the United States nonetheless also opens up space for contradictions in Cubena's novels. The opposition between overt racist violence and mestizaje created in the quote above hints at how racial mixture in Latin America has been deployed in a similar way as "the dynamite bomb" in the United States. The methods differ, but the end goal of controlling and killing Black people remains the same. This binary opposition, however, also obscures the fact that overt racial violence is not the prerogative of the United States alone. In his desire to counter racial disavowal, Cubena erases overt racist violence from the Latin American sphere.

As they seek to call attention to the realities of racism that are often silenced in Latin America, Cubena's novels concurrently critique and idealize race relations in the United States. In *Los nietos,* a West Indian expatriate living in the United States called Simón writes a letter to his Panamanian grandmother:

ESPOUSING LIBERAL INDIVIDUALISM IN CUBENA'S WORK 209

> Lo bueno de por acá es el orden en todo, la facilidad para estudiar de día o de noche, la limpieza, los empleos que pagan bien. . . . Pero, el invierno con su frío es horrible. . . . Otro asunto muy desagradable por acá es la KKK. . . . Pero te voy a confesar algo, a pesar de todos los problemas acá hay esperanza de que la situación cambie y mejore para la gente decente . . . a decir verdad, este país es el menor de todos los males.[62]

> The good thing here is that there is order in everything, it's easy to study at night or during the day, it's clean, jobs pay well. . . . But the winter with its cold weather is horrible. . . . Another very unpleasant issue here is the KKK. . . . But I will confess something to you, despite all the problems, here there is hope that things will change and improve for the decent people . . . to tell you the truth, this country is the lesser of all evils.

Simón suggests that, all things considered, Black people have it better in the United States than in Panama. When asked why he spends so much time in the United States, Litó similarly answers in *Chombo*: "entre dos males, el menor" (it's the lesser of two evils).[63] In the passage above, Simón intimates that the United States is a meritocracy where it is easy for a Black person to climb the social ladder. While elsewhere overt racist violence is presented as emblematic of US race relations, here the KKK is trivialized and reduced to "another unpleasant issue" among many others, like the cold North American winters. In the process, the novel succumbs to the politics of respectability, made apparent through Simón's belief that in the United States "for the decent people" there is hope.

That Cubena's novels idealize race relations in the United States becomes more apparent in the following passage from *Los nietos*, in which the West Indian character Elsa Gordon contends that African Americans have achieved more in terms of racial equality than West Indians in Panama and Afro-Latin Americans in general. She affirms:

> [En los Estados Unidos] a pesar de Los Enmascarados, grupos de filosofía nazi, y la brutalidad de algunos policías, la gente de ascendencia africana tiene más y mejores oportunidades para triunfar, lo cual se le niega sutil y, con frecuencia, brutalmente fuera de los Estados Unidos. Pues, ¿en qué siglo tendremos un candidato chombo como presidente? Ya los afronorteamericanos tuvieron su Jesse Jackson.[64]

210   DECOLONIAL IMAGINARIES AND COLORBLIND LOGICS

> [In the United States] despite the KKK, groups that practice Nazi philosophy, and the brutality of some policemen, people of African descent have more and better opportunities to triumph, which are subtly, and frequently, brutally negated to them outside of the United States. In fact, in which century will we have a chombo [derog. for West Indian] candidate for president? African Americans already had their Jesse Jackson.

According to Elsa's logic, having a Black presidential candidate is a sign that things have improved for Black people in the United States, a fact belied by Barack Obama's presidency. As it disregards the actual experiences of Black Americans, Elsa's argument also echoes colorblind rhetorics that equate racism with prejudice. For Elsa, the problem is not that the police are a racist institution, but that "some policemen" happen to be brutal. In the attempt to call attention to racism in Panama through comparisons with the United States, the novel thus obfuscates the structural dimensions of racism.

Not only in the passage above but in the novel as a whole, racism is mainly represented as being synonymous with individual prejudice. This prejudice, in turn, is posited as being innate. In *Los nietos*, even white characters who have been adopted and raised within Black families, such as Carnaval and Diploma, end up despising Black people and leaving Panama to join the Nazi Party in Adolf Hitler's Germany. To further complicate matters, *Chombo* and *Los nietos* both include an imaginary myth about the origins of "white evil" that describes white people as freaks of nature and original sinners. In the myth, Kwafufo, described as "la más depravada oveja blanca de toda Africa negra" (the most depraved white sheep of all Black Africa), rapes his daughter Kwaikó, described as "una muchacha demente" (a demented girl), who later gives birth to an ancestral lineage of albino hermaphrodites without pinkie fingers.[65] These albinos are then all associated with the enslavement of Black people in a move that reinscribes both ableism and anti-Blackness.

Literary critic Sheila Carter has contended that Cubena's association of racism with "mental and moral degeneracy" suggests "the affirmation that racial hatred is evidence of irrational behavior."[66] Yet racism is not a matter of irrational behavior. In understanding racism as irrational and a question of individual prejudice, the novels reproduce colorblind logics. Viewing racism as irrational disconnects racism from social reality.[67] While racist white characters like Carnaval and Diploma simply

ESPOUSING LIBERAL INDIVIDUALISM IN CUBENA'S WORK 211

appear irrational, white people are actively invested in reproducing racism because of the material, political, psychological, and symbolic advantages that racism provides for us. White supremacy is a political system deliberately set up to maximize the collective advantages of white people through the collective dispossession of Black people and people of color. There is nothing irrational about it.

Coming Together

As Cubena's novels denounce racism, the principal solution to racialized conditions of existence that they advocate, alongside education, is unity among Black people. The importance of unity is immediately visible in *Los nietos*, which opens at a New York airport in an imagined future. It is 1999 and a group of West Indian expats awaits impatiently their return to Panama, where they will celebrate USAmericans handing over the Panama Canal. There is much chatter at the airport. Suddenly, someone utters a strange word: "sodinu," which is the Spanish word *unidos* (united) spelled backward.[68] The mysterious word *sodinu* reappears throughout the novel as the characters attempt to discover its meaning to no avail, a gesture which symbolizes the lack of unity that reigns between the Afro-Panamanian and the West Indian characters. This motif reflects larger political concerns in Cubena's thought. In an interview, Cubena addressed the importance he attributes to unity among Black people: "[We Black people] must recognize and accept our common identity, and the key word is respect and then UNITY. If we don't respect and accept ourselves unity will not be possible, and then the slow death will continue in the 'favelas,' in the Chorrillos, and in all the ghettoes around the world."[69] Yet in Cubena's novels unity translates into an enforced homogeneity that is in conflict with the author's agenda of fostering unity between Afro-Panamanians and West Indians in particular.

Rather than envisioning spaces where Black solidarity can thrive, the works insist on viewing West Indians as the sole victims of racism in Panama and as embodying an emancipatory Blackness that the Afro-Panamanian characters must one-sidedly emulate in order for racism to be undermined. In the process, the novels display a discrepancy in the representation of West Indian and Afro-Panamanian characters. Cubena aims to challenge negative stereotypes about West Indians, but the means that he employs to achieve this goal reinscribe racialized,

212   DECOLONIAL IMAGINARIES AND COLORBLIND LOGICS

gendered, and sexual hierarchies rather than challenging the divide-and-conquer tactics of white nationalism. The West Indian characters have realistic names, such as Litó, Nenén, Victor, and James Duglin; they are represented as virtuous, articulate, proud, and knowledgeable; and they are the principal victims of racial discrimination. They are also middle class and well educated. Litó is a brilliant young man educated in the prestigious Instituto Nacional, his sister Chabela is a professional nurse, and his brother Victor is a medical doctor. By contrast, the Afro-Panamanian characters have mocking names, such as Fulabuta Simeñíquez, Karafula Barrescoba, Bolanieve Barrescoba, and Carbón Barrescoba/Mierdsié Leblancú (all telling names in Spanish, several of which evoke the characters' desire to be white); they are given a flat characterization; are ridiculed as self-hating, cruel, ignorant, irrational, and sexually deviant; and are perpetrators of anti-West Indian hatred.

This negative and grotesque characterization typifies virtually all Afro-Panamanian characters, who are problematically depicted as self-hating "racists." For example, Fulabuta Simeñíquez is a fanatical member of the right-wing Patriotic Party, is proud that her five children are all fathered by white US soldiers, and engages in frequent verbal abuse against West Indian characters.[70] Fulabuta's husband Arnulfo (a reference to former Panamanian president Arnulfo Arias, responsible for passing the Constitution that in 1941 denied citizenship to non-Spanish speaking Black people) reads Hitler's *Mein Kampf*, dreams of becoming Panama's Führer, and proposes the establishment of concentration camps for West Indians. Karafula Barrescoba, who appears both in *Chombo* and *Los nietos*, vehemently despises West Indians, obsessively applies powder to her face so as to appear white, and names her five dolls Nievita, Lechita, Marfilita, Albita, and Espumita, all telling names that reference whiteness.[71]

Afro-Panamanians are consistently portrayed as perpetrators of racism and never as its victims. This colorblind move places the blame for racism onto its victims and silences the fact that racism is not synonymous with prejudice, but requires the control of social and political institutions for its reproduction, a control that Afro-Panamanians do not have. As they conflate racism and prejudice, the novels thus problematically suggest that Black people *can* be racist. Offering valuable insights into the operations of racism, Andile Mngxitama writes, "Essentially, blacks, by virtue of their historically evolved positionality, can't be racist. Racism is a concept which seeks to both describe and explain how whites have come to oppress and dominate blacks. Properly conceived, racism

ESPOUSING LIBERAL INDIVIDUALISM IN CUBENA'S WORK   213

locates white power and privilege on the historical reality organised upon white-on-black violence (slavery, colonialism, imperialism)."[72] Cubena's novels nonetheless depict Afro-Panamanians as fundamentally racist, while the racism that white people wage against them is rendered invisible.

In the attempt to critique Black complicity with anti-Blackness, Cubena's novels reproduce the anti-Blackness that they aim to challenge. In an interview, Cubena denounced what he views as Afro-Panamanians' complicity with racism, which is also thematized in his novels, stating: "Some Latinos of African descent . . . are often times collaborators in the spread and propaganda of racist ideas, racial stereotypes, and historical misconceptions with regard to Afro-Hispanics. They have contributed very much to the 'divide et impera' practice that has kept oppressed groups divided and subservient."[73] Cubena here echoes Fanon's sentiment that "the enemy of the Negro is often not the white man but a man of his own color."[74] In Cubena's novels, however, the representation of Afro-Panamanians as principal perpetrators of racism takes responsibility away from white people, the actual chief culprits for the maintenance of white supremacy in Panama. What further complicates Cubena's treatment of intraracial conflict is his understanding that Afro-Panamanians are preventing "national unity." Rather than questioning national unity as a viable category for Black liberation, Cubena upholds it as the highest value. The discourse of national unity also remains firmly in place in his novels, which romanticize the nation as a site of emancipatory politics. Instead of undoing the racist terms of engagement, then, Cubena reverses them: it is not West Indians who hinder national unity in Panama, but Afro-Panamanians.

This reversal is emblematic of the larger representational strategies that Cubena's novels deploy to contest anti–West Indian propaganda. The works attempt to denaturalize positive associations with whiteness and negative association with Blackness (that is, West Indian Blackness). The novels endow white people, and whiteness itself, with the demeaning characteristics that white people have attributed to Black people and Blackness. Although this strategy allows Cubena to render stereotypes visible, it does not challenge stereotypes per se. Instead, it remains trapped within the Manichean allegory, which Abdul R. Jan-Mohamed defines as "a field of diverse yet inter-changeable oppositions between white and black, good and evil, superiority and inferiority, civilization and savagery, intelligence and emotion, rationality and sensuality, self and Other, subject and object."[75] By depicting characters

214 DECOLONIAL IMAGINARIES AND COLORBLIND LOGICS

as good and evil according to their race, Cubena merely inverts the racial hierarchy without undoing the symbolic power that defines these elements in their binary relations. To further complicate matters, white and Afro-Panamanian characters are generally endowed with other negative attributes besides racial prejudice, such as alcoholism and drug consumption. The novels also stigmatize Afro-Panamanian characters by associating them with promiscuity, pedophilia, rape, incest, or prostitution. Anita Gallers argues that this allows Cubena to construct racism itself as a perversion.[76] However, white supremacy is not an individual perversion. It is, as Charles Mills writes, a "political system."[77] While associations with drug use or sexual deviancy are intended to enhance the characters' despicability, they deflect the reader's attention away from racism. These associations also stigmatize and criminalize sex work by placing it in proximity to rape or pedophilia.

Whereas Afro-Panamanian characters are represented as sexually deviant, West Indian characters are divested of any sexual desire in the novels. Cubena through this strategy contends with the fact that white people have projected onto Black people their own sexual fears and desires, so that racism operates, as Toni Morrison writes, through "the transference to blackness of the power of illicit sexuality, chaos, madness, impropriety, strangeness, and helpless, hapless desire."[78] In response to these racist projections, Cubena's novels attempt to delink Blackness from the racist myth that Black people, in Fanon's terms, "have tremendous sexual powers."[79] Building on Fanon, Darieck Scott writes in *Extravagant Abjection* that "Negrophobia is essentially a sexual phobia, because blackness is primarily associated in Western (and Western-influenced) cultures with perverse, nonnormative sexuality."[80] Seeking to destabilize the sexual phobia that structures anti-Blackness, Cubena does not provide any physical descriptions of West Indian characters, especially of women, a strategy that Fanon employs in his own work. What renders Cubena's move questionable is that these representational strategies are confined solely to West Indian characters, while Afro-Panamanians are portrayed as hypersexual so that, to cite Roberto Strongman in a different context, Black people are "rendered as hypersexual degenerates."[81] Despite Cubena's intentions, the works ultimately end up tethering Blackness to sexual deviance.

Cubena's fictional works also deploy nonnormative genders and sexualities as a strategy to further stigmatize both white and Afro-Panamanian characters. Homosexuality is made to stand in for immorality as it is deployed in the same way that the novels mobilize alcoholism or pedophilia. The works are replete with homophobic epithets and associations between homosexuality and degeneracy.[82] In Cubena's short story "La Depravada" (The Depraved), the relationship between depravity and homosexuality is already established in the title, which refers to Genevieve, the Californian protagonist who leaves her lover Obtalá Cubena, an autobiographical character, for a European woman. In *Chombo*, homosexuality is associated with criminal behavior, sexual harassment, and pedophilia. In *Los nietos*, Lesbiaquiña (the name is a compound of the words *lesbian* and *white*), an Afro-Panamanian woman who has a white USAmerican lover, is brutally decapitated in an act of poetic justice as the autobiographical character Litó rejoices at the news of her death. In the same novel, AIDS is defined as "la enfermedad de los maricones" (the illness of faggots),[83] LGBTQ people are accused of having spread the disease, and Felicidad Dolores, who symbolizes Africa, considers AIDS to be "el último castigo de orixa Omolú para muchos de los descendientes de los que cobardemente permitieron que los navíos negreros zarparan de la costa africana con millares de niñas y niños africanos" (the last curse of the orisha Omolú for many of the descendants of those people who cowardly permitted that slave ships leave the African coast with thousands of children).[84] These associations rest upon the assumption that the reader agrees with Cubena's understanding of homosexuality as a perversion. If the reader does not, they might be inclined to read the works for what they can teach us about the ways that regressive gender and sexual politics are bound to reproduce regressive racial politics. As the works conflate Blackness with heterosexuality, they silence the very existence of a Black LGBTQ community. The assumption is that only heterosexual Black people are "authentically Black," that there is such a thing as racial authenticity, and that West Indians are the only Black people in Panama who hold the key to it.

Climbing the Social Ladder

Having been unwilling to construct a fictional world in which Afro-Panamanians and West Indians are equally burdened by racism and work together in solidarity to overcome it, *Los nietos* nonetheless ends with a letter announcing that Afro-Latinos have finally, almost magically, come together: "Por fin, nosotros, los nietos de Felicidad Dolores nos hemos organizado. Sí, los afrolatinos estamos **UNIDOS**" (Finally, we, the grandchildren of Felicidad Dolores, have organized ourselves. Yes, we Afro-Latinos are **UNITED**).[85] Reiterating the importance of achieving unity, the letter makes a final call to Black people in Panama and Latin America more broadly, this time exhorting them to work toward "Progress Through Education."[86] The phrase, written in English in the original text, is repeated several times throughout the novel. In this particular paragraph, the phrase is attributed to George Westerman (1910–1988), an influential Panamanian intellectual of West Indian descent. Previously, the slogan is mentioned in relation to a professor of Latin who teaches in a Catholic school. This reveals that "education" here must be understood as formal education, especially higher education, which both *Chombo* and *Los nietos* depict as intrinsically liberatory. The novels thus reproduce colorblind logics that locate the ultimate goal of antiracism in the individual, behavioral sphere. Remember how in the "ESCUDO CUBENA" (Cubena Shield) that opens both novels, the book (a symbol of education) is counterpoised to slavery and its ongoing legacies. The book is not described as a tool that serves to combat the legacies of slavery at a structural level, but as the principal means to combat "mental slavery." Neither is mental slavery posited as a means to a larger end, as a method whose aim, to cite Biko, is "to completely transform the system."[87] Overcoming mental slavery here becomes an end in itself, so that the problem in Cubena's formulation is not structural racism, but Black people's own behaviors and attitudes.

Through their emphasis on education, the novels advocate for behavioral changes in Black individuals, rather than for the abolition of the racist infrastructure. In *Chombo*, Afro-Panamanians desire white partners and white children as a way to experience greater proximity to whiteness. The Afro-Panamanian character Fulabuta Simeñíquez is ridiculed for attempting to "whiten" herself by having a relationship with a white USAmerican. The West Indian characters criticize this behavior and contend that Black people should "mejorar la raza negra por medio de la educación—la única manera—y no por el racista e irracional mestizaje como aconsejaba Fulabuta Simeñíquez" (improve the Black race through education—the only way—and not through the racist and irrational mestizaje as Fulabuta Simeñíquez advised).[88] The emphasis on education as a way to "improve the Black race" presupposes that Black people need improvement. The opposition between "mestizaje" and "education" constructed in the novels meanwhile fails to consider the extent to which the two do not exist in opposition as missionary schools institutionalized precisely "mental slavery." The education system, like mestizaje, has been a racist tool in the hands of the white supremacist state used to assimilate Black and colonized people and divest them of their history, beliefs, and the means of resistance that they entail. Cubena's novels carry on this assimilationist project.

This becomes evident through the works' paradoxical treatment of Euro-American culture. As we saw, Fanon argues that the pursuit of a national culture that existed before colonialism is motivated by the desire on the part of colonized intellectuals "to shrink away from that Western culture in which they all risk being swamped."[89] However, the inclusion of African history and mythology in Cubena's works does not preclude a valorization of Western culture. *Chombo*, *Los nietos*, and several short stories are infused with frequent references to European literary texts, music, and art. In the short story "La Depravada" (The Depraved), the autobiographical protagonist Obatalá Cubena is a highly educated and well-traveled medical doctor who has studied at the most prestigious US universities and is a great admirer of European philosophy, literature, and classical music. Similarly, in "La fiesta" (The Party), Cubena is a young writer who is proud of having read *Don Quijote* three times in one year and challenges his white US colleagues into naming the inventors of the telephone, television or airplane. Richard Jackson contends that "in this story the author with gentle humor chides customs of some of his American associates, while at the same time showing off, as he does in several of his stories, his erudition of which he is justly proud."[90] The West Indian characters in *Los nietos*, too, display with pride their knowledge about a vast array of European artists: they read Victor Hugo's *Les Misérables*, enjoy Tchaikovsky's music, and appreciate Leonardo da Vinci's artwork.

Through these characters' erudition, which is made to contrast sharply with the "ignorance" of Afro-Panamanians, Cubena challenges racist discourses that depict West Indians as unassimilated and essentially unrefined. In the process, the works do not question the validity of Eurocentric notions of knowledge and cultural refinement per se. Instead, they reinscribe Euromodernity, which Lewis R. Gordon describes as "the constellation of convictions, arguments, policies, and a worldview promoting the idea that the only way legitimately to belong to the present and as a consequence the future is to be or become European."[91] Euromodernity, according to Gordon, confines Black people either to the past or to what Fanon calls "a zone of nonbeing."[92] In this light, it acquires great significance that the Africa that Cubena's

218   DECOLONIAL IMAGINARIES AND COLORBLIND LOGICS

works portray is trapped in the past, engulfed in imperial nostalgia, while Euro-American culture is depicted as the way to the future. By insinuating that West Indians are "finos" and knowledgeable because they are well versed in European art or literature, the works reify Euro-centric constructions of finesse and sophistication as being intrinsically linked to Western intellectualism. European traditions are ultimately valued as the summit of universal culture that Black characters need to master.

The dichotomic representation of virtuous West Indians struggling against villainous Afro-Panamanians has ironic consequences given that the West Indian characters' knowledge of Euro-American culture is depicted as a positive attribute, while Afro-Panamanian characters are derided for desiring whiteness. Afro-Panamanian characters are scorned and branded as blanqueados (whitened), yet the West Indian characters display their extensive knowledge of European culture with pride. While Cubena's works contest ideologies of whitening and mes-tizaje, then, they also reinforce hegemonic notions of identity, culture, history, and sexuality, failing "to move the terms of the debate beyond the binary of inferiority/superiority and Black/white."[93] The reader is inclined to perceive the Afro-Panamanian characters as being "ignorant" not only because they ignore, or refuse to acknowledge, their African heritage, but also because they do not know the difference between Picasso and Verdi. Yet assuming that the Afro-Panamanian characters actually "learned their lesson," would education—the pillar of Cubena's antiracist project—render them more tolerant? The works' conceptual-ization of racial prejudice as innate excludes this possibility.

Cubena's works reveal how antiracist projects grounded in liberal individualism and heteropatriarchy are bound to replicate the values of whiteness. The representation of West Indian immigrants as hard-working patriots invested in self-betterment and education achieves a valorization of a marginalized group that continues to be discrimi-nated against in Panama. But it also reproduces the ideology of the self-regulating subject, the individual who can freely choose their own destiny, giving ammunition to colorblind arguments that depict West-ern societies as meritocracies. What the works advocate is not a radical dismantlement of the racist infrastructure, but the reform of Black individuals who are exhorted to pull themselves up by their prover-bial bootstraps and "mejorar la raza negra por medio de la educación" (improve the Black race through education).[94] This sustains the myth

ESPOUSING LIBERAL INDIVIDUALISM IN CUBENA'S WORK   219

that undoing racism and anti-Blackness is a question of individual work ethic and educational achievement, rather than a question of ending the world as we know it.

Other scholars have viewed Cubena's works as existing in opposition to those of Afro-Panamanian writers such as Beleño who, according to Watson, "chose a nationalistic and imperialistic agenda over a racial one."[95] However, Cubena's novels also privilege national solidarity over racial solidarity and remain indebted to the nationalist, imperialistic, and heteropatriarchal ideologies that informed the work of his literary predecessor. They celebrate colonial conquest, Eurocentrism, and assimilation into the nation-state, even as they also confront the anti-Blackness and white supremacy intrinsic to these racial projects. Cubena's insistence on locating value and self-consciousness solely within a specific Black community (West Indian) and a particular kind of Blackness (heterosexual, patriotic, middle class, and well versed in Anglo-European culture) has ironic dimensions. His preoccupation with unity among people of African descent translates into a monolithic vision of Blackness that not only collapses Blackness and heterosexuality, excluding LGBTQ people from the Black community Cubena envisions, but also fails to value the struggles and experiences of Afro-Panamanians. As Cubena's works reinscribe an African presence into the history and racial heritage of the Panamanian nation, they concurrently marginalize and appropriate Afro-Panamanian history to challenge racist representations of West Indians as being the only Black people in Panama. At the same time, they ironically also represent West Indians as the sole bearers of an "authentic" Blackness. In doing so, they reproduce an epistemology of disavowal as Blackness in Cubena's fiction is not the condition of being "overdetermined from without,"[96] as Fanon puts it, but something that only some Black people *have*.

6

Encountering the Other in Chicana Literature

Through our multi-layered experiences as mestizas, women of color, working-class and gay people we claim multicultural education as a centerpiece of the mestiza nation. In 1920 José Vasconcelos, a Mexican philosopher, envisioned a mestizo nation, a cosmic race, a fifth race embracing the four major races of the world. We are creating ways of educating ourselves and younger generations in this mestiza nation to change how students and teachers think and read by de-constructing Euro-Anglo ways of knowing; to create texts that reflect the needs of the world community of women and people of color; and to show how lived experience is connected to political struggles and art making.
 —Gloria Anzaldúa, "The New Mestiza Nation:
  A Multicultural Movement"

In this country, lesbianism is a poverty—as is being brown, as is being a woman, as is being just plain poor. The danger lies in ranking the oppressions. *The danger lies in failing to acknowledge the specificity of the oppression.*
 —Cherríe Moraga, "La Güera"

In "The New Mestiza Nation: A Multicultural Movement," an essay based on a talk delivered at St. Olaf College in 1992, Gloria Anzaldúa reclaims a space that validates her experiences as a queer woman of color in academia. As she condemns academia for being a bastion of white supremacy and endeavoring to use her as a token, Anzaldúa warns intellectuals of color against using the same hegemonic "theories, concepts, and assumptions" that were created to subjugate colonized

221

peoples.[1] Critiquing US multiculturalism for homogenizing and erasing the histories of people of color, Anzaldúa resists neoconservative mystifications that posit white people as injured and people of color as powerful. In contrast with dominant US multiculturalism, the multiculturalism that Anzaldúa envisions is grounded in her lived experiences of racial oppression and makes visible the complex ways that race, class, gender, and sexuality intersect and define inequality. At the same time, Anzaldúa's reliance on José Vasconcelos's theory of mestizaje for her own theorization of the Chicana subject as mestiza speaks both to the insidiousness of colorblindness and to its malleability as the master's tools are constantly redeployed to create resistant counternarratives.

Chicana writers' embracing of a mestiza identity grounded in the affirmation of indigeneity is a consequence of the forced displacement of Indigenous people produced by European and US colonialisms. While it arises from deep and noble impulses, a reliance on indigenist aesthetics creates paradoxes in Chicana literary imaginaries that reveal a disjunction between the politics advocated in Chicana feminist theory and the content of Chicana literary practice. I argue that, as they provide powerful critiques of colonialism and heteropatriarchy, Chicana indigenist imaginaries that blur the boundaries between the Chicanx self and the Indigenous Other also reproduce the logics of white feminism and dominant multiculturalism that they contest and reinscribe a pernicious anti-Blackness. I examine these paradoxes in this chapter not to discredit Chicana feminism, but rather to illustrate the importance of using the generative insights of Chicana feminism to more fully theorize the intersectional and relational dimensions of racial subordination.

In interrogating Chicana indigenist imaginaries, I do not mean to suggest that Chicana literature is monolithic. Neither do I intend to question Chicanx indigeneity per se. The term *indigenism*, according to Guisela Latorre, refers to consciously adopting an Indigenous identity for political purposes, while *indigeneity* indicates expressions that derive organically from an immersion in Indigenous communities.[2] Chicanx identity, Latorre argues, exists at the intersection of indigenism and indigeneity. However, here I employ the terms indigenism and indigenist imaginary not to refer to Chicanx identity, but to specifically describe aesthetic and discursive formations within Chicanx literature and theory in which Indigenous people, stories, traditions, symbols, and myths figure centrally.

Black and Chicana feminists have taken white feminists to task for being chief agents of white supremacy. Critiquing the exclusionary

ENCOUNTERING THE OTHER IN CHICANA LITERATURE

practices of the white women who organized the 1979 Second Sex Conference, Audre Lorde argued that "it is a particular academic arrogance to assume any discussion of feminist theory without examining our many differences, and without a significant input from poor women, Black and Third World women, and lesbians."[3] Lorde here points to the white feminist fallacy of obscuring differences between women and insisting on what Chela Sandoval will later call "a unified female subject."[4] Offering further crucial insights into the gendered workings of racial power, Kimberlé Crenshaw argues that conflating differences between women is especially problematic in the context of gender-based violence, "fundamentally because the violence that many women experience is often shaped by other dimensions of their identities, such as race and class."[5] Crenshaw first developed the theory of intersectionality in "Demarginalizing the Intersection of Race and Sex: A Black Feminist Critique of Antidiscrimination Doctrine, Feminist Theory and Antiracist Politics" (1989), where she shows that, as legal racial discrimination cases tend to privilege the experiences of Black men and sex discrimination cases center the experiences of white women, the law marginalizes the experiences of Black women, who are burdened by multiple oppressions.[6] Simply including Black women in the structure of analysis that already exists does not resolve the problem, Crenshaw contends, because "the intersectional experience is greater than the sum of racism and sexism," so that analyses which do not consider intersectionality fail to grasp the complex ways in which Black women are subordinated.[7] In the epigraph, Cherríe Moraga also contends that a decolonial feminist practice requires attentiveness to differential oppression, not as a way to engage in an Olympics of oppression, which Moraga rejects, but because social movements cannot be productively built without acknowledging "*the specificity of the oppression*."[8] It is in light of arguments about the importance of centering differences between women developed within Black and Chicana feminisms that I interrogate Chicana indigenist imaginaries. While in the previous chapter I showed how regressive gender and sexual politics undermine the antiracist agenda of Cubena's works, here I call attention to how the seemingly progressive gender and sexual politics of Chicana indigenism display an alliance to dominant ontologies and epistemologies grounded in anti-Indigeneity and anti-Blackness.

Chicanx indigenism cannot be understood outside the history of racialized oppression to which Chicanxs have been subjected in the United States. With the 1848 Treaty of Guadalupe Hidalgo that settled the Mexican-American War, the United States seized a vast portion of

Mexico's northern territories, including what are today the US states of California, Arizona, New Mexico, Texas, and parts of Colorado. The treaty formally protected the rights of Mexicans living in the annexed territories, such as the right to keep land and property. However, US legislators violated the treaty, arguing that Mexicans were Indians and therefore did not deserve the rights of white citizens.[9] The white supremacist assault against people of Mexican descent continued relentlessly in the twentieth century as Chicanx pupils, for example, were also forced to attend segregated schools like African American children.[10]

Mobilizing against the racial discrimination that shaped their social existence, during the 1969 National Chicano Youth Liberation Conference in Denver, Colorado, a group of young Chicanx intellectuals, against the backdrop of the Chicano Movement, produced the groundbreaking document *El Plan Espiritual de Aztlán* (The Spiritual Plan of Aztlán). Accompanied by a program advocating "economic, cultural and political independence," *El Plan* brought to light pressing problems that affected the Chicanx community, from racism to economic exploitation.[11] It also emphasized self-determination, defined nationalism as central to collective organizing, and reclaimed a Chicanx Indigenous identity shadowed by centuries of Spanish and Anglo domination. In *El Plan*, Chicanx students declared: "With our heart in our hands and our hands in the soil, we declare the independence of our mestizo nation. We are a bronze people with a bronze culture. Before the world, before all of North America, before all our brothers in the bronze continent, we are a nation, we are a union of free pueblos, we are *Aztlán*."[12] In defining *gabachos* as occupiers and foreigners in North America, *El Plan* refused the Anglo-American definition of "native" as synonymous with white that confines Chicanxs to the status of foreigners. The references to "La Raza" (The Race) and "La Raza de Bronce" (The Bronze Race), which in *El Plan* signify Chicanxs as a people and revolutionary agents, derive from Vasconcelos's *La raza cósmica* and signal the continuity between Mexican and Chicanx nationalisms.

Notably, the proclamation of a "bronze continent" and "mestizo nation" that animates *El Plan* does not include an affirmation of Blackness. Even as the Chicano Movement was inspired by the Black Power Movement, Chicanx mestizaje was contingent on a recovery of indigeneity and on discourses of sovereignty that excluded people of African descent from the imagined Chicanx "mestizo nation," replicating the exclusion of Blackness that defined Mexican indigenismo. The

ENCOUNTERING THE OTHER IN CHICANA LITERATURE

disavowal of Blackness that animates *El Plan*, and the construction of Chicanx mestizaje in the works examined in this chapter, support Jared Sexton's argument that "any politics of resurgence and recovery is bound to regard the slave as the position of the unthought."[13] Within "the union of free pueblos" there is no space for Black people, even as enslaved Africans were precisely the people who "plant the seeds, water the fields, and gather the crops." Within Aztlán, the primordial home of the Aztecs that Chicanxs claimed as their own, Black USAmericans and Black Mexicans are both relegated to the realm of the unthought, disappeared in a mestizaje that, to some extent, evokes the "browning" logics of eugenicist theorizations of mestizaje discussed in chapter 2.

While *El Plan* was unable to envision Black people as members of the Chicanx community, it propelled a recovery of ancient Mesoamerican mythology as Chicanxs turned to the past to understand and confront racial struggles in the present. Myth functioned as a cohesive force for Chicanxs and operated in conjunction with history to generate what Lee Bebout calls *mythohistorical interventions*, namely "the seizing of historical agency to refashion the world and the ways in which experience is ordered."[14] Making such an intervention, *El Plan* reconceptualized the US territory by defining Anglos as occupiers in the United States and explicitly claiming Aztlán as the Chicano homeland.[15] Prior to the Chicano Movement, Mexican Americans had largely rejected their Indigenous roots and had privileged their Spanish heritage.[16] The Chicano Movement produced the reverse as the turn to the Indigenous evident in Chicano Movement art and literature represented a rejection of Eurocentrism and USAmerican cultural imperialism.[17] Rafael Pérez-Torres writes that "the logic used in the nineteenth century to dispossess the Mexican in the United States would become one of the strategic arguments mustered to stake a claim for inclusion in the twentieth. Chicanos became Natives. Identification with the Indian gave birth to a Chicano/a critical subaltern identity in solidarity with other Indigenous groups throughout the Americas."[18] Forsaken by Mexico and marginalized in the United States, Chicanxs found in their Aztec ancestors, and to a smaller extent in the Maya, a highly sophisticated culture whose military, artistic, and architectural achievements surpassed that of Europe and other Mesoamerican civilizations. Privileging the Aztec and the Maya as ancestors, of course, was not a gesture free of contradictions since it valorized militaristic cultures and mirrored romanticizing approaches to Indigenous peoples that characterized hegemonic mestizaje in post-revolutionary Mexico.

By privileging an Aztec lineage, Chicanxs paradoxically celebrated an imperialistic civilization that also subjugated other peoples by exercising military and technological dominance.[19]

Chicanx indigenism has been accompanied by self-reflexivity since its early days. The commitment to Indigenous mythology and assertation of an Indigenous identity have been neither uniform nor unchallenged among Chicanx artists and intellectuals. Already during the Chicano Movement some argued that the return to myth was counterproductive. In the words of Francisco A. Lomelí, "The Chicano Movement, then, split into two: those who resorted to myth for grounding a foundational cultural identity and those who regarded myth as a useless vehicle of distraction from hard social issues."[20] According to Rudolfo Anaya, some Chicanxs argued that they did not need ancient stories but "direct political mobilization, perhaps revolution."[21] In his novel *Heart of Aztlán* (1976), however, Anaya portrays mythology as important for organized political action. Critiques that focus on the relationship between Chicanx indigeneity and Native American communities also have a long history. In the late 1970s, Ricardo Sánchez argued that Chicano Movement indigenism relied on a limited contact with living Indigenous peoples. He criticized the poet Alurista for romanticizing Indigenous peoples in his poetry and for being "so hot on indigenismo," but failing to attend a conference on the Navajo reservation although he had tickets. Sánchez bitingly wondered if Alurista feared Indigenous people "born of blood and fetal flesh" because they are not perfect and angelic.[22]

The critique of Chicano Movement indigenism has perhaps nowhere been articulated as compellingly as in Chicana feminism, which in part emerged in response to the heteropatriarchy of the Chicano Movement.[23] In the manifesto "Queer Aztlán: The Reformation of the Chicano Tribe" (2001), Moraga criticized the invocation of Aztlán as the Chicanx homeland for having benefited only heterosexual men while relegating Chicanas to the traditional roles of mothers and wives. She also faulted Chicano nationalists for disregarding differences among Chicanxs as a commitment to heteropatriarchy produced exclusionary constructions of Chicanx identity. Moraga writes:

> In reaction against Anglo-America's emasculation of Chicano men, the male dominated Chicano Movement embraced the most patriarchal aspects of its Mexican heritage. For a generation, nationalist leaders used a kind of 'selective memory,' drawing exclusively from those aspects of Mexican and Native

cultures that served the interests of male heterosexuals. At times, they took the worst of Mexican machismo and Aztec warrior bravado, combined it with some of the most oppressive male-conceived idealizations of 'traditional' Mexican womanhood and called that cultural integrity.[24]

Chicana writers have de-romanticized the Chicano Movement pantheon by reinterpreting Mesoamerican mythology in a feminist light and exposing those aspects of Aztec and Maya cultures that oppressed women. Yet "a kind of 'selective memory'" also informs Chicana indigenism, which both challenges and reproposes the problematic relationship to Indigenous peoples that characterize Mexican and Chicano indigenisms.

Chicana indigenist imaginaries exhibit surrogate "Indian" characters who empower the Chicana protagonists, enable reflections on Chicana subjectivity and history, facilitate the construction of a Chicana Indigenous genealogy, and make possible a powerful critique of heteropatriarchy. Producing knowledge that is also relevant to the literary works examined herein, Toni Morrison argues in *Playing in the Dark* that an Africanist presence pervades white US literary imaginaries. She contends that Africanist characters in works by white US authors act as enablers and surrogates. Africanist figures in these texts are not included to critique anti-Black racism; rather, they are instruments that allow white writers to reflect upon their own identity, longings, and desires. In Morrison's own words, "The fabrication of an Africanist persona is reflective; an extraordinary meditation on the self; a powerful exploration of the fears and desires that reside within the writerly conscious."[25] In constructing Africanist characters, Morrison shows, white writers rely on several "techniques of 'othering,'" including "metaphoric condensation, fetishizing strategies, the economy of the stereotype, allegorical foreclosure."[26] In sharp contrast with the white US literature that Morrison examines, Chicana indigenist imaginaries disrupt the language of white supremacy. Yet they also rely on various "techniques of 'othering'" in representing *both* Black and Indigenous people. Albeit less frequently than Indigenous characters, Black characters also appear in Chicana literature as backdrops that are instrumental to the construction of a Chicana identity. I contend that both an Africanist and an Indigenist presence haunts Chicana indigenist imaginaries.

My assessment of Chicana indigenism is indebted to the work of scholars who have previously offered poignant critiques of the paradoxes

228 DECOLONIAL IMAGINARIES AND COLORBLIND LOGICS

that inform it. One of the first scholars to systematically unearth the Eurocentric logics animating Chicanx literature that represents Indigenous myths and people, Sheila Marie Contreras argues in *Blood Lines* that Chicanx indigenism "relies upon an already established signifying order, one launched by the narratives of travel and exploration and later professionalized in the consolidation of anthropology as an academic discipline."[27] Contreras shows that, as Chicanx indigenism often remains indebted to dominant ways of acquiring knowledge about Indigenous cultures (i.e. mainly through the archives of anthropology and archaeology), it reproduces some of the colonial logics and representational strategies that it attempts to disrupt. In Contreras's terms, "Even as Chicana/o indigenist discourse puts forth its critiques of racial domination, colonial violence, and land removal, it remains embedded within the very 'circuits' of knowledge and power that have advanced imperialist agendas."[28] Chicanx indigenism, Contreras contends, both disrupts and reinscribes a representation of Indigenous peoples grounded in primitivism and mythologization.[29]

In an earlier essay, María Josefina Saldaña-Portillo critiques Chicana indigenism for reproducing liberal logics. She writes that Anzaldúa's "model of representation" in *Borderlands/La Frontera: The New Mestiza* (1987) "mirrors liberal models of choice that privilege her position as a US Chicana: she goes through her backpack and decides what to keep and what to throw out, and she chooses to keep signs of Indigenous identity as ornamentation and spiritual revival."[30] While Anzaldúa responded to this critique that she felt Saldaña-Portillo had misread or not read enough of her work, she conceded:

> I claim a mestizaje (mixed-blood, mixed culture) identity. In participating in this dialogue I fear violating Indian cultural boundaries. I'm afraid that what I say may unwittingly contribute to the misappropriation of Native cultures, that I (and other Chicanas) will inadvertently contribute to the cultural erasure, silencing, invisibility, racial stereotyping, and disenfranchisement of people who live in real Indian bodies. I'm afraid that Chicanas may unknowingly help the dominant culture remove Indians from their specific tribal identities and histories. . . . I hate that a lot of us Chicanas/os have Eurocentric assumptions about indigenous traditions. We do to Indian cultures what museums do—impose western attitudes, categories, and terms by decontextualizing objects, symbols and isolating them,

disconnecting them from their cultural meaning and intentions, and then reclassifying them within western terms and contexts.[31]

Chicana indigenist imaginaries, Anzaldúa self-critically suggests, reproduce pastiche aesthetics that "remove Indians from their specific tribal identities and histories." The reference to "people who live in real Indian bodies" makes clear that Anzaldúa considered her own relationship to indigeneity precarious and perceived her positionality as being different from that of "real" (her word) Indigenous people. This recognition, however, did not prevent Anzaldúa from conflating a mestiza and Indigenous subjectivity in her work. In her critique of multiculturalism, Anzaldúa emphasizes that "Others can't be lumped together, our issues collapsed, our differences erased."[32] Literary imaginaries that confound the Chicanx self and the Indigenous Other nevertheless collapse differences among Indigenous peoples, disguise hierarchies of power, and provide limited spaces for theorizing a Chicanx responsibility for "cultural erasure, silencing, invisibility, racial stereotyping, and disenfranchisement of people who live in real Indian bodies."

To illustrate these arguments, this chapter examines two important works of Chicana literature that at first might appear to have little in common beyond their parallel concern with Chicana indigenenity and references to the Zapatista Movement: Graciela Limón's novel *Erased Faces* (2001) and Cherríe Moraga's play *The Hungry Woman: A Mexican Medea* (2001). In attending to Indigenous struggles outside US borders and envisioning transnational Chicana-indígena alliances, *Erased Faces* makes an original contribution to Chicanx and hemispheric American literature.[33] Critiquing Anzaldúa for confining the Indigenous to a mythological past in *Borderlands/La Frontera*, Saldaña-Portillo argues that "the indígena . . . demands new representational models that include her among the living."[34] *Erased Faces* offers precisely such a new representational model, as the living Indigenous subject is central to Limón's narrative. And yet, the novel also revives old colonial tropes of travel, spiritual awakening, and white saviorism. The metaphysical journey into the Mexican jungle undergone by the protagonist Adriana Mora, an Afro-Chicana photographer from Los Angeles, reproduces a familiar narrative: among Indigenous people, the foreigner is bound to be spiritually enlightened and discover her mission in life. *Erased Faces* shows that including the Indigenous "among the living" does not change the unequal relationship between the Chicana and the Indigenous subject that, I argue, often undergirds Chicana literary representations of

230 DECOLONIAL IMAGINARIES AND COLORBLIND LOGICS

Indigenous peoples. Neither does it change the instrumental function that Blackness serves in the novel, which appropriates Blackness to construct the Afro-Chicana protagonist as fundamentally innocent. In its deployment of Blackness for the sake of Chicana feminist critique, the novel follows in the footsteps of white feminism's common instrumentalization of Blackness, which in white feminist writing often serves, to cite Sabine Broeck, "largely symbolic purposes for representations of oppression, violence, and discrimination."[35] Rather than functioning as an effective conduit for the critique of anti-Blackness, as we shall see, Adriana's Blackness paradoxically serves as a conduit for racial disavowal.

Moraga's formally innovative play *The Hungry Woman* at first appears far removed from the Latin American indigenismo to which *Erased Faces* is indebted.[36] The play is a radical work of dissent that rejects Eurocentric forms (such as progressive plot lines, the story arc, and the single protagonist) and content (such as the white male heterosexual hero, celebration of imperialism, and erasure of people of color and their histories). Moraga considers drama a privileged site for bringing actors and audiences to consciousness about histories and desires that have been marginalized and repressed through colonialism. In contrast with mainstream theater, which has been used as a tool for domination, Moraga's plays strive to produce "a literature toward liberation."[37] Moraga not only brings to the stage the stories of queer Chicanas who are ignored in mainstream venues, but she also writes *for* queer women of color and not to entertain white people. Her plays affirm Brown bodies, lesbian desire, and decolonial politics as legitimate subjects of theater and confront the audience with strong and erotic female characters. Nonetheless, *The Hungry Woman* relies on colonial representations of Indigenous peoples and reproduces an unsettling anti-Blackness. Both *Erased Faces* and *The Hungry Woman* are beholden to liberal modes of representation as they mobilize race to critique heteropatriarchy in ways that replicate the logics of colorblindness and the white feminism that they aim to contest, "*failing to acknowledge the specificity of the oppression*"[38] that Moraga warns against.

Encountering the Living Indígena: Graciela Limón's *Erased Faces*

Set against the backdrop of the 1994 Zapatista uprising in Chiapas, Graciela Limón's novel *Erased Faces* narrates the life stories of Adriana Mora, an Afro-Chicana photographer from Los Angeles who travels to

ENCOUNTERING THE OTHER IN CHICANA LITERATURE 231

Mexico to craft a photo history of Maya women; Juana Galván, a Tzeltal woman who makes a living selling crafts in San Cristóbal de las Casas, Chiapas; and Orlando Flores, a young Lacandón man who works as a servant but later rebels against his cruel mestizo boss and becomes a fugitive. As the story develops, Adriana and Juana enter a romantic relationship and eventually join the Zapatista Movement, the history of which is central to the narrative. The Ejército Zapatista de Liberación Nacional (Zapatista Army of National Liberation, EZLN), the novel contends, did not surface suddenly but is the product of a five hundred-year battle for Indigenous dignity and freedom that continues today.

Erased Faces opens with daunting images of persecution and warfare. Chased by rabid dogs, an unnamed "she" and a group of Lacandón women and men run for their lives in the Mexican jungle. As the dogs advance, the nameless woman drops to the ground. It is not fear that causes her paralysis but "the pain of having lost something that was precious to her."[39] The reader is thus immediately confronted with dread, pain, and loss—important themes in the novel. We soon learn that the threatening scene is a dream. As is often the case in indigenista novels, dreams are significant and revelatory in *Erased Faces*: for the Lacandón characters, dreams represent a gateway to uncovering previous lives.

Our dreamer is not a Lacandón, however, but Adriana Mora. Frightened and sweating, the young Afro-Chicana wakes up in a palapa (a thatched-roof dwelling) next to her "cameras, tripod, note pad, canvas jacket with its pockets stuffed with lenses she used to capture the faces and bodies of Lacandon women."[40] Adriana's paraphernalia and her status as an outsider in the Mexican jungle evoke the vexed relationship between the Western anthropologist and Indigenous people, even as Adriana's endeavor is not formally related to research: "Wanting to be accomplished in her profession, to publish her work, she had chosen to come to the jungle to create a photo history of the women of the Lacandona."[41] At first, the villagers do not allow Adriana to take pictures of them because, as the Lacandón elder Chan K'in explains, reproducing an Indigenous person's image entails possessing their spirit. The Indigenous women nevertheless soon trust her. The narrator assures us: "They knew why she dwelled among them."[42] Yet Adriana does not refrain from immortalizing the women in the most intimate situations. Observing an unnamed thirteen-year-old mother about to breastfeed her child, Adriana "rapidly pointed her lens at the girl's hand as it uncovered a full breast."[43] The photojournalist's intrusive gaze fetishizes the bodies of Indigenous people as she aims to "capture the dark mahogany tones of

232 DECOLONIAL IMAGINARIES AND COLORBLIND LOGICS

the women's skin."[44] Accompanied by written notes that include details on her subjects, Adriana's pictures are deeply embedded in ethnography and colonial epistemologies. "As she took each picture," the narrator states, "she concentrated on faces while trying to capture the dense jungle background."[45] Adriana's pictures, which represent Indigenous people in what they construct as being their "natural" setting, evoke those of Swiss photographer and anthropologist Gertrude Duby Blom, one of the first Europeans to "study" the Lacandones, who have been in the crosshairs of anthropologists for over a century.[46]

The Mexican Instituto Nacional Indigenista (INI), whose questionable approaches to Indigenous peoples you might recall from chapter 2, sponsored Blom's early trips into the Lacandón jungle, with Blom's first expedition being requested by the governor of Chiapas himself.[47] Reproducing the paternalistic agenda of the INI and the Mexican state that controlled it, Blom, who captured the Lacandones in more than 55,000 photographs, lamented changes in the Lacandón people's "way of life" and in their environment while she herself contributed to some of these changes. From 1950, together with her husband, the Danish archeologist Frans Blom, until her death in 1993—coincidentally, the year in which *Erased Faces* opens—Gertrude Blom lived in San Cristóbal de las Casas, where she bought a mansion and founded Casa Na Bolom (House of the Jaguar).[48] A museum and research center on the Lacandón people, Na Bolom, to cite Juan Felipe Herrera, "was constructed with an exoticized web of Mayas, always on the verge of extinction, always banished from the policed and authentic beat of 'civilized' time and space."[49] In *Mayan Drifter: Chicano Poet in the Lowlands of America* (1997), Herrera retells his 1992 journey into Chiapas in search of K'ayum Ma'ax, a Lacandón elder whom he had met in 1970, when he was an anthropology student at UCLA. In the hybrid memoir, Herrera describes how Na Bolom exoticizes the Maya, effectively rendering them museum pieces, while living Maya people exist at its margins, as exploited maids and as objects of desire paraded for tourists. Na Bolom, Herrera writes, "opposed deep changes for the Maya. If it favored la revolución, it was only in the same manner as the PRI did—that is, in its rhetoric and gestures in the name of the indigenous peoples of Chiapas."[50] At Na Bolom the "Indian" is displayed, objectified, and "preserved" for posterity, while living Indigenous people are exploited and excluded. Ironically, the Maya whose ancestors are portrayed on the Na Bolom walls sweep the floors and wash the bed sheets for Mexican and mostly foreign anthropology students, researchers, and tourists. That

ENCOUNTERING THE OTHER IN CHICANA LITERATURE   233

Herrera himself in 1992 begins his journey into the Lacandón jungle at Na Bolom, and that *Mayan Drifter* reproduces some the objectifying representations of Indigenous peoples that he critiques, including through ethnographic photographs of Lacandón people immortalized in the jungle, speaks to the profound ways that anthropology continues to shape the representation of Indigenous peoples in Chicanx literature at large.[51]

If the "colonial dependency" that the museum fostered, as Herrera writes, "was not part of the Bolom conversation,"[52] neither is the objectifying way that Limón and Herrera represent Indigenous people part of the conversation in *Erased Faces* and *Mayan Drifter*. Adriana never questions her camera, and neither do the people she photographs. Instead, they quickly "trusted her enough to allow her to take photographs of them as they toiled in the jungle or fished in the river."[53] Adriana, like Herrera, appears oblivious to the fact that photography, as Mireille Miller-Young writes, "did not arise on the margins of empire but was at its core."[54] Ethnography, Miller-Young also reminds us, "was a key method in maintaining discourses of power, truth, and control."[55] Rather than destabilizing the colonial ways of knowing codified within anthropology, Limón and Herrera reinscribe them. While Herrera, however, incorporates a critique of Chicanx indigeneity by showing that in Chiapas he inhabits the privileged positionality of a white man, Adriana Mora is precluded from thinking self-critically about her positionality through her racial construction as Black, which in the novel serves to sustain, rather than challenge, colorblindness.

Adriana, whose telling last name "Mora" references her Blackness, is an injured character. Having told us about Adriana's nightmare and the reasons for her presence in the Mexican jungle, the omniscient narrator quickly directs our attention to her Blackness (she has "thick lips" and "curled hair") and to her suffering ("ever since she could remember, she had felt lost, separated, alone, always filled with fear").[56] The daughter of a Mexican man of African descent and a mestiza woman who migrated to Los Angeles from Campeche, Adriana was taunted as a child because of her Blackness, including by people in her own barrio. Now, at twenty-four years old, "sometimes she still felt as she had when she was a child."[57] Adriana's injury is concomitantly racialized and shown to transcend racial meaning: when Adriana is four years old, her mother kills her father before taking her own life, a dramatic element that appears added to the plot merely to further construct Adriana as injured and therefore innocent.

234   DECOLONIAL IMAGINARIES AND COLORBLIND LOGICS

Adriana's injury is important at the narrative level, for the novel posits the commonality of anguish as a leveling vehicle for interracial coalition. When Juana tells her about an upcoming Zapatista meeting, Adriana asks: "Why are you telling me this? I'm not one of your people." Juana replies: "No, you're not, but soon you will be, and we're certain that you will not betray us. Besides, you, too, have suffered, haven't you? . . . Join us, Adriana."[58] Suffering facilitates Adriana's acceptance within a community of Indigenous people. Adriana, too, has suffered. She can be trusted. She is "like us." In this way, the novel reproduces the deployment of suffering as an analogizing colorblind tool that is often present in white writing. The crime novels of white South African author Deon Meyer featuring the serial white protagonist Benny Griessel, for example, routinely deploy this strategy to disavow Griessel's white privilege and the novels' own complicity with racism. In *The Woman in the Blue Cloak* (2017), the character Vaughn Cupido, who is Coloured, says to Benny: "Colour only applies to whites who have never suffered. You don't have colour, Benna."[59] Suffering is presumed to erase Benny's whiteness, just as Adriana's suffering is posited as neutralizing difference, making Adriana "one of [our] people." In both cases, the colorblind argument that seeks to render invisible racialized hierarchies of power is placed in the mouth of a character of color, Juana in *Erased Faces* and Vaughn in Meyer's novel, rendering it more effective as tool of racial disavowal.

Erased Faces thus presents us with a protagonist who is deeply wounded, essentially virtuous, and ultimately not accountable for any harm occurring to the Indigenous people around her. As asymmetries of power disappear in sentimentalism, this colorblind move positions Adriana in troubling proximity to injured white figures of the white imagination. Robyn Wiegman shows how Forrest Gump, a quintessential injured white character, is "strategically disaffiliated" from racism as he moves through the Civil Rights Movement.[60] *Forrest Gump* (1994) features a protagonist with disabilities for whom responsibility for white supremacy is suspended. His injury makes Gump not only innocent and "good," but is posited as being comparable to the structural injury that Black people experience under white supremacist terror. The symbolic evocation of anti-Black racism in little Forrest's sitting alone on the school bus on the verge of the Civil Rights Movement cannot be overlooked.

What I am suggesting here is that Adriana Mora's Blackness, like Forrest Gump's and Benny Griessel's injuries, is strategic. The racialized suffering that Adriana experiences as a Black woman is a means to an

ENCOUNTERING THE OTHER IN CHICANA LITERATURE 235

end that serves to place her in figurative proximity to the Indigenous people she encounters in Mexico, thereby freeing the Chicana protagonist of responsibility for exploiting Indigenous people and reproducing racial inequality. In *Erased Faces*, as Christina Sharpe writes in a different context, "Black suffering forms the backdrop against which another kind of 'human drama' (capital H) is staged."[61] Black suffering is appropriated in the novel to stage the persistent Chicanx drama of Indigenous (un)belonging. Rather than making visible how the structural positionality of Black people is unique, Adriana's Blackness achieves exactly the opposite as it presumes that Black people's suffering is equivalent to the suffering of non-Black people of color. It makes sense, then, that Adriana's Blackness is mentioned only briefly, early in the novel, and placed alongside injuries that transcend racial meaning, and then is never mentioned again. Adriana's Blackness does not seem to be relevant to her experiences past her childhood. She never experiences racism as an adult, neither in the United States nor in Mexico, nor is she concerned in the slightest about her African or Afro-Mexican roots, in contrast to the search for her Indigenous roots, which propels the narrative. And since the novel, as we will see, argues that all oppressions are the same, it effectively exploits Blackness and turns it into an emblem, a symbolic marker of injury as a conduit to innocence.

In complicating Adriana's mestizaje through her Blackness, the novel precludes the possibility that in her new milieu Adriana might have to contend with white privilege or be forced to critically consider her positionality vis-à-vis the Indigenous people she encounters. This sets her apart from Chicanx characters who experience a momentary destabilization of identity while traveling in Mexico. Teresa, the protagonist of Ana Castillo's novel *The Mixquiahuala Letters* (1986), grapples with being read as an outsider during her journey through Mexico. Despite the "Indian in [her]," she is perceived as a tourist and foreigner.[62] In Alma Luz Villanueva's short story "Free Women" (1994), locals similarly consider the four middle-class Chicana protagonists vacationing in Mexico as gringas.[63] In *Mayan Drifter*, Herrera is compelled to rethink his racial identity in terms of relationality in the midst of an Indigenous demonstration in Chiapas and concedes: "I was the only Ladino man out in the plaza."[64] The category *Chicano* holds no significance in Chiapas, where Herrera is perceived as a white man. Among dispossessed Maya, Herrera questions his subalternity, even as he ultimately also falls into the trap of analogizing his suffering as Chicano in the United States to the suffering experienced by Indigenous peoples in

236 DECOLONIAL IMAGINARIES AND COLORBLIND LOGICS

Mexico. Differently from what occurs in these works, Adriana is spared the trauma of misrecognition in Mexico. Rather than experiencing an identity crisis that propels her to recognize her situational privilege, Adriana merely undergoes a symbolic identity shift that places her in even *closer proximity* to Indigenous people: thanks to the Lacandón elder Chan K'in, she discovers that she is the descendant of a brave Mexica woman. There is no sign by the end of the novel that Adriana has learned an Indigenous language or adopted any Indigenous values or customs. Adriana's indigenenity, as if often the case in Chicanx literature, is constructed merely through lineage.

In privileging Adriana's perspective, *Erased Faces* displays a commitment to modes of representation that envisage the superiority of the Western subject. As the novel portrays Adriana's immediate inclusion into a community of Indigenous peoples, it is unable to imagine Indigenous characters who challenge her intrusive presence. Adriana is constantly reassured that she is a full member of the Maya communities that she encounters. Yet as the narrative insists on positing a colorblind sameness between Adriana and the Indigenous characters, it cannot avoid calling attention to differences among them. Colonial modes of representation are inscribed through Adriana and the Indigenous characters' asymmetrical characterization. Replicating the surrogate role that Indigenous characters often play in white savior narratives, Juana facilitates Adriana's entry into an Indigenous community. Their differential representation is striking. Adriana has a complex interiority, yet we know little about Juana's and Orlando's inner lives. Adriana is associated with literacy, technology, and psychological complexity, while Juana is compared to animals, nature, and instinctual behavior. Even as they purport to value orality, indigenista novels ultimately valorize literacy and remain anchored in Eurocentric notions of Indigenous peoples. *Erased Faces* is no exception as it reproduces colonial images of Indigenous peoples as illiterate, spiritual, virtuous, and close to nature.

Adriana's unique position among Indigenous people who look for her, attend to her, and provide her with the love she longs for summons colonial relationships of subordination. The Indigenous characters guide Adriana on her path to self-discovery: Adriana does not need to take the first step in asking Chan K'in to interpret her dreams; every morning, the elder wants to know what Adriana has dreamed. Chan K'in does little else in the novel but provide Adriana with spiritual nourishment and knowledge about his own Indigenous traditions and history. He seems to exist for Adriana and the reader's enlightenment alone. Asymmetries

ENCOUNTERING THE OTHER IN CHICANA LITERATURE

of power are also reflected in spatial relations. In the mountain, Adriana sleeps in a palapa with a net covering and a basin, while everybody else sleeps on hammocks outside. The novel suggests that Adriana is occasionally "shown privilege"[65] through the unsolicited generosity of others, but presumes that she does not *have* privilege.

Adriana does not seem disturbed by her paradoxical position as a newly minted "insider" who is afforded comforts that others around her do not have. Like Forrest Gump, she also seems "unable to read the historical archive [she] is moving through."[66] Adriana is not self-critical about her ethnographic endeavor and the impact of her presence among Indigenous people, whom the narrator describes as "the tribe."[67] Adriana's anxieties are immediately appeased as she is reassured that she is good, much needed, and *one of them*. Given that Adriana does not self-consciously grapple with the significance of her actions, she fails to construct what Carl Gutiérrez-Jones calls a *critical race narrative*. Examining Louise Erdrich's *Tracks* and John Rechy's *The Miraculous Day of Amalia Gómez*, Gutiérrez-Jones shows that, although the characters in both novels suffer racial injuries, they are not primarily constructed as victims; rather, they critically mediate between their actions and their context as they struggle with questions of responsibility.[68] By contrast, Adriana rarely contends with her situational privilege as a US photographer and traveler among Indigenous people in the Mexican jungle. In this way, she ironically resembles white savior figures, who are generally oblivious to how their status and behavior perpetuate inequalities.[69]

The novel falls prey to the allure of white saviorism even as the redeemer is now an Afro-Chicana woman. As in white savior narratives such as those that structure the films *Dances with Wolves* (1990) and *Avatar* (2009), Adriana is made to play a central role among a community of racialized Others, who seem to necessitate the help of an outsider to liberate themselves. Adriana is not simply accepted into the Lacandón community; she is *invited* to join the Zapatista struggle, as becomes clear in this dialogue between Juana and Adriana:

> "Join us, Adriana."
> "What good could I be to you? I'm not a native, much less do I have training in what you are planning." [. . .]
> "We are about to embark on a plan for which we've been preparing for many years, one that will return to us what was snatched away long ago. It will be painful, and it will cause anguish, but it must take place. All of our actions should be

238 DECOLONIAL IMAGINARIES AND COLORBLIND LOGICS

chronicled in writing as well as in images for the world to see. You can do that for us." [. . .]

"Will the people accept me?"

"They already have. This is why I'm here speaking to you."[70]

The move from Adriana's inclusion to leadership is a swift one. The request that Adriana record the Zapatista struggle through writing and pictures meanwhile suggests that Indigenous communities are unable to do this by themselves.

The silencing of literacy and literature among Indigenous people in *Erased Faces* is ironic given that the novel incorporates fragments of Zapatista writings into its dialogues without giving due credit. Before she leaves the village to join the EZLN, Adriana is concerned that she might be seen as "an intruder, a foreigner."[71] Chan K'in quickly reassures her:

> That is not the case, *niña.* You are part of us. We used to be like stones, like plants along the road. We had no word, no face, no name, no tomorrow. We did not exist. But now we have a vision; we know the road on which we are to embark, and we invite you to come and seek, to find yourself, and to find us. We are you, and you are us, and through you the world will come to know the truth.[72]

In this passage, the novel projects onto Chan K'in Adriana's quest for self-discovery, posited here as operating in conjunction with her *finding* of the Indigenous Other. As Chan K'in reassures Adriana that she is "part of us," his response includes words that were pronounced on July 21, 1996, in the Zapatista community of Aguascalientes II in Oventic, Chiapas, a fact that the novel does not disclose. In the "Closing Remarks at the First Intercontinental *Encuentro* for Humanity and against Neoliberalism," Marcos and the EZLN announce:

> LET US INTRODUCE OURSELVES. We are the Zapatista National Liberation Army. For ten years, we lived in these mountains, preparing to fight a war. In these mountains, we built an army. Below, in the cities and plantations, we did not exist. Our lives were worth less than those of machines and animals. We were like stones, like weeds in the road. We were silenced. We were faceless. We were nameless. We had no future. We did not exist. For the powers that be, known internationally by the term

ENCOUNTERING THE OTHER IN CHICANA LITERATURE   239

> "neoliberalism," we did not count, we did not produce, we did
> not buy, we did not sell. We were a cipher in the accounts of
> big capital.[73]

Rather than communicating dependency on foreign help, the communiqué shows that self-determination defines the tactics of the Zapatistas. The novel silences the Zapatistas' long-term commitment to self-representation through writing, appropriating the words of the communiqué to seal Adriana's inclusion in the Zapatista Movement and elevate her position within it: "We are you, and you are us, and through you the world will come to see the truth."[74] Notwithstanding that Marcos is himself a mestizo whose past position of leadership within the Zapatistas educes the realities of white privilege and paternalism, Marcos's words and the context in which they were pronounced constitute an indictment of neoliberalism. Adriana's endeavor in the jungle, in contrast, signals global capitalism's ongoing dependence on the exploitation of Indigenous peoples.

As the novel positions Adriana in the missionary role of savior, it encroaches upon Indigenous struggles for self-representation. The novel does not simply obfuscate the intrinsically racialized dimension of Indigenous women's oppression, but also fails to provide an intersectional analysis of racial subordination. Replicating the liberal rhetorics that underpin colorblindness discourse, Orlando conflates different types of oppression: "I see that to the men who want to be our masters, being *una india* or *un indio*, being poor and forced to scratch a life out of a piece of dry dirt, being a *manflora* [derog. for lesbian] or a man who loves men, being anyone contrary, is all the same."[75] Discrimination based on race, class, and sexuality is here literally posited as being "all the same."

The novel also mobilizes racism to critique homophobia in ways that obscure the operations of racial power. When Juana dies in the Acteal massacre, in which Mexican paramilitaries executed forty-five innocent Maya women and children while they were praying inside a church, the soldier who kills her shouts "the hateful word *manflora*, lover of women."[76] The historical Acteal massacre in 1997 targeted Indigenous women who were believed to sympathize with the Zapatista Movement, yet Juana's death is depicted as the product of homophobia. Adriana describes the reasons for Juana's death as follows:

> *Juana's murder was caused by hatred, but it was even more than*
> *loathing because dangling from it, like poisonous snakes, was*

240   DECOLONIAL IMAGINARIES AND COLORBLIND LOGICS

the repugnance and disgust for women like us. Her love for me was discovered. . . . She was erased because she had been strong, because she had been a leader, because she was una india, but most of all because she had committed the forbidden act: She had been in love with another woman.[77]

The novel occludes the central role that white supremacist violence played in the massacre of the Indigenous women that henchmen of the Mexican state killed in Acteal. As the novel deploys homosexuality as yet another colorblind tool that seeks to erase racialized differences, a gesture embodied in Adriana's description of the assassins' hatred for *"women like us,"* Juana's erasure by the paramilitary soldier is epistemologically matched by the text's erasure of white supremacy.

The narrative is consistently concerned with valorizing Adriana's role among the Indigenous people she photographs and with indirectly valorizing *Erased Faces*, which itself attempts to advocate and speak for oppressed Maya women. The final chapter, tellingly titled "She asked me to be the lips through which their silenced voices will speak," sees Adriana in an airplane traveling from Merida to Los Angeles, to where she is permanently returning after having spent five years in Chiapas. During the flight, Adriana describes in her diary a dream in which Juana appeared to her: *"She told me that until she and I meet again in our next life, she will always be with me when I show my photographs, while I speak to others about la gente in Lacandona, about the atrocities in Acteal and in all the other places of misery. She asked me to be the lips through which their silenced voices could speak."*[78] Adriana's photographs—and indirectly Limón's novel—here become "the lips" through which silenced Indigenous people can speak. As it revives the vexed agenda of Latin American indigenista novels, *Erased Faces* infringes upon Indigenous struggles for self-representation and liberation, endowing a Chicana character with the power to represent and give voice to Indigenous communities. So fundamentally colonial is the relationship between Adriana and the Indigenous characters that the reader is made to forget that Adriana is a Black woman. Adriana's Blackness, after all, bears no relevance to her experiences in Mexico, her actions, or her politics. The anti-Blackness that structures social life in Mexico, including among Indigenous peoples, is thereby also rendered invisible in the novel.

Adriana's presence in the jungle, as we have seen, remains inescapably loaded with the weight of history and racial meaning. Yet the novel constantly displaces racism *elsewhere*, away from Adriana and her camera,

ENCOUNTERING THE OTHER IN CHICANA LITERATURE 241

and away from the reader. After she captures images of the Zapatista uprising, Adriana finally becomes recognized as a photographer: "The publication of her work spread, opening promising doors for her work beyond the United States, extending to Europe, Canada and Australia, all of which resulted in stipends on which she and Juana were able to live."[79] As Adriana's venture into the Lacandón jungle is not problematized but ultimately sanctioned by the Indigenous community, the young Chicana, like Forrest Gump, is also allowed to "participate innocently in the new order of global capital."[80] However, unlike Gump's shrimp business, Adriana Mora's endeavor does not appear to be commercial at all. As they are described as "a unique way of alerting the world to the anguish that was tormenting Chiapas,"[81] Adriana's pictures are endowed with much more than monetary value. While Gump is merely disaffiliated from whiteness, Adriana's photography enables a leadership position within a community of racialized Others who are organizing against white supremacy. Her pictures are not exploitative and objectifying, the novel insists, but "a graphic and undeniable testimony of truth."[82] Since evil is embodied by a series of villainous characters in the novel, neither Adriana nor the reader is asked to feel responsible for racism. And yet, Adriana has the privilege to enter a community of racialized Others and leave not only unscarred, but also transformed. On the flight back to Los Angeles, "Adriana . . . felt serene; she understood her mission. She touched Juana's bracelet as she looked out her window."[83] The adventure in the jungle is appealing as long as it is not permanent. The outsider leaves Mexico empowered with new knowledge, a flourishing career, and self-confidence, toward a bright future. Among Indigenous people, the Chicana was bound to find her Indigenous roots, "her mission," and, ultimately, herself.

Between Aztlán and a Hard Place: Cherríe Moraga's *The Hungry Woman*

In the foreword to *The Hungry Woman*, Cherríe Moraga leads the reader into a dream in which she is about to undergo an initiation ceremony alongside Native American women belonging to different nations:

> *In the dream, I am to be initiated in a ceremony. We are many women from many nations. We prepare ourselves. We dress. I am nervous about what is appropriate. There may be a test of some kind and I realize there are basic answers I have not memorized:*

242 DECOLONIAL IMAGINARIES AND COLORBLIND LOGICS

basic elements of my cultura (the proper names for things, the language that comes with knowledge) that escape me.[84]

Rather than being at peace, Moraga at first is apprehensive. As she dresses, covers her head with a huipil, and ties it with a Guatemalan cloth, she feels discomfort, realizing that her headdress is *"a kind of 'Chicana invention.'"*[85] Moraga's unfamiliarity with *"basic elements of [her] cultura"* signals the denial of access to Indigenous knowledge that European and US colonizers have imposed upon Chicanxs. The dream is filled with anxiety as Moraga is *"not even quite convinced of [her] place in the circle of those mixed-blood lodge sisters."*[86] She feels like an outsider.

Moraga's apprehensions, however, are quickly placated as she learns that entry into this Indigenous community does not require any demonstration of knowledge or proof of ancestry; in a simple *"ritual of inclusion into this extended nation of women . . . [e]ach woman sits across from a kind of elder Maestra and each initiate, with few words spoken, is simply 'brought in.'"*[87] Moraga's Maestra is Déborah, an O'odham woman to whom Moraga has spoken only once before. Déborah tells Moraga that, since they both share ancestral ties to the Sonora Desert, Moraga's heritage might also be O'odham. Similar to Adriana Mora, who in the Lacandón jungle discovers that she has Mexica ancestors, Moraga's presence in the ceremony is legitimized through Déborah's announcement of Moraga's possible O'odham heritage.

The more Moraga's inclusion process advances, the more the Indigenous characters are placed in a subordinate position as the narrative is contingent upon a representation of Indigenous peoples as generous, loving, and willing to unconditionally accept others in their space. Moraga describes Déborah as follows:

> Now kneeling face to face with Déborah in ceremony, she exhibits the same generosity as in our first meeting. I don't remember what is said, only that she retains the same direct calmness in her approach to me, in her complete confidence in me. She places a simple cotton dress folded into a square into my arms. "It is for the sweatlodge," she tells me; and I am pleased to be given something that draws me more solidly into that circle. . . . As we leave the ceremonial structure, I experience a profound sense of well-being, a full sense of belonging. My step meets the ground more solidly.[88]

ENCOUNTERING THE OTHER IN CHICANA LITERATURE   243

Like Adriana Mora, who in Chiapas quickly realizes that the Indigenous people she encounters "trusted her,"[89] Moraga is granted *complete confidence.*"[90] Yet as Moraga is drawn *"more solidly into that circle,"* she is, like Adriana, also placed in the unequal position of being nurtured and attended to while she undergoes a process of spiritual growth. Meanwhile, Déborah's calmness, generosity, and welcoming attitude conjure colonial representations of Indigenous people. As I showed in the introduction, Christopher Columbus's representation of the Taino people as welcoming and "generous with all that they possess"[91] served to silence the violent European theft of Indigenous land and Indigenous resistance to European invasion. In contrast with Columbus's letter, there is no explicit assertion of racial superiority in Moraga's narrative. Déborah's characterization nonetheless conjures naivety and servility as she asks Moraga for permission to enter her space, comforts her, gives her a dress for the sweat lodge as well as displays *"generosity," "calmness"* and *"complete confidence"* in the initiate.

Similar to what occurs in *Erased Faces* and in white fantasies á la *Dances with Wolves*, Moraga constructs a narrative of entry into a racialized community that culminates with the outsider's unchallenged inclusion, indigenization, and spiritual transformation. The dream, however, does not end with Moraga's inclusion. Just as Moraga finally *"experience[s] a profound sense of well-being, a full sense of belonging,"* a disturbing presence interrupts the ceremony:

> *Suddenly, the ceremony is disrupted. A non-Native man wants to claim a rightful place in the ceremony. The scene suddenly becomes a kind of college campus where toddlers (white kids) require my attention. I am outraged by the situation in front of me, while at the same time sense, in the background, that my own blood child, who is not with me, is somehow endangered. The ceremony degenerates into estupideces and complete chaos. But upon awakening, the horror y lo ridículo of the dream's conclusion have little hold on me.*
>
> *I awaken full of ceremony, like medicine. It is as close to joy as I can imagine.*[92]

A male outsider, implicitly racialized as white, ruins the peaceful ceremony. The white man obviously does not belong in a community of Indigenous women. Moraga's outrage indicates an antiracist stance against cultural appropriation. In the meantime, the anxiety about her

244   DECOLONIAL IMAGINARIES AND COLORBLIND LOGICS

own legitimacy is projected onto a disturbing external element. The presence of the white man reassures the initiate that she is not engaging in appropriation and serves to seal her status as an insider. Moraga no longer needs to be concerned about her *"maybe-Indianness."*[93] She is now a full member in the circle of Indigenous women.

In the second part of the foreword, Moraga creates a bridge between dream and myth, which she describes as "an opening into the past, told in character and image, that can provide a kind of road map to our future."[94] She writes that *The Hungry Woman* was inspired by a journey into the Mexican southlands that she undertook in the 1980s in search of her roots. Once in Mexico, Moraga was confronted with "the daily, and often painful, reminder of [her] own cultural outsiderhood as a U.S.-born Mexican of mixed parentage."[95] During the journey, Moraga undergoes a process of (re)education and turns to Mesoamerican myth as a usable past that can provide valuable directions for the future. Moraga contends that Aztec and Maya temples in Mexico provided her with access to "a collective racial memory" and she came to the realization that her gods and her people are the same thing.[96] This tension between indigeneity as heritage and indigeneity as practice—and the slippage between mythological deities, living Indigenous people, and the Chicanx subject—undergird the representational politics of *The Hungry Woman.*[97]

Set during the second decade of the twenty-first century, an imagined dystopian future, *The Hungry Woman* tells the story of Medea, a queer Chicana curandera (traditional healer), midwife, and former leader in the Chicano Movement. A civil war has "balkanized" half of the United States into various independent nations which have seceded to stop US imperial expansion and white cultural imperialism.[98] These nations include Africa-America, located in the South; the Mexicano Nation of Aztlán, which includes former Mexican territories; the Union of Indian Nations, "which shares, in an uneasy alliance with its Chicano neighbors, much of the Southwest and also occupies the Great Plains and Rocky Mountain regions," the Hawai'i Nation, and the First Nations Peoples confederacy in former Alaska.[99] In an implicit critique of the racial essentialism articulated in *El Plan Espiritual de Aztlán,* citizenship in these new nations is based on political affiliation rather than on "blood quantum." However, as we shall see, the play also falls back onto privileging ancestry as instrumental for the articulation of a Chicanx Indigenous politics over solidarity with Black and Indigenous communities in the United States. In the process, *The Hungry Woman* both

ENCOUNTERING THE OTHER IN CHICANA LITERATURE

appropriates Blackness and excludes Black people from the Chicanx community it envisions.

The revolution is soon followed by a counterrevolution, as the new nations institute hierarchies between male and female, and straight and queer, so that LGBTQ people are unilaterally sent into exile. Having been in a lesbian relationship, Medea is forced into exile to Phoenix, where she lives with her son Chac-Mool, her lover Luna, and her grandmother Mama Sal. Other characters in the play include Luna's girlfriend, Savannah, described as "African-American with Native ancestry;" Medea's husband and Chac-Mool's father, Jasón; Medea's unnamed Puerto Rican caretaker; and the chorus of four Cihuateteo, spirits of warrior women who died in childbirth according to the Aztec myth, who are distinguished by the four directions and "pre-colonial colors," and whose name Moraga misspells as Cihuatateo, a spelling that I will maintain to respect Moraga's authorial decision.

The Aztec myth of the Hungry Woman, the Mesoamerican tale of La Llorona, and Euripides's tragedy *Medea* are all creatively reimagined in *The Hungry Woman*.[100] The play opens in the present, with Medea in a prison psychiatric ward for having killed her son, and successively reconstructs the events that led to Chac-Mool's murder. Prior to Medea's incarceration, alternations of jealousy, moments of genuine passion and tenderness, and an unquenched desire for something that seems unattainable strain Medea and Luna's seven-year-long relationship. The conflict between the two partners reaches a pinnacle when Jasón demands custody of Chac-Mool to secure his political ascent in Aztlán. While Medea and Chac-Mool are Yaqui, Jasón is primarily of Spanish descent and does not have the "blood quantum" required for land ownership in Aztlán. Medea initially agrees to follow Jasón, but then refuses when he demands that she disavow her relationship with Luna. At this point in the play, Chac-Mool is soon to be thirteen, the age in which a boy can participate in ceremonies that will indoctrinate him into Aztlán's heteropatriarchy. An optimistic character, Chac-Mool believes that he can change Aztlán's culture of patriarchy and homophobia. Before his planned departure, however, Medea takes her child's life. The tragic murder suggests that no simple redemption is possible between patriarchy-ruled Aztlán and the queer people who live at its margins. A glimpse of hope is found in the ending as Chac-Mool returns from the dead to take his mother home.

The opening scene of *The Hungry Woman* sets the stage for a series of correlations between Mesoamerican deities and the Chicanx

246   DECOLONIAL IMAGINARIES AND COLORBLIND LOGICS

characters that will recur throughout the play. The audience is led into a mythical indigenist space. Lights slowly illuminate a massive stone figure of Coatlicue, the Aztec goddess of creation and destruction. Four Cihuatateo surround the statue, while *"Pre-Columbian Meso-American music"* plays in the background.[101] Cihuatateo East immediately creates a bond between Coatlicue and Medea based on their common condition as mothers: Coatlicue gave birth to Huitzilopochtli, the god of war, while Medea birthed Chac-Mool, a male warrior.

The play concurrently places the Mesoamerican Indigenous subject in the constancy of mythical time and evokes the historical Zapatista uprising through metonymic displacement. Having established a connection between Coatlicue and Medea, Cihuatateo East now wears a nurse's cap, while Cihuatateo North puts on a black ski mask, which signals the iconic Zapatista mask. Savannah protests that neoliberalism has destroyed unionized jobs, environmental protection, health standards, and living wages, but thankfully the Maya in Chiapas have led an international response. The conversation continues as follows:

> MAMA SAL: The Zapatistas took on the PRI and the PAN y hasta el partido de la TORTILLA [even the party of the TORTILLA] and the Mexican president got shot and bueno [well] . . . the rest is history. Pan-indigenismo tore América apart and Aztlán was born from the pedacitos [little pieces].
>
> SAVANNAH: Uniting the disenfranchised diaspora of Indian-mestizos throughout the Southwest.
>
> MAMA SAL: We were contentos [happy] for awhile—
>
> SAVANNAH: Sort of. Until the revolutionaries told the women, put down your guns and pick up your babies. . . . And then en masse, all the colored countries—
>
> MAMA SAL: Threw out their jotería [queer folk].
>
> SAVANNAH: Queers of every color and shade and definition.
>
> MAMA SAL: Y los homos became peregrinos . . . como nomads, just like our Aztec ancestors a thousand years ago. . . .
>
> SAVANNAH: And we made a kind of gypsy ghetto for ourselves in what was once a thriving desert.[102]

Creating a genesis for the play's imaginary insurrection that culminates in the establishment of Aztlán, in which Chicanxs constitute a "disenfranchised diaspora of Indian-mestizos," the dialogue invokes the 1994 Zapatista uprising as instrumental for propelling pan-indigenism and

ENCOUNTERING THE OTHER IN CHICANA LITERATURE 247

uniting Chicanxs. That the Zapatistas continue to struggle precisely against mestizo dominance in Mexico is ignored in the passage, which brings together "Indians" and "mestizos" in ways that conceal the workings of racial power south and north of the US–Mexico border. The parallel invoked between "los homos" (homosexual people) and "our Aztec ancestors" also excludes those members of the LGBTQ community who, like Savannah herself, cannot claim Aztec ancestry—or at least the play never suggests that she can.

The only Black character in the play, Savannah is made to reproduce colorblind logics and silence anti-Blackness. Phoenix, which Savannah defines as "a kind of gypsy ghetto," is a strip of barren land located between Aztlán and what remains of Gringolandia (the United States). The imaginary Phoenix evokes both actual Native American reservations and poor African American neighborhoods. Described as "a city-in-ruin, the dumping site of every kind of poison and person unwanted by its neighbors," Phoenix faces problems similar to those plaguing Native American reservations: the land is polluted, the soil is arid, and the education system does not teach children about their own history and culture.[103] Luna laments: "who gives a shit about the environment here."[104] Meanwhile, the constant sirens and police helicopters that unsettle everyday life in Phoenix evoke the criminalization and over-policing of predominantly Black neighborhoods, which are also disproportionately exposed to environmental hazards, including air pollution, industrial facilities, and toxic waste. Yet as Phoenix is described as a "gypsy ghetto" inhabited by "queers of every color and shade and definition," the play mystifies the racial dimensions of spatial segregation and environmental pollution. Powerfully placing these words in the mouth of Savannah, it silences how Black people in particular are subjected to segregation and police terror.

As it appropriates the voice of a Black character to disavow its own anti-Blackness, the play also evokes like-race comparisons that pervade white gay rights discourses. In the attempt to appeal to racialized equal protection precedents, Janet Halley explains, LGBTQ advocates often engage in what she calls imitations of identity by arguing "that homophobia is like racism" or that "homosexuals are like racial minorities."[105] These arguments facilitate diverting resources from Black people and people of color to LGBTQ constituencies who, collectively, are more likely to be white and middle class.[106] These analogizing arguments, Chandan Reddy writes, "posit a fundamental identity between unlike subjects otherwise incommensurate."[107] They also tend to exploit the

248　　　　　　DECOLONIAL IMAGINARIES AND COLORBLIND LOGICS

histories and struggles of Black people to advance the cause of LGBTQ constituencies that are not Black, as is the case in *The Hungry Woman*. Writing about Bill Clinton's "gays in the military" campaign, Hortense J. Spillers argues that discourses which analogized "gay sexuality to the situation of black soldiers in the armed forces of the Truman era" failed to consider "that black people cannot conceal the color of their skin."[108] Arguments that liken sexuality to race (and often, as in this case, specifically invoke Black people) render invisible the unique position that Black people inhabit in the racial hierarchy as well as the oppression faced by people who are *both* Black and queer. Further, they silence the particular vulnerability of Black trans women, who face exorbitant murder rates in the United States, whether they are homosexual or heterosexual. It bears mentioning in this context that Moraga has not simply been unconcerned with the experiences of transgender people, but also outright hostile to them, a fact encapsulated in her statement: "I do not want to keep losing my macha daughters to manhood. . . . I do not want butch lesbians to become a dying breed, headed for extinction."[109] In Moraga's work, including in *The Hungry Woman,* cis Chicana "butch lesbians" remain the privileged subject of Moraga's feminist politics. As this occurs at the expense of other racialized and gendered subjects, Moraga's works reproduce their own hierarchies and exclusions.

In "Learning to Live Without Black Familia: Cherríe Moraga's Nationalist Articulations," Sharpe traces some of the political changes that occur in Moraga's early writing, from the publication of *This Bridge Called My Back* (1981) to *The Last Generation* (1993), to show how Moraga's shift from coalitional to nationalist politics and concomitant expulsion of what Sharpe calls "black familia" reproduces racially exclusionary logics. Sharpe argues that in Moraga's work the boundaries of Chicana ethnic identity are at times constructed, and policed, through her usage of Blackness. Sharpe writes, "I am uncomfortable with Moraga's nationalist discourse and how she sometimes works out questions of inside and outside on the bodies of black and 'mulatto' people."[110] Sharpe shows how in *The Last Generation* Moraga disavows the links between the Black Power Movement and the Chicano Movement. Rather than serving as vehicles for coalitional politics or a critique of anti-Blackness, Black characters such as the "intruder" in Moraga's story "Pesadilla," which appears in *Loving in the War Years* (1983), represent "that which must be expelled."[111] In a similar way, Savannah in *The Hungry Woman* is represented as an intruder, literally as a homewrecker, rather than a member of the extended Chicanx family. She is

ENCOUNTERING THE OTHER IN CHICANA LITERATURE 249

the character that must be expelled so that Moraga and Luna's relationship, and Moraga's articulation of a Chicana identity *as* Indigenous, may continue.

Moraga's depiction and deployment of Savannah is entangled with the reproduction of colorblind logics that concurrently reproduce and silence anti-Blackness. *The Hungry Woman* both appropriates Blackness and posits it as Other. Although she is also an Indigenous woman of mixed-race heritage, like Medea herself, Savannah's Blackness sets her apart from the other characters. In the cast of characters, women who are not Chicanas are described in terms of their background and their relationship to the Chicanx characters. Savannah is merely described as "LUNA's girlfriend, African-American with Native ancestry."[112] While we immediately learn that the character is played by Cihuatateo West, we do not learn her actual name. Medea does not refer to Savannah by her name either. Wanting to know about the nature of Luna's relationship with Savannah, Medea asks Luna during a fight: "And your negra?"[113] Savannah is merely a "negra" in Medea's eyes, even as Medea lives in a public housing project, a setting that for a US audience inevitably evokes associations with poor Black communities. Medea's anti-Blackness is never challenged by other characters. At this point in the play, Savannah is also only spoken about as she disappears after the first act.

If the play appropriates the voice of a Black character to disavow anti-Blackness, including its own, and advance its own gender and sexual politics, the figure of the undocumented migrant in *The Hungry Woman* is also subordinated to the construction of a Chicana identity and instrumental to the play's critique of heteropatriarchy. The play mobilizes narratives about Latin American immigrants' crossings into the United States not to centrally problematize the racist logics of US citizenship, but to critique the masculinist politics of the Chicano Movement and further construct the Chicana subject as Indigenous. In a key scene, Luna is stopped and interrogated at the border for attempting to enter Aztlán without a permit and for breaking into a museum. During the interrogation, Luna appears dressed in a sack, with bare legs and feet. The guard ties Luna's hands behind her back while a big spotlight shines into her face:

> BORDER GUARD: Why did you cross the border?
> LUNA: I was on my way to her. [. . .]
> BORDER GUARD: But you hadn't a work permit.
> LUNA: I was denied one.

250   DECOLONIAL IMAGINARIES AND COLORBLIND LOGICS

BORDER GUARD: You knew it was illegal.

LUNA: Yes.

BORDER GUARD: Then—

LUNA: I longed for Aztlán.

BORDER GUARD: Why did you break into the museum?

LUNA: I wanted to free them.

BORDER GUARD: Who?

LUNA: Those little female figures. Those tiny breasts and thick thighs, those ombligos y panzas de barro [navels and bellies of clay].

BORDER GUARD: Who were they to you, these figurines?

LUNA: Ancient little diosas [goddesses], the size of children's toys. They were trapped, sir, behind the museum glass. They belonged to us. . . . I wanted to free my little sisters, trapped by history. I broke the glass.

BORDER GUARD: You stole them?

LUNA: No, m'am, I only wanted to hold them in my hands and feel what they had to teach me about their maker.

BORDER GUARD: And...?

LUNA: We were not as we are now. We were not always fallen from the mountain.[114]

Luna's humble sack-dress, tied hands, and exhausting interrogation evoke the intimidation that Latin American refugees and migrants suffer at the hand of USAmerican officials at the US–Mexico border. Providing an interesting reading of this scene, Irma Mayorga argues that "The interrogation scene positions Luna's lesbian sexuality as both 'toxic' and 'illegal,' language that echoes the rhetoric of racialized xenophobia—a political move on the part of the play's dramaturgy that links her treatment and violation as a queer identity to the hostility met by Mexican nationals or Mexican-descended US citizens attempting to cross through US boundaries."[115] As it equates Luna's illegitimate sexuality with legal status, the play evinces the precariousness that defines undocumented immigrants' everyday lives in the United States. Yet it also obfuscates the privileges of citizenship and how undocumented women are especially vulnerable to violence.[116] In the wake of Arizona's SB 1070, which legitimized racial profiling in ways that adversely affect Chicanx and Native American communities, the setting "Phoenix" summons the specter of white supremacist violence. In the play, however, it is evoked to critique the gender and sexual politics of the Chicano Movement. The border setting is deployed in a similar manner.

ENCOUNTERING THE OTHER IN CHICANA LITERATURE 251

The border interrogation scene is also crucial for understanding the play's indigenist politics. Luna tells the Border Guard that she took the figurines from the museum because she wanted "to free them." She did not intend to steal them—for one can only steal what belongs to somebody else—but hold them, so that she may grasp what these icons reveal about her own history. The Indigenous figurines are behavioral and cultural models. They are indigenist surrogates that teach Luna that Chicanxs are a fallen civilization with a grand past. But in the attempt to give back to Chicanxs symbols and stories that have been denied to them by centuries of colonization, the play does not question the process that has rendered the "Indian" a museum piece in the first place. Instead, the play reproduces, to cite Jodi A. Byrd, "the erasure of indigenous peoples and the subsequent normalization of the history of displaying them, dead or alive, in museums for the benefit of future civilized generations."[117] In transposing objects from the museum to the stage, the play re-creates a rupture: What has happened since these figurines were made? What happened to the people who made them? Are they extinct? And what does Luna's eagerness to free these Indigenous figurines suggest about saviorism and Indigenous agency? Luna has no doubt that the figurines have been trapped and need her rescuing. *The Hungry Woman* carries on the entrapping by partaking in the museumification of Mexico's Indigenous peoples, who are treated largely as a collection of myths, symbols, and icons adapted to reinterpret a contemporary Chicana reality. In this way, the play follows in the footsteps of Mexican and Chicano indigenismo's concern with lo indígena, things that are Indigenous, over el/la indígena, the living Indigenous subject. Luna is sure that the figurines belong to her. After all, they exist to impart lessons about *her* people: "We were not always fallen from the mountain." Indigenous objects and the Chicana subject once again become merged as one.

The identification between the human and the divine that is recurrent in Chicana literature de-historicizes the relationship between Chicanxs and Indigenous people, relegating the Mesoamerican Indigenous both to the past and to the margins of history. As a repressed side of mestiza consciousness, the Indigenous is posited as always already inhabiting the Chicana, even as the Indigenous exists mainly in a mythological realm that remains unknowable. Evincing the centrality of archaeology to Chicana decolonial imaginaries, Moraga first saw the Cihuateteo statues at the Anthropology Museum in Mexico City.[118] Comparably, Anzaldúa first encountered the statue of Coatlicue in the Museum of

252   DECOLONIAL IMAGINARIES AND COLORBLIND LOGICS

Natural History in New York City, although in *Borderlands/La Frontera* she describes Coatlicue as a powerful archetype "that inhabits my psyche."[119] In situating Indigenous subjectivity within Chicanas' embodied and collective memory, as inhabiting their "psyche," Anzaldúa and Moraga conceal the actual mechanisms that enable them to learn about Indigenous traditions. In *A Xicana Codex of Changing Consciousness* (2011), Moraga describes an unnamed elderly woman: "She taught me how to smoke rolled tobacco like you're praying to some god; although I knew it before. Somehow. When she taught me I remembered, like with most things she taught me, that it was a matter of remembering."[120] The unnamed elderly woman who taught Moraga how to pray while smoking rolled tobacco, the passage suggests, did not really teach her anything about Indigenous practices because Moraga "knew it before."

While Moraga claims that acquiring Indigenous knowledge is merely a matter of remembering what her body already knows, representations of Mesoamerican Indigenous people in *The Hungry Woman* are rooted in colonial epistemologies that suggest otherwise. Although Moraga criticized Chicano Movement writers for extolling "Aztec warrior bravado,"[121] *The Hungry Woman* features a chorus of Aztec warriors, albeit now for the purpose of feminist critique. The Cihuatateo fulfill several functions in the play. They assume the role of narrators and comment on the action, like the chorus in Greek tragedies, and play the role of other characters, including Jasón and Savannah. Most importantly, through the Cihuatateo the play creates a connection between an ancestral Mesoamerican Indigenous lineage and the Chicanx present as the indigenist presence serves to ultimately construct and reflect upon the Chicanx subject as itself Indigenous. In this way, Indigenist personae in Chicana literature evoke the servile role that Africanist characters fulfill in white US writing, as described by Morrison in *Playing in the Dark*.

In a scene that precedes the second part of Luna's interrogation, the Cihuatateo are described as follows:

> *The CIHUATATEO dance as warrior women. They draw out maguey thorns, the size of hands, from their serpent's sashes. They pierce and slash themselves, wailing. They encircle MEDEA with the ghostly white veil of La Llorona. It is a river in the silver night. MEDEA and the sounds of the children's cries drown beneath it.*[122]

Connecting Medea's murder of her son to the story of La Llorona, the wailing woman who cries incessantly for the children she killed, the

ENCOUNTERING THE OTHER IN CHICANA LITERATURE 253

Cihuatateo perform the ritual of bloodletting, an autosacrificial act which becomes the prelude to Medea's sacrifice of Chac-Mool. The play thus creatively reenacts a religious Indigenous ritual on stage. The ancient Aztecs, who considered blood sacred and necessary to the continuation of life, pierced their tongues and other parts of the body with thorns of the maguey plant to petition the gods for fertility.[123] The practice also existed among the Maya. However, in a different part of *The Hungry Woman*, Moraga writes that the ritual of bloodletting is restricted to men because women bleed naturally every month.[124] Performed by a chorus of female deities, the ritual appears contradictory. The Cihuatateo's performance of piercing and slashing themselves with oversized thorns seems included to achieve sensational effects.

The Cihuatateo, who dance, chant, and perform traditional rituals, function as a folkloric and spiritual element in the play. According to the stage directions, the Cihuatateo wear "the faces of the dead in form of skulls. Their hands are shaped into claws. Their breasts appear bare and their skirts are tied with the cord of snake. They are barefoot with their ankles wrapped in shell rattles. The chorus performs in the traditional style of Aztec danzantes."[125] Moraga's choice to feature a chorus of dead deities may initially seem to be a subversive strategy aimed at critiquing representations of the Indigenous as confined to the past, but there is no evidence of such a critique in the play. The representation of the Cihuatateo instead conjures the dominant inclusion of Indigenous characters as a spectacular element, evoking what Helen Pringle describes as *scientific ethnopornography*, which is "not merely a procedure for the collection of certain materials about the 'natives'; it is also a practice of representation through which to make a spectacle of them."[126] The neo-Aztec costumes and performances are a folkloric and nostalgic rendering of a seemingly extinct civilization as imagined by a mestizo population. An audience member who has been to Mexico City may recognize the costumes of the Cihuatateo as being similar to those worn by Mexican artists performing in the Zocalo for tourists eager to experience an "authentic" version of indigeneity. Still, the danza azteca does not exist only for the entertainment of tourists in Mexico, where participation in the dance continues to grow. For Chicanxs, who have been forcibly disconnected from their roots, the danza azteca also represents an important way to unearth and reconnect to Indigenous spirituality. Nonetheless, the transposition of this practice to the stage in Moraga's play is indebted to the valorization of the same remote Aztec past and mythology that undergirds Mexican nationalism.

254   DECOLONIAL IMAGINARIES AND COLORBLIND LOGICS

But even as the play constantly draws connections between Meso-american deities and Chicanxs, *The Hungry Woman* argues through the figure of Chac-Mool that indigeneity is not merely a matter of embodied memory, ancestry or "blood," but is a *practice*. Since the Spanish and Anglo colonization to which Chicanxs have been subjected has interrupted traditional modes of knowledge acquisition, Chac-Mool has to learn how to harvest and worship. In an attempt to reconnect with his Indigenous roots, Chac-Mool gets a tattoo on his arm, a process that re-creates the Aztec sacrificial ritual of skin piercing:

> CHAC-MOOL: I don't remember if this is the right way to pray. I was never officially taught. It is not allowed. Everything relies on memory. We no longer have any records, nothing is written down. But I heard. I heard about Aztlán and the piercing of the skin as prayer.[127]

Chac-Mool's statement "It is not allowed" constitutes a poignant critique of European and US cultural imperialism. Since Indigenous practices are neither documented in books nor taught in schools, Chac-Mool must undergo a (re)learning process. Tattooing his skin is Chac-Mool's way to write down his history and adopt spiritual practices in a creative manner. Chac-Mool's tattoo depicts the eponymous messenger between the world of humans and deities that in Aztec iconography is represented carrying a bowl on his belly, which he uses to transport sacrificed hearts to the gods. In constructing the character of Chac-Mool, the play blurs the boundaries between different Indigenous peoples and traditions, mirroring the pastiche aesthetics of dominant multiculturalism. Chac-Mool is Yaqui and traces his lineage from the Aztec people, while acquiring citizenship in Aztlán requires him to participate in a Sun Dance, a Native American religious practice. As it constructs Medea and Chac-Mool's ethnicity as Yaqui, the play silences the fact that, during the Yaqui Indian wars of 1880–1910, white USAmericans and Mexicanos with economic interests in Sonora collaborated in the genocide of the Yaqui.[128]

Structuring its criticism of Chicano indigenism largely around the figure of Jasón, *The Hungry Woman* reinscribes the racial essentialism of *El Plan Espiritual de Aztlán* even as it critiques it. After Medea abandons Jasón and takes Chac-Mool with her, Jasón marries a young Apache woman so that he can meet the requirement of authenticity necessary for land ownership in Aztlán. When he discovers that his wife cannot have children, Jasón demands custody of Chac-Mool, whom he

ENCOUNTERING THE OTHER IN CHICANA LITERATURE   255

intends to use to secure his political ascension in Aztlán. When Chac-Mool attempts to cross into Aztlán, the Border Guard interrogates him:

> CHAC-MOOL: [My father] wants me back. To make a man outta me, to keep the Indian in him.
> BORDER GUARD: He's not an Indian?
> CHAC-MOOL: Not enough, according to my mother.
> BORDER GUARD: And that's a problem?
> CHAC-MOOL: In Aztlán it is. God, I thought you knew the place.[129]

While *El Plan Espiritual de Aztlán* resorted to racial measures of authenticity in affirming "the call of our blood is our power," *The Hungry Woman* challenges "blood quantum" and phenotype as primary measures of indigeneity, suggesting through the character of Chac-Mool that being Indigenous is based on lived cultural and spiritual practices. At the same time, the play also contradicts this vision of indigeneity. While the play's critique of essentialism is attached to Jasón, it does not seem to apply to the Chicana characters. Medea insists that she is "more Indian" than Jasón because she has Yaqui ancestry and is "more Indian" than Luna because of her hairless body. She also argues that, because she has passed on her "Yaqui blood" to Chac-Mool, their bond is more significant than the child's relationship with his father. In Medea's understanding, Chac-Mool is Indigenous *thanks to her* and she expects him to express gratitude by remaining in Phoenix, even as Medea paradoxically refuses to transmit Indigenous knowledge to her son although she is a curandera.

The Hungry Woman constructs a pastiche Indigenous Chicanx identity that blends different Mesoamerican and Native American traditions. And yet the play itself articulates a critique of appropriation:

> CHAC-MOOL: Luna told me they just finished building a strip of casinos along Cuahtemoc [*sic*] Boulevard.
> MAMA SAL: Casinos? In Aztlán?
> CHAC-MOOL: With neon, glitter and the works.
> SAVANNAH: I guess they figure the Indians are making a killing on gambling throughout the Union, why not the Chicanos, too? No one's gonna leave them in the dust of socialism.
> MAMA SAL: Wannabes. First it's the sweat lodge, then the sundance. Ni saben su propia tradición indígena [They don't even know their own Indigenous tradition].[130]

Medea is both Yaqui and Chicana, yet "Indians" and "Chicanos" are treated as separate groups in this passage. Although gambling is not a Native American tradition, unlike what Mama Sal suggests, here it is associated with sacred elements of Native American cultures, such as the sweat lodge and Sun Dance. Gambling is also stigmatized as a capitalistic endeavor, rather than portrayed as a means of economic survival for Native American communities that must be understood within the specific contexts of colonialism, land dispossession, and the poverty that reigns on reservations. Mama Sal's comment about Indigenous traditions, which significantly is expressed in Spanish, reveals an anxiety about the crossing of inappropriate boundaries and conjures a statement that Anzaldúa made in an interview: "The goal of spirituality is to transform one's life. In order to achieve this goal we 'borrow' Native American spirituality and apply it to our situation. But we often misuse what we've borrowed by using it out of context. Chicanas/os are not critical enough about how we borrow from lo indio. Some Indian Americans think all Chicanas/os plunder native culture as mercilessly as whites."[131] As Mama Sal's critique of Chicanxs as "wannabes" evokes real-life divisions between Chicanx and Native American communities, it makes you wonder why Chac-Mool's initiation into Aztlán entails precisely a Sun Dance, or why Moraga's initiation into the circle of "*mixed-blood lodge sisters*"[132] described in the foreword occurs in a sweat lodge.

As *The Hungry Woman* excludes both Black people and Native Americans from the Chicanx community that it envisions, it privileges a nationalist construction of Chicanx identity that continues to rely on ancestry and ancient myth, rather than a politics of solidarity with other oppressed communities. In the process, it posits land ownership and sovereignty as shared paths toward liberation for Chicanxs, Native Americans, and African Americans. Describing the civil war that has divided the United States into smaller nations and which provides the backdrop to the play, Moraga writes, "The revolution established economic and political sovereignty for seceding nations with the ultimate goal of defending aboriginal rights throughout the globe."[133] Envisioning the protection of "aboriginal rights" as the ultimate goal of revolution, Moraga misrecognizes what Sexton calls "'the true horror of slavery' as de-culturalization or the loss of sovereignty."[134] In conflating the positionality of Indigenous people, whose structural position is dependent on a history of genocide and loss of sovereignty, and Black people, whose political ontology continues to be determined by slavery, Moraga de facto relegates the slave to "the position of the unthought."[135] Bound

ENCOUNTERING THE OTHER IN CHICANA LITERATURE   257

to what Sexton terms a "dialectics of loss and recovery" rather than "a politics with no (final) recourse to foundations of any sort,"[136] *The Hungry Woman* cannot imagine abolishing the plantation that is the United States. It can only envision its reform.

As Chicana indigenism is invested in creating powerful decolonial imaginaries, its entanglement with politics of indigeneity and authenticity means that it cannot be understood outside complex notions of power. While critics have lamented that the indígena has been relegated to the margins of Chicana literature, this chapter has shown that the inclusion of living Indigenous characters does not resolve the tensions at the heart of Chicana indigenism. Rather than relying mainly on Aztec and Maya mythology, the construction of a Chicana Indigenous identity in *Erased Faces* depends on the encounter with living Maya people. However, the relationship between the Chicana and the Indigenous subject, dead or alive, remains unchanged as the Indigenous continues to be a source of love, knowledge, and renewal for the Chicana, a surrogate that ultimately enables Chicana writers "to think about themselves."[137] While indigenism is put at the service of feminism in Chicana literature, the employment of the Indigenous as a vehicle for social critique, literary creation, political mobilization, and spiritual awakening is a priori entangled with Eurocentric understandings of the Indigenous as *usable*. White writers like Michel de Montaigne and Jean-Jacques Rousseau inaugurated the invocation of the "Indian" as a means to critique Western society.[138] Constructing the Indigenous subject as the ultimate racial insider-outsider whose identity boundaries are flexible is central to both white discourses of racial disavowal and to Chicana indigenist imaginaries that seek to counter de-indigenization and white disavowal. What remains constant in the early Chicano indigenismo of Alurista's *Floricanto en Aztlán*, the neo-indigenismo of *Erased Faces*, and the radical Chicana feminism of *Borderlands/La Frontera* and *The Hungry Woman* is the usage of the Indigenous as an instrument for counterhegemonic poetics and a disavowal of Mexicano complicity in the genocide of Indigenous peoples of the Southwest as Chicanx mestizaje reinscribes the mystification of colonial violence of state-sponsored mestizaje.

In reproposing some of the representational strategies and ideological pitfalls that it contests, Chicana indigenism demands a deeper engagement with the intersectional and relational dimensions of racism and reveals the embeddedness of colorblind discourse within the colonial archive. Chicana indigenist imaginaries construct equivalences between Chicanx and Mesoamerican Indigenous subjects (and objects), while they disavow the significance of citizenship, class, education, nationality, or mobility in envisioning the positionality of the Chicana. In a priori relieving the Chicana subject from responsibility for racism while conflating different kinds of oppression and different Indigenous subjectivities and histories, Chicana indigenist imaginaries collude with the colorblind logics of the white feminism and multiculturalism they aim to oppose. As they collapse the Chicana self and the Indigenous Other while disavowing a possible historical, ideological, or symbolic affinity with the colonizer, Chicana indigenist imaginaries reproduce an epistemology of disavowal as they construct the Chicanx subject as always already innocent. Mexican and Mexican American historical complicity with slavery and the oppression of Indigenous people is erased in the process.[139]

Even as they create a narrative of inclusion within Indigenous communities, both Limón's and Moraga's works display an anxiety about the Chicana characters' legitimacy in Indigenous spaces. In making visible these anxieties, the works articulate a particular kind of ethic. Rather than hiding their doubts, Moraga in the foreword to *The Hungry Woman* and Adriana Mora in *Erased Faces* invite readers to bear witness to their anxieties about legitimacy. The acknowledgment of the Chicana's status as outsider in these works, however, does not warrant the Indigenous characters' resistance to the Chicana's presence in their ceremonies and communities. The candid acknowledgment of one's outsider status, or the manifestation of what might be a particular kind of guilt, merely serve to indicate that the Chicana is not guilty. The display of anxiety over one's legitimacy signals that the characters *mean well*. In the process, although they insist on a politics of absolute identification with the Indigenous, the works cannot avoid calling attention to differences between Indigenous and Chicanx characters inscribed through differential characterization.

As they collapse Chicana and Indigenous subjectivities, *Erased Faces* and *The Hungry Woman* also silence the specificity of Black women's struggles, while they appropriate Blackness for the benefit of Chicana feminist politics. Ironically, the works suggest that homosexuality can elide differences between women, yet also demonstrate that this process of analogization reproduces epistemic violence. Anzaldúa warned against romanticizing homosexuality as a potential equalizer. In the keynote address delivered at the Lesbian Plenary Session of the 1988

ENCOUNTERING THE OTHER IN CHICANA LITERATURE 259

National Women's Studies Association conference, Anzaldúa states: "If we were to ask white lesbians to leave their whiteness at home, they would be shocked, having assumed that they have de-conditioned the negative aspects of being white out of themselves by virtue of being feminist or lesbian. But I see that whiteness bleeds through all the baggage they port around with them."[140] Although they are written by women of color, the works examined in this chapter also posit homosexuality as an equalizer that can elide differences between women. And yet, the Chicana characters' relationship to Black, Indigenous, and undocumented women are shaped by asymmetries of power that their sexuality is unable to supersede. To acknowledge this does not mean minimizing the significance of white privilege, but rather the opposite. It implies recognizing that race is relational and racial positionality may shift when borders are crossed—with one important exception: Black people alone remain at the bottom of the racial hierarchy regardless of where they are in the world. Fanon puts this succinctly: *"Wherever he goes, the Negro remains a Negro."*[141] In the imaginative world of Chicana literature, too, Blackness often remains the locus of abjection, appropriation, and silencing.

EPILOGUE

An Undying Colonialism

They know how to hold on to their privilege, could they have held it this long otherwise?
—George Jackson, *Blood in My Eye*

The step backward has a new name today. It is called the "white backlash." But the white backlash is nothing new. It is the surfacing of old prejudices, hostilities and ambivalences that have always been there. It was caused neither by the cry of Black Power nor by the unfortunate recent wave of riots in our cities. The white backlash of today is rooted in the same problem that has characterized America ever since the black man landed in chains on the shores of this nation. The white backlash is an expression of the same vacillations, the same search for rationalizations, the same lack of commitment that have always characterized white America on the question of race.
—Martin Luther King Jr., *Where Do We Go from Here: Chaos or Community?*

In decolonization, there is therefore the need of a complete calling into question of the colonial situation.
—Frantz Fanon, *The Wretched of the Earth*

The inauguration of Donald Trump as president of the United States was merely one week away when my Countering Colorblindness across the Disciplines graduate seminar met for the first time in Nashville on January 12, 2017. I was quickly made to realize that a course about colorblindness required a degree of justification unlikely during Barack

261

Obama's presidency as a student soon asked, "Is colorblindness still relevant in the age of Trump?" Turning this query on its head, *Colorblind Tools* has demonstrated that colorblindness is a constitutive tool of racial power that white people have mobilized since the inception of colonial conquest and the transatlantic slave trade. What appears as a new epoch of neofascism is merely the cumulation of centuries of undying colonialism and slavery. While many scholars contend that racism since World War II has been radically reformulated to the extent that it has been termed *the new racism*, I have shown that present-day racism is fundamentally tied to the past. In this way, I have pushed against the dominant emphasis on historical change that has pervaded racial theory for over half a century, arguing instead for the importance of centering the substance of unrelenting anti-Black violence and white privilege.

Today, the demonization of Black and Brown people delivered in colorblind language continues to serve the manufacturing of political consent across national borders. To illustrate this point, we need look no further than to Trump's 2016 electoral campaign. That crime was at an all-time low in the United States did not stop Trump from bringing up crime in a Republican nomination acceptance speech that aimed to divide people of color while exploiting white people's fears of losing privileges. In the speech, delivered in July 2016, Trump specifically targeted Black and Latinx people, providing a false picture of the United States as a country at the mercy of uncontrolled racialized crime and violence. The criminalization of Black people is packaged in colorblind language in the speech, as cities with a large African American population—Washington, Baltimore, and Chicago—are made to embody violent crime. Undocumented Latinx immigrants, who do not have the right to vote, were more explicit targets as Trump argued that "illegal immigrants with criminal records . . . are tonight roaming free to threaten peaceful citizens."[1] While many white USAmericans hire immigrants illegally, Trump branded as illegal the victims of such exploitation. Undocumented immigrants in the United States contribute billions in taxes, yet this did not stop Trump from depicting Latinx immigrants as detrimental to the economy and as threats to the jobs of the working classes—people whose interests are not represented by the Republican party, but whose anxieties were conveniently leveraged during Trump's campaign.[2] What else, then, could have been expected the day of Trump's nomination than a speech from his daughter Ivanka that disavowed Trump's racism and invoked the bootstraps ideology

AN UNDYING COLONIALISM · 263

and the colorblind tool of *merit*? Conveniently silencing Trump's white supremacist agenda and the Trump Management Corporation's long-standing systematic discrimination against Black people, Ivanka Trump represented her father as an ethical and hard-working man whose companies are "true meritocracies" and who "hires the best person for the job." Trump, his daughter Ivanka confidently stated, "is colorblind and gender neutral."[3]

Colorblindness continued to prove productive beyond Trump's electoral campaign. Swiftly passed after Trump's election, Executive Order 13763—which banned citizens from seven Muslim-majority countries from traveling to the United States, including refugees fleeing the war in Syria—is couched in colorblind language.[4] Without mentioning the word Muslim, it prevented citizens from Muslim-majority nations Iran, Iraq, Libya, Somalia, Sudan, Syria, and Yemen from entering the United States. Conveniently named "Protecting the Nation from Foreign Terrorist Entry into the United States," the ban projected the threat of terrorism onto foreign racialized Others, while protecting US terrorism abroad and at home. White USAmerican terrorists have killed almost twice as many USAmericans as Islamic extremists have done since September 11, 2001. Yet no legislation protecting against homegrown white terrorists exists.

Racialized xenophobia couched in colorblind language also continues to serve as a nation-building tool. Although neoliberalism has partially eroded national sovereignty and complicated the relationship between nation and race, the entanglement between race-making and nation-state building persists. Nationalist rhetoric—whether in Europe, the United States, or Brazil—still relies on the scapegoating of racialized Others as a means to garner consent, thereby constantly reproposing on the political stage an *us* versus *them* dichotomy that infers white superiority. This is visible also in South Africa, where xenophobia only targets Black immigrants and is best described as Afrophobia, and where white people as a collective are the main beneficiaries of a xenophobia that excludes us.[5] Like elsewhere, propaganda against immigrants in South Africa serves the manufacturing of consent and protects white interests.

In Italy, the demonization of immigrants fulfills the same functions. It also continues to serve as a nation-building tool. The case of the far-right political party Lega Nord (Northern League), which managed to garner votes in the South and became a majority party in the Italian government in 2018, is instructive here. Originally, in the 1990s, the Northern League built its constituency in the North by targeting southern Italians, whom the party branded as inferior, living off governmental assistance, and prone to corruption, while it represented northerners as modern, hard-working, and virtuous.[6] In this way, the Northern League concealed and reproduced the subordinate relationship between the North and South that has existed since the 1861 so-called unification of Italy, an annexation that the North violently imposed upon the South.[7] Redirecting their propaganda toward Black migrants and refugees has allowed the Northern League, which strategically dropped the term Northern from its name, to expand its voting constituency in the South and acquire stronger legitimacy in the Italian government. Anti-Blackness couched in the language of immigration has functioned as a nation-building tool to the extent that southern Italians no longer face systemic discrimination in northern Italy, while northern and southern Italians have united over targeting Black people. That anti-Blackness is as prevalent in the South as it is in the North, and that southern Italians have been co-opted into supporting a party that does not have their interests at heart, speaks powerfully to the enduring power of racist propaganda disguised as cultural nationalism.

Targeting Black immigrants has enabled the Italian government to deflect attention away from its responsibility for maintaining a neo-colonial order in Africa and the Middle East that has caused the displacement of millions of people, just as targeting West Indian immigrants allowed the white elite in early twentieth-century Panama to hide their own complicity with US imperialism. Comparable to the disavowal of racist intent that accompanied the hostility against West Indians in Olmedo Alfaro's Panama, the enmity against Black people is rarely acknowledged as being racist in the Italian media and public discourse. Behind closed doors, though, at plenty of white Italian families' dinner tables and social gatherings, the anti-Blackness is loud and bold. What it means to be Italian meanwhile remains associated with whiteness, as the principle of jus sanguinis ("right of blood") grants even third-generation descendants of Italians who have no ties to the country the right to an Italian passport, while the children of immigrants born and raised in Italy remain excluded from citizenship until the age of eighteen,[8] reminding us again of Panama in the 1930s, when West Indian children born in the country were allowed to apply for citizenship only at twenty-one years of age.[9]

Just as targeting Black and Latinx people continues to ensure the presence of a vast exploitable pool of cheap labor in the United States, demonizing Black people achieves the same results in Italy. Many Black people who live in Italy work for very little pay and live in dilapidated and overcrowded buildings without services, yet they are constantly misrepresented as a burden on the economy and as having privileges that Italian citizens do not have. The manner in which Black people are treated in present-day Italy demonstrates that the African in Europe continues to be, to cite Frantz Fanon, "a thing tossed into the great sound and fury."[10] Despite fully knowing that Black people are sold in slave markets and face harrowing conditions in Libyan prisons, the Italian government continues to fund the Libyan military.[11] While they represent themselves as bastions of "civility" and democracy, Italy and the European Union at large are doing everything in their power to keep Black people out of Europe, including financing slavery in the twenty-first century.

While Black people remain subjected to the daily terror of gratuitous white violence, white people ironically argue that *we* are the victims of racism. Fabricated and propagated by the South African government during apartheid, the swart gevaar (Black peril) propaganda has achieved renewed and global traction in our time. The myth of the "assailed white race" is evident in numerous crime novels by white South African authors that portray white people as subjects under siege, propaganda videos by US white supremacist David Duke falsely claiming that "white genocide" is rampant in South Africa, Australian home affairs minister Peter Dutton's 2018 outlandish statement that white South African farmers are being "persecuted," or Trump's equally concerning 2018 tweet proclaiming the alleged "large scale killing of farmers" in South Africa.[12] In reality, white South African farmers are "*far less likely* to be the targets of crime than the general population."[13] The white discourse about farm murders thus reveals itself as a racist tactic. These present-day reverberations of the swart gevaar propaganda seek to turn white people—the perpetrators of anti-Black violence and dispossession—into victims. They do so to deliberately mystify the ongoing reality of Black suffering and white privilege in South Africa and worldwide. They also demonstrate that white people continue to act together across national boundaries to protect our privileges. President Cyril Ramaphosa's mere mention that he would redistribute land to Black South Africans was met with white threats and attempts to police how redistribution should be undertaken reverberating from the United Kingdom to the United States, no matter that white South Africans have nothing to fear as Ramaphosa's declaration was little more than an electoral gimmick. In the process, just like during plantation

266   EPILOGUE

slavery, white people try by all means to render invisible the inexorable ways that Black people and people of color threaten the racist status quo through collective organizing and mobilization. On July 4th, 2020, *millions* of people took to the streets all over the United States to protest against the police and the state-sanctioned racist violence that defines them as an institution, yet not one single article on the entire CNN online frontpage mentioned the protests the following day.

As I finish writing this book amid what has been described as a resurgence of fascist politics and Trump's election as the product of a white backlash against the Obama presidency, I am reminded of the words that Martin Luther King Jr. pronounced in his last book, *Where Do We Go from Here: Chaos or Community?* (1967). Faced with violent white resistance to desegregation that starkly revealed white people's unwillingness to put into practice the mandates of *Brown v. Board of Education*, King refused to capitulate to the myth of a nascent white backlash and identified these white tactics as persistent strategies of racial domination. The white backlash, King argues, is the expression of the "same search for rationalizations, the same lack of commitment that have always characterized white America on the question of race." King reminds us of the consistency with which white people, as a collective, concurrently support and disavow racism. We should not take for granted that many of the rhetorical moves, indeed rationalizations, that Rijno Johannes van der Riet made in 1810 to defend slavery for Khoena children are still deployed to control, criminalize, and incarcerate Black people today—miles across the Atlantic. We also cannot forget the words of George Jackson, who in *Blood in My Eye* (1972) writes: "We will never have a complete definition of fascism, because it is in constant motion, showing a new face to fit any particular set of problems that arise to threaten the predominance of the traditionalist, capitalist ruling class. But if one would be forced for the sake of clarity to define it in a word simple enough for all to understand, that word would be 'reform.'"[14] Jackson makes visible the entanglement between fascism, camouflage, and reform, warning us against confusing modifications in appearance ("a new face") with shifts in substance. Rather than obsessing about how racism changes, it is more productive to consider how disavowal, camouflage, and consmetic change are themselves instrumental for the maintenance of the racist infrastructure. After all, it would be wrong to view the Trump presidency as fundamentally different from that of Obama, which witnessed the unrelenting mass incarceration of Black people and mass deportation of Latinx immigrants. Meanwhile, US president Joe Biden continues to exploit fears of crime to fund the genocidal police at exorbitant rates, just as vice president Kamala Harris continues to demonize and oppose immigrants arriving south of the US–Mexico border. Clearly, the "Trump era" did not end with Trump's presidency. One thing is certain: it is neither through colorblindness nor through reform that anti-Blackness and white supremacy are challenged. Reform is how white supremacy reproduces itself. Outside abolition there is nothing but the permanence of racism—a permanence to which the white disavowal of racism has been instrumental for over five hundred years.

ACKNOWLEDGMENTS

This book has been over a decade in the making. Many people have helped me along the way and it gives me great joy to be able to thank them here. It truly takes a village to write a book and, while all remaining errors are my sole responsibility, if there is something useful in this book, the merit is not mine alone.

This book originated at the University of California, Santa Barbara (UCSB). I owe a huge debt of gratitude to my advisors, Carl Gutiérrez-Jones and George Lipsitz, and committee members, Abdul JanMohamed and Francisco Lomelí, for their brilliance, generous mentorship, and trust in my work. It was my greatest fortune to pursue a PhD in the UCSB Comparative Literature Program, which allowed me to truly follow my research interests and structure my coursework across disciplines, departments, and universities as I pleased. I wish the same freedom for every graduate student out there. Thank you to Sydney Lévy and Catherine Nesci, who chaired the program while I was there. Being a teaching assistant in the Department of Black Studies at UCSB was a true gift that continues to nourish my scholarship and pedagogy. Thank you in particular to Gaye Johnson, Chris McAuley, and Jeffrey Stewart. During my doctoral studies, I was blessed with wonderful teachers. Much gratitude goes especially to Gerardo Aldana, Stephanie Batiste, Leo Cabranes-Grant, Reg Daniel, the late Harry Garuba, Randal Johnson, Juan Pablo Lupi, Jorge Marturano, Ellen McCracken, Christina McMahon, Mantoa Motinyane, the late Cedric Robinson, Emiko Saldívar, Chela Sandoval, Darieck Scott, Kelwyn Sole, Roberto Strongman, and Howard Winant. Cedric Robinson and Harry Garuba have left an unbridgeable void. May they rest in power and in poetry.

At the University of Freiburg, I am indebted to Wolfgang Hochbruck, who mentored me and exhorted me to pursue a PhD when this first-generation student did not know what a PhD is. Thank you also to Rebecca Davies, who taught me English, Greta Olson, who encouraged me to thread my own path in literary analysis, and Walter Bruno Berg, who introduced me to Latin American literature. During my MA

270 ACKNOWLEDGMENTS

studies, an academic exchange fellowship allowed me to spend the 2002–03 academic year at the University of Texas at Austin, where it all began. Sincere thanks to Chiquita Collins, James Cox, Miguel Levario, John González, Domino Perez, Lisa Sánchez González, and Arnoldo Carlos Vento for the lessons.

My appreciation goes to my colleagues in the Department of English at Vanderbilt University as well as colleagues in the Department of African American and Diaspora Studies, Latino and Latina Studies Program, and Center for Latin American Studies. I am especially grateful for the generous and affirming mentorship of Mark Schoenfield. Thank you also to Vera Kutzinski and Ruth Hill for being supportive mentors. I thank Ifeoma Nwankwo for her frankness and sustaining guidance. Houston Baker, Jay Clayton, Colin Dayan, Lynn Enterline, Jen Fay, Earl Fitz, Jane Landers, Lorraine López, William Luis, Allison Schachter, Rachel Teukolsky, Ben Tran, and Mark Wollaeger provided much-appreciated support and advice. Always greeting me with a chat, Rick Hilles was the best office neighbor one can wish for. Much gratitude to Lucius Outlaw for the generosity and for modeling close reading in the classroom. The friendship, wit, and brilliance of Hortense Spillers have been a true gift. I am eternally grateful to her.

Joining the faculty in the Department of English at the University of Johannesburg has been a dream come true. Many thanks especially to Sikhumbuzo Mngadi for the guidance and patience. Thank you also to my colleagues Victoria Collis-Buthelezi, Minesh Dass, Ronit Frenkel, Lucy Valerie Graham, Siphiwo Mahala, Zamansele Nsele, and Thabo Tsehloane for making me feel at home and to Nosi Seranyane for the support. I am excited to be part of this community.

I am deeply indebted to the many people who generously read and offered feedback on portions of this manuscript: Candice Amich, Pavneet Aulakh, Pallavi Banerjee, Franco Barchiesi, Lee Bebout, RJ Boutelle, Sabine Broeck, Annie Castro, Jerry Flores, Daniel HoSang, Christina Jackson, Janine Jones, Vera Kutzinski, Sabrina Liccardo, Lorraine López, Jessica Lopez Lyman, Anne Garland Mahler, Chris McAuley, Tatiana McInnis, Lucy Mensah, Khwezi Mkhize, N. Michelle Murray, David Platzer, Alison Reed, Maythe Ruffino, Akshya Saxena, Allison Schachter, Haerin Shin, Tendayi Sithole, Unathi Slasha, Anand Taneja, Jamie Thomas, and LaTonya Trotter. This book would not be the same without you.

It has been a great experience to publish this book with Northwestern University Press. Thank you to my editors Gianna Mosser, who solicited

ACKNOWLEDGMENTS 271

the manuscript and ensured that it was off to a strong start, Trevor Perri, who graciously accompanied it through the peer review process, and Faith Wilson Stein, who pushed it across the finish line. Thank you also to Olivia Aguilar, Anne Gendler, Dino Robinson, Elizabeth Station, Anne Tappan Strother, and JD Wilson for the assistance. I am honored that *Colorblind Tools* is part of the Critical Insurgencies series. Thank you to series editors Michelle Wright and Jodi Byrd for believing in this work. Much appreciation and gratitude goes also to the three anonymous readers for generously reading the manuscript and for their generative feedback and critique.

Invitations to present my work always humble and inspire me. Abdul JanMohamed took a chance on me and invited me early on to speak about this project at the Postcolonial and Minority Studies Program at Emory University. Christina Jackson invited me to speak about colorblindness in the Africana Studies Program at Gettysburg College. Daniel HoSang invited me to present portions of this work at the Countering Colorblindness across the Disciplines symposium at the University of Oregon, where my work was also nurtured through intellectual community with coparticipants Glenn Adams, Devon Carbado, Kimberlé Crenshaw, William Darity, Lynn Fujiwara, Alison Gash, Leah Gordon, Cheryl Harris, Luke Harris, Michael Hames-García, Loren Kajikawa, Brian Klopotek, George Lipsitz, Joseph Lowndes, Sharon Luk, Ernesto Martinez, Chandan Reddy, Milton Reynolds, Dwanna Robertson, Lani Teves, Barbara Tomlinson, and Priscilla Yamin. Sam Naidu invited me to speak about colorblindness and South African literature in the Department of Literary Studies in English at Rhodes University. I am also glad to have had the opportunity to talk about racism and South African philosophy in the Department of Philosophy at Rhodes University. Camalita Naicker invited me to give a talk on this project in the Department of Historical Studies at the University of Cape Town. I am thankful to have been selected to speak about Chicana indigenism at the Young Scholars Symposium in the Institute for Latino Studies at the University of Notre Dame, where I especially benefited from Davíd Carrasco's insights. Aretha Phiri invited me to the Revising the Black Atlantic colloquium at the Stellenbosch Institute for Advanced Study. Thank you also to Hamilton Carroll, Lisa Lowe, Elizabeth Maddock Dillon, and Hortense Spillers for offering feedback on this project at the Futures of American Studies Institute and to Donald Pease for his interest in my work.

Financial support has been instrumental to the writing of this book. I am grateful for a Chancellor's Fellowship that allowed me to pursue a doctorate at UC Santa Barbara and (thanks also to the wonderful UC Intercampus Exchange Program and UCSB Education Abroad Program) enabled me to spend almost two years completing course-work and conducting research at the University of California, Berkeley, University of California, Los Angeles, and the University of Cape Town. Thank you also for a summer research grant to conduct research at the Instituto de Pesquisas e Estudos Afro-Brasileiros (IPEAFRO) in Rio de Janeiro, a language grant for the study of isiZulu, and a disser-tation completion fellowship from the UCSB Comparative Literature Program. I have been incredibly fortunate to receive both an Andrew W. Mellon Postdoctoral Fellowship and a Rhodes Postdoctoral Fellowship that enabled me to work on this manuscript at Rhodes University in Makhanda, where I thank Sam Naidu for the support. Thank you also to the Faculty of Humanities at the University of Johannesburg for sponsoring the indexing of this book.

This book would not exist without the work of archivists and librari-ans. Thank you especially to Deborah Lilton at the Jean and Alexander Heard Libraries at Vanderbilt University, and to the librarians at the Universitätsbibliothek Freiburg, Nettie Lee Benson Latin American Collection at UT Austin, the Bancroft Library at UC Berkeley, the African Studies Library at the University of Cape Town, the Amazwi South African Museum of Literature in Makhanda, and the UNESCO Archives. A special shout-out goes to Elisa Larkin Nascimento and Tatiane Lima at IPEAFRO. Many thanks to Aurelia Álvarez Urbajtel at the Archivo Manuel Álvarez Bravo for granting me permission to use Manuel Álvarez Bravo's photograph *Instrumental* on the cover. I could not have asked for a more fitting image.

I have been blessed with friends who carry, uplift, and inspire me. Much love to Simona Alessandro, Bachir "Black Son" Ali, Faquir Ali, Kaio de Almeida, Claudia Bozzaro, Aina Cabra Riart, Jaber Camara da Silva, Tinomutenda Chaka, Lorena Cinquemani, Barbara D'Amico, Ilana Dann Luna, Robson Dias, Gaby Eppler, Gabriel "Chef4Souls" Ferrão, Elsa Filosa, Christine Freudenberg, Vitor Granado, Ismael Huerta, Carmelo Incarbone, Phurah Jack, Juju & Leo, Patrick Kiame, Sabrina Liccardo, Judith Lienhart, Leonel "Blaze 5th" Manuel, Koketso Mashabela, Ntokozo Mbokazi, Ana Morente Luis, Sabaka "Kuvas" Muianga, Camalita Naicker, Lerato Ngwenya, Zamansele Nsele, Alison Reed, Maythe Ruffino, Haerin Shin, Genny Termini, Christiane Trefz, LaTonya Trotter, and Lêla Vianna Valerio. To the many others whose names are not listed here: you know who you are. Ein spezielles

ACKNOWLEDGMENTS

Danke geht an Eduard Czerwinski und Ralf Czerwinski. I appreciate you all.

The support of my family and loved ones means everything to me. Grazie di cuore a mia madre, Concetta Palazzo, e a mio padre, Francesco Milazzo, per l'amore incondizionale e per credere in me. My brothers, Mario and Mattia, are my greatest blessings. Grazie ai miei nonni, zii e cugini. Angela Firrarello, sei la sorella che non ho avuto. Cono Davide Cinquemani, sei unico e sei famiglia. The love of Katharina Czerwinski continues to sustain me. Unathi Slasha, keeper of the key, thank you for bringing so much joy into my life.

This book is not mine alone. It is the product of many conversations and is indebted to the people who have opened their doors to me, accompanied me, and made a multitude of joys and lessons across four continents possible. I am grateful to them and to God. From the bottom of my heart, thank you.

An early version of chapter 1 was published as "White Supremacy, White Knowledge, and Anti-West Indian Discourse in Panama: Olmedo Alfaro's *El peligro antillano en la América Central*" in *The Global South* 6, no. 2 (Fall 2012): 65–86. Portions of chapter 3 appeared in "The Rhetorics of Racial Power: Enforcing Colorblindness in Post-Apartheid Scholarship on Race" in *Journal of International and Intercultural Communication* 8, no. 1 (February 2015): 7–26, and in "On the Transportability, Malleability, and Longevity of Colorblindness: Reproducing White Supremacy in Brazil and South Africa" in *Seeing Race Again: Countering Colorblindness Across the Disciplines*, edited by Kimberlé Crenshaw, Luke Harris, Daniel HoSang, and George Lipsitz (Oakland: University of California Press, 2019), 105–27. Parts of chapter 4 were published in "On White Ignorance, White Shame, and Other Pitfalls in Critical Philosophy of Race" in *Journal of Applied Philosophy* 34, no. 4 (August 2017): 557–72. A few paragraphs of chapter 4 and the epilogue appeared in "Mark Mathabane's *K*ffir Boy*, Black Consciousness, and the Fallacies of Liberalism" in *ARIEL* 52, no. 3–4 (July–October 2021): 29–62.

NOTES

Introduction

EPIGRAPHS: Césaire, *Notebook of a Return to the Native Land*, 44; Fanon, *Toward the African Revolution*, 37; Spillers, *Black, White, and in Color*, 379.

1. Most sources that I have encountered argue that Jaén was seventeen years old when he was murdered (see, for example, "Riots in Colon When Police Officer Shot Fleeing Youth" and "West Indians Riot After Police Killing"), while a source first published in the United States says that he was nineteen years old (see "Panama Mob Stones Police Chief's Home After Boy Is Killed"). Notice also that I use the term West Indian rather than Afro-Caribbean to avoid confusion as Panama is part of the extended Caribbean.

2. On the murder, court case, and uprising see Lasso, "Race and Ethnicity in the Formation of Panamanian National Identity"; "Riots in Colon When Police Officer Shot Fleeing Youth"; and "West Indians Riot After Police Killing." On Delgado's 1933 indictment, see "File Indictment Against Head of the Colon Police Force."

3. Lasso, "Race and Ethnicity in the Formation of Panamanian National Identity," 84.

4. Lasso, 70 (my emphasis). See also Watson, *The Politics of Race in Panama*, 14.

5. On the murder and its aftermath, see Harney and Moten, "Michael Brown"; and Mirzoeff, "The Murder of Michael Brown."

6. Wilson cited in Mirzoeff, 65–66. For the full transcript of the hearing see *State of Missouri v. Darren Wilson*.

7. Mirzoeff, "The Murder of Michael Brown," 60.

8. Cited in Lasso, "Race and Ethnicity in the Formation of Panamanian National Identity," 83.

9. Wilson in "Exclusive: Watch George Stephanopoulos' Full Interview."

10. "Exclusive: Watch George Stephanopoulos' Full Interview."

11. Martinot and Sexton, "The Avant-Garde of White Supremacy," 171.

12. Harney and Moten, "Michael Brown," 84.

13. On the 2020 protests against racism and police violence see, for example, Hill, *We Still Here*; Hinton, *America on Fire*; and Elliott-Cooper, *Black Resistance to British Policing*.

14. Micol Seigel writes that "any analysis of US policing must consider its constitutive relationship to the racialization of Black and Brown subjects, not only theoretically but also in history, with the US police's structural formation as an antiblack force" (*Violence Work*, 21). On the history of the US police, see also Mitrani, *The Rise of the Chicago Police Department*. On police violence and anti-Blackness, see, for example, Sexton and Martinot, "The Avant-Garde of White Supremacy"; Abu-Jamal, *Have Black Lives Ever Mattered?*; Woods, *Blackhood Against the Police Power*; and Alves, *The Anti-Black City*.

15. On abolition see, for example, Jackson, *Blood in My Eye*; Davis, *Are Prisons Obsolete?*; James, *The New Abolitionists*; Gilmore, *Change Everything*; and Kaba, *We Do This 'Til We Free Us*.

16. Césaire, *Notebook of a Return to the Native Land*, 22; Wilderson, "Frank B. Wilderson, 'Wallowing in the Contradictions.'"

17. Wilderson, *Afropessimism*, 92. See also Warren, "The Will of the American God," 52.

18. Mills, *The Racial Contract*, 1.

19. Martinot and Sexton, "The Avant-Garde of White Supremacy," 173.

20. Newton, "A Functional Definition of Politics," 149.

21. Foucault, *The History of Sexuality*, 86. Notice that, while I find this specific formulation about power useful, I consider Foucault's theorization of power as diffused and coming from everywhere not simply useless for understanding the operations of white supremacy and anti-Blackness, but actually dangerous given that it conceals how white people do exercise power *over* Black people and people of color in a white supremacist society. For these reasons, I refrain from using Foucault's theories about power in this book.

22. While I borrow the term *racial power* from Claire Jean Kim, my understanding of the term differs from hers. Kim defines racial power as "the systematic tendency of the racial status quo to reproduce itself." She adds, "I conceive of racial power not as something that an individual or group exercises directly or intentionally over another individual or group but rather as a systemic property, permeating, circulating throughout, and continuously constituting society. I do not use the phrase 'White racial power' because it erroneously suggests that Whites possess and deliberately exercise racial power against others when in fact Whites, too, are

NOTES TO PAGES 6–10

constituted *qua* Whites by the operation of racial power" (*Bitter Fruit*, 9). In contrast with Kim, I use the term racial power as synonymous with *white racial power* to highlight that white people, collectively and systematically, exercise power against Black people and people of color.

23. Robinson, *Forgeries of Memory and Meaning*, xii.

24. Robinson, xii-xiii.

25. Robinson, xiii.

26. Jung, *Beneath the Surface of White Supremacy*, 14.

27. Du Bois, *The Souls of Black Folk*, 12.

28. I expand upon the distinction between slavery, which structures anti-Blackness, and colonialism, the mode of white supremacy, in the second part of this introduction.

29. Lorde, *Sister Outsider*, 113.

30. Sorentino, "Mistresses as Masters?," 70.

31. Jones-Rogers, *They Were Her Property*, xv.

32. See, for example, Wetherell and Potter, *Mapping the Language of Racism*; Augoustinos, Tuffin, and Rapley, "Genocide or a Failure to Gel?"; and McReary, "Colour-Blind."

33. See, for example, Fredrickson, *White Supremacy*; Marx, *Making Race and Nation*; Hamilton et al., *Beyond Racism*; Winant, *The World is a Ghetto*; Ansell, "Casting a Blind Eye"; Daniel, *Race and Multiraciality in Brazil and the United States*; Willoughby-Herard, *Waste of a White Skin*; and Vargas, *The Denial of Antiblackness*.

34. On relationality as method see, for example, Goldberg, "Racial Comparisons, Relational Racisms"; Sexton, "People-of-Color-Blindness"; Molina, *How Race is Made in America*; and Molina, HoSang, and Gutiér-rez, *Relational Formations of Race*.

35. Robinson, *Forgeries of Memory and Meaning*, xii, xiii (my emphasis).

36. Said, *Orientalism*, 6.

37. Spillers, *Black, White, and in Color*, 380 (italics in the original).

38. On *Graham v. Connor* see Obasogie and Newman, "The Futile Fourth Amendment."

39. See the testimony of Darren Wilson in *State of Missouri v. Darren Wilson*.

40. On colorblindness in the United States see, for example, Zuberi and Bonilla-Silva, "Toward a Definition of White Logic and White Methods"; Crenshaw, "Color Blindness, History, and the Law"; Lipsitz, *How Racism Takes Place*; and Crenshaw et al., *Seeing Race Again*. On colorblindness in Brazil see, for example, Nascimento, *Brazil: Mixture or Massacre?*; Nascimento, *The Sorcery of Color*; and Milazzo, "On the Transportability,

278   NOTES TO PAGES 10–12

Malleability, and Longevity of Colorblindness." On colorblindness in South
Africa see, for example, Mngxitama, "Blacks Can't Be Racist"; Ansell, "Cast-
ing a Blind Eye"; Milazzo, "The Rhetorics of Racial Power"; and Modiri,
"Race as/and the Trace of the Ghost."

41. In *Represent and Destroy*, Jodi Melamed demonstrates the importance of literary studies in reproducing liberal orders and "disseminating
racial discourse" (3) in post–World War II United States. At the same time,
she shows that a race-radical literary tradition has disrupted and denatural-
ized the relationship between what Melamed calls "state antiracisms" (xviii)
and capitalism, providing powerful alternatives to US multiculturalism.

42. Moya, *The Social Imperative*, 8.

43. In his theorization of "cultural artifacts as socially symbolic acts" (5),
Fredric Jameson in *The Political Unconscious* draws from Louis Althusser's
definition of ideology as "the imaginary representation of the subject's relationship to his or her real conditions of existence" (Althusser, *Lenin and
Philosophy and Other Essays*, 162).

44. Inaugurated by Emma Pérez in *The Decolonial Imaginary*, the term
"decolonial imaginary" has proven generative beyond historical scholarship. Pérez conceptualizes a decolonial imaginary as "a rupturing space,
the alternative to that which is written in history. . . . [It] is that time lag
between the colonial and the postcolonial, that interstitial space where
differential politics and social dilemmas are negotiated" (*The Decolonial
Imaginary*, 6). In this book, I borrow the term *decolonial imaginary* to signify specifically literary imaginaries that produce "differential politics" and
create alternative narratives which deconstruct and destabilize racist ideologies and dominant versions of history.

45. Shange, *Progressive Dystopia*, 15.

46. Wilderson, *Red, White and Black*, 58.

47. Rampolokeng, "Rapmaster" in *Horns for Hondo* and *End Beginnings*.

48. Césaire, *Discourse on Colonialism*, 32.

49. Murakawa, *The First Civil Right*, 7.

50. The term "the new racism" was coined by British scholar Martin
Barker, who in *The New Racism* (1981) argues that racism has been fundamentally reformulated since the 1970s so that anti-immigrant propaganda
no longer relies on explicitly racist language or arguments about biology,
but on "a much more subtle form of racism than that which we stereotyp-
ically recognize as such" (4). At the center of this purported "new racism,"
which Barker argues is not an exclusively British phenomenon, is a "pseudo-
biological culturalism" (23) that portrays the nation as a culturally uniform
entity and views (racialized) immigrants as undesirable not because they

NOTE TO PAGE 12

are intrinsically inferior, but because they threaten the British way of life. Given that the nation in these racist arguments is constructed as fixed, homogeneous, and unchangeable, the allegedly new racist arguments about cultural difference, Barker contends, resemble older arguments about biology.

Building on Barker's work, in *'There Ain't No Black in the Union Jack'* (1987), Paul Gilroy analogously argues that there is a "new racism" (13) and contends that "ideologies of legality and of blacks as a high-crime group are . . . constitutive of the new racism" (13). Gilroy postulates the deployment of "new, cultural definitions of 'race'" (60) as central to contemporary racism. More specifically, Gilroy argues that the novelty of this racism "lies in the capacity to link discourses of patriotism, nationalism, xenophobia, Englishness, Britishness, militarism and gender difference into a complex system which gives 'race' its contemporary meaning. These themes combine to provide a definition of 'race' in terms of culture and identity" (43). The framing of post–World War II racism as "new" leads to theoretical impasses, such as Gilroy's argument in *Against Race* (2000) that the "New Racism" is now over because the era of molecular biology has ushered in an even *newer* era in which "the time of 'race' may be coming to a close even while racisms appear to proliferate" (44). Such arguments detach race from racism, further concealing the operations of racial power.

While Barker and Gilroy focus on the British context, French philosopher Pierre-André Taguieff similarly argues in *The Force of Prejudice* (2001), first published in French in 1987, that "previously unseen forms of 'racism'" have developed since the early 1970s that testify to "the novelty of racist discourses in France" and in Europe at large (3). Taguieff contends that racist discourse has been reformulated since the 1970s and is now "culturalized" or "mentalized,'" by which he means that there has been a "'racialization' of the lexicons of culture, religion, traditions, and mentalities," a phenomenon that he calls *racial biologization* (4). Like Barker, Taguieff argues that racist discourses about culture have newly substituted biological formulations, yet function in the same manner as biology because they treat culture as a fixed trait. (Later in this introduction, I will show how the arguments of Barker, Gilroy, Taguieff, and other scholars who have postulated the rise of a new racism/cultural racism/colorblind racism actually draw from Frantz Fanon's talk "Racism and Culture" [1956]).

Following the trend of conceptualizing contemporary racism as drastically different from racism in the past, Howard Winant argues in *The World is a Ghetto* (2001) that there has been a radical shift in racial dynamics

NOTE TO PAGE 12

since the end of World War II. Winant conceptualizes the existence of a "racial break," a post–World War II "'new world racial system,' [which] in sharp contrast to the old structures of explicit colonialism and state-sponsored segregation, now presents itself as 'beyond race,' 'colorblind,' multicultural and post-racial" (xiv). This racial break, according to Winant, has witnessed the "birth" of colorblindness. In response to global decolonization movements of the 1950s and 1960s, Winant argues, there has been a shift from racial domination to racial hegemony, so that racism "can now operate as a taken-for-granted, almost unconscious common sense" (xiv). Implicit in Winant's theorization of the racial break is the argument that racism today is largely maintained without resorting to coercion given that hegemony, in Antonio Gramsci's terms, presumes active consent (*Prison Notebooks*, 271). In this way, Winant follows in Gramsci's footsteps and presumes "that all subjects are positioned in such a way as to have their consent solicited and to be able to extend their consent 'spontaneously'" (Wilderson, "Gramsci's Black Marx," 229). The theory of the racial break, then, both envisions the current racial order as completely different from its predecessors and sidelines the central roles that white violence and coercion continue to play in maintaining the racist status quo.

Eduardo Bonilla-Silva comparably argues in *Racism Without Racists* (2017 [2003]) that colorblindness "emerged as a new racial ideology in the late 1960s concomitantly with the crystallization of the 'new racism' as America's new racial structure" (16). During this period, Bonilla-Silva contends, "new rationalizations emerged to justify the new racial order" (16). Since the 1960s, he argues, white USAmericans have deployed four new rationalizations to silence and justify racism, which Bonilla-Silva describes as the central frames of colorblind racism: abstract liberalism, naturalization, cultural racism, and minimization of racism (74). While Bonilla-Silva correctly emphasizes the importance of these four frames to white racist discourse, as we will see, none of these strategies are new.

Similar arguments postulating the rise of a new racism have been made across disciplines and national contexts and in too many works to list them all here. For more examples, see: Omi and Winant, *Racial Formation in the United States*; Balibar, "Is There a 'Neo-Racism?'"; Sniderman et al., "The New Racism"; van Dijk, *Racism and the Press*; Gilroy, *The Black Atlantic*; Wetherell and Potter, *Mapping the Language of Racism*; Wieviorka, *The Arena of Racism*; Bobo, Kluegel, and Smith, "Laissez-Faire Racism"; Ansell, *New Right, New Racism*; Carr, *'Color-Blind' Racism*; Cole, *The New Racism in Europe*; Winant, *The New Politics of Race*; Collins, *Black Sexual Politics*; Goldberg, "Racisms Without Racism" and *Are We All Postracial Yet?*;

NOTES TO PAGES 12–15 281

Desai, "The Challenge of New Colorblind Racism in Art Education"; Pascale, "Nuevas formas de racismo"; Thornton and Luker, "The New Racism in Employment Discrimination"; Melamed, *Represent and Destroy*; López, *Dog Whistle Politics*; de Machedo, Roso, and de Lara, "Mulheres, saúde e uso de crack"; Mbembe, *Critique of Black Reason*; Noon, "Pointless Diversity Training"; and Ruiters, "Non-Racialism."

51. Omi and Winant, *Racial Formation in the United States*, 55.

52. For further critiques of the theory of racial formation see Elias and Feagin, *Racial Theories in Social Science*; and Saucier and Woods, *Conceptual Aphasia in Black*.

53. Omi and Winant, *Racial Formation in the United States*, 2 (my emphasis).

54. See Bonilla-Silva, "'We are all Americans!" and "From Bi-racial to Tri-racial."

55. Alcoff, *The Future of Whiteness*, 114.

56. See, for example, Barker, *The New Racism*; Taguieff, *The Force of Prejudice*; Gilroy, '*There Ain't No Black in the Union Jack*'; and Balibar, "Is There a 'Neo-Racism?'" Barker and Taguieff do not mention Fanon in their respective texts. Balibar brings him up once, but not with regard to the argument about the "new racism" that Balibar is making. Meanwhile, Gilroy only mentions Fanon in passing, stating: "The evolution of racism from vulgar to cultural forms described by Fanon has introduced a new variety which stresses complex difference rather than simple hierarchy" (*'There Ain't No Black in the Union Jack'*, 40).

57. Fanon, *Toward the African Revolution*, 32.

58. Fanon, 32.

59. Fanon, 32.

60. Fanon, 35.

61. For continuities between eugenics and contemporary racism see Fields and Fields, *Racecraft*. Medicine also continues to rely on a biological understanding of race. See Perez-Rodriguez and de la Fuente, "Now is the Time for a Postracial Medicine"; and Feagin, "Systemic Racism and 'Race' Categorization in Medical Research and Practice." See chapter 2 in this book for some works in other fields that continue to reproduce the myth that race is a genetic reality.

62. Fanon, *Toward the African Revolution*, 33.

63. Fields and Fields, *Racecraft*, 2.

64. Leach, "Against the Notion of a 'New Racism.'"

65. Young, *Colonial Desire*, 25.

66. Malcolm X cited in Lipsitz, *How Racism Takes Place*, 21.

282   NOTES TO PAGES 15–17

67. Fanon, *Toward the African Revolution*, 33.

68. The terms are attributed to the following authors, among others: "cultural racism" (Fanon 1956, Gilroy 1987, Taguieff 2001 [1987]); "culturalist racism" (Gilroy 1990 and 1993); "new racism" (Barker 1982, Gilroy 1987 and 1993, Ansell 1997, Bonilla-Silva 1999, Bonilla-Silva and Dietrich 2011); "New Racism" (Gilroy 2000); "symbolic racism" (Kinder and Sears 1981); "racial biologization" (Taguieff 2001 [1987]); "aversive racism" (Dovidio and Gaertner 1998); "postmodern racism" (Flecha 1999); "differentialist racism" (Taguieff 2001 [1987], Martin 2013); "laissez-faire racism" (Bobo and Kluegel 1997); "neo-racism" (Balibar and Wallerstein 1991); "racial hegemony" (Winant 2001); "color-blind racism" or "colorblind racism" (Carr 1997, Bonilla-Silva 2003); "racism without racists" (Bonilla-Silva 2017 [2003]); "racisms without racism" (Goldberg 2008); "racism without races" (Balibar 2008); "post-racialism" (Winant 2001, 2004); "post-racial racism" (Haney López 2010); "the New Racial Domain" (Manning 2006); "racism 2.0" (Wise 2009); "post-racial liberalism" (Wise 2010); "colorblind white dominance" (Haney López 2011); "race after race" (Gray 2019); "postrace" (Mukherjee, Banet-Wesier, and Gray 2019).

69. Farley, "Toward a General Theory of Antiblackness," 103.

70. Gilmore, *Golden Gulag*, 247.

71. Ture and Hamilton, *Black Power*, 4.

72. Hartman, *Lose Your Mother*, 6.

73. Abu-Jamal, *Have Black Lives Ever Mattered?*, 33.

74. See, for example, Davis, *Are Prisons Obsolete?*; and Abu-Jamal, *Live from Death Row* and *Have Black Lives Ever Mattered?*

75. The entanglement between slavery, theft, and the carceral state is not, of course, merely a US phenomenon. In the words of Fred Moten, "even though these terms [*abolition* and *reconstruction*] index the specific history in the United States, their continued relevance and resonance will be international as well as intranational insofar as the ongoing aggressive constitution of the modern nation-state as a carceral entity extends histories of forced migration and stolen labor and insofar as the imperial suppression of movements that would excavate new aesthetic, political, and economic dispositions . . . is a global phenomenon" ("Black Op," 1745). On mass incarceration in the United States see, for example, Davis, *Are Prisons Obsolete?*; Alexander, *The New Jim Crow*; and Childs, *Slaves of the State*.

76. See Abu-Jamal, *Live from Death Row*; and Alexander, *The New Jim Crow*.

77. See Bukhari, *The War Before*, 104; and Abu-Jamal, *Live from Death Row*.

NOTES TO PAGES 17–20

78. On the Marikana massacre see, for example, Marinovich, *Murder at Small Koppie*.

79. Ramaphosa cited in Kings, "Is the Marikana Miners' Blood on All Our Hands?"

80. Tutu, "Chairman's Foreword," 23.

81. Bhekizizwe Peterson argues that notions of reconciliation and forgiveness in post-1994 South Africa rely on a series of "repressions" that reproduce "abuse, poverty, injustice and alienation" ("Dignity, Memory and the Future Under Siege," 214).

82. Alves, *The Anti-Black City*, 7.

83. Cerquiera et al., *Atlas da violência 2017*, 32. On police violence in Brazil and the murder of Black people, see also da Silva, "Ninguém"; Amnesty International, *You Killed My Son*; and Alves, *The Anti-Black City*.

84. Pezão cited in Lisboa, "Governador do Rio diz que assassinato de cinco jovens não foi racismo."

85. Smith, *Afro-Paradise*, 9.

86. Smith, 9.

87. Marcos, *Conversations with Don Durito*, 1.

88. See Ejército Zapatista de Liberación Nacional, "Declaration of War." On NAFTA and its effects on Mexico's Indigenous people see also Bacon, *Illegal People*.

89. Rapalo, "Thousands Displaced as Territory Disputes Continue in Chiapas."

90. Ricardo Wilson writes that "in 1579 Yanga, by all existing accounts African-born, led a group of fellow enslaved persons from the African continent to escape a sugar plantation near the city of Veracruz. The maroons formed a community in the mountainous region of nearby Orizaba and lived relatively undisturbed for thirty years" (*The Nigrescent Beyond*, 9). On the Yanga community, see also Landers, "Leadership and Authority in Maroon Settlements in Spanish America and Brazil." On Blackness and racial inequality in Mexico, see also Sue, *Land of the Cosmic Race*.

91. McGarrity and Cárdenas, "Cuba," 110.

92. Moore, "Afro-Cubans and the Communist Revolution," 211. See also: Moore, *Pichón*.

93. On racism in Cuba see, for example, Sawyer, *Racial Politics in Post-Revolutionary Cuba*; and Clealand, *The Power of Race in Cuba*.

94. Arroyo, "Racial Theory and Practice in Panama," 156. On racism in Panama, see also Barrow, *No me pidas una foto*; Barrow and Priestly, *Piel oscura Panamá*; and Watson, *The Politics of Race in Panama*.

95. Barrow, "Racism Was Central to the Invasion," 82.

284   NOTES TO PAGES 20–24

96. Sharpe, *In the Wake*, 55.

97. Redazione ANSA, "Attack on Egyptian Boys 'Xenophobia.'"

98. Sharpe, *In the Wake*, 59.

99. Associated Press, "1,600 Migrants Lost at Sea in Mediterranean This Year."

100. On anti-Black racism in Italy see, for example, Khouma, *I Was an Elephant Salesman* and *Noi Italiani Neri*; Soumahoro, *Umanitá in rivolta*; Naletto, *Rapporto sul razzismo in Italia*; Hawthorne, "In Search of Black Italia" and "*L'Italia Meticcia?*"

101. Mills, *The Racial Contract*, 18.

102. Doane cited in Mills, "White Ignorance," 28.

103. Ellison, *Invisible Man*, 3.

104. Ellison, 14.

105. Fanon, *Toward the African Revolution*, 37.

106. See Gordon, *Bad Faith and Antiblack Racism*.

107. Crenshaw, "Race, Reform, and Retrenchment," 112.

108. See Stavrakakis, *The Lacanian Left*, 130.

109. Wilderson, *Afropessimism*, 162.

110. See Lipsitz, *How Racism Takes Place*.

111. Department of Rural Development and Land Reform of the Republic of South Africa, *Land Audit Report*, 2. For demographics, see: Statistics South Africa, *Mid-year Population Estimates 2017*. On racial inequality in South Africa see, for example, Ntsebeza and Hall, *The Land Question in South Africa*; Emery, "Class and Race Domination and Transformation in South Africa"; Mngxitama, "Blacks Can't Be Racist"; Barchiesi, *Precarious Liberation*; South African Human Rights Commission (SAHRC), *Research Brief on Race and Inequality in South Africa, 2013–2017*; and Moorosi, "Colour-blind Educational Leadership Policy."

112. These numbers are reported in Rooks and Oerlemans, "South Africa: A Rising Star?," 1210.

113. Vargas, "The Liberation Imperative of Black Genocide," 271.

114. Salata, "Race, Class and Income Inequality in Brazil." On racial inequality in Brazil, see also Nascimento, *Brazil: Mixture or Massacre?*; Telles, *Race in Another America*; Twine, *Racism in a Racial Democracy*; Williams, *Sex Tourism in Bahia*; Silva and Paixão, "Mixed and Unequal"; Smith, *Afro-Paradise*; and Alves, *The Anti-Black City*.

115. Articulação dos Povos Indígenas do Brasil (APIB) and Rede de Cooperação Amazônica (RCA), "The Human Rights Situation of Indigenous Peoples in Brazil," 9.

NOTES TO PAGES 25–27

116. Zizumbo-Colunga and Martínez, "Is Mexico a Post-Racial Country?", 1. Zizumbo-Colunga and Martínez write that Mexico's Institute of Statistics (INEGI) for the first time used a color palette to measure the skin tone of individuals in 2017. In citing this scholarship, I do not mean to suggest that race is equivalent to skin color. While race is *not* synonymous with skin color, a fact to which I will return in A Note on Method, this specific method of data collection has benefits in the Mexican context, in which the correlation between race and class status continues to be denied. For the relationship between skin color and social status in the Latin American context, see Telles and PERLA, *Pigmentocracies*. On racial inequality in Mexico, see also: Casas, Saldívar, Flores, and Sue, "The Different Faces of Mestizaje"; and Navarrete, *México racista*.

117. See, for example, Sawyer, *Racial Politics in Post-Revolutionary Cuba*; and Clealand, *The Power of Race in Cuba*.

118. See, for example, Barrow, *No me pidas una foto*; Barrow and Priestley, *Piel oscura Panamá*; and Watson, *The Politics of Race in Panama*.

119. See Malcolm X, "If You Stick a Knife in My Back" (video), *YouTube.com*, https://www.youtube.com/watch?v=XiSiHRNQlQo.

120. Warren, "Black Time," 56.

121. See Warren, "Black Time," 60–61; and Mills, "White Time," 27–28.

122. Tlali, *Between Two Worlds*, 160. The novel was previously published as *Muriel at Metropolitan*.

123. Lipsitz, *How Racism Takes Place*, 4.

124. The number of South Africans living on less than $1 per day more than doubled between 1996 (1.9 million or 4.5%) and 2004 (4.3 million or 9.1%). See Legassick, *Towards Socialist Democracy*, 506–8.

125. Césaire, *Discourse on Colonialism*, 11.

126. Césaire, 43.

127. Alvarez, *Native America and the Question of Genocide*, 15; Abu-Jamal and Vittoria, *Murder Incorporated*, 36; and Wilderson, *Red, White and Black*, 10.

128. Fenelon and Trafzer, "From Colonialism to Denial of California Genocide," 5.

129. Stannard, *American Holocaust*, 95.

130. Churchill, *A Little Matter of Genocide*, 1, 151.

131. Burnett cited in Horsman, *Race and Manifest Destiny*, 279.

132. See, for example, Churchill, *A Little Matter of Genocide*; Reed, "The American Indian in the White Man's Prison"; and Taylor, *Toxic Communities*.

286   NOTES TO PAGES 27–29

133. De Zurara, *The Chronicle of the Discovery and Conquest of Guinea,* *Vol. 1*, 111.

134. Lovejoy, "The Impact of the Atlantic Slave Trade on Africa," 368.

135. James, *The Black Jacobins*, 8.

136. James, 8, 9.

137. James, 6–7.

138. Pérez, *Cuba*, 72.

139. Pérez, 37.

140. Jaffe, *European Colonial Despotism*, 36.

141. Magubane, *Race and the Construction of the Dispensable Other*, 180.

142. I use the terms Khoe (singular) and Khoena (plural) instead of the more common terms Khoi and Khoikhoi because, as June Bam writes, "Khoena was the name by which the indigenous people nearest to the Cape of Good Hope preferred to call themselves" (*Ausi Told Me*, xxii). Also, Khoena is gender neutral, while Khoikhoi means "men of men" (*Ausi Told Me*, xxii).

143. Jaffe, *European Colonial Despotism*, 36.

144. Jaffe, 49.

145. Cited in Jaffe, 49.

146. Jaffe, 54.

147. Robinson, *Black Marxism*, 27. Robinson contends that the roots of European racialism are to be found in the formative period of European society, "which extends into the medieval and feudal ages as 'blood' and racial beliefs and legends" (*Black Marxism*, 67). "Racism," Robinson argues, "was not simply a convention for ordering the relations of European to non-European peoples but has its genesis in the 'internal' relations of European peoples" (2). The slave trade and colonialism, according to Robinson, marked not the birth of racism but rather its exacerbation (71).

148. Marriott, *Whither Fanon?*, 20.

149. Painter, *The History of White People*, 1, 79.

150. Lafont, "How Skin Color Became a Racial Marker," 90.

151. Painter, *The History of White People*, 79–80.

152. See Quijano, "Coloniality of Power."

153. Harris, "Whiteness as Property," 1716.

154. On racial capitalism see Alexander, *Sow the Wind*; and Robinson, *Black Marxism*.

155. See, for example, Wynter, "Unsettling the Coloniality of Being/Power/Truth/Freedom"; Wilderson, *Red, White and Black*; Walcott, "The Problem of the Human"; and King, *The Black Shoals*. In *Becoming Human,*

NOTES TO PAGES 29–32 287

Zakiyyah Iman Jackson complicates the argument that Black people are excluded from the category of the Human. Jackson argues that, through a process that she terms *ontological plasticity*, Blackness is posited as infinitely malleable and "produced as sub/super/human at once, a form where form shall not hold: potentially 'everything and nothing' at the register of ontology" (3). Eurocentric humanism, Jackson writes, depends on using Blackness as a prop to construct whiteness (4). In *Playing in the Dark*, which Jackson does not cite, Toni Morrison theorizes this phenomenon within the context of white US literature, showing precisely how white writers use Black characters self-reflectively as props to define and elevate whiteness. A kind of plasticity defines Blackness within these texts, in which, as Morrison argues, "images of blackness can be evil *and* protective, rebellious *and* forgiving, fearful *and* desirable—all the self-contradictory features of the self" (59, italics in the original).

156. Robinson, *Black Marxism*, 81.

157. Davis cited in Robinson, *Black Marxism*, 75.

158. Robert Fogel and Stanley Engerman write, "The Catholic Church not only rationalized the possession of slaves by others, but was itself a major owner of slaves. Even before the Jesuits began to encourage the importation of Africans into the New World, the Church actively promoted slavery" (*Time on the Cross*, 30).

159. Fanon, *Black Skin, White Masks*, 2.

160. Walcott, "The Problem of the Human," 93.

161. Wilderson, *Red, White and Black*, 43.

162. Sexton, "The *Vel* of Slavery," 584.

163. Sexton, 591.

164. Sexton, 593.

165. Warren, "Black Time," 56. See also Wilderson, *Red, White and Black*.

166. Warren, *Ontological Terror*, 72 (italics in the original).

167. Warren, 72.

168. See Crenshaw et al., *Critical Race Theory*.

169. Du Bois, *Black Reconstruction*, 4. On colorblindness and slavery in the US Constitution see also Lipsitz, "The Sounds of Silence," 27.

170. US Citizenship and Immigration Services, *The Declaration of Independence and Constitution*.

171. US Citizenship and Immigration Services.

172. Morrison, *Playing in the Dark*, 57.

173. HoSang, *A Wider Type of Freedom*, xii.

174. Patterson, *Slavery and Social Death*, 160.

288   NOTES TO PAGES 32–36

175. Du Bois, *The World and Africa*, 58. On slavery and capitalism, see also Marx, *The Poverty of Philosophy*, 94; Williams, *Capitalism and Slavery*; Fogel and Engerman, *Time on the Cross*; and Robinson, *Black Marxism*.

176. See Buck-Morss, *Hegel, Haiti, and Universal History*, 21.

177. Kant, *Physische Geographie*, 316. For the English translation, see Kant, *Natural Science*, 576. On racism in Kant's work, see Eze, "The Color of Reason"; Mills, "Kant's *Untermenschen*" in *Black Rights/White Wrongs*, 91–112; and Neugebauer, "The Racism of Hegel and Kant."

178. Voltaire cited in Cohen, *The French Encounter with Africans*, 88.

179. See US Citizenship and Immigration Services, *The Declaration of Independence and Constitution*; and Stanton, *"Those Who Labor for My Happiness."*

180. Costa, *The Brazilian Empire*, 57.

181. Fanon, *Black Skin, White Masks*, 172.

182. Spillers, *Black, White, and in Color*, 206.

183. Cited in James, *The Black Jacobins*, 17.

184. James, 17.

185. Millin, *White Africans Are Also People*, 30.

186. Hartman, *Scenes of Subjection*, 21.

187. Memmi, *The Colonizer and the Colonized*, 79.

188. Here, I am paraphrasing Ella Shohat and Robert Stam who, in a very useful formulation, write that racist stereotypes "are not an error of perception but rather a form of social control" (*Unthinking Eurocentrism*, 198).

189. Marriott, *Whither Fanon?*, 67.

190. JanMohamed, "The Economy of Manichean Allegory," 61.

191. Memmi, *The Colonizer and the Colonized*, 85.

192. Moten, *Black and Blur*, 1.

193. Quijano, "Coloniality and Modernity / Rationality," 28.

194. I use the term Briticist deliberately to call attention to the differential manner in which scholars of British literature describe themselves vis-à-vis scholars of USAmerican literature (Americanists) and other literary traditions. Briticists insist that they are not Briticists, but rather Early Modernists, Victorianists, Romanticists, and so on. This temporal differentiation makes it possible for Briticists to continue to dominate many English departments in the United States and elsewhere, while not appearing to be disproportionately overrepresented.

195. See Crenshaw, Harris, HoSang, and Lipsitz, "Introduction" in *Seeing Race Again*.

NOTES TO PAGES 36–38   289

196. Zuberi and Bonilla-Silva, "Toward a Definition of White Logic and White Methods," 18.

197. Wallerstein, *Open the Social Sciences*, 13.

198. Wallerstein, 28.

199. The English translation is my own. The original Italian text reads as follows:

> Una scienza affatto nuova, eppure gigante, è sorta ad un tratto, o Signore, dal germe fecondo delle scuole moderne, sui ruderi dei vecchi e dei nuovi pregiudizi. È la scienza dell'antropologia, che studia l'uomo col mezzo e coi metodi delle scienze fisiche, che ai sogni dei teologhi, alle fantasticherie dei metafisici, sostituisce pochi aridi fatti . . . . . ma fatti.
>
> Uno dei più curiosi problemi, che si agitava insoluto prima della sua comparsa, è quello della origine e della pluralità delle stirpi umane: se, cioè, nelle razze umane esistano delle disuguaglianze profonde, che si manifestarono fino dall'origine loro, e perdurarono immutate sotto il variare dei tempi e dei climi, lasciando nella storia e nei destini dei popoli l'eterno loro conio.
>
> Gli è un grave problema.
>
> Si tratta di vedere se vi sia, o no, un legame tra la storia e la natura, tra l'uomo primitivo e tutta la serie degli esseri vivi, da cui la nostra vanità ci vorrebbe le mille miglia lontani.
>
> Si tratta di sapere se noi bianchi, che torreggiamo orgogliosi sulla vetta della civiltà, dovremo un giorno chinare la fronte innanzi al muso prognato del negro ed alla gialla e terrea faccia del mongòlo; se, infine, noi dobbiamo il nostro primato al nostro organismo o agli accidenti del caso. E vuolsi anche una buona volta decidere se possiamo, senza paura, come senza audacia sfrontata, attenerci, più che alle tradizioni, alla sola autorità dei nostri tempi, la Scienza (Lombroso, *L'uomo bianco e l'uomo di colore*, 9–10).

200. To "prove" that white people are, in his words, "i re della natura" (the kings of nature, 20), Lombroso in *L'uomo bianco e l'uomo di colore* says surprisingly little about white people. Instead, he says a lot about everybody else, especially Black people, about whom he writes absurdities such as, "Perfino il sangue appare differente nel Negro e si coagula appena estratto dalla vena" (Even the blood appears different in the Negro,

290   NOTES TO PAGES 38–44

and coagulates as soon as it is extracted from the veins, 20), or argues that Black children are not born dark-skinned but their skin becomes dark "solo dopo il tredicesimo anno" (only after the thirteenth year of life, 28). These are the kinds of fabrications that Lombroso presented as scientific facts. Having dehumanized everyone who is not white, it becomes easy for Lombroso to represent white people as superior by comparison.

201. DeLoughrey and Handley, "Introduction," 8.

202. Columbus and Jane, *The Four Voyages of Columbus*, 7, 9. The original Spanish text reads as follows:

> La gente d'esta ysla y de todas las otras que he fallado y he avido noticia, andan todos desnudos, hombres y mugeres, así como sus madres los paren. . . . ellos no tienen fierro, ni azero, ni armas, ni so(n par)a ello, no porque no sea gente bien dispuesta y de formosa estatura, salvo que son muy te(merosos) á maravilla. . . . verdad es que, después de que se aseguran y pierden este miedo, ellos son tanto sin engaño y tan liberales de lo que tienen, que no lo creería sino el que lo viese. ellos de cosa que tengan, pidiéndogela, jamás dizen de no; antes, convidan la persona con ello, y muestran tanto amor que darían los corazones, y, quier sea cosa de valor, quier sea de poco precio, luego por qualquiera cosica, de qualquiera manera que sea que se lo dé, por ello se an contentos (Columbus and Jane, 7–9).

203. Du Toit and Giliomee, *Afrikaner Political Thought*, 53.

204. Van der Riet,"Letter from Landdrost R. J. van der Riet of Stellenbosch to fiscal J. A. Truter, 1 April 1810," 53–55.

205. Jaffe, *European Colonial Despotism*, 45.

206. Jaffe, 45

207. Wynter, "1492," 33 (italics in the original).

208. King, *The Black Shoals*, 61.

209. Coetzee, *White Writing*, 17.

210. Nieuhof cited in Coetzee, 17.

211. My emphasis.

212. Abu-Jamal and Vittoria, *Murder Incorporated*, 44.

213. On racist discourses of Black cultural deficiency and deviance see, for example, Spillers, "Mama's Baby, Papa's Maybe"; Kelley, *Yo' Mama's Disfunktional!*; and Shange, *Progressive Dystopia*.

214. JanMohamed, "The Economy of Manichean Allegory," 61.

215. Lombroso, *L'uomo bianco e l'uomo di colore*. My translation.

NOTES TO PAGES 47–60   291

216. Wilderson, *Afropessimism*, 220 (italics in the original).
217. See Blake, "Why Black Lives Matter in the Humanities."
218. Morrison, *Playing in the Dark*, 46.
219. Bell, *Faces at the Bottom of the Well*, ix.
220. Zuberi and Bonilla-Silva, "Toward a Definition of White Logic and White Methods," 7.
221. See Gotanda, "A Critique of 'Our Constitution is Colorblind.'"
222. Fanon, *Black Skin, White Masks*, 87 (italics in the original).
223. See Obasogie, "Do Blind People See Race?"
224. Lipsitz, *How Racism Takes Place*, 21.
225. Césaire, *Discourse on Colonialism*, 45.

Chapter 1
EPIGRAPHS: Césaire, *Discourse on Colonialism*, 42–43 (italics in the original). Ritter cited in Primer Congreso del Negro Panameño, *Memorias*, 17.
1. Rydell, *All the World's a Fair*, 224, 209. For the conference proceedings see Race Betterment Foundation, *Official Proceedings of the Second National Conference*.
2. Williams, "The Greatest Migration in History," 4.
3. Williams, 4.
4. See Missal, *Seaway to the Future*, 181.
5. Griffith cited in Rydell, *All the World's a Fair*, 231.
6. I put the word *miscegenation* in scare quotes here to signal that race is not a biological or genetic reality and, consequently, neither is "racial mixture" a biological or genetic fact, but is itself a construction grounded in the history of racism. The word miscegenation was invented in 1864 to indicate what was believed to be "the fertile fusion and merging of races" (Young, *Colonial Desire*, 8). While I do not consistently place words such as miscegenation, racial mixture, or racial purity in scare quotes throughout the book, these terms should obviously be taken with a grain of salt.
7. Nascimento, *Brazil: Mixture or Massacre?*, 76.
8. Vasconcelos, *La raza cósmica*, 16. My translation.
9. Alfaro, *El peligro antillano*, 14–15 (italics in the original).
10. All translations of *El peligro antillano* from the Spanish original to English are mine.
11. Melamed, *Represent and Destroy*, 4.
12. Melamed, 4.
13. Pimentel, "Alfaro Paredes Olmedo." A report from the US Committee on Military Affairs submitted to the US House of Representatives

292   NOTES TO PAGES 60–64

on January 20, 1900, shows that Ecuador's Minister of Foreign Relations requested "permission for Olmedo Alfaro, eldest son of the President of Ecuador, to enter the Military Academy at West Point" (House of Representatives, "Señor Olmedo Alfaro"). The permission was granted.

14. Alfaro, *El peligro antillano*, 12.

15. Guerrón-Montero, "Racial Democracy and Nationalism in Panama," 210; Conniff, *Black Labor on a White Canal*, 12.

16. Conniff, 12. Conniff himself reproduces this myth by writing that Panamanians "had inherited from colonial times an ethic . . . of interracial harmony that discouraged segregation. . . . After the United States began building the canal, however, Panama's elite displayed some of the race prejudices that had been latent earlier" (*Black Labor on a White Canal*, 11).

17. Lindsay-Poland, *Emperors in the Jungle*, 12. Conniff, 147; Senior, *Dying to Better Themselves*, 105. US imperialism in Panama was a manifestation of the Monroe Doctrine, declared by President James Monroe in his 1823 State of the Union address, which stipulated that the United States would not tolerate any attempt by Europe to interfere with US interests in Latin America (Missal, *Seaway to the Future*, 22).

18. See Alexander Craft, *When the Devil Knocks*, 8.

19. Lasso, "Race and Ethnicity in the Formation of Panamanian National Identity," 83.

20. Lasso, 84.

21. Davis, "Panama," 205; Alexander Craft, *When the Devil Knocks*, 8.

22. Conniff, *Black Labor on a White Canal*, 4.

23. Sale, *Le leggi razziali in Italia e il Vaticano*, 72.

24. Pimentel, "Alfaro Paredes Olmedo."

25. Alfaro, *El peligro antillano*, 3.

26. Pimentel, "Alfaro Paredes Olmedo."

27. Pimentel.

28. Alfaro, *El peligro antillano*, 3.

29. Alfaro, 3.

30. Alfaro, 7.

31. Alfaro, 15–16.

32. This has been amply documented, for example, in Du Bois, *Black Reconstruction*; Cox, *Caste, Class, and Race*; and Roediger, *The Wages of Whiteness*.

33. Bell, *Faces at the Bottom of the Well*, 7.

34. Historian David McCullough writes that visitors to the Canal "could not help but be amazed, even astounded, at the degree to which the entire system, not simply the construction, depended on black labor. There were

NOTES TO PAGES 65–69 293

not only thousands of West Indians down amid the turmoil of Culebra Cut or at the lock sites but black waiters in every hotel, black stevedores, teamsters, porters, hospital orderlies, cooks, laundresses, nursemaids, janitors, delivery boys, coachmen, icemen, garbage men, yardmen, mail clerks, police, plumbers, house painters, grave diggers. A black man walking along spraying oil on still water, a metal tank on his back, was one of the most familiar of all sights in the Canal Zone. Whenever a mosquito was seen in a white household, the Sanitary Department was notified and immediately a black man came with chloroform and a glass vital to catch the insect and take it back to a laboratory for analysis" (*The Path Between the Seas*, 575).

35. Cited in Davis, *Slavery and Beyond*, 148.

36. Newton, *The Silver Men*, 125.

37. Rydell, *All the World's a Fair*, 224, 209.

38. Alexander Craft, *When the Devil Knocks*, 39–40.

39. Zumoff, "The 1925 Tenants' Strike in Panama," 2.

40. Senior, *Dying to Better Themselves*, 166–67. On West Indian activism and mobilization in the Canal Zone see also Corinealdi, "Envisioning Multiple Citizenships."

41. Senior, 167.

42. Senior, 167.

43. Walcott, *The Long Emancipation*, 1.

44. Senior, *Dying to Better Themselves*, 298.

45. Senior, 65.

46. Senior, 4, 65. The new constitution of 1946 finally granted West Indians full citizenship, but it denied the right to language and self-determination (Watson, *The Politics of Race in Panama*, 14).

47. Alfaro, *El peligro antillano*, 16, 17.

48. Walcott, *The Long Emancipation*, 50.

49. Alfaro, *El peligro antillano*, 17.

50. Krauze cited in Hale, "Does Multiculturalism Menace?", 499. The translation from the Spanish original is mine.

51. Alfaro, *El peligro antillano*, 7.

52. Alfaro, 7.

53. Alfaro, 14–15.

54. Kelley, *Yo' Mama's Disfunktional!*, 16.

55. Alfaro, *El peligro antillano*, 3.

56. Kim, *Bitter Fruit*, 19.

57. Zuberi and Bonilla-Silva, "Toward a Definition of White Logic and White Methods," 18.

58. Alfaro, *El peligro antillano*, 4.

59. Alfaro, 4.

60. Alfaro, 5.

61. Alfaro, 3.

62. Bryce, *The Relations of the Advanced and the Backward Races of Mankind*, 25.

63. Alfaro, *El peligro antillano*, 8 (my emphasis).

64. Alfaro, 7.

65. Alfaro, 10–12.

66. Alfaro uses the term *morenos*, a term that, as mentioned, is often used euphemistically to refer to Black people in Panama and which literally means "browns," brown people, or dark-skinned people.

67. Alfaro, *El peligro antillano*, 9–10.

68. Said, *Orientalism*, 7.

69. Goffman, *On the Run*, 5–6.

70. Said, *Orientalism*, 7.

71. Van Maanen and de Rond, "The Making of a Classic Ethnography," 399. For incisive critiques of Goffman's *On the Run* see, for example, Sharpe, "Black Life, Annotated"; and Rios, "Book Review."

72. JanMohamed, "The Economy of Manichean Allegory," 64–65.

73. Kelley, *Yo' Mama's Disfunktional!*, 16.

74. Wilderson, *Red, White and Black*, 56.

75. Morrison, *Playing in the Dark*, 13.

76. Alfaro, *El peligro antillano*, 15.

77. Roberts, *Freedom as Marronage*, 29, 28.

78. Van der Riet, "Letter from Landdrost R. J. van der Riet of Stellenbosch to fiscal J. A. Truter, 1 April 1810," 53.

79. La Barre cited in Trouillot, *Silencing the Past*, 72.

80. Reid, *Afro-Latin America*, 38.

81. Pike, "Black Rebels," 244.

82. Pike, 245.

83. Pike, 250.

84. Pike, 266. However, Lancelot Lewis writes that "as late as 1796, the name of a town known as Palenque appears in a document in reference to a black settlement established by runaway slaves who resisted all military excursions against them until the authorities saw fit to recognize their autonomy and granted them their freedom" (*The West Indian in Panama*, 10).

85. D'Anghera, *De Orbe Novo*, 286.

86. Van Sertima, *They Came Before Columbus*, 23–24; Lewis, *The West Indian in Panama*, 3.

NOTES TO PAGES 77–82

87. Lewis, 3.

88. Fortune, *Obra selecta*, 100.

89. Lewis, *The West Indian in Panama*, 6.

90. Conniff and Davis, *Africans in the Americas*, 114.

91. De la Rosa, "El negro en Panamá," 229.

92. Davis, "Panama," 203.

93. Conniff, *Black Labor on a White Canal*, 3.

94. Lewis, *The West Indian in Panama*, 22.

95. Conniff, "Afro-West Indians on the Central American Isthmus," 147.

96. Conniff, 153.

97. Senior, *Dying to Better Themsleves*, 153.

98. Alfaro, *El peligro antillano*, 5.

99. Conniff, *Black Labor on a White Canal*, 3–5, 149.

100. Frank cited in Senior, *Dying to Better Themselves*, 106.

101. Senior, 106–7. Europeans from Greece, Italy, and Spain, a smaller part of the silver workforce, were also labelled as silver workers. They were considered inferior to white USAmericans but superior to Black workers with regard to pay, living conditions, and so forth. These silver workers were also spatially segregated from Black workers (Senior, 108).

102. Conniff, *Black Labor on a White Canal*, 5, 34.

103. Primer Congreso del Negro Panameño, *Memorias*, 37.

104. Smith, "Buscando las raíces afro-panameñas," 24.

105. Wilderson, *Red, White and Black*, 140.

Chapter 2

EPIGRAPHS: Nascimento, *Africans in Brazil*, 149 (italics in the original). Jackson, *Becoming Human*, 121.

1. Gilliam, "From Roxbury to Rio—and Back in a Hurry," 176.

2. Gilliam, 176.

3. Gilliam, 176.

4. As the country with the second-largest population of African descent in the world and the alleged cradle of racial democracy in the Americas, Brazil has captured the imagination of African American intellectuals ever since the nineteenth century. Before the Civil Rights Movement, the absence of de jure segregation, antimiscegenation laws, or white suprema-cist organizations such as the KKK, led African American intellectuals into idealizing the position of Black people in Brazilian society. Several African American intellectuals, including W. E. B. Du Bois, and publications such as the *Chicago Defender* reinforced the myth of Brazil as a racial paradise

296   NOTES TO PAGE 82

and often appeared oblivious of the institutionalized racism that characterized the nation, as documented in David Hellwig's unique anthology *African American Reflections on Brazil's Racial Paradise*.

The idealization of Brazil is visible also in Nella Larsen's classic novel of the Harlem Renaissance *Passing* (1929), which represents Brazil as a desirable alternative to life in the United States. Clare and Irene, the protagonists of a story which is seen through the eyes of the latter, are mirror figures with opposite personality traits and conflicting perspectives on racial and gender identity. While Clare crosses the color line and then risks her life to reconnect with her Black community, Irene passes occasionally to obtain the social advantages that Jim Crow society reserves solely to white people. The possibility of passing, however, is foreclosed to Irene's husband Brian, who is dark-skinned. Brian longs for an existence free of racial discrimination and repeatedly expresses a desire to move to Brazil. As Irene states, "Brian doesn't care for ladies. . . . It's South America that attracts him" (42). When Irene refuses to educate her small children about racism, Brian states that she should allow the family to move to Brazil, where there would simply be no need to address the issue. However, Irene is not capable of grasping the extent of racial oppression faced by her husband in the United States and rejects his proposal to move: "That strange, and to her fantastic, notion of Brian's of going off to Brazil . . . how it frightened her, and—yes, angered her!" (57). Throughout the novel, Brazil remains an unfulfilled dream, a sensual object of desire, a utopia—a vision of the country that would later be challenged in another classic novel, Gayl Jones's *Corregidora* (1975), which denounces the sexual violence that white slave owners inflicted upon enslaved Black women and men, a violence that defined the history and meaning of mestiçagem in Brazil.

5. Gilliam, "A Black Feminist Perspective on the Sexual Commodification of Women in the Global Culture," 166.

6. One way that racial fluidity supports white dominance in Brazil is through what Edward Telles calls a *mulatto escape hatch*, which enables social ascent for selected few light-skinned people of African descent while keeping access to power firmly in white hands (*Race in Another America*, 146). A certain kind of microlevel fluidity also characterizes racial identification in the United States, where a small number of light-skinned people of color are perceived as white if they achieve high economic status. In the United States, just as in Brazil, this fluidity supports, rather than challenges, racial disparities (Saperstein and Penner, "Racial Fluidity and Inequality in the United States," 678).

7. Fernández, "La Raza and the Melting Pot," 127.

NOTES TO PAGE 82

8. Fernández, 140.

9. Fernández, 140–41.

10. For example, journalist Gregory Rodriguez's *Mongrels, Bastards, Orphans, and Vagabonds: Mexican Immigration and the Future of Race in America* (2007) also argues that Latinx immigrants will positively impact the US racial landscape. Rodriguez formulates his faith in the potential of Mexican Americans as pioneers of a revolution that will completely alter US race relations as follows:

> Mexican Americans are forcing the United States to reinterpret the concept of the melting pot to include racial as well as ethnic mixing. Rather than abetting the segregationist ethos of a country divided into mutually exclusive groups, Mexican Americans continually continue to blur the lines between "us" and "them." Just as the emergence of the mestizo undermined the Spanish racial system in colonial Mexico, Mexican Americans, who have always confounded the Anglo American racial system, will ultimately destroy it, too. (xvii)

Similar to how Israel Zangwill in *The Melting-Pot* (1908) extolled Eastern Europeans for abandoning their heritage and becoming USAmerican (and, by implication, white), Rodriguez portrays Mexican Americans as a new "model minority," even as Mexican Americans, unlike Eastern Europeans, are not collectively allowed to partake in the privileges of whiteness in the United States. In Rodriguez's view, the presence of Mexican immigrants, who are increasingly marrying outside their ethnoracial community, will bring a new element to US society that goes beyond cultural assimilation to include the crucial element of "miscegenation" (which Rodriguez erroneously assumes does not exist in the United States). However, miscegenation has not managed to halt white supremacy in Mexico, nor will it dismantle white supremacy in the United States. Instead of undermining "the Spanish racial system," a selected number of light-skinned Mexican mestizos acquired the privileges of whiteness that were previously reserved only for Europeans. Rodriguez, then, broaches mestizaje as yet another ingredient that will leave white supremacy intact.

Ronald Fernandez similarly argues in *America Beyond Black and White: How Immigrants and Fusions Are Helping Us Overcome the Racial Divide* (2007) that immigrants will positively transform racial classification in the United States and render the country more tolerant of racial mixture. He writes, "the one-drop rule never dominated in Latin America. Equally

298   NOTES TO PAGES 83–84

important for all Hispanics, mestizaje never implied homogeneity, the racial purity imagined by Anglo Protestant America. . . . Imagine this: forty million Hispanic Americans joining hands around recognition of mestizaje and the encounter with Europe, Africa, Asia, and Iberia" (185). As he lies about race relations in Latin America and portrays mestizaje as a counter-hegemonic ideology, Fernández also suggests that reporting more than one race or the inclusion of the category "Other" on the US census are positive outcomes, although African American leaders have criticized these measures for being damaging for the purposes of monitoring and redress (see Anderson and Fienberg, "Race and Ethnicity and the Controversy Over the US Census," 94–95).

11. Nascimento, *Africans in Brazil*, 149. Numerous scholars have established that mestizaje is anti-Black and anti-Indigenous. On mestizaje see, for example, Nascimento, *Brazil: Mixture or Massacre?*; Paschel, *Becoming Black Political Subjects*; da Silva, *Toward a Global Idea of Race*; Sue, *The Land of the Cosmic Race*; and Wilson, *The Nigrescent Beyond*.

12. For critiques of multiraciality in the United States see, for example, Gordon, *Her Majesty's Other Children*; Sexton, *Amalgamation Schemes*; and Valentine, "Racial Mixedness in the Contemporary United States and South Africa."

13. Douglass cited in Mount, "Historical Ventriloquy," 141.

14. Williams, "The Recursive Outcomes of the Multiracial Movement," 89–90.

15. See Anderson and Fienberg, "Race and Ethnicity and the Controversy Over the US Census"; Williams, *Mark More Than One*; and Sexton, *Amalgamation Schemes*.

16. Williams, "The Recursive Outcomes of the Multiracial Movement," 90.

17. Spillers, *Black, White, and in Color*, 302 (italics in the original).

18. Spillers, 302.

19. Spillers, 308.

20. Lund, *The Impure Imagination*, xv.

21. See Gqola, *What is Slavery to Me?* and Valentine, "Racial Mixedness in the Contemporary United States and South Africa" on white appropriations of racial mixture discourses in post-apartheid South Africa.

22. Frenkel and MacKenzie, "Conceptualizing 'Post-Transitional' South African Literature in English," 5. See also, Milazzo, "The Rhetorics of Racial Power."

23. Jackson, *Becoming Black*, 121.

24. Andrews, *Afro-Latin America*, 118–19; Nunes, *Cannibal Democracy*, 6; Paschel, *Becoming Black Political Subjects*, 7.

NOTES TO PAGES 84–88

25. Nascimento, *Brazil: Mixture or Massacre?* 5, 43.

26. Moura cited in Nascimento, *Brazil: Mixture or Massacre?* 8–9.

27. Sue, *Land of the Cosmic Race*, 13.

28. Andrews, *Afro-Latin America*, 119.

29. Andrews, 119.

30. Andrews, 120. I put "freed" in scare quotes because, as Christina Sharpe writes, "Contrary to the plantation romance (that enslaved people were happy and remained with the master and mistress out of loyalty and devotion), the formerly enslaved faced a present in which their freedom was only nominal. So, however traumatic staying might be, it is no small wonder that numbers of the formerly enslaved were unable to leave. That is, notwithstanding legal emancipation, the very force of the law, trauma, sexual violence, the need or compulsion to work, and familial ties kept people bound to awful material psychic configurations" (*Monstrous Intimacies*, 37). The conditions in Brazilian cities were not better than on plantations, leading to a "freedom" for Black people that remains ephemeral to this day.

31. Andrews, *Afro-Latin America*, 122.

32. Andrews, 122

33. Andrews, 122–24.

34. Andrews, 129–30. See also Helg, *Our Rightful Share*; and Pappademos, *Black Political Activism and the Cuban Republic*.

35. Gimeno Martín, "Las luchas por el indigenismo," 32.

36. On this shift, see Morrison, *Cuba's Racial Crucible*, 153–54; Paschel, *Becoming Black Political Subjects*, 30; and da Silva, *Toward a Global Idea of Race*, 238.

37. Alberto, *Terms of Inclusion*, 10.

38. Da Silva, *Toward a Global Idea of Race*, 238.

39. Andrews, *Afro-Latin America*, 119.

40. Da Silva, *Toward a Global Idea of Race*, 239.

41. Cornejo Polar, "*Mestizaje*, Transculturation, Heterogeneity," 116.

42. Cornejo Polar, "*Mestizaje* and Hybridity," 760.

43. Sexton, *Amalgamation Schemes*, 200.

44. Paschel, *Becoming Black Political Subjects*, 7–8.

45. Casas et al., "The Different Faces of Mestizaje," 47. On the formal shift from mestizaje to multiculturalism see also Wade, "Mestizaje, Multiculturalism, Liberalism, and Violence," 333.

46. Casas et al., "The Different Faces of Mestizaje," 47.

47. Sexton, *Amalgamation Schemes*, 5.

48. "The Race Problem in Latin America" is the third lecture that Vasconcelos delivered as part of the Harris Foundation Lectures at the

University of Chicago in 1926, following "Similarity and Contrast" and "Democracy in Latin America." The three lectures were collected under the title *The Latin-American Basis of Mexican Civilization* and published alongside Manuel Gamio's lecture "The Indian Basis of Mexican Civilization" in the volume *Aspects of Mexican Civilization*.

49. Hooker, *Theorizing Race in the Americas*, 11.

50. Hooker, 155.

51. Rosaldo, "Foreword," xv.

52. To my knowledge, the only work that examines the report (in the report's French translation, rather than the English original) is Jerry Dávila's essay "Entre dois mundos: Gilberto Freyre, a ONU e o apartheid sul-africano." I thank Dávila for sending me the French version of Freyre's report.

53. Freyre, "Letter to Ezekiel Gordon," April 23, 1954.

54. Palthey, "Télégramme adressé le 10 Mars 1954 par le Directeur du Personnel des Nations Unies à Monsieur le Docteur Gilberto Freyre." The translation from the French original is mine.

55. Vasconcelos, *La raza cósmica*, 43–44.

56. Sexton, *Amalgamation Schemes*, 201.

57. Saldaña-Portillo, *Indian Given*, 203.

58. The university was called Universidad Nacional at the time.

59. Coerver, Pasztor, and Buffington, "José Vasconcelos," 519–23.

60. See Wyman and Muirhead, "Jim Crow Comes to Central Illinois."

61. Shabazz, *Spatializing Blackness*, 34.

62. See Arvin, *Possessing Polynesians*; and Anderson, "Racial Hybridity, Physical Anthropology, and Human Biology in the Colonial Laboratories of the United States."

63. Arvin, 69.

64. Arvin, 102.

65. Vasconcelos, "The Race Problem in Latin America," 80.

66. Vasconcelos, 89.

67. Vasconcelos, 97.

68. Vasconcelos, 85.

69. Vasconcelos, 86–87.

70. Vasconcelos, 87.

71. On the politics of the English language in India, see Saxena, *Vernacular English*.

72. On practices of racialized containment in colonial Mexico, see Nemser, *Infrastructures of Race*.

73. Vasconcelos, "The Race Problem in Latin America," 79.

NOTES TO PAGES 94–101

74. Vasconcelos, 77.

75. See Instituto Nacional de Estadística y Geografía, "Encuesta Intercensal 2015."

76. Vasconcelos, "The Race Problem in Latin America," 89.

77. Vasconcelos, 90.

78. Vasconcelos, 77.

79. Vasconcelos, 77.

80. Vasconcelos, 83.

81. Vasconcelos, 92.

82. Vasconcelos, 84.

83. On racism in the Philippines and against Filipino Americans see, Rodríguez, *Suspended Apocalypse*.

84. Vasconcelos, "The Race Problem in Latin America," 87.

85. Vasconcelos, 87.

86. Vasconcelos, 100–101.

87. Vasconcelos, 101.

88. Serna, *México, un pueblo testimonio*, 87.

89. Gimeno Martín, "Las luchas por el indigenismo," 39.

90. Portillo, "Who Is the Indian in Aztlán?," 409.

91. Instituto Nacional Indigenista (INI), *Memoria 1995–2000*, 17. The translation from the Spanish original is mine.

92. On the Zapatista Movement see, for example, Hayden, *The Zapatista Reader*; Marcos, *Our Word Is Our Weapon*; and Ramírez, Carlsen, and Arias, *The Fire and the Word*.

93. Vasconcelos, "The Race Problem in Latin America," 77.

94. Rivera-Barnes, "Ethnological Counterpoint," 50.

95. Yelvington, "The Invention of Africa in Latin America and the Caribbean," 51 (my emphasis).

96. Lahaye Guerra, "El antirracismo de Fernando Ortiz."

97. Lowe, *The Intimacies of Four Continents*, 35.

98. Hoeg, *Science, Technology, and Latin American Narrative in the Twentieth Century and Beyond*, 69.

99. Attwell, *Rewriting Modernity*, 18.

100. Pérez-Torres, *Mestizaje*, 30.

101. Lund, *The Impure Imagination*, xiii.

102. Pratt, *Imperial Eyes*, 245.

103. Da Silva, *Toward a Global Idea of Race*, 29.

104. Wilderson, "As Free as Whiteness Will Make Them" (italics in the original).

105. Ortiz, *Contrapunteo*, 260.

302   NOTES TO PAGES 101–110

106. Ortiz, *Cuban Counterpoint*, 102–3.

107. On the 1912 uprising, Club Atenas, and Afro-Cuban activism in the Republic more broadly, see Pappademos, *Black Political Activism and the Cuban Republic*. On the 1912 uprising see also Helg, *Our Rightful Share*.

108. Miller, *Rise and Fall of the Cosmic Race*, 75.

109. Ortiz, "Por la integración cubana de blancos y negros," 257. All translations from the Spanish original into English are mine.

110. Ortiz, 256.

111. Guridy, *Forging Diaspora*, 85, 180.

112. Ortiz, "Por la integración cubana de blancos y negros," 256–57.

113. Ortiz, 259, 260.

114. Ortiz, 259.

115. The lecture first appeared in English translation as "The Relations between Whites and Blacks in Cuba" (1944).

116. Ortiz, *Hampa afro-cubana: Los negros brujos*, 400.

117. Castellanos, "The Evolution of Criminology in Cuba," 220.

118. Fonticoba, "Fernando Ortiz e Israel Castellanos," 3.

119. On Lombroso see, for example, Gibson, *Born to Crime*.

120. On the No Museo Lombroso organization see: http://www.nolombroso.org/it/.

121. Ortiz, "Por la integración cubana de blancos y negros," 263.

122. Ortiz, 258.

123. Ortiz, 262.

124. Biko, *I Write What I Like*, 20.

125. Ortiz, "Por la integración cubana de blancos y negros," 263.

126. Ortiz, 263.

127. Ortiz, *Hampa afro-cubana: Los negros brujos*, 20–21. The translation that follows is mine.

128. Lombroso, *L'uomo bianco e l'uomo di colore*, 56–57.

129. Ortiz, "Por la integración cubana de blancos y negros," 263–64.

130. Ortiz, 264.

131. Ortiz, 264.

132. Ortiz, 264.

133. Ortiz, 264.

134. Paton, "Black Consciousness," 9.

135. Paton, 9.

136. Ortiz, "Por la integración cubana de blancos y negros," 265 (italics in the original).

137. Ortiz, 265.

138. Ortiz, 265.

NOTES TO PAGES 110–118

139. Biko, *I Write What I Like*, 20.
140. Da Silva, *Toward a Global Idea of Race*, 31.
141. Woods, *Blackhood Against the Police Power*, 15.
142. Ortiz, "Por la integración cubana de blancos y negros," 262.
143. Ortiz, *Cuban Counterpoint*, 53.
144. See, for example, Nascimento, *Brazil: Mixture or Massacre?* and Telles, *Race in Another America*.
145. Nascimento, *Brazil: Mixture or Massacre?*, 3.
146. Aidoo, *Slavery Unseen*, 104.
147. Freyre, *Casa-grande e senzala*, 265.
148. See Freyre, 109, 117.
149. Freyre cited in Needell, "Identity, Race, Gender, and Modernity," 57–58.
150. Nascimento, *Brazil: Mixture or Massacre?*, 38.
151. Nascimento, 63.
152. Nascimento, 63.
153. The central role that female slaveowners played in subjugating slaves and maintaining the institution of slavery, of course, is not a Brazilian peculiarity. On slave owning women in the US South, see Jones-Rogers, *They Were Her Property*.
154. Telles, *Race in Another America*, 193.
155. UNESCO, "The Race Problem," 1.
156. Palthey, "Télégramme adressé le 10 Mars 1954 par le Directeur des Nations Unies."
157. Dávila, "Entre dois mundos," 141.
158. Freyre, "Report," 2.
159. Freyre, 2.
160. Wynter, "Unsettling the Coloniality of Being/Power/Truth/Freedom," 301.
161. Freyre, "Report," 34, 8.
162. Freyre, 4.
163. Freyre, 4.
164. Freyre, 5.
165. Freyre, 5–6.
166. Freyre, 6.
167. Freyre, 42.
168. UNESCO, *International Social Science Bulletin*, 462.
169. Saucier and Woods, "Introduction," 5–6.
170. Ture and Hamilton, *Black Power*, 4.
171. Ture, *Stokely Speaks*, 38.

304 NOTES TO PAGES 118–129

172. Wilderson, *Red, White and Black*, 12.
173. Freyre, "Report," 37.
174. Freyre, 37.
175. Vasconcelos, "The Race Problem in Latin America," 89.
176. Freyre, "Report," 36, 37.
177. Freyre, 36.
178. Freyre, 22.
179. Freyre, 38.
180. Freyre, 37.
181. Freyre, 28–29.
182. Freyre, 33–34.
183. Freyre, 33.
184. Freyre, 32.
185. Vasconcelos, "The Race Problem in Latin America," 86.
186. Freyre, "Report," 43.
187. Fernandes, "Apresentação: o gênio da formação social brasileira," 9.
188. Lehman, "Gilberto Freyre," 211.
189. Lund and McNee, "Gilberto Freyre e o sublime brasileiro," 7.
190. Krauze, "Latin America's Talent for Tolerance."
191. Rodriguez, *Brown*, 136, 142.
192. Fields and Fields, *Racecraft*, 4.
193. Esteva-Fabregat, *Mestizaje in Ibero-America*; and Wirth, "The Revolutionary Encounter," 25.
194. See, for example, Fields and Fields, *Racecraft*; Perez-Rodriguez and de la Fuente, "Now is the Time for a Postracial Medicine"; and Feagin, "Systemic Racism and 'Race' Categorization in Medical Research and Practice."
195. Macharia, *Frottage*, 19.
196. Gilroy, *The Black Atlantic*, 2, 4.
197. Jackson, *Becoming Human*, 121.
198. Gilroy, *The Black Atlantic*, 31.
199. I examine the politics of hybridity in *The Black Atlantic* in depth in a forthcoming article titled "The Ruse of Impurity: Paul Gilroy's *The Black Atlantic* and the Politics of Hybridity."
200. Pérez-Torres, *Mestizaje*, 30.
201. Gordon, *Her Majesty's Other Children*, 67 (my emphasis).

Chapter 3
EPIGRAPHS: Biko, *I Write What I Like*, 89–90. Slasha, "Black Paint," verses 56–66.

NOTES TO PAGES 130–132

1. Ndlovu, *The Soweto Uprisings*, 59.

2. On the protests at South African universities, see, for example, Naicker, "From Marikana to #feesmustfall"; and Gibson, "The Specter of Fanon." On police repression in the Jan Smuts student residence at Rhodes University, see Ebrahim, "Students at UCKAR are Calling on the Police to Answer for Alleged Brutality."

3. Thabo is not his real name. Frustrated by the scarcity of reports on the repression at the Jan Smuts student residence, in June 2017, while I was a postdoctoral fellow at Rhodes University, I decided to interview a student who lived in the residence and whose contact information I received from a common friend. The student was made aware of my intention to include his perspective in this book and was sent this paragraph prior to its inclusion in the manuscript. While the student did not request it, I have decided to use a pseudonym to protect his privacy.

4. February, "From Redress to Empowerment," 81; Department of Higher Education and Training (DHET), *Statistics on Post-School Education and Training in South Africa: 2020*, 90. The racial categories generally used by the South African government, including in these statistics, are: African/Black, Coloured, Indian/Asian, and White.

5. Naicker, "From Marikana to #feesmustfall," 56.

6. Department of Higher Education and Training (DHET), *Statistics on Post-School Education and Training in South Africa: 2020*, 26.

7. Department of Higher Education and Training (DHET), 25.

8. Affirmative action programs in the country have been the result of the 1990s settlement between the National Party (NP) and the African National Congress (ANC), in which the ANC negotiated for a clause in the Constitution which stipulates that "to promote the achievement of equality, legislative and other measures designed to protect or advance persons, or categories of persons, disadvantaged by unfair discrimination may be taken" (February, "From Redress to Empowerment," 76).

9. See Zuberi and Bonilla-Silva, "Toward a Definition of White Logic and White Methods."

10. John H. Stanfield writes, "Anointed as the best and the brightest, intellectuals of color and White neoliberal intellectuals who embrace the doctrines of colorblindness and the declining significance of race make prestigious academic careers for themselves even though it is apparent to even the casual observer that race is more than alive and well in America" ("The Gospel of Feel-Good Sociology," 281).

11. Harney and Moten, *The Undercommons*, 40.

12. Harney and Moten, 30.

306   NOTES TO PAGES 133–141

13. On the student occupations see, for example, Pureza, "Brazil's Student Upsurge."

14. Bernardino-Costa and Blackman, "Affirmative Action in Brazil," 373.

15. Martins, Madeiro, and Nascimento, "Paving Paradise," 807.

16. See Kamel, *Não somos racistas*, 9.

17. National Center for Education Statistics, "Status and Trends," 89.

18. See www.studentmarch.org/.

19. Garrison-Wade and Lewis, "Affirmative Action," 24.

20. Feder, "The Constitution and Racial Diversity in K-12 Education," 4.

21. *Parents Involved*, Syllabus, 1.

22. On how white women have invoked discourses of motherhood to support white supremacy in the United States, see McRae, *Mothers of Massive Resistance*.

23. Westley, "White Normativity and the Racial Rhetoric of Equal Protection," 98.

24. Westley, 97.

25. See Erasmus, "Apartheid Race Categories," 1.

26. Garuba, "Closing Reflections on 'Revisiting Apartheid's Race Categories,'" 174.

27. Oppenheimer and David, "The New Affirmative Action," 51.

28. Seekings, *Race, Discrimination, and Diversity in South Africa*, 26.

29. Maré, "Non-Racialism in the Struggle Against Apartheid," 27.

30. Ruggunan and Maré, "Race Classification at the University of KwaZulu-Natal," 56.

31. Maré, "Non-Racialism in the Struggle Against Apartheid," 23.

32. Alexander, "Affirmative Action and the Perpetuation of Racial Identities," 94.

33. Oppenheimer and Ansara, "The New Affirmative Action," 50.

34. Maré, *Declassified*, 55.

35. Jansen, "Intellectuals, the State and Universities in South Africa," 149.

36. *Parents Involved*, Syllabus, 5.

37. Harlan cited in Carr, *"Color-Blind" Racism*, ix.

38. Harlan cited in Carr, ix–x.

39. See Harris, "The Story of Plessy v. Ferguson."

40. Crenshaw, "Color Blindness, History, and the Law," 282–83.

41. Crenshaw, 284.

42. Gotanda, "A Critique of 'Our Constitution is Colorblind,'" 265.

43. Nascimento, *The Sorcery of Color*, 513.

44. Ture and Hamilton, *Black Power*, 47.

45. Biko, *I Write What I Like*, 25

NOTES TO PAGES 142–150

46. Malcolm X, *Malcolm X Speaks*, 165.

47. See Mngxitama, "Blacks Can't Be Racist."

48. See van Gelder, "Inside the Kommando Camp That Turns Boys' Doubts to Hate."

49. Magnoli, *Uma gota de sangue*, 143–44 (my translation).

50. Nascimento, *Brazil: Mixture or Massacre?*, 66.

51. Kamel, *Não somos racistas*, 18. All translations from the original Portuguese text are mine.

52. Kamel, 18.

53. Kamel, 23.

54. See Nascimento, *Quilombo*.

55. *Parents Involved*, Syllabus, 4.

56. Kamel, *Não somos racistas*, 51.

57. Kamel, 26.

58. Kamel, 40.

59. Kamel, 40.

60. Kamel, *Não somos racistas*, 43.

61. Maré, *Declassified*, 150.

62. Kamel, *Não somos racistas*, 24.

63. Kamel, 77.

64. *Parents Involved*, Kennedy, 17.

65. Maré, *Declassified*, 111.

66. Nuttall, *Entanglement*, 31.

67. Nuttall, 31. In an earlier article titled "City Forms and Writing the 'Now' in South Africa" (2004), Nuttall also argues that scholarship on creolization produced outside South Africa proves useful to theorizing social relations in the post-apartheid present.

68. Cooppan, "W(h)ither Post-Colonial Studies?," 29.

69. Jolly, "Rehearsals of Liberation," 17.

70. Jolly, 17.

71. Jolly, 17.

72. Jolly, 17.

73. Jolly, 19–20.

74. Jolly, 22.

75. Jolly, 23.

76. Jolly, 23.

77. Mamdani, *Citizen and Subject*, 7.

78. Biko, *I Write What I Like*, 97.

79. Jolly, "Rehearsals of Liberation," 24 (my emphasis).

80. Jolly, 22, 27–28.

308   NOTES TO PAGES 151–154

81. Soudien, "The Modern Seduction of Race," 20.

82. Derrida, "Racism's Last Word," 291; Soudien, 20.

83. Erasmus, "Apartheid Race Categories," 1.

84. Biko, *I Write What I Like*, 48.

85. Mngxitama, "Blacks Can't Be Racist," 9.

86. Soudien, "The Modern Seduction of Race," 35.

87. Erasmus, "Confronting the Categories," 244.

88. Mngxitama writes that liberal humanism is deliberately invoked to maintain white dominance: "Whiteness is so pervasive it has become invisible, that is to say normalized—the 'normative state of existence.' This normative state of existence is also a powerful tool of silencing. 'Why can't we all just get along?' someone asks innocently, while another claims that 'colour is just skin deep, in fact we are human beings ultimately.' Blacks are under pressure to accept this, and therefore fail to bracket off whiteness. . . . The arsenal of strategies which function to normalise and make invisible whiteness (with all its unearned privileges), generally falter when whiteness is exposed, because to point out that whites are white is to call for accounting" ("Blacks Can't Be Racist," 16).

89. Wilderson, *Afropessimism*, 164.

90. *Parents Involved*, Stevens, 39.

91. Kamel, *Não somos racistas*, 65.

92. Maré, *Declassified*, 96.

93. Kamel, *Não somos racistas*, 74.

94. See Nascimento, *Brazil: Mixture or Massacre?*

95. Kamel, *Não somos racistas*, 41.

96. Kamel, 47.

97. Maré, *Declassified*, 169.

98. Maré, 22.

99. On the history of the ANC, see Turok, *The Historical Roots of the ANC*.

100. *Parents Involved*, Syllabus, 3.

101. *Parents Involved*, Thomas, 18.

102. On the discourse of white injury see, for example, Gutiérrez-Jones, *Critical Race Narratives*; Carroll, *Affirmative Reaction*; and Wiegman, *Object Lessons*.

103. Seekings, "The Continuing Salience of Race," 1. The silencing of racism is a recurring pattern in Seekings's scholarship. In *Class, Race, and Inequality in the South African City* (2010), for example, Seekings also silences white domination. He states that the post-apartheid city "remains deeply divided by class and, for the most part and for whatever reason, race

NOTES TO PAGES 155–159

also," yet describes this inequality as being *not* the consequence of structural racism but the product of "'neo-liberal' policies with regard to urban structure" (13). Neoliberalism, in Seekings's conception, is unrelated to racial exploitation. In its fixation on silencing race, Seekings's scholarship reveals itself as a racial project.

104. Seekings, *Race, Discrimination, and Diversity in South Africa*, 24.

105. Seekings, 26.

106. Statistics South Africa, *Quarterly Labor Force Survey*, 23, 24, 10.

107. Seekings, *Race, Discrimination, and Diversity in South Africa* 25.

108. Seekings, 3–4.

109. Seekings, 3.

110. Zuberi and Bonilla-Silva, "Toward a Definition of White Logic and White Methods," 144.

111. Seekings, *Race, Discrimination, and Inequality in South Africa*, 25.

112. Seekings and Nattrass, *Class, Race, and Inequality in South Africa*, 6.

113. Lipsitz, *How Racism Takes Place*, 2.

114. Lipsitz, 4.

115. Kelley, *Yo' Mama's Disfunktional!*, 92.

116. West, "Only 2% of Companies Listed on the JSE Are Under 100% Black Leadership."

117. Seekings and Nattrass, *Class, Race, and Inequality in South Africa*, 308.

118. Seekings and Nattrass, 45.

119. Seekings and Nattrass, 6; Maré, *Declassified*, 63, 35.

120. Kamel, *Não somos racistas*, 79. The literal meaning of "se pareçem" is "look alike."

121. Maré, *Declassified*, 115, 104.

122. Posel, "Races to Consume," 158. See also Posel and van Wyk, *Conspicuous Consumption in Africa*.

123. South African Institute of Race Relations (IRR), "Affirmative Action is Killing Babies."

124. Lipsitz, *The Possessive Investment in Whiteness*, 15.

125. For a book funded by the IRR that enforces colorblindness, see Holborn, *The Long Shadow of Apartheid*. Holborn condemns affirmative action, arguing that it reinforces "racial categorization" and creates "racial division" (4). She also views former president Jacob Zuma's "refusal to start a debate on racism" and other "efforts to reduce the prominence of race in public discourse" as positive trends that, she argues, have led to improvements in race relations in the country (5).

310   NOTES TO PAGES 159–168

126. See Soudien, *Realising the Dream.*
127. Maré, *Declassified*, 27.

Chapter 4
EPIGRAPHS: Biko, *I Write What I Like*, 19. Wilderson, *Afropessimism*, 220.
1. Paton, "Black Consciousness," 9.
2. Paton, 9.
3. Paton, 9.
4. Biko, *I Write What I Like*, 89.
5. Paton, "Black Consciousness," 10. On Paton's statement see also Biko, *I Write What I Like*, 89.
6. Paton, 10.
7. Biko, *I Write What I Like*, 82.
8. The so-called architect of apartheid Hendrick Verwoerd made clear that he viewed separate development as a central means through which whites could maintain power: "We want to keep South Africa White . . . 'keeping it White' can only mean one thing, namely, White domination, not 'leadership,' not 'guidance,' but 'control,' 'supremacy.' If we are agreed that it is the desire of the people that the white man should be able to protect himself by retaining White domination, we say that it can be achieved by separate development" (Verwoerd in More, "Biko," 51).
9. Wilderson, "Biko and the Problematic of Presence," 101.
10. Biko, *I Write What I Like*, 89.
11. Biko, 89.
12. Biko, 20.
13. Ture, *Stokely Speaks*, 38.
14. Biko, *I Write What I Like*, 19.
15. Curry, "Concerning the Underspecialization of Race Theory in American Philosophy," 44.
16. Baldwin, "What Price Freedom?", 84.
17. Vice's article was written for an academic readership. It was through McKaiser's intervention that it first reached a larger audience. See McKaiser, "Hoe moet 'whiteys' in dié vreemde plek leef?" (How Should "Whiteys" Live in This Strange Place?) and McKaiser, "Confronting Whiteness."
18. Vice, "Why My Opinions on Whiteness Touched a Nerve."
19. Vice, "How Do I Live in this This Strange Place?," 323.
20. Vice, 323.
21. Vice, 324.
22. Vice, 338.

23. Vice, 334.

24. Alcoff, "What Should White People Do?," 13.

25. Alcoff, 12.

26. See Lott, *Love and Theft*.

27. See Malan, *My Traitor's Heart*.

28. Vice, "Reflections on 'How Do I Live in This Strange Place?,'" 503.

29. Vice, "How Do I Live in This Strange Place?," 334, 338.

30. Vice, 325.

31. Vice, 331.

32. Gutiérrez-Jones, *Critical Race Narratives*, 34.

33. Wiegman, *Object Lessons*, 183.

34. Tabensky, "The Oppressor's Pathology," 82.

35. Tabensky, 86.

36. Tabensky, 78.

37. Sullivan, *Revealing Whiteness*, 231.

38. Vice, "How Do I Live in This Strange Place?," 326.

39. Vice, 323.

40. Vice, 323 (italics in the original).

41. Vice, 326.

42. Lipsitz, *How Racism Takes Place*, 2 (my emphasis).

43. Benatar, "Why Samantha Vice Is Wrong on Whiteness."

44. Benatar.

45. Benatar.

46. Sullivan, *Revealing Whiteness*, 63.

47. Sullivan, 63.

48. Vice, "How Do I Live in This Strange Place?," 330.

49. Palmer, "Otherwise than Blackness," 248–249 (italics in the original).

50. Vice, "How Do I Live in This Strange Place?," 325, 327, 329, 329, 330.

51. Vice, 325.

52. Biko, *I Write What I Like*, 66.

53. Biko, 66.

54. Biko, 61.

55. Biko, 61, 62, 71.

56. Biko, 23.

57. Biko, 22–23.

58. Vice, "How Do I Live in This Strange Place?," 323.

59. Vice, 324 (italics in the original).

60. Vice, 337.

61. Vice, 331.

62. Vice, 334 (italics in the original).

312   NOTES TO PAGES 179–190

63. Vice, 332.

64. Vice, 328 (italics in the original).

65. Biko, *I Write What I Like*, 87–88.

66. Lorde, *Sister Outsider*, 127.

67. Lorde, 130.

68. Lorde, 130.

69. See Sullivan, *Good White People*, 128.

70. See Mills, *The Racial Contract*, for white supremacy as a political system.

71. Ahmed, "Declarations of Whiteness."

72. Ahmed.

73. Ahmed.

74. See Zuberi and Bonilla-Silva, "Toward a Definition of White Logic and White Methods."

75. See Harris, "Whiteness as Property."

76. Biko, *I Write What I Like*, 149.

77. Vice, "How Do I Live in This Strange Place?," 335.

78. Biko, *I Write What I Like*, 23.

79. Vice, "How Do I Live in This Strange Place?," 337–38.

80. Vice, 340.

81. Mngxitama, "End to Whiteness a Black Issue."

82. Tabensky, "Pitfalls of Negritude," 4.

83. Tabensky, 4.

84. Vice, "Essentializing Rhetoric and Work on the Self," 104–5.

85. Baldwin, "The Fire Next Time," 341.

86. Vice, "How Do I Live in This Strange Place?," 335.

87. Biko, *I Write What I Like*, 19.

88. Baldwin, "What Price Freedom?," 84 (italics in the original).

Chapter 5

EPIGRAPHS: Cubena, "Interview with Dr. Carlos Guillermo Wilson," 127. Biko, *I Write What I Like*, 146.

1. *Negrismo* and *Negritud* refer to literary and cultural movements that emerged in the Hispanophone Caribbean at the beginning of the twentieth century. Literary works that are described as *negrista* center Blackness but are written by white or mestizo writers, in contrast with works within the Negritud tradition, which are written by Black writers. Negrista poetry often represents Black people in stereotypical ways, as inherently hypersexual or musical beings, whereas works in the Negritud tradition attempted to

NOTES TO PAGES 190–196

provide a humanizing perspective that included a critique of racism and discrimination. Thematically, however, the boundaries between the literature of negrismo and Negritud are often blurry. With regard to fiction, Shirley Jackson in *La novela negrista en Hispanoamérica* identifies anti-abolitionist novels by white and mestizo Latin American writers as the first examples of negrista literature in Latin America. To be precise, she names *El Periquillo Sarniento* (1816) by the Mexican writer José Joaquín Férnandez de Lizardi as the first negrista novel. Other prominent early negrista works are Gertrudis Gómez de Avellaneda's *Sab* (1841) and Cirilio Villaverde's *Cecilia Valdés, o la loma del ángel* (1882). There are several parallels with regard to themes and representational strategies between Latin American negrismo and indianismo as well as indigenismo, which I engage in the next chapter.

2. Notice that, while throughout the book I refer to the author as Cubena, the name he has chosen for himself, he published his early work using only the name Carlos Guillermo Wilson. In the bibliography, all his works are listed under Cubena for consistency.

3. Gilroy, *The Black Atlantic*, 87.

4. Lowe, *The Intimacies of Four Continents*, 3–4.

5. Armstrong, *How Novels Think*, 3.

6. Armstrong, 10.

7. Hartman, *Scenes of Subjection*, 116.

8. Hartman, 122.

9. Hartman, 118, 119.

10. Wright, *Becoming Black*, 229.

11. Ferguson, *Aberrations in Black*, 3.

12. Ferguson, 45.

13. Fortune, *Obra selecta*, 343.

14. Fortune cited in Cubena, "Aspectos de la prosa panameña contemporánea," 143, 145.

15. Cubena, "La poesía afro-panameña," 23, 26.

16. All translations from Cubena's works included in this chapter are mine.

17. See Manzano, *Autobiografía de un esclavo*; and Sousa, *Obras poéticas*.

18. Fanon, *Toward the African Revolution*, 26.

19. Branche, *Colonialism and Race in Luso-Hispanic Literature*, 170. See also Davis, "Panama," 204.

20. Soley, *Culture and Customs of Panama*, 57.

21. Soley, 57, 65; Miró, *Itinerario de la poesia en Panamá*, 143.

22. The Spanish word *cara* can denote both "face" and "(physical) appearance."

314   NOTES TO PAGES 196–203

23. Escobar, "Nieblas," 146.

24. See Navarro, *Vida e obra de Gaspar Octavio Hernández*.

25. Miró, *Itinerario de la poesia en Panamá*, 73.

26. Cubena, "Aspectos de la prosa panameña contemporánea," 144.

27. Hérnandez cited in Watson, *The Politics of Race in Panama*, 31 (italics in the original).

28. See Watson, 41.

29. Cubena, "Aspectos de la prosa panameña contemporánea," 95, 97.

30. Beleño, *Gamboa Road Gang/Los forzados de Gamboa*, 149. The translation from the Spanish original is mine.

31. See Jackson, *Black Writers in Latin America*, 180; and Watson, *The Politics of Race in Panama*, 73.

32. Watson, 72.

33. Birmingham-Pokorny, "Introduction," 15.

34. hooks, *Ain't I a Woman*, 35.

35. Jackson, *Black Writers in Latin America*, 181.

36. In the shield portrayed in *Chombo* the chain has six rings, rather than seven, and the Efik are not mentioned.

37. In the shield portrayed in *Chombo* there are only three stars, which symbolize "los tres lares donde habita la familia de CUBENA [the three locations in which the CUBENA family lives]: AFRICA—JAMAICA—PANAMA."

38. In *Chombo*, Cubena mentions Black people in general in this passage.

39. In *Chombo*, Cubena describes this character as patient and strong and as characterizing all people of African descent.

40. Cubena, *Chombo*, 7 (italics in the original). The third novel of the "trilogy" that Cubena mentions here is *La misión secreta* (The Secret Mission, 2005), which foreshadows the 2014 centenary of the completion of the Canal. The novel narrates the story of Panamanian characters of West Indian descent living in the United States and intercalates numerous tales about enslaved Black people as well as Africans participating in the conquest of Latin America. On *La misión secreta* see Watson, *The Politics of Race in Panama*.

41. Jackson, *Black Writers and the Hispanic Canon*, 78–79.

42. On Black South African fiction written during apartheid and its aesthetics see, for example, Nkosi, "Fiction by Black South Africans"; and Ndebele, "The Rediscovery of the Ordinary."

43. Mutloatse cited in Seroke, "Black Writers in South Africa," 305.

44. Cubena, *Chombo*, 9.

45. Cubena, 9.

NOTES TO PAGES 203–213

46. Cubena, 12.

47. Cubena, 12. The same argument is advanced in *Los nietos*, in which the West Indian character Elsa Gordon emphasizes that Africans have profoundly influenced Spanish history, culture, and racial makeup (Cubena, *Los nietos*, 56).

48. Guillén, *Obra poética*, 114.

49. Ellison, *Collected Essays*, 500.

50. As V. Y. Mudimbe explains in *The Invention of Africa*, "Although in African history the colonial experience represented but a brief moment from the perspective of today, this moment is still charged and controversial, since . . . it signified . . . radically new types of discourses on African traditions and cultures" (1).

51. Biko, *I Write What I Like*, 29.

52. Hartman, *Lose Your Mother*, 7.

53. Fanon, *The Wretched of the Earth*, 209.

54. Cubena, *Los nietos*, 55.

55. Cubena, 55.

56. See Watson, *The Politics of Race in Panama*, 91.

57. Cubena, *Los nietos*, 30.

58. Cubena, 182.

59. Wade, *Race and Ethnicity in Latin America*, 87.

60. Cubena, *Chombo*, 28.

61. These poems by Guillén are included in the collections *Tengo* (1964) and *Summa Poética* (2006).

62. Cubena, *Los nietos*, 206–7.

63. Cubena, *Chombo*, 18.

64. Cubena, *Los nietos*, 57.

65. Cubena, *Chombo*, 98–99.

66. Carter, "Women in Carlos Guillermo Wilson's *Chombo*," 22.

67. See Gotanda, "A Critique of 'Our Constitution is Color-Blind,'" 257.

68. Cubena, *Los nietos*, 31.

69. Cubena, "Interview with Dr. Carlos Guillermo Wilson," 22.

70. Cubena, *Chombo*, 50–51.

71. According to Tomás Wayne Edison, Karafula's name recalls the Panamanian slang "cara fula" (pale face), a clear reference to her obsession with whiteness ("Humor and Satire," 502). This character and Fulabuta reappear also in *Los nietos*, in which Fulabuta is obsessed with burned charcoal and engages in lascivious sexual behavior (Cubena, *Los nietos*, 158).

72. Mngxitama, "Blacks Can't Be Racist," 7.

73. Cubena, "Interview with Dr. Carlos Guillermo Wilson," 19.

316   NOTES TO PAGES 213–223

74. Fanon, *Toward the African Revolution*, 17.

75. JanMohamed, "The Economy of Manichean Allegory," 63.

76. Gallers, *Enslavement and Masculinity in Afro-Hispanic Narrative*, 123.

77. Mills, *The Racial Contract*, 7.

78. Morrison, *Playing in the Dark*, 81.

79. Fanon, *Black Skin, White Masks*, 121.

80. Scott, *Extravagant Abjection*, 6.

81. Strongman, *Queering Black Atlantic Religions*, 106.

82. For example, LGBTQ characters are referred to as "amujerados," "cuecos," and "maricones" (*Cuentos* 46–7) or "cojos" (*Los nietos*, 42), "amaricados" (*Chombo*, 64), and even "cuecos de mierda" (*Los nietos*, 151)—all homophobic epithets.

83. Cubena, *Los nietos*, 205; 213.

84. Cubena, 205.

85. Cubena, 231.

86. Cubena, 231.

87. Biko, *I Write What I Like*, 49.

88. Cubena, *Chombo*, 76.

89. Fanon, *The Wretched of the Earth*, 209.

90. Jackson, *Black Writers in Latin America*, 188.

91. Gordon, "Black Aesthetics, Black Value," 20.

92. Fanon, *Black Skin, White Masks*, 2.

93. Wright, *Becoming Black*, 67.

94. Cubena, *Chombo*, 76.

95. Watson, *The Politics of Race in Panama*, 47.

96. Fanon, *Black Skin, White Masks*, 87.

Chapter 6

EPIGRAPHS: Anzaldúa, *The Gloria Anzaldúa Reader*, 204. Moraga, "La Güera," 24 (italics in the original).

1. Anzaldúa, *The Gloria Anzaldúa Reader*, 204.

2. Latorre, *Walls of Empowerment*, 2–3.

3. Lorde, *Sister Outsider*, 94.

4. Sandoval, "U.S. Third World Feminism," 8.

5. Crenshaw, "Mapping the Margins," 1242.

6. Crenshaw, "Demarginalizing the Intersection of Race and Sex," 140.

7. Crenshaw, 140.

8. Moraga, "La Güera," 24 (italics in the original).

NOTES TO PAGES 224–227

9. Menchaca, "Chicano Indianism," 584.

10. Menchaca, 598. The *Mendez v. Westminster* case set the precedent for *Brown v. Board of Education*.

11. Anaya and Lomelí, *Aztlán*, 27–30.

12. Anaya and Lomelí, 27.

13. Sexton, "The *Vel* of Slavery," 592.

14. Bebout, *Mythohistorical Interventions*, 4.

15. The existence of Aztlán has been the object of numerous investigations but its specific geographic location remains in the realm of speculation. Described in the 902 *Códice Ramirez* as "a paradisiacal place where the ancestral Aztecs lived in comfort and ease" (Pina, "The Archaic, Historical, Mythicized Dimension of Aztlán," 52), Aztlán might have been north of the Gulf of California, in what today is the Southwest of the United States. Whether or not Aztlán existed, scholars agree that the Aztecs migrated into central Mexico from the north (Smith, *The Aztecs*, 39). Moreover, Anaya writes, "The migration and quest of the original inhabitants of Aztlán can be viewed in the context of world mythology: like the Jews migrating from Egypt in the time of their Exodus to settle in the promised land, the Aztecs migrated south to establish the new nation of Tenochtitlan" ("Aztlán," 36). In reclaiming Aztlán as homeland, Chicanxs defined themselves as residing in their place of origin.

16. Pérez-Torres, "Refiguring Aztlán," 29.

17. Moya, *The Social Imperative*, 86.

18. Pérez-Torres, *Mestizaje*, 9.

19. José Limón has argued that the result has been "a dense, richly allusive but ultimately opaque and politically limited poetics keyed not on social engagement, but on inwardness, indigenous purity, and metaphysical transcendence" (*Mexican Ballads, Chicano Poems*, 109–10). Similarly, Ana María Alonso contends that, in relying on Aztec mythology in the literary construction of a mestiza consciousness, Anzaldúa privileged an Indigenous group that is often problematically considered more "advanced" or "civilized" than others ("Conforming Disconformity," 481). On Chicana feminism and indigenism see also Contreras, *Blood Lines*; and Perez, "New Tribalism and Chicana/o Indigeneity in the Work of Gloria Anzaldúa."

20. Lomelí, "Introduction. Revisiting the Vision of Aztlán," 7.

21. Anaya, "Aztlán," 39.

22. Sánchez cited in Bruce-Novoa, *Chicano Authors*, 233.

23. See Moya, "Chicana Feminisms and Postmodernist Theory," 446–47.

24. Moraga, "Queer Aztlán," 242.

25. Morrison, *Playing in the Dark*, 17.

NOTES TO PAGES 227–232

26. Morrison, 58.

27. Contreras, *Blood Lines*, 14.

28. Contreras, 9.

29. Contreras, 164.

30. Saldaña-Portillo, "Who Is the Indian in Aztlán?," 420.

31. Anzaldúa et al., "Speaking across the Divide," 12, 14.

32. Anzaldúa, *The Gloria Anzaldúa Reader*, 203–4.

33. Ignacio López-Calvo has argued that *Erased Faces* is concerned with politics of feminist transnational solidarity. He has lauded the novel for moving beyond the nation state and constructing a "fruitful dialogue" between Chicana feminism and the Zapatista Movement ("Chicanismo Meets Zapatismo," 67).

34. Saldaña-Portillo, "Who Is the Indian in Aztlán?," 420. See also Saldaña-Portillo, *The Revolutionary Imagination in the Americas and the Age of Development*.

35. Broeck, *Gender and the Abjection of Blackness*, 5.

36. Literary *indianismo* and *indigenismo* were popular literary movements, burgeoning in the nineteenth and early twentieth centuries respectively, in Latin American countries with a large Indigenous population, such as Brazil, Ecuador, Guatemala, Mexico, and Peru. Literary indigenismo, which flourished especially after the 1930s, owes much to social realism. It aspired to be a countercurrent to indianismo, which portrayed Indigenous people as "primitive" and passive beings in exotic and erotically charged settings (Rosenthal, "Race Mixture and the Representation of Indians," 123). José Carlos Mariátegui argues in *Siete ensayos de interpretación de la realidad peruana* (1928) that indigenista novels aspired to be a countercurrent to indianismo and involve social criticism through the exposure of Indigenous people's exploitation. However, as the product of white and mestiza/o writers, indigenista works also provide distorted and paternalistic representations of Indigenous peoples. *Erased Faces*, as we will see, reproposes the paternalism that typified both literary indianismo and indigenismo.

37. Moraga, *A Xicana Codex of Changing Consciousness*, 35.

38. Moraga, "La Güera," 24 (italics in the original).

39. Limón, *Erased Faces*, 2.

40. Limón, 2.

41. Limón, 4.

42. Limón, 13.

43. Limón, 31.

44. Limón, 31.

45. Limón, 31.

NOTES TO PAGES 232–240

46. Palau, "Ethnography Otherwise," 11.

47. Blom, ¿Hay razas inferiores?, 8.

48. Blom, Imágenes Lacandonas, 86.

49. Herrera, Mayan Drifter, 35.

50. Herrera, 54.

51. I examine the politics of Mayan Drifter in a forthcoming essay titled "'To Go into America as I Go into Myself'": Chicanx Indigenism, the Indigenous Other, and the Ethnographic Gaze in Juan Felipe Herrera's Mayan Drifter."

52. Herrera, 54.

53. Limón, Erased Faces, 13.

54. Miller-Young, "Exotic/Erotic/Ethnopornographic," 43.

55. Miller-Young, 43.

56. Limón, Erased Faces, 4.

57. Limón, 4.

58. Limón, 38–39.

59. Meyer, The Woman in the Blue Cloak, 46.

60. Wiegman, Object Lessons, 161.

61. Sharpe, In the Wake, 53.

62. Castillo, The Mixquiahuala Letters, 52.

63. Villanueva, Weeping Woman. On "Free Women," see Contreras, Blood Lines, 158–61.

64. Herrera, Mayan Drifter, 76.

65. Limón, Erased Faces, 51.

66. Wiegman, Object Lessons, 164.

67. Limón, Erased Faces, 14.

68. Gutiérrez-Jones, Critical Race Narratives, 172.

69. Julio Cammarota argues that the white savior displays a "privilege of ignorance by failing to see how the maintenance of his or her higher status in relation to the oppressed perpetuates inequalities" ("Blindsided by Avatar," 256).

70. Limón, Erased Faces, 39.

71. Limón, 39.

72. Limón, 41 (italics in the original).

73. Marcos, Our Word Is Our Weapon, 109 (my translation). The novel also adopts parts of this same communiqué in another dialogue without attribution (see Erased Faces, 38).

74. Limón, Erased Faces, 39.

75. Limón, 100–101 (italics in the original).

76. Limón, 242 (italics in the original).

77. Limón, 253–54 (italics in the original).

320   NOTES TO PAGES 240–245

78. Limón, 256 (italics in the original).

79. Limón, 239.

80. Wiegman, *Object Lessons*, 171.

81. Limón, *Erased Faces*, 239.

82. Limón, 239.

83. Limón, 257.

84. Moraga, *The Hungry Woman*, vii (italics in the original).

85. Moraga, viii (italics in the original).

86. Moraga, viii (italics in the original).

87. Moraga, vii (italics in the original).

88. Moraga, ix (italics in the original).

89. Limón, *Erased Faces*, 13.

90. Moraga, *The Hungry Woman*, ix (italics in the original).

91. Columbus and Jane, *The Four Voyages of Columbus*, 7–9.

92. Moraga, *The Hungry Woman*, ix (italics in the original).

93. Moraga, viii (italics in the original).

94. Moraga, ix.

95. Moraga, x.

96. Moraga, x.

97. This slippage between deities and people is not unique to Moraga's work. It can be found also in Anzaldúa's *Borderlands/La Frontera*, for example, and in various theoretical works on Chicana feminism. For example, Norma Alarcón writes that the "native woman has many names . . . Coatlicue, Cihuacoátl, Ixtacihúatl, and so on" ("Chicana Feminism," 66). On this slippage see Contreras, *Blood Lines*, 120.

98. Moraga, *The Hungry Woman*, 6.

99. Moraga, 6.

100. Euripides's tragedy *Medea*, just like Moraga's play, tells a story of revenge. Leaving behind her father and people, Medea leaves home to follow her husband Jason, who forsakes her after the birth of their two children and betrays her with a woman called Glauce. Creon, Glauce's father and ruler of Corinth, orders that Medea be exiled to prevent her from injuring the children. Medea begs not to be banished and finally asks for one day of delay. The tragedy culminates with Medea murdering her two children to avenge Jason's betrayal and prevent the children from being enslaved. Finally, Medea flees to Athens. Medea's story presents similarities with the Mesoamerican legend of La Llorona (the Weeping Woman), which is rooted in a syncretic combination of Mesoamerican and Spanish folklore (Rebolledo, *Women Singing in the Snow*, 62). In one version of the tale, La Llorona is an Indigenous woman who marries a wealthy Spaniard.

NOTES TO PAGES 246–253

After her husband abandons her for a woman of his social class, La Llorona drowns their children in a river to exact revenge upon her husband and is condemned to search for the soul of her lost children for eternity (Perez, "Caminando con la Llorona," 101). In *The Hungry Woman*, Moraga connects the betrayal suffered by Medea and La Llorona to the Aztec creation myth of the Hungry Woman, "a woman with mouths all over her body and insatiable hunger" (45). According to the myth, the Aztec gods Quetzalcoatl and Tezcatlipoca seize the woman's body in two parts and use the halves to make the sky and the earth. Since the woman does not stop crying for food, the spirits begin to make grass and flowers from the brown of her skin. However, the woman's hunger can never be satisfied and sometimes she can still be heard crying. In *The Hungry Woman*, it is Luna, Medea's lover, who narrates the myth while she "makes love to Medea with her mouth" (44) as the woman's hunger for food is reenacted as Luna's lust for Medea.

101. Moraga, *The Hungry Woman*, 9 (italics in the original).

102. Moraga, 23–24. All translations from the Spanish original are mine.

103. Moraga, 6. On environmental racism in Native American reservations see Taylor, *Toxic Communities*, 47.

104. Moraga, 35.

105. Halley, "'Like-Race' Arguments," 47.

106. Moraga, *The Hungry Woman*, 58.

107. Reddy, "Time for Rights?," 154.

108. Spillers, *Black, White, and in Color*, 379.

109. Moraga, *A Xicana Codex of Changing Consciousness*, 186.

110. Sharpe, "Learning to Live Without Black Familia," 242.

111. Sharpe, 250.

112. Moraga, *The Hungry Woman*, 8.

113. Moraga, 81.

114. Moraga, 58–60.

115. Mayorga, "Invisibility's Contusions," 166–67.

116. See Crenshaw, "Mapping the Margins," 1248–9.

117. Byrd, *The Transit of Empire*, 44.

118. Moraga, "An Interview with Cherríe Moraga."

119. Anzaldúa, *Borderlands/La Frontera*, 69.

120. Moraga, *A Xicana Codex of Changing Consciousness*, 4.

121. Moraga, "Queer Aztlán," 242.

122. Moraga, *The Hungry Woman*, 63 (italics in the original).

123. See Smith, *The Aztecs*, 221.

124. This interpretation of bloodletting as a male prerogative is also supported by Davíd Carrasco, who writes that male Maya leaders pierced their

penises because they aspired to experience a totality by imitating women menstruating and giving birth (*Religions of Mesoamerica*, 136).

125. Moraga, *The Hungry Woman*, 8.

126. Pringle cited in Sigal, Tortorici, and Whitehead, "Introduction," 7.

127. Moraga, *The Hungry Woman*, 21.

128. See Guidotti-Hernández, *Unspeakable Violence*, 31.

129. Moraga, *The Hungry Woman*, 77.

130. Moraga, 24–25.

131. Anzaldúa et al., "Speaking across the Divide," 3–4.

132. Moraga, *The Hungry Woman*, viii (italics in the original).

133. Moraga, 6.

134. Sexton, "The *Vel* of Slavery," 591.

135. Sexton, 592.

136. Sexton, 589.

137. Morrison, *Playing in the Dark*, 51.

138. See Contreras, *Blood Lines*, 18; and Deloria, *Playing Indian*, 4.

139. Nicole Guidotti-Hérnandez argues in *Unspeakable Violence* that Chicanx historiography has ignored the ways in which Mexicanos and Chicanxs in the Southwest have also enacted "colonial aggression" against Indigenous peoples (14). Raising similar concerns, B. V. Olguín writes that "Throughout the past century and a half, Mexican and Mexican American encounters with Native Americans have included outright acts of colonial violence and coordinated warfare against Indian people and specific Indian nations" (31–32). See also Contreras, *Blood Lines*, 34.

140. Anzaldúa, *The Gloria Anzaldúa Reader*, 152.

141. Fanon, *Black Skin, White Masks*, 133 (italics in the original).

Epilogue

EPIGRAPHS: Jackson, *Blood in My Eye*, 45; King, *Where Do We Go from Here*, 72; Fanon, *The Wretched of the Earth*, 37.

1. Trump, "Transcript: Donald Trump at the G.O.P. Convention.".

2. Research from the Institute on Taxation and Economic Policy (ITEP) conducted in 2016 shows, for example, that undocumented immigrants in the United States contribute an estimated $11.64 billion a year in state and local taxes (Gee et al., *Undocumented Immigrants' State and Local Tax Contributions*, 1).

3. Ivanka Trump cited in Drabold, "Read Ivanka Trump's Speech at the Republican Convention."

NOTES TO PAGES 263–266

4. United States, Executive Office of the President [Donald J. Trump], "Executive Order 13769."

5. See Mngxitama, "Whites are Tourists, Blacks are Kwerekweres."

6. Huysseune, "Come interpretare l'altro," 175, 177–79, 182; Testa and Armstrong, "'We Are Against Islam!,'" 4.

7. Gramsci, *Prison Notebooks*, 71. See also Gramsci, *The Southern Question*, 16.

8. Love and Varghese, "Race, Language, and Schooling in Italy's Immigrant Policies," 7.

9. Senior, *Dying to Better Themselves*, 91.

10. Fanon, *Toward the African Revolution*, 15.

11. See Ayoub, "How the EU is Responsible for Slavery in Libya."

12. See Duke, "White Genocide in South Africa" (video); and "US President Donald Trump's Tweet on Land Seizures."

13. Holmes, "Tucker Carlson" (my emphasis).

14. Jackson, *Blood in My Eye*, 118.

BIBLIOGRAPHY

Abu-Jamal, Mumia. *Have Black Lives Ever Mattered?* San Francisco: City Lights, 2017.

Abu-Jamal, Mumia. *Live from Death Row*. New York: Harper Perennial, 1995.

Abu-Jamal, Mumia, and Stephen Vittoria. *Murder Incorporated: Empire, Genocide, Manifest Destiny. Book One*. San Francisco: Prison Radio, 2018.

Ahmed, Sara. "Declarations of Whiteness: The Non-Performativity of Anti-Racism." *Borderlands* 3, no. 2 (2004). www.borderlands.net.au/vol3no2 _2004/ahmed _declarations.htm.

Aidoo, Lamonte. *Slavery Unseen: Sex, Power, and Violence in Brazilian History*. Durham, NC: Duke University Press, 2018.

Alarcón, Norma. "Chicana Feminism: In the Tracks of 'the' Native Woman." In *Between Woman and Nation: Nationalisms, Transnational Feminisms, and the State*, edited by Caren Kaplan, Norma Alarcón, and Minoo Moallem, 63–71. Durham, NC: Duke University Press, 1999.

Alberto, Paulina L. *Terms of Inclusion: Black Intellectuals in Twentieth-Century Brazil*. Chapel Hill: University of North Carolina Press, 2011.

Alcoff, Linda Martín. *The Future of Whiteness*. Cambridge, England: Polity Press, 2015.

Alcoff, Linda Martín. "What Should White People Do?" *Hypatia* 13, no. 3 (Summer 1998): 6–26.

Alexander, Michelle. *The New Jim Crow: Mass Incarceration in the Age of Colorblindness*. New York: New Press, 2010.

Alexander, Neville. "Affirmative Action and the Perpetuation of Racial Identities in Post-Apartheid South Africa." *Transformation* 63 (2007): 92–108.

Alexander, Neville. *Sow the Wind: Contemporary Speeches*. Braamfontein, South Africa: Skotaville Publishers, 1985.

Alexander Craft, Renée. *When the Devil Knocks: The Congo Tradition and the Politics of Blackness in Twentieth-Century Panama*. Columbus: The Ohio State University Press, 2015.

Alfaro, Olmedo. *El peligro antillano en la América Central: La defensa de la raza*. 2nd ed. Panama City: Imprenta Nacional, 1925.

Alonso, Ana M. "Conforming Disconformity: 'Mestizaje,' Hybridity, and the Aesthetics of Mexican Nationalism." *Cultural Anthropology* 19, no. 4 (2004): 459–90.

Althusser, Louis. *Lenin and Philosophy and Other Essays*. New York: Monthly Review Press, 1972.

Alurista. *Floricanto en Aztlán*. Los Angeles: UCLA Chicano Studies Research Center Press, 2012.

Alvarez, Alex. *Native America and the Question of Genocide*. Lanham, MD: Rowman and Littlefield, 2014.

Alves, Jaime Amparo. *The Anti-Black City: Police Terror and Black Urban Life in Brazil*. Minneapolis: University of Minnesota Press, 2018.

Amnesty International. *You Killed My Son: Homicides by Military Police in the City of Rio de Janeiro*, August 3, 2015. https://www.amnesty.org/en /documents/amr19/2068/2015/en/.

Anaya, Rudolfo. "Aztlán: A Homeland without Boundaries." In Anaya and Lomelí, *Aztlán*, 31–42.

Anaya, Rudolfo. *Heart of Aztlán*. Albuquerque: University of New Mexico Press, 1976.

Anaya, Rudolfo, and Francisco Lomelí, eds. *Aztlán: Essays on the Chicano Homeland, Revised and Expanded Edition*. Albuquerque: University of New Mexico Press, 2017.

Anderson, Margo, and Stephen Fienberg. "Race and Ethnicity and the Controversy over the US Census." *Current Sociology* 48, no. 3 (July 2000): 87–110.

Andrews, George Reid. *Afro-Latin America: 1800–2000*. Oxford: Oxford University Press, 2004.

Ansell, Amy E. "Casting a Blind Eye: The Ironic Consequences of Color-Blindness in South Africa and the United States." *Critical Sociology* 32, no. 2–3 (2006): 333–56.

Ansell, Amy E. *New Right, New Racism: Race and Reaction in the United States and Britain*. London: Palgrave, 1997.

Anzaldúa, Gloria. *Borderlands/La Frontera: The New Mestiza*. San Francisco: Aunt Lute Books, 1987.

Anzaldúa, Gloria. *The Gloria Anzaldúa Reader*. Edited by AnaLouise Keating. Durham, NC: Duke University Press, 2009.

Anzaldúa, Gloria, Simon J. Ortiz, Inéz Hernández-Avila, and Domino Perez. "Speaking across the Divide." *Studies in American Indian Literatures* 15, no. 3–4 (2003): 7–22.

BIBLIOGRAPHY

Armstrong, Nancy. *How Novels Think: The Limits of Individualism from 1719–1900*. New York: Columbia University Press, 2006.

Arroyo, Justo. "Racial Theory and Practice in Panama." In *African Presence in the Americas*, edited by Carlos Moore, Tanya R. Saunders, and Shawna Moore, 155–62. Trenton, NJ: Africa World Press, 1995.

Articulação dos Povos Indígenas do Brasil (APIB) and Rede de Cooperação Amazônica (RCA). "The Human Rights Situation of Indigenous Peoples in Brazil." September 2016. https://uprdoc.ohchr.org/uprweb /downloadfile.aspx?filename=3972&file=CoverPage.

Arvin, Maile. *Possessing Polynesians: The Science of Settler Colonial Whiteness in Hawai'i and Oceania*. Durham, NC: Duke University Press, 2019.

Associated Press. "1,600 Migrants Lost at Sea in Mediterranean This Year." *VOA News*, November 25, 2021. https://www.voanews.com/a/migrants -lost-at-sea-in-mediterranean-this-year/6328210.html.

Attwell, David. *Rewriting Modernity: Studies in Black South African Literary History*. Athens: Ohio University Press, 2006.

Augoustinos, Martha, Keith Tuffin, and Mark Rapley. "Genocide or a Failure to Gel? Racism, History and Nationalism in Australian Talk." *Discourse and Society* 10, no. 3 (July 1999): 351–78.

Ayoub, Joey. "How the EU Is Responsible for Slavery in Libya." *Al Jazeera*, November 29, 2017. https://www.aljazeera.com/opinions/2017/11/29/ how-the-eu-is-responsible-for-slavery-in-libya.

Bacon, David. *Illegal People: How Globalization Creates Migration and Criminalizes Immigrants*. Boston: Beacon Press, 2008.

Baldwin, James. "The Fire Next Time." In *James Baldwin: Collected Essays*, edited by Toni Morrison, 287–347. New York: Library of America, 1998.

Baldwin, James. "What Price Freedom?" In *The Cross of Redemption: Uncollected Writings*, edited by Randall Kenan, 82–87. New York: Vintage International, 2010.

Balibar, Etienne. "Is There a 'Neo-Racism'?" In *Race, Nation, Class: Ambiguous Identities*, edited by Immanuel Wallerstein and Etienne Balibar, 17–28. New York: Verso, 1991.

Bam, June. *Ausi Told Me: Why Cape Herstoriographies Matter*. Johannesburg: Fanele, 2021.

Barchiesi, Franco. *Precarious Liberation: Workers, the State, and Contested Social Citizenship in Postapartheid South Africa*. Albany: SUNY Press, 2011.

Barker, Martin. *The New Racism: Conservatives and the Ideology of the Tribe*. London: Junction Books, 1981.

Barrow, Alberto S. N. *No me pidas una foto: Desvelando el racismo en Panamá*. Panama City: Universal Books, 2001.

Barrow, Alberto S. N. "Racism Was Central to the Invasion." In *The United States' Invasion of Panama: The Truth Behind Operation "Just Cause,"* by The Independent Commission of Inquiry on the U.S. Invasion of Panama, 81–83. Boston: South End Press, 1991.

Barrow, Alberto S. N., and George Priestley. *Piel oscura Panamá: Ensayos y reflexiones al filo del centenario*. Panama City: Editorial Universitaria, 2003.

Bebout, Lee. *Mythohistorical Interventions: The Chicano Movement and Its Legacies*. Minneapolis: University of Minnesota Press, 2011.

Beleño, Joaquín C. *Curundú: Novela*. Panama City: Eds. del Ministerio de Educación, Depto. de Bellas Artes y Publicaciones, 1963.

Beleño, Joaquín C. *Gamboa Road Gang/Los forzados de Gamboa*. Panama City: Editora Lemania, 1969.

Beleño, Joaquín C. *Luna verde: Diario dialogado*. Panama City: Ediciones Estrella de Panamá, 1961.

Bell, Derrick A. *Faces at the Bottom of the Well: The Permanence of Racism*. New York: Basic Books, 1992.

Benatar, David. "Why Samantha Vice Is Wrong on Whiteness." *Politicsweb*, September 16, 2011. https://www.politicsweb.co.za/news-and-analysis/why-samantha-vice-is-wrong-on-whiteness.

Bernardino-Costa, Joaze, and Ana Elisa De Carli Blackman. "Affirmative Action in Brazil and Building an Anti-Racist University." *Race, Ethnicity, and Education* 20, no. 3 (2017): 372–84.

Bhabha, Homi K. *The Location of Culture*. London: Routledge, 1994.

Biko, Steve. *I Write What I Like: A Selection of His Writings*. Chicago: University of Chicago Press, 2002.

Birmingham-Pokorny, Elba D., ed. *Denouncement and Reaffirmation of the Afro-Hispanic Identity in Carlos Guillermo Wilson's Works*. Miami: Ediciones Universal, 1993.

Blake, Felice. "Why Black Lives Matter in the Humanities." In Crenshaw et al., *Seeing Race Again*, 307–326.

Blom, Gertrude Duby. *¿Hay razas inferiores?* Mexico City: Colección Metropolitana, 1974.

Blom, Gertrude Duby. *Imágenes Lacandonas*. San Cristóbal de las Casas: Tezontle, 1999.

Blumenbach, Johann Friedrich. *On the Natural Varieties of Mankind / De generis humani varietate nativa*. New York: Bergman Publishers, 1969.

Bobo, Lawrence, James R. Kluegel, and Ryan A. Smith. "Laissez-Faire Racism: The Crystallization of a Kinder, Gentler Anti-Black Ideology." In

BIBLIOGRAPHY

Racial Attitudes in the 1990s: Continuity and Change, edited by Steven A. Tuch and Jack K. Martin, 15–44. Westport, CT: Praeger, 1997.

Bonilla-Silva, Eduardo. "From Bi-racial to Tri-racial: Towards a New System of Racial Stratification in the USA." *Ethnic and Racial Studies* 27, no. 6 (2004): 931–50.

Bonilla-Silva, Eduardo. "The New Racism: Racial Structure in the United States, 1960–1990s." In *Race, Ethnicity, and Nationality in the United States: Toward the Twenty-First Century*, edited by Paul Wong, 55–101. New York: Routledge, 1999.

Bonilla-Silva, Eduardo. *Racism without Racists: Color-Blind Racism and the Persistence of Racial Inequality in America*, 5th ed. Lanham, MD: Rowman and Littlefield, 2017.

Bonilla-Silva, Eduardo. "We Are All Americans! The Latin Americanization of Racial Stratification in the USA." *Race and Society*, no. 5 (2000): 3–16.

Bonilla-Silva, Eduardo, and David Dietrich. "The New Racism: The Racial Regime of Post–Civil Rights America." In *Covert Racism: Theories, Institutions, and Experiences*, edited by Rodney D. Coates, 41–68. Boston: Brill, 2011.

Branche, Jerome. *Colonialism and Race in Luso-Hispanic Literature*. Columbia: University of Missouri Press, 2006.

Briggs, Charles L. "Communicability, Racial Discourse, and Disease." *Annual Review of Anthropology*, no. 34 (2005): 269–91.

Broeck, Sabine. *Gender and the Abjection of Blackness*. Albany: SUNY Press, 2018.

Bruce-Novoa, Juan. *Chicano Authors: Inquiry by Interview*. Austin: University of Texas Press, 1980.

Bryce, James. *The Relations of the Advanced and the Backward Races of Mankind*. Oxford, England: Clarendon Press, 1902.

Buck-Morss, Susan. *Hegel, Haiti, and Universal History*. Pittsburgh: University of Pittsburgh Press, 2009.

Bukhari, Safiya. *The War Before: The True Life Story of Becoming a Panther, Keeping the Faith in Prison, and Fighting for Those Left Behind*. New York: Feminist Press, 2010.

Byrd, Jodi A. *The Transit of Empire: Indigenous Critiques of Colonialism*. Minneapolis: University of Minnesota Press, 2011.

Cammarota, Julio. "Blindsided by the Avatar: White Saviors and Allies out of Hollywood and in Education." *Review of Education, Pedagogy and Cultural Studies* 33, no. 3 (2011): 242–59.

Carr, Leslie G. *"Color-Blind" Racism*. New York: Sage Press, 1997.

Carrasco, Davíd. *Religions of Mesoamerica*. 2nd ed. Long Grove, IL: Waveland Press, 2013.

Carroll, Hamilton. *Affirmative Reaction: New Formations of White Masculinity*. Durham, NC: Duke University Press, 2011.

Casas, Regina Martínez, Emiko Saldívar, René D. Flores, and Christina A. Sue. "The Different Faces of Mestizaje: Ethnicity and Race in Mexico." In Telles and PERLA, *Pigmentocracies*, 36–80.

Castellanos, Israel. "The Evolution of Criminology in Cuba." *Journal of Criminal Law and Criminology (1931–1951)* 24, no. 1 (1933): 218–29.

Castillo, Ana. *The Mixquiahuala Letters*. Tempe, AZ: Bilingual Review Press, 1992.

Cerqueira, Daniel, Renato Sergio de Lima, Samira Bueno, Luis Iván Valencia, Olaya Hanashiro, Pedro Henrique G. Machado, and Adriana dos Santos Lima. *Atlas da violência 2017*. Brasilia: Ipea e FBSP, 2017. www.ipea.gov.br/portal/images/170609_atlas_da_violencia_2017.pdf.

Césaire, Aimé. *Discourse on Colonialism*. Translated by Joan Pinkham. New York: Monthly Review Press, 2000.

Césaire, Aimé. *Notebook of a Return to the Native Land*. Translated by Clayton Eshelman and Annette Smith. Middletown, CT: Wesleyan University Press, 2001.

Childs, Dennis. *Slaves of the State: Black Incarceration from the Chain Gang to the Penitentiary*. Minneapolis: University of Minnesota Press, 2015.

Churchill, Ward. *A Little Matter of Genocide: Holocaust and Denial in the Americas, 1492 to the Present*. San Francisco: City Lights, 1997.

Clealand, Danielle P. *The Power of Race in Cuba: Racial Ideology and Black Consciousness During the Revolution*. Oxford: Oxford University Press, 2017.

Coerver, Don M., Suzanne B. Pasztor, and Robert M. Buffington. "José Vasconcelos." In *Mexico: An Encyclopedia of Contemporary Culture and History*, edited by Don M. Coerver, Suzanne B. Pasztor, and Robert M. Buffington. Santa Barbara, CA: ABC-CLIO, 2004.

Coetzee, J. M. *White Writing: On the Culture of Letters in South Africa*. Braamfontein, South Africa: Pentz Publishers, 2007.

Cohen, William B. *The French Encounter with Africans: White Response to Blacks, 1530–1880*. Bloomington: Indiana University Press, 2003.

Cole, Jeffrey. *The New Racism in Europe: A Sicilian Ethnography*. Cambridge: Cambridge University Press, 1997.

Collins, Patricia Hill. *Black Sexual Politics: African Americans, Gender, and the New Racism*. New York: Routledge, 2004.

BIBLIOGRAPHY   331

Columbus, Christopher, and Lionel Cecil Jane. *The Four Voyages of Columbus: A History in Eight Documents, Including Five by Christopher Columbus, in the Original Spanish, with English Translations*. Mineola, NY: Dover Publications, 1988.

Conniff, Michael L. *Black Labor on a White Canal: Panama, 1904–1981*. Pittsburgh: University of Pittsburgh Press, 1985.

Conniff, Michael L., and Thomas Davis. *Africans in the Americas: A History of the Black Diaspora*. New York: St. Martin's Press, 1994.

Contreras, Sheila M. *Blood Lines: Myth, Indigenism and Chicana/o Literature*. Austin: University of Texas Press, 2008.

Cooppan, Vilashini. "W(h)ither Post-Colonial Studies? Towards the Transnational Study of Race and Nation." In *Postcolonial Theory and Criticism*, edited by Laura Chrisman and Benita Parry, 1–35. Cambridge, England: D. S. Brewer, 2000.

Corinealdi, Kaysha. "Envisioning Multiple Citizenships: West Indian Panamanians and Creating Community in the Canal Zone Neocolony." *The Global South* 6, no. 2 (Fall 2012): 87–106.

Cornejo Polar, Antonio. "*Mestizaje* and Hybridity: The Risks of Metaphors— Notes." In *The Latin American Cultural Studies Reader*, edited by Ana Del Sarto, Alicia Ríos, and Abril Trigo, 760–64. Durham, NC: Duke University Press, 2004.

Cornejo Polar, Antonio. "*Mestizaje*, Transculturation, Heterogeneity." In *The Latin American Cultural Studies Reader*, edited by Ana Del Sarto, Alicia Ríos, and Abril Trigo, 116–19. Durham, NC: Duke University Press, 2004.

Costa, Emília Viotti da. *The Brazilian Empire: Myths and Histories*. 2nd ed. Chapel Hill: University of North Carolina Press, 2000.

Cox, Oliver C. *Caste, Class, and Race: A Study in Social Dynamics*. New York: Monthly Review Press, 1948.

Crenshaw, Kimberlé Williams. "Color Blindness, History, and the Law." In *The House That Race Built: Black Americans, U.S. Terrain*, edited by Wahneema Lubiano, 280–88. New York: Pantheon Books, 1997.

Crenshaw, Kimberlé. "Demarginalizing the Intersection of Race and Sex: A Black Feminist Critique of Antidiscrimination Doctrine, Feminist Theory and Antiracist Politics." *University of Chicago Legal Forum*, no. 140 (1989): 139–67.

Crenshaw, Kimberlé. "Mapping the Margins: Intersectionality, Identity Politics, and Violence against Women of Color." *Stanford Law Review* 43, no. 6 (July 1991): 1241–99.

332   BIBLIOGRAPHY

Crenshaw, Kimberlé, Neil Gotanda, Gary Peller, and Kendall Thomas, eds. *Critical Race Theory: The Key Writings That Formed the Movement*. New York: New Press, 1995.

Crenshaw, Kimberlé Williams, Luke Charles Harris, Daniel Martinez HoSang, and George Lipsitz, eds. *Seeing Race Again: Countering Color-blindness Across the Disciplines*. Berkeley: University of California Press, 2019.

Cubena. [Wilson, Carlos Guillermo]. "Aspectos de la prosa panameña contemporánea." PhD diss., University of California Los Angeles, 1975.

Cubena. [Wilson, Carlos Guillermo]. *Chombo*. Miami: Ediciones Universal, 1981.

Cubena. [Wilson, Carlos Guillermo]. *Cuentos del negro Cubena*. Guatemala City: Editorial Landívar, 1977.

Cubena. [Wilson, Carlos Guillermo]. "Interview with Dr. Carlos Guillermo Wilson." Interview by Elba D. Birmingham-Pokorny. *Confluencia* 6, no. 2 (Spring 1991): 127–133.

Cubena. [Wilson, Carlos Guillermo]. *La misión secreta*. Alexandria, VA: Alexander Street Press, 2005.

Cubena. [Wilson, Carlos Guillermo]. *Los nietos de Felicidad Dolores*. Miami: Ediciones Universal, 1991.

Cubena. [Wilson, Carlos Guillermo]. "La poesía afro-panameña." In *Papers of the 3rd Conference of Latin-Americanists*. Kingston, Jamaica: University of the West Indies at Mona, 1980.

Curry, Tommy J. "Concerning the Underspecialization of Race Theory in American Philosophy: How the Exclusion of Black Sources Affects the Field." *The Pluralist* 5, no. 1 (Spring 2010): 44–64.

Dabashi, Hamid. *Can Non-Europeans Think?* Chicago: Chicago University Press, 2015.

D'Anghiera, Peter M. *De Orbe Novo: The Eight Decades of Peter Martyr D'Anghera*, vol. 1. Translated by Francis A. MacNutt. New York: G. P. Putnam's Sons, 1912.

Daniel, Reginald G. *Race and Multiraciality in Brazil and the United States: Converging Paths?* University Park: Pennsylvania State University Press, 2006.

Dávila, Jerry. "Entre dois mundos: Gilberto Freyre, a ONU e o apartheid sul-africano." *História Social*, no. 19 (Segundo semestre de 2010): 135–48.

Davis, Angela. *Are Prisons Obsolete?* New York: Seven Stories Press, 2003.

Davis, Darién J. "Panama." In *No Longer Invisible: Afro-Latin Americans Today*, edited by Minority Rights Group, 202–14. London: Minority Rights Group, 1995.

BIBLIOGRAPHY 333

Davis, Darién J. *Slavery and Beyond: The African Impact on Latin America and the Caribbean*. Lanham, MD: Rowman and Littlefield, 1994.

Dead Prez. "They Schools." Track 3 on *Let's Get Free*. Loud Records and Columbia Records, 2000.

Deloria, Philip J. *Playing Indian*. New Haven: Yale University Press, 1998.

DeLoughrey, Elizabeth, and George B. Handley. "Introduction: Toward an Aesthetics of the Earth." In *Postcolonial Ecologies: Literatures of the Environment*, edited by Elizabeth DeLoughrey and George B. Handley, 3–41. Oxford: Oxford University Press, 2011.

Department of Higher Education and Training (DHET). *Statistics on Post-School Education and Training in South Africa: 2020*. https://www.dhet .gov.za/DHET%20Statistics%20Publication/Statistics%20on%20Post -School%20Education%20and%20Training%20in%20South%20Africa %202020.pdf.

Department of Rural Development and Land Reform of the Republic of South Africa. *Land Audit Report*, November 2017. https://www.sapeople .com/wp-content/uploads/2018/02/land_audit_report_05jan2018_final .pdf.

Derrida, Jacques. "Racism's Last Word." Translated by Peggy Kamuf. *Critical Inquiry* 12 (Autumn 1985): 290–99.

Desai, Dipti. "The Challenge of New Colorblind Racism in Art Education." *Art Education* 63, no. 5 (September 2010): 22–28.

de Zurara, Gomes Eanes. *The Chronicle of the Discovery and Conquest of Guinea, Volume One*. Cambridge: Cambridge University Press, 2010.

Dovidio, John F., and Samuel L. Gaertner. "On the Nature of Contemporary Prejudice: The Causes, Consequences, and Challenges of Aversive Racism." In *Confronting Racism: The Problem and the Response*, edited by Jennifer Lynn Eberhardt and Susan T. Fiske, 3–32. Newbury Park, CA: Sage, 1998.

Drabold, Will. "Read Ivanka Trump's Speech at the Republican Convention." *Time*, July 22, 2016. https://time.com/4417579/republican -convention-ivanka-trump-transcript/.

Du Bois, W. E. B. *Black Reconstruction: An Essay Toward a History of the Part Which Black Folk Played in the Attempt to Reconstruct Democracy in America*. New York: Harcourt, Brace and Company, 1935.

Du Bois, W. E. B. *The Souls of Black Folk*. New Haven: Yale University Press, 2015.

Du Bois, W. E. B. *The World and Africa: An Inquiry into the Part Which Africa Has Played in World History*. New York: International Publishers, 1965.

334 BIBLIOGRAPHY

Duke, David. "White Genocide in South Africa" (video). *dailymotion.com*. Last accessed April 2, 2022. www.dailymotion.com/video/x4i8tz0.

du Toit, André, and Hermann Giliomee, eds. *Afrikaner Political Thought: Analysis and Documents, Volume One: 1780–1850*. Berkeley: University of California Press, 1983.

Ebrahim, Shaazia. "Students at UCKAR are Calling on the Police to Answer for Alleged Brutality." *Daily Vox*, October 27, 2016. https://www.thedailyvox.co.za/students-uckar-calling-police-answer-alleged-brutality/.

Edison, Tomás W. "Humor and Satire: Ammunitions in Carlos Guillermo Wilson's Resistance Novel *Chombo*." *College Language Association Journal* 43, no. 4 (June 2000): 494–511.

Ejército Zapatista de Liberación Nacional (EZLN). "Declaration of War." In *Zapatistas! Documents of the New Mexican Revolution*, 35–37. New York: Autonomedia, 1994. http://lanic.utexas.edu/project/Zapatistas/Zapatistas_book.pdf.

Elias, Sean, and Joe R. Feagin. *Racial Theories in Social Science: A Systemic Racism Critique*. New York: Routledge, 2016.

Elliott-Cooper, Adam. *Black Resistance to British Policing*. Manchester, England: Manchester University Press, 2021.

Ellison, Ralph W. *Invisible Man*. New York: Vintage, 1995.

Ellison, Ralph W. *The Collected Essays of Ralph Ellison*. New York: Modern Library, 1995.

El Plan Espiritual de Aztlán. In Anaya and Lomelí, *Aztlán*, 27–30.

Emery, Alan. "Class and Race Domination and Transformation in South Africa." *Critical Sociology* 34, vol. 3 (2008): 409–43.

Erasmus, Zimitri. "Apartheid Race Categories: Daring to Question Their Continued Use." *Transformation* 79 (2012): 1–12.

Erasmus, Zimitri. "Confronting the Categories: Equitable Admissions without Apartheid Race Classification." *South African Journal of Higher Education* 24, no. 2 (2010): 244–57.

Escobar, Federico. "Nieblas." In *Itinerario de la poesia en Panamá, Tomo I*, edited by Rodrigo Miró Grimaldo, 146–147. Panama City: Biblioteca de la Nacionalidad, 1999.

Esteva-Fabregat, Claudio. *Mestizaje in Ibero-America*. Tucson: University of Arizona Press, 1994.

"Exclusive: Watch George Stephanopoulos' Full Interview with Police Officer Darren Wilson." *ABC News*, November 23, 2014. https://abcnews.go.com/GMA/video/exclusive-watch-george-stephanopoulos-full-interview-police-officer-27186831.

BIBLIOGRAPHY

Eze, Emmanuel C. "The Color of Reason: The Idea of Race in Kant's Anthropology." In *Postcolonial African Philosophy: A Critical Reader*, edited by Emmanel C. Eze, 103–40. Hoboken, NJ: Blackwell, 1997.

Fanon, Frantz. *Black Skin, White Masks*. Translated by Charles Lam Markmann. London: Pluto Press, 2008.

Fanon, Frantz. *Toward the African Revolution: Political Essays*. Translated by Haakon Chevalier. New York: Grove Press, 1967.

Fanon, Frantz. *The Wretched of the Earth*. Translated by Constance Farrington. New York: Grove Press, 1963.

Farley, Anthony Paul. "Toward a General Theory of Antiblackness." In *Antiblackness*, edited by Moon-Kie Jung and João H. Costa Vargas, 82–105. Durham, NC: Duke University Press, 2021.

Feagin, Joe. "Systemic Racism and 'Race' Categorization in Medical Research and Practice." *American Journal of Bioethics* 17, no. 9 (August 2017): 54–56.

February, Judith. "From Redress to Empowerment: The New South African Constitution and Its Implementation." In *The Next Twenty-Five Years: Affirmative Action in Higher Education in the United States and South Africa*, edited by David L. Featherman, Martin Hall, and Marvin Krislov, 74–86. Ann Arbor: University of Michigan Press, 2010.

Feder, Jody. "The Constitution and Racial Diversity in K-12 Education: A Legal Analysis of the Supreme Court Ruling in *Parents Involved in Community Schools v. Seattle School District No. 1*." United States Congressional Research Service, 2007.

Fenelon, James, and Clifford Trafzer. "From Colonialism to Denial of California Genocide to Misrepresentations: Special Issue on Indigenous Struggles in the Americas." *American Behavioral Scientist* 58, no. 1 (2014): 3–29.

Ferguson, Roderick A. *Aberrations in Black: Toward a Queer of Color Critique*. Minneapolis: University of Minnesota Press, 2004.

Fernandes, Luis. "Apresentação: o gênio da formação social brasileira." In *Gilberto Freyre e a formação do Brasil: artigos em homenagem ao centenário de nascimento de Gilberto Freyre*, edited by Aldo Rebelo, 5–9. Brasília: Centro de Documentação e Informação, 2000.

Fernández, Carlos A. "La Raza and the Melting Pot: A Comparative Look at Multiethnicity." In *Racially Mixed People in America*, edited by Maria P. P. Root, 126–43. New York: Sage Press, 1992.

Fernandez, Ronald. *America Beyond Black and White: How Immigrants and Fusions Are Helping Us Overcome the Racial Divide*. Ann Arbor: University of Michigan Press, 2007.

Fields, Karen E., and Barbara J. Fields. *Racecraft: The Soul of Inequality in American Life*. New York: Verso, 2012.

"File Indictment Against Head of the Colon Police Force." *The Daily Gleaner*, January 6, 1933, 11.

Flecha, Ramón. "Modern and Postmodern Racism in Europe: Dialogic Approach to Anti-Racist Pedagogies." *Harvard Educational Review* 69, no. 2 (1999): 150–172.

Fogel, Robert W., and Stanley L. Engerman. *Time on the Cross: The Economics of American Negro Slavery*. New York: Little, Brown and Company, 1974.

Fonticoba, Tania De Armas. "'Fernando Ortiz' e 'Israel Castellanos' en la genealogía de la criminología en Cuba." *Derecho y Cambio Social* 8, no. 25 (2011): 1–13. www.derechoycambiosocial.com/revista025/criminologia_en_cuba.pdf.

Fortune, Armando. *Obra selecta*. Panama City: Instituto Nacional de Cultura, 1993.

Foucault, Michel. *The History of Sexuality, Volume I: An Introduction*. New York: Vintage, 1990.

Fredrickson, George M. *White Supremacy: A Comparative Study in American and South African History*. Oxford: Oxford University Press, 1981.

Frenkel, Ronit, and Craig MacKenzie. "Conceptualizing 'Post-Transitional' South African Literature in English." *English Studies in Africa* 53, no. 1 (2010): 1–10.

Freyre, Gilberto. *Casa-grande e senzala: formação da família brasileira sob o regime de economia patriarcal*. Rio de Janeiro: Livraria José Olympio, 1958.

Freyre, Gilberto. "Letter to Ezekiel Gordon (April 23, 1954)." United Nations Archives, S-0724-0008-0007-00001 NSL.

Freyre, Gilberto. "Report on the Most Important and Most Effective Methods for Eliminating Racial Conflicts, Tensions, and Discriminatory Practices Employed with Positive Results in Countries in Different Geographical Regions, in Particular Countries Where Conditions Approximate Most Closely Those in the Union of South Africa." United Nations Commission on the Racial Situation in the Union of South Africa, June 1, 1954. United Nations Archives, S-0724-0008-0007-00001 NSL.

Fry, Peter. *A persistência da raça: ensaios antropológicos sobre o Brasil e a África austral*. Rio de Janeiro: Civilização Brasileira, 2005.

Gallers, Anita. "Enslavement and Masculinity in Afro-Hispanic Narrative." PhD diss., Yale University, 2000.

BIBLIOGRAPHY

García Canclini, Néstor. *Culturas híbridas: Estrategias para entrar y salir de la modernidad*. Mexico City: Grijalbo, 1990.

García Canclini, Néstor. *Hybrid Cultures: Strategies for Entering and Leaving Modernity*. Minneapolis: University of Minnesota Press, 1995.

Garrison-Wade, Dorothy F., and Chance W. Lewis. "Affirmative Action: History and Analysis." *Journal of College Admission*, no. 184 (Summer 2004): 23–26.

Garuba, Harry. "Closing Reflections on 'Revisiting Apartheid's Race Categories.'" *Transformation*, no. 79 (2012): 173–77.

Gee, Lisa Christensen, Matthew Gardner, Misha E. Hill and Meg Wiehe. *Undocumented Immigrants' State and Local Tax Contributions*. Washington, DC: Institute on Taxation and Economic Policy, 2017.

Gibson, Mary. *Born to Crime: Cesare Lombroso and the Origins of Biological Criminology*. Westport, CT: Praeger, 2002.

Gibson, Nigel C. "The Specter of Fanon: The Student Movements and the Rationality of Revolt in South Africa." *Social Identities* 23, no. 5 (2017): 579–99.

Gilliam, Angela M. "A Black Feminist Perspective on the Sexual Commodification of Women in the Global Culture." In *Black Feminist Anthropology: Theory, Politics, Praxis, and Poetics*, edited by Irma McClaurin, 150–86. New Brunswick, NJ: Rutgers University Press, 2001.

Gilliam, Angela M. "From Roxbury to Rio—and Back in a Hurry." In *African American Reflections on Brazil's Racial Paradise*, edited by David Hellwig, 173–81. Philadelphia: Temple University Press, 1992.

Gilmore, Ruth Wilson. *Change Everything: Racial Capitalism and the Case for Abolition*. Chicago: Haymarket Books, 2021.

Gilmore, Ruth Wilson. *Golden Gulag: Prisons, Surplus, Crisis, and Opposition in Globalizing California*. Berkeley: University of California Press, 2007.

Gilroy, Paul. *Against Race: Imagining Political Culture beyond the Color Line*. Cambridge, MA: Belknap Press of Harvard University Press, 2000.

Gilroy, Paul. *The Black Atlantic: Modernity and Double Consciousness*. Cambridge, MA: Harvard University Press, 1993.

Gilroy, Paul. "Nationalism, History and Ethnic Absolutism." *History Workshop* 30 (Autumn 1990): 114–120.

Gilroy, Paul. *'There Ain't No Black in the Union Jack': The Cultural Politics of Race and Nation*. London: Hutchinson, 1987.

Gimeno Martín, Juan Carlos. "Las luchas por el indigenismo: Postindigenismo, movimientos indios y antropología en la Mesoamérica contemporánea." In *El indigenismo americano II*, edited by Cristina Mature and Azucena Palacio, 31–50. Valencia, Spain: Universitat de València, 2001.

Goffman, Alice. *On the Run: Fugitive Life in an American City*. Chicago: University of Chicago Press, 2014.

Goldberg, David T. *Are We All Postracial Yet?* Cambridge, England: Polity Press, 2015.

Goldberg, David T. "Racial Comparisons, Relational Racisms: Some Thoughts on Method." *Ethnic and Racial Studies* 37, no. 7 (September 2009): 1272–82.

Goldberg, David T. "Racisms Without Racism." *PMLA* 123, no. 5 (October 2008): 1712–16.

Gómez de Avellaneda, Gertrudis. *Sab*. Manchester: Manchester University Press, 2011.

Gordon, Lewis R. *Bad Faith and Antiblack Racism*. Atlantic Highlands, NJ: Humanities Press, 1995.

Gordon, Lewis R. "Black Aesthetics, Black Value." *Public Culture* 30, no. 1 (2018): 19–34.

Gordon, Lewis R. *Her Majesty's Other Children: Sketches of Racism from a Neocolonial Age*. Lanham, MD: Rowman and Littlefield, 1997.

Gotanda, Neil. "A Critique of 'Our Constitution Is Colorblind.'" In Crenshaw et al., *Critical Race Theory*, 258–75.

Gqola, Pumla D. *What Is Slavery to Me? Postcolonial/Slave Memory in Post-Apartheid South Africa*. Johannesburg: Wits University Press, 2010.

Graham, Richard, ed. *The Idea of Race in Latin America, 1870–1940*. Austin: University of Texas Press, 1990.

Gramsci, Antonio. *Selections from the Prison Notebooks*. Edited and translated by Quintin Hoare and Geoffrey Nowell Smith. New York: International, 1971.

Gramsci, Antonio. *The Southern Question*. Translated by Pasquale Verdicchio. New York: Bordighera Press, 2015.

Grey, Herman. "Race after Race." In Mukherjee, Banet-Wiser, and Gray, *Racism Postrace*, 23–36.

Guerrón-Montero, Carla. "Racial Democracy and Nationalism in Panama." *Ethnology* 45, no. 3 (Summer 2006): 209–228.

Guidotti-Hernández, Nicole M. *Unspeakable Violence: Remapping U.S. and Mexican National Imaginaries*. Durham, NC: Duke University Press, 2011.

Guillén, Nicolás. *Obra poética*. Havana: Editora de Arte y Literatura, 1974.

Guillén, Nicolás. *Summa poética*. Madrid: Cátedra, 2006.

Guillén, Nicolás. *Tengo*. Havana: Editora del Consejo Nacional de Universidades, Universidad Central de las Villas, 1964.

Guridy, Frank A. *Forging Diaspora: Afro-Cubans and African Americans in a World of Empire and Jim Crow*. Chapel Hill: University of North Carolina Press, 2010.

Gutiérrez-Jones, Carl S. *Critical Race Narratives: A Study of Race, Rhetoric, and Injury*. New York: New York University Press, 2001.

Haggerty, Daniel. "White Shame: Responsibility and Moral Emotions." *Philosophy Today* 53, no. 3 (Fall 2009): 304–16.

Hale, Charles R. "Does Multiculturalism Menace? Governance, Cultural Rights and the Politics of Identity in Guatemala." *Journal of Latin American Studies* 34, no. 3 (August 2002): 485–524.

Halley, Janet. "'Like-Race' Arguments." In *What's Left of Theory? New Work on the Politics of Literary Theory*, edited by Judith Butler, John Guillory, and Kendall Thomas, 40–73. New York: Routledge, 2000.

Hamilton, Charles V., Lynn Huntley, Neville Alexander, Antonio Sérgio Alfredo Guimarães, and Wilmot James, eds. *Beyond Racism: Race and Inequality in Brazil, South Africa, and the United States*. Boulder, CO: Lynne Rienner Publishers, 2001.

Haney López, Ian F. "Colorblind White Dominance." In *Covert Racism: Theories, Institutions, and Experience*, edited by Rodney D. Coates, 85–109. Leiden, Germany: Brill, 2011.

Haney López, Ian F. *Dog Whistle Politics: How Coded Racial Appeals Have Reinvented Racism and Wrecked the Middle Class*. Oxford: Oxford University Press, 2014.

Haney López, Ian F. "Post-Racial Racism: Racial Stratification and Mass Incarceration in the Age of Obama." *California Law Review* 98, no. 3 (June 2010): 1023–74.

Harney, Stefano, and Fred Moten. "Michael Brown." *Boundary 2* 42, no. 4 (November 2015): 81–87.

Harney, Stefano, and Fred Moten. *The Undercommons: Fugitive Planning and Black Study*. New York: Minor Compositions, 2013.

Harris, Cheryl I. "The Story of *Plessy v. Ferguson*: The Death and Resurrection of Racial Formalism." In *Constitutional Law Stories*, edited by Michael C. Dorf, 181–222. New York: Foundation Press, 2004.

Harris, Cheryl I. "Whiteness as Property." *Harvard Law Review* 106, no. 8 (June 1993): 1707–91.

Hartman, Saidiya. *Lose Your Mother: A Journey Along the Atlantic Slave Route*. New York: Farrar, Straus and Giroux, 2007.

Hartman, Saidiya. *Scenes of Subjection: Terror, Slavery and Self-Making in Nineteenth-Century America.* Oxford: Oxford University Press, 1997.

Hawthorne, Camilla. "In Search of Black Italia." *Transition* 123, no. 123 (2017): 152–74.

Hawthorne, Camilla. "*L'Italia Meticcia?*: The Black Mediterranean and the Racial Cartographies of Citizenship." In *The Black Mediterranean: Bodies, Borders, and Citizenship*, edited by The Black Mediterranean Collective, 169–198. London: Palgrave Macmillian, 2021.

Hayden, Tom, ed. *The Zapatista Reader.* New York: Thunder's Mouth Press, 2022.

Helg, Aline. *Our Rightful Share: The Afro-Cuban Struggle for Equality, 1886–1912.* Chapel Hill: University of North Carolina Press, 1995.

Hellwig, David. *African American Reflections on Brazil's Racial Paradise.* Philadelphia: Temple University Press, 1992.

Herrera, Juan F. *Mayan Drifter: Chicano Poet in the Lowlands of America.* Philadelphia: Temple University Press, 1997.

Hill, Marc Lamont. *We Still Here: Pandemic, Policing, Protest, and Possibility.* Chicago: Haymarket Books, 2020.

Hinton, Elizabeth. *America on Fire: The Untold History of Police Violence and Black Rebellion Since the 1960s.* New York: Liveright Press, 2021.

Hoeg, Jerry. *Science, Technology, and Latin American Narrative in the Twentieth Century and Beyond.* Bethlehem, PA: Lehigh University Press, 2000.

Holborn, Lucy. *The Long Shadow of Apartheid: Race in South Africa since 1994.* Johannesburg: South African Institute of Race Relations, 2010.

Holmes, Carolyn. "Tucker Carlson, Those South African White Rights Activists Aren't Telling You the Whole Truth." *Washington Post*, May 15, 2019. https://www.washingtonpost.com/politics/2019/05/15/tucker -carlson-those-south-african-white-rights-activists-arent-telling-you -whole-truth/.

Hooker, Juliet. *Theorizing Race in the Americas: Douglass, Sarmiento, Du Bois, and Vasconcelos.* Oxford: Oxford University Press, 2017.

hooks, bell. *Ain't I a Woman: Black Women and Feminism.* New York: Routledge, 2015.

Horsman, Reginald. *Race and Manifest Destiny: The Origins of American Racial Anglo-Saxonism.* Cambridge, MA: Harvard University Press, 1981.

HoSang, Daniel Martinez. *A Wider Type of Freedom: How Struggles for Racial Justice Liberate Everyone.* Oakland: California University Press, 2021.

BIBLIOGRAPHY   341

House of Representatives. "Señor Olmedo Alfaro." H.R. Rep No. 56–86 (January 20, 1900).

Huysseune, Michel. "Come interpretare l'altro: Il Mezzogiorno nel discorso della Lega Nord." *Meridiana*, no. 63 (2008): 173–92.

Instituto Nacional de Estadística y Geografía. *Encuesta Intercensal 2015.* https://www.inegi.org.mx/programas/intercensal/2015/.

Jackson, George L. *Blood in My Eye*. Baltimore: Black Classic Press, 1990.

Jackson, Richard L. *Black Writers and the Hispanic Canon*. Woodbridge, CT: Twayne, 1997.

Jackson, Richard L. *Black Writers in Latin America*. Albuquerque: University of New Mexico Press, 1979.

Jackson, Shirley M. *La novela negrista en hispanoamérica*. Madrid: Pliegos, 1986.

Jackson, Zakiyyah Iman. *Becoming Human: Matter and Meaning in an Antiblack World*. New York: New York University Press, 2020.

Jaffe, Hosea. *European Colonial Despotism: A History of Oppression and Resistance in South Africa*. London: Karnak House, 1994.

James, C. L. R. *The Black Jacobins: Toussaint L'Ouverture and the San Domingo Revolution*. New York: Vintage, 1989.

James, Joy, ed. *The New Abolitionists: (Neo)Slave Narratives and Contemporary Prison Writings*. Albany: SUNY Press, 2005.

Jameson, Fredric. *The Political Unconscious: Narrative as Socially Symbolic Act*. Ithaca, NY: Cornell University Press, 1981.

JanMohamed, Abdul R. "The Economy of Manichean Allegory: The Function of Racial Difference in Colonialist Literature." *Critical Inquiry* 12, no. 1 (Autumn 1985): 59–87.

Jansen, Jonathan D. "Intellectuals, the State and Universities in South Africa." In *The Poverty of Ideas: South African Democracy and the Retreat of Intellectuals*, edited by William M. Gumede and Leslie Dikeni, 143–52. Johannesburg: Jacana, 2009.

Jolly, Rosemary. "Rehearsals of Liberation: Contemporary Postcolonial Discourse and the New South Africa." *PMLA* 110, no. 1 (January 1995): 17–29.

Jones, Gayl. *Corregidora*. Boston: Beacon Press, 1975.

Jones-Rogers, Stephanie E. *They Were Her Property: White Women as Slave Owners in the American South*. New Haven, CT: Yale University Press, 2019.

Jung, Moon-Kie. *Beneath the Surface of White Supremacy: Denaturalizing U.S. Racisms Past and Present*. Palo Alto, CA: Stanford University Press, 2015.

BIBLIOGRAPHY

Kaba, Mariame. *We Do This 'Til We Free Us: Abolitionist Organizing and Transforming Justice.* Chicago: Haymarket Books, 2021.

Kamel, Ali. *Não somos racistas: uma reacão aos que querem nos transformar numa nacão bicolor.* Rio de Janeiro: Nova Frontera, 2006.

Kant, Immanuel. *Natural Science.* Edited by Eric Watkins. Cambridge: Cambridge University Press, 2012.

Kant, Immanuel. *Physische Geographie.* https://korpora.zim.uni-duisburg-essen.de/kant/aa09/Inhalt9.html.

Kelley, Robin D. G. *Yo' Mama's Disfunktional! Fighting the Culture Wars in Urban America.* Boston: Beacon Press, 1998.

Khouma, Pap. *I Was an Elephant Salesman: Adventures between Dakar, Paris, and Milan.* Bloomington: Indiana University Press, 2010.

Khouma, Pap. *Noi italiani neri: Storie di ordinario razzismo.* Milan: Dalai Editore, 2010.

Kim, Claire J. *Bitter Fruit: The Politics of Black-Korean Conflict in New York City.* New Haven, CT: Yale University Press, 2000.

Kinder, Donald R., and David O. Sears. "Prejudice and Politics: Symbolic Racism Versus Racial Threats to the Good Life." *Journal of Personality and Social Psychology* 40, no. 3 (1981): 414–431.

King, Tiffany Lethabo. *The Black Shoals: Offshore Formations of Black and Native Studies.* Durham, NC: Duke University Press, 2019.

King, Martin Luther, Jr. *Where Do We Go from Here: Chaos or Community?* Boston: Beacon Press, 2010.

Kings, Sipho. "Is the Marikana Miners' Blood on All Our Hands?" *Mail & Guardian*, August 15, 2014. https://mg.co.za/article/2014-08-14-is-the-marikana-miners-blood-on-all-our-hands/.

Krauze, Enrique. "Latin America's Talent for Tolerance." *New York Times*, July 10, 2014. https://www.nytimes.com/2014/07/11/opinion/enrique-krauze-latin-americas-talent-for-tolerance.html?_r=0.

Lafont, Anne. "How Skin Color Became a Racial Marker: Art Historical Perspectives on Race." *Eighteenth-Century Studies* 51, no. 1 (Fall 2017): 89–113.

Landers, Jane. "Leadership and Authority in Maroon Settlements in Spanish America and Brazil." In *Africa and the Americas: Interconnections During the Slave Trade*, edited by José C. Curto and Renée Soulodre-La France, 173–184. Trenton, NJ: Africa World Press, 204.

Larsen, Nella. *Passing.* New York: Penguin, 1997.

Lasso, Marixa de Paulis. "Race and Ethnicity in the Formation of Panamanian National Identity." *Revista Panameña de Política*, no. 4 (Julio-Diciembre 2007): 61–92.

BIBLIOGRAPHY 343

Latorre, Guisela. *Walls of Empowerment: Chicana/o Indigenist Murals of California*. Austin: University of Texas Press, 2008.

Lawson, Edward. "Letter to Jean A. Ramos about 'Experts on Race Questions,'" March 23, 1954. United Nations Archives, S-0724-0006-0005-00002 NSL.

Leach, Colin W. "Against the Notion of a 'New Racism.'" *Journal of Community and Applied Social Psychology* 15 (2005): 432–445.

Legassick, Martin. *Towards Socialist Democracy*. Pietermaritzburg, South Africa: UKZN Press, 2007.

Lahaye Guerra, María Rosa de. "El antirracismo de Fernando Ortiz (primera parte)." *Cuba Debate*, October 28, 2011. http://www.cubadebate.cu/noticias/2011/10/28/el-antirracismo-de-fernando-ortiz-primera-parte/.

Lehmann, David. "Gilberto Freyre: The Reassessment Continues." *Latin American Research Review* 43, no. 1 (2008): 208–218.

Lewis, Lancelot. *The West Indian in Panama: Black Labor in Panama, 1850–1914*. Lanham, MD: University Press of America, 1980.

Limón, Graciela. *Erased Faces*. Houston: Arte Público Press, 2001.

Limón, José E. *Mexican Ballads, Chicano Poems: History and Influence in Mexican-American Social Poetry*. Berkeley: University of California Press, 1992.

Lindsay-Poland, John. *Emperors in the Jungle: The Hidden History of the U.S. in Panama*. Durham, NC: Duke University Press, 2003.

Linnaeus, Carolus. *Systema Naturae*. Nieuwkoop, Netherlands: Hes and De Graaf, 2003.

Lipsitz, George. *How Racism Takes Place*. Philadelphia: Temple University Press, 2011.

Lipsitz, George. *The Possessive Investment in Whiteness: How White People Profit from Identity Politics*. Philadelphia: Temple University Press, 2006.

Lipsitz, George. "The Sounds of Silence: How Race Neutrality Preserves White Supremacy." In Crenshaw et al., *Seeing Race Again*, 23–51.

Lisboa, Vinícius. "Governador do Rio diz que assassinato de cinco jovens não foi racismo." *Agência Brasil*, November 30, 2015. https://agenciabrasil.ebc.com.br/geral/noticia/2015-11/governador-diz-que-assassinato-de-5-jovens-nao-foi-racismo.

Lizardi, José Joaquín Férnandez de. *El Periquillo Sarniento*. Madrid: Cátedra, 2007.

Lombroso, Cesare. *L'uomo bianco e l'uomo di colore: Lettura sull'origine e le varietà delle razze umane*. Padua: Editrice F. Sacchetto, 1871.

Lombroso, Cesare. *L'uomo delinquente studiato in rapporto alla antropologia, alla medicina legale ed alle discipline carcerarie*. Milano: Hoepli, 1876.

Lombroso, Cesare. *Criminal Man*. Translated by Mary Gibson and Nicole Hahn Rafter. Durham, NC: Duke University Press, 2006.

Lomelí, Francisco A. "Introduction. Revisiting the Vision of Aztlán: Origins, Interpretations, and Theory vis-à-vis Fact and Fiction." In Anaya and Lomelí, *Aztlán*, 1–24.

López-Calvo, Ignacio. "Chicanismo Meets Zapatismo: U.S. Third World Feminism and Transnational Activism in Graciela Limón's *Erased Faces*." *Chasqui* 33, no. 2 (2004):64–74.

Lorde, Audre. *Sister Outsider: Essays and Speeches*. Berkeley, CA: Crossing Press, 1984.

Lott, Eric. *Love and Theft: Blackface Minstrelsy and the American Working Class*. Oxford: Oxford University Press, 2013.

Love, Stephanie, and Manka M. Varghese. "Race, Language, and Schooling in Italy's Immigrant Policies, Public Discourses, and Pedagogies." *International Journal of Multicultural Education* 14, no. 2 (2012): 1–19.

Lovejoy, Paul E. "The Impact of the Atlantic Slave Trade on Africa: A Review of the Literature." *Journal of African History* 30, no. 3 (1989): 365–94.

Lowe, Lisa. *The Intimacies of Four Continents*. Durham, NC: Duke University Press, 2015.

Lund, Joshua. *The Impure Imagination: Toward a Critical Hybridity in Latin American Writing*. Minneapolis: University of Minnesota Press, 2006.

Lund, Joshua, and Malcolm McNee. *Gilberto Freyre e os estudos latino-americanos*. Pittsburgh: Instituto Internacional de Literatura Iberoamericana, University of Pittsburgh, 2006.

Lund Joshua, and Malcolm McNee. "Gilberto Freyre e o sublime brasileiro." In Lund and McNee, eds., *Gilberto Freyre e os estudos latino-americanos*, 7–34.

Macharia, Keguro. *Frottage: Frictions of Intimacy across the Black Diaspora*. New York: New York University Press, 2019.

Machedo, Fernanda dos Santos de, Adriane Roso, and Michele Pivetta de Lara. "Mulheres, saúde e uso de crack: a reprodução do novo racismo na/pela mídia televisiva." *Saúde e Sociedade* 24, no. 4 (October–December 2015): 1285–98.

Magnoli, Demétrio. *Uma gota de sangue: história do pensamento racial*. São Paulo: Editora Contexto, 2009.

Magubane, Bernard M. *Race and the Construction of the Dispensable Other*. Pretoria: UNISA Press, 2007.

Malan, Rian. *My Traitor's Heart: A South African Exile Returns to Face His Country, His Tribe, and His Conscience*. New York: Grove Press, 2000.

Malcolm X. *Malcolm X Speaks: Selected Speeches and Statements*. Edited by George Breitman. New York: Grove Press, 1965.

Mamdani, Mahmood. *Citizen and Subject: Contemporary Africa and the Legacy of Late Colonialism*. Princeton, NJ: Princeton University Press, 1996.

Manzano, Juan F. *Autobiografía de un esclavo*. Barcelona: Linkgua, 2014.

Marable, Manning. "Globalization and Racialization." *Synthesis/Regeneration*, no. 39 (Winter 2006). http://www.greens.org/s-r/39/39-06.html.

Marcos. *Conversations with Don Durito: Stories of the Zapatistas and Neoliberalism*. New York: Autonomedia, 2006.

Marcos. *Our Word Is Our Weapon: Selected Writings*. Edited by Juana Ponce de Leon. New York: Seven Stories Press, 2001.

Maré, Gerhard. *Declassified: Moving Beyond the Dead-End of Race in South Africa*. Johannesburg: Jacana, 2015.

Maré, Gerhard. "Non-Racialism in the Struggle against Apartheid." *Society in Transition* 34, no. 1 (2003): 13–37.

Mariátegui, José C. *Siete ensayos de interpretación de la realidad peruana*. Barcelona: Linkgua, 2014.

Marinovich, Greg. *Murder at Small Koppie: The Real Story of the Marikana Massacre*. Johannesburg: Penguin South Africa, 2016.

Marriott, David. *Whither Fanon? Studies in the Blackness of Being*. Palo Alto, CA: Stanford University Press, 2018.

Martin, Peter. "Racism, Differentialism, and Anti-Racism in Everyday Ideology: A Mixed-Methods Study in Britain." *International Journal of Conflict and Violence* 7, no. 1 (2013): 57–73.

Martinot, Steve, and Jared Sexton. "The Avant-Garde of White Supremacy." *Social Identities* 9, no. 2 (2003): 169–181.

Martins, Sérgio da Silva, Carlos Alberto Madeiros, and Elisa Larkin Nascimento. "Paving Paradise: The Road from 'Racial Democracy' to Affirmative Action in Brazil." *Journal of Black Studies* 34, no. 6 (July 2004): 787–816.

Marx, Anthony. *Making Race and Nation: A Comparison of South Africa, the United States, and Brazil*. Cambridge: Cambridge University Press, 1998.

Marx, Karl. *The Poverty of Philosophy*. New York: International, 1963.

Mayorga, Irma. "Invisibility's Contusions: Violence in Cherríe Moraga's *Heroes and Saints* and *The Hungry Woman* and Luis Valdez's *Zoot Suit*." In *Violence in American Drama: Essays on Its Staging, Meanings and Effects*, edited by Alfonso Ceballos Muñoz, Ramón Espejo Romero, and Bernardo Muñoz Martinez, 157–71. Jefferson, NC: McFarland, 2011.

Mbembe, Achille. *Critique of Black Reason*. Translated by Dubois Laurent. Durham, NC: Duke University Press, 2017.

McCullough, David. *The Path Between the Seas: The Creation of the Panama Canal, 1870–1914*. New York: Simon and Schuster, 1978.

McGarrity, Gayle, and Osvaldo Cárdenas. "Cuba." In *No Longer Invisible: Afro-Latin Americans Today*, edited by Minority Rights Group, 77–107. London: Minority Rights Publications, 1995.

McKaiser, Eusebius. "Confronting Whiteness." *Mail & Guardian*, September 2, 2011. mg.co.za/article/2011-07-01-confronting-whiteness.

McKaiser, Eusebius. "Hoe moet 'whiteys' in dié vreemde plek leef?" *Beeld*, June 25, 2011, 5.

McRae, Elizabeth Gillespie. *Mothers of Massive Resistance: White Women and the Politics of White Supremacy*. Oxford: Oxford University Press, 2018.

McReary, Tyler. "Colour-Blind: Discursive Repertoires Teachers Used to Story Racism and Aboriginality in Urban Prairie Schools." *Brock Education* 21, no. 1 (Fall 2011): 16–33.

Melamed, Jodi. *Represent and Destroy: Rationalizing Violence in the New Racial Capitalism*. Minneapolis: University of Minnesota Press, 2011.

Memmi, Albert. *The Colonizer and the Colonized*. Translated by Howard Greenfield. London: Souvenir Press, 1965.

Menchaca, Martha. "Chicano Indianism: A Historical Account of Racial Repression in the United States." *American Ethnologist* 20, no. 3 (1993): 583–603.

Meyer, Deon. *The Woman in the Blue Cloak*. London: Hodder and Staughton, 2017.

Milazzo, Marzia. "Mark Mathabane's *K*ffir Boy*, Black Consciousness, and the Fallacies of Liberalism." *ARIEL* 52, no. 3–4 (July–October 2021): 29–62.

Milazzo, Marzia. "The Master's Colorblind Tools: Hegemonic Racial Discourse and the Decolonial Imaginaries of Contemporary Afro-Panamanian, Black South African, and Chicana/o Literatures." PhD diss., University of California Santa Barbara, 2013.

Milazzo, Marzia. "On the Transportability, Malleability, and Longevity of Colorblindness: Reproducing White Supremacy in Brazil and South Africa." In Crenshaw et al., *Seeing Race Again*, 105–27.

Milazzo, Marzia. "On White Ignorance, White Shame, and Other Pitfalls in Critical Philosophy of Race." *Journal of Applied Philosophy* 34, no. 4 (August 2017): 557–72.

BIBLIOGRAPHY

Milazzo, Marzia. "The Rhetorics of Racial Power: Enforcing Colorblindness in Post-Apartheid Scholarship on Race." *Journal of International and Intercultural Communication* 8, no. 1 (February 2015): 7–26.

Milazzo, Marzia. "White Supremacy, White Knowledge, and Anti-West Indian Discourse in Panama: Olmedo Alfaro's *El peligro antillano en la América Central.*" *The Global South* 6, no. 2 (Fall 2012): 65–86.

Miller, Marilyn G. *Rise and Fall of the Cosmic Race: The Cult of Mestizaje in Latin America.* Austin: University of Texas Press, 2004.

Miller-Young, Mireille. "Exotic/Erotic/Ethnopornographic: Black Women, Desire, and Labor in the Photographic Archive." In *Ethnopornography: Sexuality, Colonialism, and Archival Knowledge,* edited by Pete Sigal, Zeb Tortorici, and Neil L. Whitehead, 41–66. Durham: Duke University Press, 2020.

Millin, Sarah G. *White Africans Are Also People.* Cape Town: Howard Timmins, 1966.

Mills, Charles W. *Black Rights/White Wrongs: The Critique of Racial Liberalism.* Oxford: Oxford University Press, 2017.

Mills, Charles W. "Global White Ignorance." In *Routledge International Handbook of Ignorance Studies,* edited by Matthias Gross and Linsey McGoey, 217–27. New York: Routledge, 2015.

Mills, Charles W. *The Racial Contract.* Ithaca, NY: Cornell University Press, 1997.

Mills, Charles W. "White Ignorance." In *Race and Epistemologies of Ignorance,* edited by Shannon Sullivan and Nancy Tuana, 11–38. Albany: SUNY Press, 2007.

Mills, Charles W. "White Time: The Chronic Injustice of Ideal Theory." *Du Bois Review* 11, no. 1 (2014): 27–42.

Miró, Rodrigo Grimaldo. *Itinerario de la poesia en Panamá, Tomo I.* Panama City: Biblioteca de la Nacionalidad, 1999.

Mirzoeff, Nicholas. "The Murder of Michael Brown: Reading the Ferguson Grand Jury Transcript." *Social Text* 34, no. 1 (2016): 49–71.

Missal, Alexander. *Seaway to the Future: American Social Visions and the Construction of the Panama Canal.* Madison: University of Wisconsin Press, 2008.

Mitrani, Sam. *The Rise of the Chicago Police Department: Class and Conflict, 1850–1894.* Champaign: University of Illinois Press, 2013.

Mngxitama, Andile. "Blacks Can't Be Racist." *New Frank Talk: Critical Essays on the Black Condition* 3. Johannesburg: Sankara Publishing, 2009.

Mngxitama, Andile. "End to Whiteness a Black Issue." *Mail & Guardian*, October 24, 2011. https://mg.co.za/article/2011-10-24-end-to-whiteness-a-black-issue/.

Mngxitama, Andile. "Whites are Tourists, Blacks are Kwerekweres." *Black Opinion*, April 3, 2019. https://blackopinion.co.za/2019/04/03/whites-tourists-blacks-kwerekweres/.

Modiri, Joel M. "Race as/and the Trace of the Ghost: Jurisprudential Escapism, Horizontal Anxiety and the Right to Be Racist in *BoE Trust Limited*." *Potchefstroom Electronic Law Journal* 16, no. 5 (2013): 581–614.

Molina, Natalia. *How Race Is Made in America: Immigration, Citizenship, and the Historical Power of Racial Scripts*. Berkeley: University of California Press, 2014.

Molina, Natalia, Daniel Martinez HoSang, and Ramón A. Gutiérrez, eds. *Relational Formations of Race: Theory, Method, and Practice*. Berkeley: University of California Press, 2019.

Moore, Carlos. "Afro-Cubans and the Communist Revolution." In *African Presence in the Americas*, edited by Carlos Moore, Tanya R. Saunders, and Shwana Moore, 199–240. Trenton, NJ: Africa World Press, 1995.

Moore, Carlos. *Pichón: Race and Revolution in Castro's Cuba*. Chicago: Lawrence Hill Books, 2008.

Moorosi, Pontso. "Colour-blind Educational Leadership Policy: A Critical Race Theory Analysis of School Principalship Standards in South Africa." *Educational Management Administration and Leadership* 49, no. 4 (2021): 644–661.

Moraga, Cherríe. *The Hungry Woman*. Albuquerque, NM: West End Press, 2003.

Moraga, Cherríe. "An Interview with Cherríe Moraga." Interview by Maria Antónia Oliver-Rotger. *Soundings: Voices from the Gap*, January 2005. http://voices.cla.umn.edu./newsite/soundings/ROTGERmaria-moraga.htm.

Moraga, Cherríe. "La Güera." In *This Bridge Called My Back: Writings by Radical Women of Color*, edited by Cherríe Moraga and Gloria E. Anzaldúa, 22–29. Albany: SUNY Press, 2015.

Moraga, Cherríe. *The Last Generation: Prose and Poetry*. Boston: South End Press, 1999.

Moraga, Cherríe. *Loving in the War Years: Lo Que Nunca Pasó por Sus Labios*. Boston: South End Press, 2000.

Moraga, Cherríe. "Queer Aztlán: The Re-formation of the Chicano Tribe." In *Re-emerging Native Women of the Americas: Native Chicana Latina Women's Studies*, edited by Yolanda Broyles-González, 236–53. Cambridge, MA: Kendall, 2001.

BIBLIOGRAPHY

Moraga, Cherríe. *A Xicana Codex of Changing Consciousness: Writings, 2000–2010*. Durham, NC: Duke University Press, 2011.

Moraga, Cherríe, and Gloria Anzaldúa, eds. *This Bridge Called My Back: Writings by Radical Women of Color*. New York: Kitchen Table, 1993.

More, Mabogo P. "Biko: Africana Existentialist Philosopher." In *Biko Lives! Contesting the Legacies of Steve Biko*, edited by Andile Mngxitama, Amanda Alexander, and Nigel C. Gibson, 45–68. London: Palgrave Macmillian, 2008.

Morrison, Karen Y. *Cuba's Racial Crucible: The Sexual Economy of Social Identities, 1750–2000*. Bloomington: Indiana University Press, 2015.

Morrison, Toni. *Playing in the Dark: Whiteness and the Literary Imagination*. New York: Vintage, 2003.

Moten, Fred. *Black and Blur*. Durham, NC: Duke University Press, 2017.

Moten, Fred. "Black Op." *PMLA* 123, no. 5 (Oct. 2008): 1743–47.

Mount, Guy Emerson. "Historical Ventriloquy: Black Thought and Sexual Politics in the Interracial Marriage of Frederick Douglass." In *New Perspectives on the Black Intellectual Tradition*, edited by Keisha N. Blain, Christopher Cameron, and Ashley D. Farmer, 139–55. Evanston, IL: Northwestern University Press, 2018.

Moya, Paula M. L. "Chicana Feminisms and Postmodernist Theory." *Signs* 26, no. 2 (Winter 2001): 441–83.

Moya, Paula M. L. *The Social Imperative: Race, Close Reading, and Contemporary Literary Criticism*. Palo Alto, CA: Stanford University Press, 2015.

Mudimbe, V. Y. *The Invention of Africa: Gnosis, Philosophy, and the Order of Knowledge*. Bloomington: Indiana University Press, 1988.

Mukherjee, Roopali, Sarah Banet-Weiser, and Herman Gray, eds. *Racism Postrace*. Durham, NC: Duke University Press, 2019.

Murakawa, Naomi. *The First Civil Right: How Liberals Built Prison America*. Oxford: Oxford University Press, 2014.

Naicker, Camalita. "From Marikana to #feesmustfall: The Praxis of Popular Politics in South Africa." *Urbanisation* 1, no. 1 (2016): 53–61.

Naletto, Grazia, ed. *Rapporto sul razzismo in Italia*. Rome: Manifestolibri, 2009.

Nascimento, Abdias. *Africans in Brazil: A Pan-African Perspective*. Trenton, NJ: Africa World Press, 1992.

Nascimento, Abdias. *Brazil: Mixture or Massacre? Essays in the Genocide of a Black People*. Dover, MA: Majority Press, 1989.

Nascimento, Abdias. *Quilombo: vida, problemas, e aspirações do negro*. Rio de Janeiro: Editora 34, 2003.

Nascimento, Elisa Larkin. *The Sorcery of Color: Identity, Race, and Gender in Brazil*. Philadelphia: Temple University Press, 2007.

National Center for Education Statistics. "Status and Trends in the Education of Racial and Ethnic Groups 2016." US Department of Education, 2016. nces.ed.gov/pubs2016/2016007.pdf.

Navarrete, Federico. *México racista: Una denuncia*. Mexico City: Grijalbo, 2016.

Navarro, Alfredo Figueroa. *Vida e obra de Gaspar Octavio Hernández, el Cisne Negro*. Panama City: Comisión del Centenario de la República, 2002.

Neugebeuer, Christian M. "The Racism of Hegel and Kant." In *Sage Philosophy: A New Orientation in African Philosophy*, edited by Odera Oruka, 259–72. Leiden: Brill,1990.

Ndebele, Njabulo S. "The Rediscovery of the Ordinary: Some New Writings in South Africa." In *Rediscovery of the Ordinary: Essays on South African Literature and Culture*, 31–54. Pietermaritzburg, South Africa: University of KwaZulu-Natal Press, 1991.

Ndlovu, Sifiso M. *The Soweto Uprisings: Counter Memories of June 1976*. London: Pan MacMillan, 2017.

Needell, Jeffrey D. "Identity, Race, Gender, and Modernity in the Origins of Gilberto Freyre's Oeuvre." *American Historical Review* 100, no. 1 (February 1995): 51–77.

Nemser, Daniel. *Infrastructures of Race: Concentration and Biopolitics in Colonial Mexico*. Austin, TX: University of Texas Press, 2017.

Newton, Huey P. "A Functional Definition of Politics: January 17, 1969." In *The Huey P. Newton Reader*, edited by David Hilliard and Donald Weise, 147–49. New York: Seven Stories Press, 2002.

Newton, Velma. *The Silver Men: West Indian Labour Migration to Panama, 1850–1914*. Kingston, Jamaica: Ian Randle Publishers, 2004.

Nkosi, Lewis. "Fiction by Black South Africans." In *Writing Home: Lewis Nkosi on South African Writing*, edited by Lindy Stiebel and Michael Chapman, 49–61. Pietermaritzburg, South Africa: University of KwaZulu-Natal Press, 2016.

Noon, Mike. "Pointless Diversity Training: Unconscious Bias, New Racism and Agency." *Work, Employment and Society* 32, no. 1 (February 2018): 198–209.

Ntsebeza, Lungisile, and Ruth Hall, eds. *The Land Question in South Africa: The Challenges of Transformation and Redistribution*. Cape Town: HSRC Press, 2007.

BIBLIOGRAPHY

Nunes, Zita. *Cannibal Democracy: Race and Representation in the Literature of the Americas*. Minneapolis: University of Minnesota Press, 2008.

Nuttall, Sarah. "City Forms and Writing the 'Now' in South Africa." *Journal of Southern African Studies* 30, no. 4 (December 2004): 731–48.

Nuttall, Sarah. *Entanglement: Literary and Cultural Reflections on Post-Apartheid*. Johannesburg: Wits University Press, 2009.

Obasogie, Osagie K. "Do Blind People See Race? Social, Legal, and Theoretical Considerations." *Law and Society Review* 44, no. 3–4 (2010): 585–616.

Obasogie, Osagie K., and Zachary Newman. "The Futile Fourth Amendment: Understanding Police Excessive Force Doctrine through an Empirical Assessment of *Graham v. Connor*." *Northwestern University Law Review* 112, no. 6 (2018): 1465–500.

Olguín, B. V. "'*Caballeros*' and Indians: Mexican American Whiteness, Hegemonic Mestizaje, and Ambivalent Indigeneity in Proto-Chicana/o Autobiographical Discourse, 1858–2008." *MELUS* 38, no. 1 (Spring 2013): 30–49.

Omi, Michael, and Howard Winant. *Racial Formation in the United States: From the 1960s to the 1990s*. New York: Routledge, 1994.

Oppenheimer, Mark, and David Ansara. "The New Affirmative Action: Abandoning Race as a Proxy for Disadvantage." *Journal of the Helen Suzman Foundation* 71 (November 2013): 46–51.

Ortiz, Fernando. *Contrapunteo cubano del tabaco y el azúcar: Advertencia de sus contrastes agrarios, económicos, históricos y sociales, su etnografía y su tranculturación*. Madrid: Cátedra, 2002.

Ortiz, Fernando. *Cuban Counterpoint: Tobacco and Sugar*. New York: Knopf, 1947.

Ortiz, Fernando. *Hampa afro-cubana: Los negros brujos (Apuntes para un estudio de etnología criminal)*. Miami: Ediciones Universal, 1973.

Ortiz, Fernando. "Por la integración cubana de blancos y negros." *Revista bimestre cubana* 51 (1943): 256–72.

Ortiz, Fernando. "The Relations between Blacks and Whites in Cuba." *Phylon* 5, no. 1 (First Quarter 1944): 15–29.

Painter, Nell Irvin. *The History of White People*. New York: Norton, 2010.

Palau, Karina Ruth-Ester. "Ethnography Otherwise: Interventions in Writing, Photography, and Sound in Mexico and Brazil." PhD diss., University of California Berkeley, 2013.

Palmer, Tyrone S. "Otherwise than Blackness: Feeling, World, Sublimation." *Qui Parle* 29, no. 2 (December 2020): 247–83.

BIBLIOGRAPHY

Palthey, George. "Télégramme adressé le 10 Mars 1954 par le Directeur des Nations Unies à Monsieur le Docteur Gilberto Freyre." March 10, 1954. United Nations Archives, S-0724-0006-0005-00002 NSL.

"Panama Mob Stones Police Chief's Home After Boy Is Killed." *The Daily Gleaner*, October 8, 1934, 6.

Pappademos, Melina. *Black Political Activism and the Cuban Republic*. Chapel Hill: University of North Carolina Press, 2011.

Parents Involved in Community Schools v. Seattle School Dist. No. 1. 551 U.S. 701, 2007. supreme.justia.com/cases/federal/us/551/701/.

Pascale, Pablo. "Nuevas formas de racismo: Estado de la cuestión en la psicología del prejuicio." *Ciencias Psicológicas* 4, no. 1 (2010): 57–69.

Paschel, Tianna S. *Becoming Black Political Subjects: Movements and Ethno-Racial Rights in Colombia and Brazil*. Princeton, NJ: Princeton University Press, 2016.

Paton, Alan. "Black Consciousness." *Reality* 4, no. 1 (1972): 9–10.

Paton, Alan. *Cry, the Beloved Country*. New York: Scribner, 2003.

Patterson, Orlando. *Slavery and Social Death: A Comparative Study*. Cambridge, MA: Harvard University Press, 1985.

Perez, Domino R. "*Caminando con La Llorona*: Traditional and Contemporary Narratives." In *Chicana Traditions: Continuity and Change*, edited by Norma Cantú and Olga Nájera-Ramírez, 100–113. Champaign: University of Illinois Press, 2002.

Perez, Domino R. "New Tribalism and Chicana/o Indigeneity in the Work of Gloria Anzaldúa." In *Routledge Handbook of Chicana/o Studies*, edited by Francisco A. Lomelí, Denise A. Segura, and Elyette Benjamin-Labarthe, 242–54. New York: Routledge, 2019.

Pérez, Emma. *The Decolonial Imaginary: Writing Chicanas into History*. Bloomington: Indiana University Press, 1999.

Pérez, Luis A. Jr. *Cuba: Between Reform and Revolution*. Oxford: Oxford University Press, 2011.

Perez-Rodriguez, Javier, and Alejandro de la Fuente. "Now Is the Time for a Postracial Medicine: Biomedical Research, the National Institutes of Health, and the Perpetuation of Scientific Racism." *American Journal of Bioethics* 17, no. 9 (September 2017): 36–47.

Pérez-Torres, Rafael. *Mestizaje: Critical Uses of Race in Chicano Culture*. Minneapolis: University of Minnesota Press, 2006.

Pérez-Torres, Rafael. "Refiguring Aztlán." *Aztlán* 22, no. 2 (1997): 15–41.

Peterson, Bhekizizwe. "Dignity, Memory and the Future Under Siege: Reconciliation and Nation-Building in Post-Apartheid South Africa." In *The New Violent Cartography: Geo-Analysis after the Aesthetic Turn*, edited by

BIBLIOGRAPHY

Samson Opondo and Michael J. Shapiro, 214–33. London: Routledge, 2012.

Pike, Ruth. "Black Rebels: The Cimarrons of Sixteenth-Century Panama." *The Americas* 64, no. 2 (October 2007): 243–66.

Pimentel, Rodolfo Pérez. "Alfaro Paredes Olmedo." In *Diccionario Biográfico Ecuador*. https://rodolfoperezpimentel.com/alfaro-paredes-olmedo-2/.

Pina, Michael. "The Archaic, Historical, Mythicized Dimension of Aztlán." In Anaya and Lomelí, *Aztlán*, 43–75.

Posel, Deborah. "Races to Consume: Revisiting South Africa's History of Race, Consumption, and the Struggle for Freedom." *Ethnic and Racial Studies* 33, no. 2, (February 2010): 157–75.

Posel, Deborah and Ilana van Wyk, eds. *Conspicuous Consumption in Africa*. Johannesburg: Wits University Press, 2019.

Pratt, Mary Louise. *Imperial Eyes: Travel Writing and Transculturation*. New York: Routledge, 2007.

Primer Congreso del Negro Panameño. *Memorias: Septiembre 10 al 13, 1981*. Panama City: Centro de Covenciones ATLAPA, 1982.

Pureza, Fernando. "Brazil's Student Upsurge." *Jacobin*, November 12, 2016. www.jacobinmag.com/2016/11/brazil-student-occupations-temer-pt-psol-education/.

Quijano, Aníbal. "Coloniality and Modernity / Rationality." In *Globalization and the Decolonial Option*, edited by Walter D. Mignolo and Arturo Escobar. New York: Routledge, 2010.

Quijano, Aníbal. "Coloniality of Power, Eurocentrism, and Social Classification." *Nepantla* 1, no. 3 (2000): 533–80.

Race Betterment Foundation. *Official Proceedings of the Second National Conference on Race Betterment*. Battle Creek, MI: Race Betterment Foundation, 1915.

Rama, Ángel. *Transculturación narrativa en América Latina*. Buenos Aires: Ediciones El Andariego, 2008.

Rampolokeng, Lesego. *Horns for Hondo*. Congress of South African Writers, 1990.

Rampolokeng, Lesego, and the Kalahari Surfers. "Rapmaster." Track 2 on *End Beginnings*. Compact disc. Rer Megacorp, 1993. https://kalaharisurfer.bandcamp.com/track/rapmaster.

Rapalo, Manuel. "Thousands Displaced as Territory Disputes Continue in Chiapas." *Al Jazeera*, December 19, 2017. https://www.aljazeera.com/news/2017/12/thousands-displaced-territorial-disputes-continue-mexicos-chiapas-171219115740491.html.

Rebelo, Aldo. *Gilberto Freyre e a formação do Brasil: artigos em homenagem ao centenario de nascimento de Gilberto Freyre*. Brasilia: Centro de Documentação e Informação, 2000.

Rebolledo, Tey D. *Women Singing in the Snow: A Cultural Analysis of Chicana Literature*. Tucson: University of Arizona Press, 1995.

Redazione ANSA. "Attack on Egyptian Boys 'Xenophobia.'" *ANSA*, August 23, 2016. http://www.ansa.it/english/news/general_news/2016/08/23/attack-on-egyptian-boys-xenophobia_a6da109f-1bba-48bb-b036-026131b841dc.html.

Reddy, Chandan. "Time for Rights? *Loving*, Gay Marriage, and the Limits of Comparative Legal Justice." In *Strange Affinities: The Gender and Sexual Politics of Comparative Racialization*, edited by Grace Kyungwon Hong and Roderick A. Ferguson, 148–74. Durham, NC: Duke University Press, 2011.

Reed, Little Rock. "The American Indian in the White Man's Prison: A Story of Genocide." In James, ed., *The New Abolitionists*, 135–50.

Rios, Victor M. "Book Review: *On the Run: Fugitive Life in an American City*." *American Journal of Sociology* 121, no. 1 (July 2015): 306–8.

"Riots in Colon When Police Officer Shot Fleeing Youth." *The Daily Gleaner*, October 10, 1934, 6.

Rivera-Barnes, Beatriz. "Ethnological Counterpoint: Fernando Ortiz and Jean Price-Mars, or Santeria and Vodou." *SAGE Open* 4, no. 2 (April–June 2014): 1–11.

Roberts, Neil. *Freedom as Marronage*. Chicago: University of Chicago Press, 2015.

Robinson, Cedric J. *Black Marxism: The Making of the Black Radical Tradition*. Chapel Hill: University of North Carolina Press, 1983.

Robinson, Cedric J. *Forgeries of Memory and Meaning: Blacks and the Regimes of Race in American Theater and Film Before World War II*. Chapel Hill: University of North Carolina Press, 2007.

Rodríguez, Dylan. *Suspended Apocalypse: White Supremacy, Genocide, and the Filipino Condition*. Minneapolis: University of Minnesota Press, 2010.

Rodriguez, Gregory. *Mongrels, Bastards, Orphans, and Vagabonds: Mexican Immigration and the Future of Race in America*. New York: Vintage, 2007.

Rodriguez, Richard. *Brown: The Last Discovery of America*. New York: Viking Press, 2002.

Roediger, Roger R. *The Wages of Whiteness: Race and the Making of the American Working Class*. New York: Verso, 2007.

BIBLIOGRAPHY

Rooks, Gerrit and Leon Oerlemans, "South Africa: A Rising Star? Assessing the X-effectiveness of South Africa's National System of Innovation." *European Planning Studies* 13, no. 8 (December 2005): 1205–26.

Rosa, Manuel de la. "El negro en Panamá." In *Presencia africana en Centroamérica*, edited by Luz M. Martínez Montiel, 217–90. Panama City: Consejo Nacional para la Cultura y las Artes, 1993.

Rosaldo, Renato. Foreword to *Hybrid Cultures: Strategies for Entering and Leaving Modernity* by Néstor García Canclini, xi-xvii. Minneapolis: University of Minnesota Press, 1995.

Rosenthal, Debra J. "Race Mixture and the Representation of Indians in the U.S. and the Andes." In *Mixing Race, Mixing Culture: Inter-American Literary Dialogues*, edited by Monika Kaup and Debra J. Rosenthal, 122–39. Austin: University of Texas Press, 2002.

Ruggunan, Shaun, and Gerhard Maré. "Race Classification at the University of KwaZulu-Natal: Purposes, Sites and Practices." *Transformation* 79 (2012): 47–68.

Ruiters, Greg. "Non-Racialism: The New Form of Racial Inequality in a Neo-Apartheid South Africa." *Journal of Asian and African Studies* 1, no. 16 (2020): 1–16.

Rydell, Robert W. *All the World's a Fair: Visions of Empire at American International Expositions, 1876–1916.* Chicago: University of Chicago Press, 1987.

Said, Edward. *Orientalism.* New York: Vintage, 1994.

Salata, André. "Race, Class and Income Inequality in Brazil: A Social Trajectory Analysis." *Dados* 63, no. 3 (2020): 1–40. https://doi.org/10.1590 /dados.2020.63.3.213.

Saldaña-Portillo, María Josefina. *Indian Given: Racial Geographies across Mexico and the United States.* Durham, NC: Duke University Press, 2016.

Saldaña-Portillo, María Josefina. *The Revolutionary Imagination in the Americas and the Age of Development.* Durham, NC: Duke University Press, 2003.

Saldaña-Portillo, María Josefina. "Who Is the Indian in Aztlán? Re-Writing Mestizaje, Indianism, and Chicanismo from the Lacandón." In *The Latin American Subaltern Reader*, edited by Ileana Rodríguez, 402–22. Durham, NC: Duke University Press, 2001.

Sale, Giovanni. *Le leggi razziali in Italia e il Vaticano.* Milan: Jaca Book, 2009.

Sandoval, Chela. *Methodology of the Oppressed.* Minneapolis: University of Minnesota Press, 2000.

Sandoval, Chela. "U.S. Third World Feminism: The Theory and Method of Oppositional Consciousness in the Postmodern World." *Genders*, no. 10 (Spring 1991): 1–24.

Saperstein, Aliya, and Andrew M. Penner. "Racial Fluidity and Inequality in the United States." *American Journal of Sociology* 118, no. 3 (2012): 676–727.

Saucier, Khalil P., and Tryon P. Woods. "Introduction: Racial Optimism and the Drag of Thymotics." In *Conceptual Aphasia in Black: Displacing Racial Formation*, edited by P. Khalil Saucier and Tryon P. Woods, 1–33. Lanham, MD: Lexington Books, 2016.

Sawyer, Mark Q. *Racial Politics in Post-Revolutionary Cuba*. Cambridge: Cambridge University Press, 2006.

Saxena, Akshya. *Vernacular English: Reading the Anglophone in Postcolonial India*. Princeton, NJ: Princeton University Press, 2022.

Scott, Darieck B. *Extravagant Abjection: Blackness, Power, and Sexuality in the African American Literary Imagination*. New York: New York University Press, 2010.

Seekings, Jeremy. "The Continuing Salience of Race: Discrimination and Diversity in South Africa." *Journal of Contemporary African Studies* 26, no. 1 (January 2008): 1–25.

Seekings, Jeremy. *Class, Race, and Inequality in the South African City*. Cape Town: Centre for Social Science Research, University of Cape Town, 2010.

Seekings, Jeremy. *Race, Discrimination, and Diversity in South Africa*. Cape Town: Centre for Social Science Research, University of Cape Town, 2007.

Seekings, Jeremy, and Nicoli Nattrass. *Class, Race, and Inequality in South Africa*. New Haven, CT: Yale University Press, 2005.

Seigel, Micol. *Violence Work: State Power and the Limits of Police*. Durham, NC: Duke University Press, 2018.

Senior, Oliver. *Dying to Better Themselves: West Indians and the Building of the Panama Canal*. Kingston, Jamaica: University of the West Indies Press, 2014.

Serna, Jesús M. Moreno. *México, un pueblo testimonio: Los indios y la nación en nuestra América*. Mexico City: CCYDEL y Plaza y Valdés, 2001.

Seroke, Jaki. "Black Writers in South Africa: Jaki Seroke Speaks to Miriam Tlali, Sipho Sepamla and Mutobi Mutloatse After Steering Committee Meeting of the African Writers' Association at Khotso House in 1981."

BIBLIOGRAPHY

In *Ten Years of Staffrider: 1978–1988*, edited by Andrias Walter Oliphant and Ivan Vladislavic, 303–9. Johannesburg: Ravan Press, 1988.

Sexton, Jared. *Amalgamation Schemes: Antiblackness and the Critique of Multiracialism*. Minneapolis: University of Minnesota Press, 2008.

Sexton, Jared. "People-of-Color-Blindness: Notes on the Afterlife of Slavery." *Social Text* 28, no. 2 (Summer 2010): 31–56.

Sexton, Jared. "The *Vel* of Slavery: Tracking the Figure of the Unsovereign." *Critical Sociology* 42, no. 4–5 (2016): 583–97.

Shabazz, Rashad. *Spatializing Blackness: Architectures of Confinement and Black Masculinity in Chicago*. Urbana, IL: University of Illinois Press, 2015.

Shange, Savannah. *Progressive Dystopia: Abolition, Antiblackness, and Schooling in San Francisco*. Durham, NC: Duke University Press, 2019.

Sharpe, Christina. "Black Life, Annotated." *The New Inquiry*, August 8, 2014. https://thenewinquiry.com/black-life-annotated/.

Sharpe, Christina. *In the Wake: On Blackness and Being*. Durham, NC: Duke University Press, 2016.

Sharpe, Christina. "Learning to Live Without Black Familia: Cherríe Moraga's Nationalist Articulations." In *Tortilleras: Hispanic and U.S. Latina Lesbian Expression*, edited by Lourdes Torres and Immaculata Petrusa, 240–57. Philadelphia: Temple University Press, 2003.

Sharpe, Christina. *Monstrous Intimacies: Making Post-Slavery Subjects*. Durham, NC: Duke University Press, 2010.

Shohat, Ella, and Robert Stam. *Unthinking Eurocentrism: Multiculturalism and the Media*. London: Routledge, 1994.

Sigal, Pete, Zeb Tortorici, and Neil L. Whitehead. "Introduction. Ethnopornography as Methodology and Critique: Merging the Ethno-, the Porno-, and the -Graphos." In *Ethnopornography: Sexuality, Colonialism, and Archival Knowledge*, edited by Pete Sigal, Zeb Tortorici, and Neil L. Whitehead, 1–37. Durham, NC: Duke University Press, 2019.

Silva, Denise Ferreira da. "Ninguém: direito, racialidade e violência." *Meritum* 9, no. 1 (2014): 67–117.

Silva, Denise Ferreira da. *Toward a Global Idea of Race*. Minneapolis: University of Minnesota Press, 2007.

Silva, Graziella Moraes, and Marcelo Paixão. "Mixed and Unequal: New Perspectives on Brazilian Ethnoracial Relations." In Telles and PERLA, *Pigmentocracies*, 172–217.

Slasha, Unathi. "Black Paint." In *Badilisha Poetry X-Change*. https://badilishapoetry.com/unathi-slasha/.

Smith, Carlos. "Buscando las raíces afro-panameñas: Pasado-presente-futuro." In *Discriminación racial en Panamá: Conferencias del primer foro en el Museo Afroantillano de Panamá*, edited by Ethelbert G. Mapp, 39–44. Panama City: Editorial Portobelo, 2000.

Smith, Christen A. *Afro-Paradise: Blackness, Violence, and Performance in Brazil*. Champaign: University of Illinois Press, 2016.

Smith, Michael. *The Aztecs*. Cambridge: Cambridge University Press, 1996.

Sniderman, Paul M., Thomas Piazza, Philip E. Tetlock, and Ann Kendrick. "The New Racism." *American Journal of Political Science* 35, no. 2 (May 1991): 423–47.

Soley, La Verne M. Seales. *Culture and Customs of Panama*. Westport, CT: Greenwood Press, 2009.

Sorentino, Sara-Maria. "Mistresses as Masters? The Textual Pleasures of the Plantation Present." *Differences* 32, no. 2 (2021): 69–93.

Soudien, Crain. "The Modern Seduction of Race: Whither Social Constructionism?" *Transformation* 79 (2012): 18–38.

Soudien, Crain. *Realising the Dream: Unlearning the Logic of Race in the South African School*. Cape Town: HSRC Press, 2012.

Soumahoro, Aboubakar. *Umanità in rivolta: La nostra lotta per il lavoro e il diritto alla felicità*. Milan: Feltrinelli, 2019.

Sousa, Cruz e. *Obras poéticas*. Rio de Janeiro: Imprensa Nacional, 1945.

South African Human Rights Commision (SAHRC). *Research Brief on Race and Inequality in South Africa, 2013–2017*. https://www.sahrc.org.za/home/21/files/RESEARCH%20BRIEF%20ON%20RACE%20AND%20EQUALITY%20IN%20SOUTH%20AFRICA%202013%20TO%202017.pdf.

South African Institute of Race Relations (IRR). "Press Release: Affirmative Action Is Killing Babies and Must Be Scrapped." June 6, 2014. irr.org.za/media/media-releases/affirmative-action-is-killing-babies-and-must-be-scrapped/view.

Spillers, Hortense J. *Black, White, and in Color*. Chicago: University of Chicago Press, 2003.

Spillers, Hortense J. "Mama's Baby, Papa's Maybe: An American Grammar Book." *Diacritics* 17, no. 2 (Summer 1987): 64–81.

Stanfield, John H., II. "The Gospel of Feel-Good Sociology: Race Relations as Pseudoscience and the Decline in the Relevance of American Academy Sociology in the Twenty-First Century." In *White Logic, White Methods: Racism and Methodology*, edited by Tukufu Zuberi and Eduardo Bonilla-Silva, 271–82. Lanham: Rowman and Littlefield, 2008.

BIBLIOGRAPHY

Stannard, David. *American Holocaust: The Conquest of the New World*. Oxford: Oxford University Press, 1992.

Stanton, Lucia. *"Those Who Labor for My Happiness": Slavery at Thomas Jefferson's Monticello*. Charlottesville: University of Virginia Press, 2012.

State of Missouri v. Darren Wilson. Grand Jury Volume 5, September 14, 2014. https://www.documentcloud.org/documents/1370569-grand-jury-volume 5.html#document/p216/a189399

Statistics South Africa. *Statistical Release P0211: Quarterly Labor Force Survey*. Quarter 2, 2017.

Statistics South Africa. *Statistical Release P0302: Mid-Year Population Estimates*. 2017.

Stavrakakis, Yannis. *The Lacanian Left: Psychoanalysis, Theory, and Politics*. Edinburgh: University of Edinburgh Press, 2007.

Stepan, Nancy L. *The Hour of Eugenics: Race, Gender, and Nation in Latin America*. Ithaca, NY: Cornell University Press, 1996.

Strongman, Roberto. *Queering Black Atlantic Religions: Transcorporeality in Candomblé, Santería, and Vodou*. Durham, NC: Duke University Press, 2019.

Sue, Christina A. *Land of the Cosmic Race: Race Mixture, Racism, and Blackness in Mexico*. Oxford: Oxford University Press, 2013.

Sullivan, Shannon. *Good White People: The Problem with Middle-Class White Anti-Racism*. Albany: SUNY Press, 2014.

Sullivan, Shannon. *Revealing Whiteness: The Unconscious Habits of Racial Privilege*. Bloomington: Indiana University Press, 2006.

Tabensky, Pedro A. "The Oppressor's Pathology." *Theoria* 57, no. 125 (December 2010): 77–98.

Tabensky, Pedro A. "Pitfalls of Negritude: Solace-Driven Tertiary Sector Reform." *South African Journal of Philosophy* 35, no. 4 (2016): 1–19.

Taguieff, Pierre-André. *The Force of Prejudice: On Racism and its Doubles*. Translated and edited by Hassan Melehy. Minneapolis: University of Minnesota Press, 2001.

Taylor, Dorceta E. *Toxic Communities: Environmental Racism, Industrial Pollution, and Residential Mobility*. New York: New York University Press, 2014.

Telles, Edward E. *Race in Another America: The Significance of Skin Color in Brazil*. Princeton, NJ: Princeton University Press, 2004.

Telles, Edward E., and the Project on Ethnicity and Race in Latin America (PERLA). *Pigmentocracies: Ethnicity, Race, and Color in Latin America*. Chapel Hill: University of North Carolina Press, 2014.

Testa, Alberto, and Gary Armstrong. "'We Are Against Islam!': The Lega Nord and the Islamic Folk Devil." *Sage Open* 2, no. 4 (2012): 1–14.

Thornton, Margaret, and Trish Luker. "The New Racism in Employment Discrimination: Tales from the Global Economy." *Sydney Law Review* 32, no. 1 (2010): 1–27.

Tlali, Miriam. *Between Two Worlds*. Peterborough, ON: Broadview Press, 2004.

Trouillot, Michel-Rolph. *Silencing the Past: Power and the Production of History*. Boston: Beacon Press, 1997.

Trump, Donald J. "Transcript: Donald Trump at the G.O.P. Convention." *New York Times*, July 22, 2016. https://www.nytimes.com/2016/07/22/us /politics/trump-transcript-rnc-address.html.

Ture, Kwame. *Stokely Speaks: From Black Power to Pan-Africanism*. Chicago: Lawrence Hill Books, 2007.

Ture, Kwame, and Charles V. Hamilton. *Black Power: The Politics of Liberation*. New York: Random House, 1967.

Tutu, Desmond M. "Chairman's Foreword." In *Truth and Reconciliation Commission of South Africa Report, Vol. 1*, 1–23. https://www.justice.gov .za/trc/report/finalreport/Volume%201.pdf.

Twine, France Winddance. *Racism in a Racial Democracy: The Maintenance of White Supremacy in Brazil*. New Brunswick, NJ: Rutgers University Press, 2005.

UNESCO. "The Race Question." *UNESCO and Its Programme, No. 1, 1950–1976*. 1–10.

UNESCO. *International Social Science Bulletin* 7, no. 3 (1955): 345–547.

United States, Executive Office of the President [Donald J. Trump]. "Protecting the Nation from Foreign Terrorist Entry into the United States." Exec. Order No. 13,769 (January 27, 2017). https://www.federalregister .gov/documents/2017/02/01/2017-02281/protecting-the-nation-from -foreign-terrorist-entry-into-the-united-states.

US Citizenship and Immigration Services. *The Declaration of Independence and Constitution of the United States of America*. https://www.uscis .gov/sites/default/files/document/guides/M-654.pdf.

"US President Donald Trump's Tweet on Land Seizures, 'Killing of Farmers' Angers South Africa." *ABC News*, October 1, 2020, www.abc.net .au/news/2021-04-12/trump-wants-pompeo-to-study-killing-of-farmers /10158114.

Valentine, Desiree. "Racial Mixedness in the Contemporary United States and South Africa: On the Politics of Impurity and Antiracist Praxis." *Critical Philosophy of Race* 4, no. 2 (2016): 182–204.

BIBLIOGRAPHY 361

van Dijk, Teun A. *Racism and the Press*. New York: Routledge, 1991.

van der Riet, Rijno Johannes. "Letter from Landdrost R. J. van der Riet of Stellenbosch to fiscal J. A. Truter, April 1, 1810 (translated from the original in the Cape Archives, St. 1/29)." In du Toit and Giliomee, *Afrikaner Political Thought*, 53–55.

van Gelder, Elles. "Inside the Kommando Camp That Turns Boys' Doubts to Hate." *Mail & Guardian*, February 24, 2012. http://mg.co.za/article /2012-02-24-the-kommando-camp-that-turns-boys-doubts-to-hate.

Van Maanen, John, and Mark de Rond. "The Making of a Classic Ethnography: Notes on Alice Goffman's *On the Run*." *Academy Management Review* 42, no. 2 (September 2016): 396–406.

Van Sertima, Ivan. *They Came Before Columbus: The African Presence in Ancient America*. New York: Random House, 2003.

Vargas, João Costa H. *The Denial of Antiblackness: Multiracial Redemption and Black Suffering*. Minneapolis: University of Minnesota Press, 2018.

Vargas, João Costa H. "The Liberation Imperative of Black Genocide: Blueprints from the African Diaspora in the Americas." *Souls* 10, no. 3 (2008): 256–78.

Vasconcelos, José. *La raza cósmica: Misión de la raza iberoamericana. Argentina y Brasil*. Mexico City: Editora Espasa-Calpe Mexicana, 1948.

Vasconcelos, José. "The Race Problem in Latin America." In *Aspects of Mexican Civilization*, by José Vasconcelos and Manuel Gamio, 75–102. Chicago: University of Chicago Press, 1926.

Vice, Samantha. "Essentialising Rhetoric and Work on the Self." *Philosophical Papers* 45, no. 1–2 (2016): 103–31.

Vice, Samantha. "How Do I Live in This Strange Place?" *Journal of Social Philosophy* 41, no. 3 (Fall 2010): 323–42.

Vice, Samantha. "Reflections on 'How Do I Live in This Strange Place?'" *South African Journal of Philosophy* 30, no. 4 (2011): 503–18.

Vice, Samantha. "Why My Opinions on Whiteness Touched a Nerve." *Mail & Guardian*, September 2, 2011. mg.co.za/print/2011-09-02-why-my-op inions-on-whiteness-touched-a-nerve.

Villanueva, Alma L. *Weeping Woman: La Llorona and Other Stories*. Tempe, AZ: Bilingual Review Press, 1994.

Villaverde, Cirilo. *Cecilia Valdés, o la loma del ángel*. Madrid: Cátedra, 2001.

Wade, Peter. "Mestizaje, Multiculturalism, Liberalism, and Violence." *Latin American and Caribbean Ethnic Studies* 11, no. 3 (2016): 323–43.

Wade, Peter. *Race and Ethnicity in Latin America*. London: Pluto Press, 1997.

Walcott, Rinaldo. *The Long Emancipation: Moving Toward Black Freedom*. Durham, NC: Duke University Press, 2021.

Walcott, Rinaldo. "The Problem of the Human: Black Ontologies and 'the Coloniality of Our Being.'" In *Postcoloniality–Decoloniality–Black Critique*, edited by Sabine Broek and Carsten Junker, 93–109. Frankfurt: Campus Verlag, 2014.

Wallerstein, Immanuel. *Open the Social Sciences: Report of the Gulbenkian Commission on the Restructuring of the Social Sciences*. Palo Alto, CA: Stanford University Press, 1996.

Warren, Calvin L. "Black Time: Slavery, Metaphysics, and the Logic of Wellness." In *The Psychic Hold of Slavery: Legacies in American Expressive Culture*, edited by Soyica Diggs Colbert, Robert J. Patterson, and Aida Levy-Hussein, 55–68. New Brunswick, NJ: Rutgers University Press, 2016.

Warren, Calvin L. *Ontological Terror: Blackness, Nihilism, and Emancipation*. Durham, NC: Duke University Press, 2018.

Warren, Calvin L. "The Will of the American God: Anti-Blackness, *Jouissance*-Sacrifice, and the Structuration of *das Ding*." In *Esoteric Lacan*, edited by Philipp Valentini and Mahdi Tourage, 47–57. London: Rowman and Littlefield, 2019.

Watson, Sonja Stephenson. *The Politics of Race in Panama: Afro-Hispanic and West Indian Literary Discourses of Contention*. Gainesville: University Press of Florida, 2014.

West, Edward. "Only 2% of the Companies Listed on the JSE Are Under 100% Black Ownership." *Independent Online (IOL)*, July 5, 2019. https://www.iol.co.za/business-report/companies/only-2-of-the-companies-listed-on-the-jse-are-under-100-black-ownership-28713477.

"West Indians Riot After Police Killing." Special Cable to *The New York Times*, October 6, 1934. http://druglibrary.net/schaffer/hemp/history/nytimes/100634.htm.

Westley, Robert. "White Normativity and the Racial Rhetoric of Equal Protection." In *Existence in Black: An Anthology of Black Existential Philosophy*, edited by Lewis R. Gordon, 91–98. New York: Routledge, 1996.

Wetherell, Margaret, and Jonathan Potter. *Mapping the Language of Racism: Discourse and the Legitimation of Exploitation*. New York: Columbia University Press, 1993.

Wiegman, Robyn. *Object Lessons*. Durham, NC: Duke University Press, 2012.

Wieviorka, Michel. *The Arena of Racism*. New York: Sage Press, 1995.

Wilderson, Frank B., III. *Afropessimism*. New York: Liveright Publishing, 2020.

BIBLIOGRAPHY 363

Wilderson, Frank B., III. "As Free as Whiteness Will Make Them: Interview with Frank B. Wilderson III." Interview by Gerardo Munoz and Ángel Octavio Álvarez, *illwill.com*, September 8, 2020. https://illwill.com/as-free-as-blackness-will-make-them.

Wilderson, Frank B., III. "Biko and the Problematic of Presence." In *Biko Lives! Contesting the Legacies of Steve Biko*, edited by Andile Mngxitama, Amanda Alexander, and Nigel C. Gibson, 95–114. London: Palgrave, 2008.

Wilderson, Frank B., III. "Frank B. Wilderson, 'Wallowing in the Contradictions,' Part 1." Interview by Percy Howard. percy3.wordpress.com/2010/07/09/frank-b-wilderson-"wallowing-in-the-contradictions"-part-1/.

Wilderson, Frank B., III. "Gramsci's Black Marx: Whither the Slave in Civil Society?" *Social Identities* 9, no. 2 (2003): 225–40.

Wilderson, Frank B., III. *Red, White and Black: Cinema and the Structure of U.S. Antagonisms*. Durham, NC: Duke University Press, 2010.

William, Henry Smith. "The Greatest Migration in History." *San Francisco Chronicle*, August 8, 1915. Supplement.

Williams, Eric E. *Capitalism and Slavery*. Chapel Hill: University of North Carolina Press, 1944.

Williams, Erica Lorraine. *Sex Tourism in Bahia: Ambiguous Entanglements*. Urbana, IL: University of Illinois Press, 2013.

Williams, Kim M. *Mark One or More: Civil Rights in Multiracial America*. Ann Arbor: University of Michigan Press, 2008.

Williams, Kim M. "The Recursive Outcomes of the Multiracial Movement and the End of American Racial Categories." *Studies in American Political Development* 31, no. 1 (April 2017): 88–107.

Willoughby-Herard, Tiffany. *Waste of a White Skin: The Carnegie Corporation and the Racial Logic of White Vulnerability*. Berkeley: University of California Press, 2015.

Wilson, Carlos Guillermo. *See* Cubena.

Wilson, Ricardo A., II. *The Nigrescent Beyond: Mexico, the United States, and the Psychic Vanishing of Blackness*. Evanston, IL: Northwestern University Press, 2020.

Winant, Howard. *The New Politics of Race: Globalism, Difference, Justice*. Minneapolis: University of Minnesota Press, 2004.

Winant, Howard. *The World Is a Ghetto: Race and Democracy since World War II*. New York: Basic Books, 2001.

Wirth, Rex. "The Revolutionary Encounter." In *Mestizaje and Globalization: Transformations of Identity and Power*, edited by Stephanie Wickstrom and Philip D. Young, 25–40. Tucson: University of Arizona Press, 2014.

Wise, Tim. *Between Barack and a Hard Place: Racism and White Denial in the Age of Obama*. San Francisco: City Lights, 2009.

Wise, Tim. *Colorblind: The Rise of Post-Racial Politics and the Retreat from Racial Equity*. San Francisco: City Lights, 2010.

Woods, Tryon P. *Blackhood against the Police Power: Punishment and Disavowal in the "Post-Racial" Era*. East Lansing: Michigan State University Press, 2019.

Wright, Michelle M. *Becoming Black: Creating Identity in the African Diaspora*. Durham, NC: Duke University Press, 2004.

Wyman, Mark, and John W. Muirhead. "Jim Crow Comes to Central Illinois: Racial Segregation in Twentieth-Century Bloomington-Normal." *Journal of the Illinois State Historical Society* 10, no. 2 (Summer 2017): 154–82.

Wynter, Sylvia. "1492: A New World View." In *Race, Discourse, and the Origin of the Americas: A New World View*, edited by Vera L. Hyatt and Rex M. Nettleford, 5–57. Washington, DC: Smithsonian Institution Press, 1995.

Wynter, Sylvia. "Unsettling the Coloniality of Being/Power/Truth/Freedom: Towards the Human, After Man, Its Overrepresentation—An Argument." *CR: The New Centennial Review* 3, no. 3 (Fall 2003): 257–337.

Yelvington, Kevin A. "The Invention of Africa in Latin America and the Caribbean: Political Discourse and Anthropological Praxis, 1920–1940." In *Afro-Atlantic Dialogues: Anthropology in the Diaspora*, edited by Kevin A. Yelvington, 35–82. Santa Fe, NM: School of American Research Press, 2006.

Young, David J. C. *Colonial Desire: Hybridity in Theory, Culture, and Race*. London: Routledge, 2005.

Zangwill, Israel. *The Melting-Pot: Drama in Four Acts*. New and revised edition. New York: Macmillan, 1916.

Zizumbo-Colunga, Daniel, and Iván Flores Martínez. "Is Mexico a Post-Racial Country? Inequality and Skin Tone across the Americas." *Latin American Public Opinion Project 2017*, www.LapopSurveys.org.

Zuberi, Tukufu, and Eduardo Bonilla-Silva. "Toward a Definition of White Logic and White Methods." In *White Logic, White Methods: Racism and Methodology*, edited by Tukufu Zuberi and Eduardo Bonilla-Silva, 3–27. Lanham: Rowman and Littlefield, 2008.

Zumoff, Jacob A. "The 1925 Tenants' Strike in Panama: West Indians, The Left, and the Labor Movement." *The Americas* 74, no. 4 (October 2017): 513–46.

INDEX

ableism, 210
abolition, 30, 42, 76, 77, 267
abolitionists, 185–86
aboriginal rights, 256
Abu-Jamal, Mumia, 16–17, 43
academia, 47; Briticists in, 288n194;
colonialism and, 36–37;
colorblindness and, 131–32, 134,
159, 305n10; instrumental in
legitimizing European imperialism
and white supremacy, 36–37;
racism and, 47; South African,
130–32; whiteness and, 47; white
racial consciousness and, 166.
*See also specific areas of study and
disciplines*
academic freedom, colorblind
discourse of, 132
Acteal massacre, 19, 239–40
ActionSA, 80
affirmative action, 145, 305n8,
309n125; in Brazil, 133–34, 135;
demonization of, 137–38, 158;
people with disabilities and, 140;
in South Africa, 130–32, 135,
152, 154–55, 158–59; undercut
by arguments based on racial
hybridity, 84; in United States,
133, 135; white backlash and, 135;
white women and, 140
Africa, 204, 315n50
African American intellectuals, 125–
26, 295–96n4
African civilization, 28, 204–5
African colonies, 9, 89; Black
anticolonial mobilization in, 121;
Black resistance in, 9
African diaspora, 199–200, 201
Africanist persona, 75, 227

African National Congress (ANC),
154, 305n8
Africans, enslaved: Middle Passage
and, 27–28; resistance of, 206;
slavery and, 27–28
Afrikaans, 129–30
Afrikaners, 84
Afro-Caribbean literature, 195
Afrocentric practices, suppressed in
Latin America, 85
Afro-Cuban culture, 19, 108
Afro-cubanismo, 99
Afro-Cubans, 25; middle-class, 98–112
Afrodescendants, hierarchization of,
193
Afro-Latin American literature, 195
Afro-Mexicans, 24–25, 91–98, 225;
elision of, 96; relegated to margins
of national discourse, 19
Afro-Panamanian poets, Blackness and,
194–96
Afro-Panamanians, 45, 58–80;
depicted as racist, 212–13; West
Indian Panamanians and, 72, 191,
211–19
Afropessimism, 11, 23–24, 49
Afrophobia, 80, 263
Aguascalientes II, 238
Ahmed, Sara, 181–82
Aidoo, Lamonte, 113, 114
Alagoas, Brazil, 122
Alcoff, Linda Martín, 13, 165; "What
Should White People Do?," 168
Alexander, Michelle, 16
Alfaro, José Eloy, 60
Alfaro, Olmedo, 58, 61–62, 91, 92,
112, 264, 294n66; background
of, 60; British and USAmerican
writers in, 71–72; complicity

365

Alfaro, Olmedo (*continued*)
with US imperialism, 60–61, 73; demonization of West Indians, 68–69, 72–73, 75–76, 80; divide-and-conquer strategy and, 72; objection to assimilation of West Indians, 70–72; *El peligro antillano en la América Central: La defensa de la raza* (The West Indian Danger in Central America: The Defense of the Race), 45, 58–80, 62–80, 191, 208; positional superiority of, 73, 74; silencing of cimarronaje by, 76–77

Alonso, Ana María, 317n19
Althusser, Louis, 278n43
Alurista, 226; *Floricanto en Aztlán*, 257
amaXhosa, 28
Anaya, Rudolf, *Heart of Aztlán*, 226
Anglo-Indian population, 93
Angola, 25, 114, 122
Angolan independence war, 122
Anthropology Museum, Mexico City, 251
anti-affirmative action arguments, 133–34
anti-apartheid struggle, 154
anti-Blackness, 7, 49, 223; colorblindness and, 11, 48; Cubena and, 210, 213, 214, 219; Freyre and, 120–22; global dimensions of, 50; the Human, category of and, 152–53; hybridity and, 125; immigration and, 264; Kamel and, 145; liberalism and, 192; Ortiz and, 98–112; in Panama, 45, 190; reinscription of, 222; reproduction of, 11; Rodriguez and, 124; silencing of, 247; Vasconcelos and, 95, 96; white investment in, 90; white liberalism and, 161–86; white supremacy and, 30
anti-Black politics, 47
anti-Black racism, 3, 51; disavowal of, 160; Escobar and, 196; liberals and, 193. *See also* anti-Blackness
anti-Black violence, 1–3; Humanness and, 30; protests against, 4; state-sanctioned, 4, 15–16, 17

anti-immigrant propaganda, populist deployment of, 69
anti-Indigeneity, 223; hybridity and, 125; state-sanctioned anti-Indigenous violence, 15
antillanos, vs. coloniales, 79
antiracism, 48, 151; appropriation of, 72, 161–86; deliberate misreading of, 72; white, 47–48, 161–86
antisemitism, 51, 159
antislavery movement, 185–86. *See also* abolition
anti–West Indian propaganda, 213
Anzaldúa, Gloria, 251–52; *Borderlands/La Frontera*, 228–29, 252, 257, 320n97; Indigenous traditions and, 251–52; on mestizaje, 228–29; on Native American spirituality, 256; "The New Mestiza Nation: A Multicultural Movement," 219–20; on romanticization of homosexuality, 258–59
apartheid, 8, 17, 46, 112, 156, 309n125, 310n8; Derrida on, 151; formal dismantlement of, 12; Paton's defense of, 162–63; racial classification and, 155
"apprenticeship," 40
appropriation, 38, 72
Argentina, European immigration to, 84
Arias, Arnulfo, 66, 191–92
Arizona, 224
Armstrong, Nancy, 192
Arroyo, Justo, 20
artificial integration, 110
Arvin, Maile, 92
assimilation, 297–99n10; mestizaje and, 92; theories of, 46; transculturation and, 89
assimilation discourses, racist paradox of, 71
assimilation policies, 98
Association of Multiethnic Americans, 82
Attwell, David, 100
Australia, 4, 8
authenticity, politics of, 257
Avatar, 237

INDEX

aversive racism, 15, 282n68

Aztec mythology, 245–46, 252–53, 257, 320–21n100

Aztecs, 94, 205, 225–26, 246, 247, 249, 254–55, 317n19. *See also* Aztec mythology

Aztlán, 224–26, 317n15

Baartman, Sara, 40

Bailey, Alison, 167

Baldwin, James, 166, 185

Bam, June, 286n142

Bantustans, 150, 163

Barbera, Salvatore "Nuccio," 20

Barker, Martin, 278–81n50, 281n56

Barnes, Ernie, 75

Barrow, Alberto, 20

Bayano, 76

Beaglehole, Ernest, 115

Bebout, Lee, 225

BEE (Black Economic Empowerment), 154–55

behavioral traits: fabrication of, 44 (*see also* stereotypes)

Beleño, Joaquín: *Curundú*, 197; *Gamboa Road Gang/Los forzados de Gamboa*, 197–98; *Luna verde*, 197

Bell, Derrick, 64; *Faces at the Bottom of the Well*, 50

Benatar, David, "Why Samantha Vice Is Wrong on Whiteness," 172–73

Bernasconi, Robert, 165

Bhabha, Homi, 125

Biden, Joe, 267

Biko, Steve, 47, 110, 141, 150, 151–52, 156, 159, 161–66, 182, 183, 185, 204; "Black Consciousness and the Quest for a True Humanity," 129; "Black Souls in White Skins?," 161, 180; cofounding of SASO, 176–77; "Our Strategy for Liberation," 189; on white liberals, 163–64; "White Racism and Black Consciousness," 175–77, 179–80

biological racism, 13–14

biologism, 124–25

biologization of culture, 44

biology, modern, 44

biomedical research, 125

Birmingham-Pokorny, Elba, 198–99

Black abolitionists, 185–86

Black anticolonial mobilization, 120–22

Black Atlantic, 125–26

Black body, enslaved, 34

Black bondage, white freedom and, 32–33

Black Brazilians, 24

Black consciousness, 48. *See also* Black Consciousness Movement

Black Consciousness Movement, 50, 120–22, 141, 151–52, 162, 164, 185, 204

Black elite, 17, 102, 125–26, 158, 295–96n4

Black empowerment, 109, 185

Black feminism, 222–23

Black immigrants, demonization of, 263–64

Black labor, 50, 65–66, 158, 163, 206, 264–65, 292–93n34

Black Liberation Collective, 135

Black liberation movements, 141–46, 151–52, 162, 184–85. *See also* *specific movements*

Black Lives Matter, 18

Black Mexicans. *See* Afro-Mexicans

Black middle class: in Brazil, 158; in Cuba, 98–112; in South Africa, 149

Black mobilization, 129–30; control of, 45; demonization of, 184

Blackness: Afro-Panamanian poets and, 194–96; Biko's definition of, 151–52; Chicana feminism and, 230; Chicana literature and, 230, 258–59; Chicanx identity and, 256–57; Chicanx mestizaje and, 224–25; criminality and, 112; in Cubena, 211, 213, 214–15, 219; disavowal of, 195, 224–25; Eurocentric humanism and, 286–87n155; heterosexuality and, 48; humanism and, 286–87n155; mestizaje and, 224–25, 235; Mexican indigenismo and, 224–25;

368INDEX

Blackness (*continued*)
in Panama, 58–80; in Panamanian
letters, 48, 194–99; Panamanian
national and racial imaginary and,
203; slavery and, 27; stereotypes
of, 214; transculturation, theory
of and, 101; Vasconcelos and, 91;
West Indianness and, 193
Black-only organizations, in South
Africa, 142
Black Panamanians, 1–2
Black Panthers, 141
Black people: commodification of, 75;
criminalization of, 74, 262; mass
incarceration of, 266; national
building and, 205–6; racial
hierarchy and, 259; recovering
histories of, 200; self-determination
and, 109–10; targeting of, 264–65;
treated as property, 29. *See also
specific groups*
Black poverty, white wealth and,
171–72
Black Power Movement, 88, 224, 248
Black Radical Tradition, 49, 164
Black refugees, 21
Black resistance, 50, 76; in African
colonies, 9, 121; demonization
of, 184; in Latin America, 76;
to Portuguese colonizers, 122;
to slavery, 27; suppression of,
87; white anxiety and, 119; to
white power, 164. *See also* Black
mobilization
Black self-determination, 176–77
Black students, higher education and,
135, 138
Black tax, 158
Black trans women, 248
Black USAmericans, 125–26, 225,
295–96n4
blindness, 51
Blom, Frans, 232
Blom, Gertrude Duby, 232
Bloom, Lawrence, 167
Blumenbach, Johann Friedrich, *De
generis humani varietate nativa* (*On
the Natural Varieties of Mankind*), 29
Boas, Franz, 92

Bocas del Toro province, Panama,
69–70
Bolívar, Simón, 63
Bolsonaro, Jair, 80, 134
Bonilla-Silva, Eduardo, 13, 36, 51, 69,
155, 278–81n50
Brazil, 6, 8, 16; abolition of slavery
and, 27; affirmative action in,
133–34, 135; African American
intellectuals and, 295–96n4;
anti-Black violence in, 4; Black
liberation movements in, 141,
143–47; Black middle class in,
158; class in, 157–58; disavowal
of racism in, 147; European
immigration to, 84; first
constitutional chapter of 1824, 33;
idealization of race relations in,
113–26, 295–96n4; mestiçagem
in, 87, 89, 112–23, 295–96n4;
passage of Lei Arinos, 117; police
violence in, 18; race in, 8, 17–
18, 24, 47, 81–82, 133, 143–47,
153, 157–58, 295–96n4, 296n6;
racial categories in, 81–82; racial
classification in, 143–47; racial
democracy in, 8, 17–18, 295–
96n4; racial fluidity in, 296n6;
racial inequality in, 24, 47, 133;
racial quotas in, 47, 153; racism
in, 81–82; right-wing politicians in,
80; segregation in, 114–15; skin
color in, 296n6; slavery in, 113–15,
116, 303n153; universities in, 132,
133, 143–44; white dominance in,
296n6; white intellectuals in, 45–
46; "whitening" of, 58; whitening
policies in, 84
Brazilian exceptionalism, 113
Brazilian House of Representatives,
123
Briticists, 288n194
British colonizers, racial mixture and,
93
British Empire, 28; abolition of slave
trade in, 42
Broeck, Sabine, 230
Brown, Michael, 2–3, 4, 10, 18
browning, 82, 126, 225

INDEX 369

brownness, as emancipatory, 82–83
Brown resistance, 50
Bryce, James, *The Relations of the Advanced and the Backward Races of Mankind*, 71–72
Burnett, Peter H., 27
Byrd, Jodi A., 251

California, 224
Cammarota, Julio, 319n69
Canada, 8
candomblé, 85
Cape Colony, 28, 40–42, 43–44
Cape of Good Hope, 28, 286n142
capitalism, 29; deracialization of, 157; racial capitalism, 29
capoeira, 85
Cardoso, Fernando Henrique, 147
Carrasco, Davíd, 321–22n124
Carter, Sheila, 210
Casa Na Bolom (House of the Jaguar), 232–33
Castillo, Ana, *The Mixquiahuala Letters*, 235
Castro, Fidel, 25
Central America: West Indian immigrants in, 58–80. *See also specific countries*
Césaire, Aimé, 1–4, 12, 15, 52, 190; *Discourse on Colonialism*, 26, 57; *Notebook of a Return to the Native Land*, 1, 4
Chac-Mool, 246, 253–56
change: obsession with, 12–13; as privileged mode through which scholars view racism, 14–15
chattel law, 31
Chauvin, Derek, 4
Chiapas, Mexico, 18, 19, 98, 231–32, 235, 238, 246
Chicago Defender, 295–96n4
Chicana decolonial imaginary, 251–52
Chicana feminism, 49, 222–23, 257–58, 318n33, 320n97; Blackness and, 230, 258–59; Chicana feminist theory, 222; intersectionality and, 257–58; relational dimensions of racism and, 257–58

Chicana identity: Black characters in Chicana literature and, 227; Indigenous identity and, 248–49; as mestiza, 222; positionality of, 252
Chicana indigenism, 48–49, 257; liberal logics reproduced by, 228–29; representation of Indigenous peoples and, 227–28. *See also* Chicana indigenist imaginaries
Chicana indigenist imaginaries, 49, 222, 227–29, 257–59; Africanist presence in, 227–28; decolonial imaginaries and, 257–58; Indigenist presence in, 227–30; techniques of othering and, 227–29
Chicana literature: Blackness and, 230, 258–59; Chicana literary imaginaries, 222; dehistoricization of relationship between Chicanx and Indigenous people in, 251–52; the human and the divine in, 251–52; the indígena and, 257 (*see also* Chicana indigenist imaginaries); the Other in, 48–49, 221–59. *See also specific authors*
Chicana self, Indigenous Other and, 258
Chicano Movement, 49–50, 205, 225, 244–45, 248, 249; Aztec warrior bravado and, 252; Black Power Movement and, 224; indigenism(o) and, 226–27 (*see also* Chicanx indigenism(o))
Chicanx cultural production, 49
Chicanx historiography, 322n139
Chicanx identity, 49, 222, 226–27, 229; Blackness and, 256–57; indigenism and, 224 (*see also* Chicanx indigenism); nationalist, 256–57; Native Americans and, 256–57
Chicanx indigenism(o), 223–27, 229, 235–36, 257
Chicanx mestizaje, 224–25, 257
Chicanx oppression, 223–24
Chicanxs, 205, 225–26, 251–52, 322n139

Chicanx subject, construction of, 49, 258

Christianity: invocation of, 42. *See also* Christianization; Roman Catholic Church

Christianization, 26, 42, 116

Cihuatateo, 246, 251, 252–53

cimarrón revolts (slave uprisings), 50, 76–77

civilization: imperialism disguised as, 26; progress and, 119

Civil Rights Movement, 12, 135, 234

class, 29, 48, 156–58

Clinton, Bill, 248

Club Atenas (Athens Club), 102, 104–5, 110

CNN, 266

Coatlicue, 246, 251–52

coded language, 32, 69

Coetzee, J. M., 192–93; *White Writing*, 43

collective Black liberation, 48

Colombia, cimarronaje (slave uprisings) in, 76

Colón, Panama, 1–2, 69–70

coloniales, vs. antillanos, 79

colonialism, 7, 26, 28–29, 34–35, 38–39, 48, 169–70; academic disciplines and, 36–37; colonial discourses, 7, 11, 257–58; contestation of, 49; critiques of, 222; Cubena and, 207–8; defense of, 46; disavowal and, 26; Freyre and, 115, 122–23; liberal humanism and, 7; official end of, 12; slavery and, 30, 277n28; in South Africa, 156; underwritten by lies, 33–34; undying, 261–67

colonialist fiction, 74, 75

colonial power(s): suppressing history of their own violence, 38–39; universities and, 132

coloniality, 52

colonos (settlers), 67

Colorado, 224

colorblind discourse, 6, 9–10, 48, 51, 52–53, 132–33, 258; of academic freedom, 132; colonial archive, 257–58; Cubena and, 207–11;

deployed to halt desegregation, 46–47; deployment of, 7–8; global popularity of, 23–24; invocation of Christianity and, 42; of neutrality, 37–38; of objectivity, 37–38; racism and, 2–3, 6, 15, 44, 263; of scientific knowledge, 37–38; slavery and, 32; time-tested, 26–43; white domination and, 15. *See also* colorblindness

colorblind jurisprudence, 135, 140

colorblindness, 11, 32, 48, 159; academia and, 131–32, 134, 159, 305n10; as act of epistemic violence, 144–45; decolonial literary imaginaries and, 11–12; definition of, 12; as engine of white supremacy, 6–7; as epistemology, 6, 52–53; epistemology of disavowal and, 22; free-market ideology and, 156–57; in Freyre, 113; historicization as a technology, 9; institutionalization of, 9, 10, 31, 49, 140, 142; in journalism, 134; law and, 6–7, 138–39; liberal humanism and, 11; literary criticism and, 50; malleability of, 52–53; meaning of the term, 51; modulated through national and transnational forces, 9; multiculturalism and, 149–50; nation building and, 57–80; nonracialism and, 154; rhetorical strategies of, 9–10; as structural rather than localized, 8; as technology, 6, 10, 39–40, 52–53, 63–64; as technology of white nation building, 63–64; as technology of white supremacy, 39–40; as tool of capacitation and incapacitation, 32; as tool of racial power, 262; in Trump's electoral campaign, 262–63; use of the term, 52; of white feminism, 49

colorblind racism, 6, 13, 15, 282n68

colorblind time, 25–26

colorblind tools, definition of, 7–8

colorblind white dominance, 15, 282n68

color-line, 7

INDEX

Columbus, Christopher (Cristoforo Colombo), 21, 26, 38–39, 43, 44, 243

Comas, Juan, 115

Comisión Nacional para el Desarrollo de los Pueblos Indígenas (National Commission for the Development of Indigenous Peoples), 98

common sense, disguise of, 9

Communist Party, Black section of, 141

Congreso Indigenista, 97

Conniff, Michael, 60, 292n16

consumption, 158

contract form, 31

Contreras, Sheila Marie, *Blood Lines*, 228

conversion. *See* Christianization

convict lease system, 16

Cooppan, Vilashini, 148

Cornejo Polar, Antonio, 86

Cortés, Hernán, 206

Crenshaw, Kimberlé, 23, 140, 223; "Demarginalizing the Intersection of Race and Sex: A Black Feminist Critique of Antidiscrimination Doctrine, Feminist Theory and Antiracist Politics," 223

criminality, Blackness and, 112

criminalization, of Black people, 74

critical philosophy of race, 47, 165, 166

critical race narrative, 237

critical race scholars, 9, 10

critical race theory (CRT), 49, 165, 166

critical whiteness studies, 47, 165, 166. *See also* whiteness studies

Cronje, Frans, 158

Cruz e Sousa, João, 195

Cuba, 6, 8, 19; Black middle class in, 98–112; European immigration to, 84–85; Jamaican and Haitian immigration to, 112; mestizaje in, 87; nationalist rhetoric in, 208; Negritud in, 48; plantations in, 28; prison population in, 19; racial inequality in, 24–25; slavery in, 108; white intellectuals in, 45–46

Cuban Communist Party, Black section of, 141

Cuban Revolution, 19

Cubena (Carlos Guillermo Wilson), 11, 48, 216–19; anti-Blackness and, 210, 213, 214, 219; Blackness and, 211, 213, 214–15, 219; Black Panamanian literary voice and, 204–5; *Chombo*, 48, 190, 191, 192, 193–94, 314n40; colonialism and, 207–8; colorblind discourse and, 207–11; denunciation of racism in Panama as well as United States, 208; reception of in the United States, 198–99; silenced in Panama, 198; West Indian Panamanians and, 191; white nationalism and, 191. *See also* Cubena (Carlos Guillermo Wilson), works of

Cubena (Carlos Guillermo Wilson), works of: ableism in, 210; African history and mythology and, 204–5; *Chombo*, 200, 201, 202, 205–19; "La Depravada" (The Depraved), 214–15, 217; education in, 216–19; "La Fiesta" (The Party), 217; heteropatriarchal homogeneity and, 193–94; homosexuality in, 214–15, 219; imperialism in, 207–8; "Interview with Dr. Carlos Guillermo Wilson," 189; inversion of racial hierarchy in, 213–14; liberal individualism in, 189–219; mestizaje in, 216–17; *La misión secreta* (The Secret Mission), 206–7; *Los nietos de Felicidad Dolores* (The Grandchildren of Felicidad Dolores), 48, 191–94, 200, 205–19, 315n47, 315n71; "La poesía afro-panameña" (Afro-Panamanian Poetry), 194–95; portrayal of Africa in, 217–18; retrospective gaze in, 206–7; sexuality in, 214–15, 219; slavery in, 199–200, 207–8; unity in, 214–15, 219; valorization of Western culture in, 217–19; West Indian identity in, 207; whiteness in, 218–19

372

INDEX

cult of whiteness: Cruz e Sousa and, 195; Hernández and, 196–97
cultural deficiency, discourse of, 155–56, 290n213
cultural hybridization, as mutual exchange, 88–89
culturalist racism, 15, 282n68
cultural racism, 6, 13–14, 15, 44, 278–81n50, 282n68
cultural studies, 125
culture, biologization of, 44
Curry, Tommy, 165

daltonico, 52
Damas, Léon, 190
Dances with Wolves, 237, 243
D'Anghiera, Peter Martyr, *De Orbe Novo*, 77
D'Annunzio, Gabriele, 21
danza azteca, 253
Darién, Panama, 70, 77
Darwinism, 44, 70
da Silva, Denise Ferreira, 86, 101
Dead Prez, "They Schools," 16
death penalty, 16
decolonial feminist practice, 223
decolonial imaginaries, 48, 49, 257–58, 278n44
decolonial movements, 115
decolonial theory, 49–50
decolonization, 30, 130, 280
deconstructionism, 151
decontextualization, 72
dehistoricization, 72
dehumanization, 34, 75–76
Delgado, José Vicente, 1–2, 6, 79–80
demographics, in United States, 13
Derrida, Jacques, 151; "Racism's Last Word," 149
desegregation: colorblind rhetoric deployed to halt, 46–47; undercutting of, 46–47; in United States, 135, 138, 144, 170; US Supreme Court and, 135–36, 138, 139–40, 170; white mobilization against, 46–47, 129–60; white resistance to, 266
de Souza, Carlos, 18

de Souza, Cleiton, 18
de Zurara, Gomes Eanes, *The Chronicle of the Discovery and Conquest of Guinea*, 27
Díaz, Porfirio, 84
La difesa della razza (The Defense of the Race), 62
differences: conflation of, 223 (*see also* racial difference)
differentialist racism, 15, 282n68
disavowal, 2–3, 38; as basis for construct of "the Negro," 29–30; as basis for idea of race, 29–30; of Blackness, 195, 224–25; epistemology of, 9, 22, 49, 95, 111, 150; foregrounding, 22–23; as global, 21–24; Lacanian sense of, 23; of racism, 5–8, 12, 21–24, 28, 80, 116, 132–33, 147, 153–55, 159–60, 207–11, 266–67; shifting conceptual lens from ignorance to, 23; as technology of racial power, 80; of white privilege, 84, 155, 156
disenfranchisement, 16
disguise, 5–6, 38
dispossession, 27, 34
dissimulation, 28–29, 38
divide-and-conquer strategy, 61–62, 64, 69, 72, 79, 122, 150, 191
the divine, in Chicana literature, 251–52
Doane, Woody, 22
Domingos Júnior, Wilton, 18
Douglass, Frederick, 83, 99
Du Bois, W. E. B., 6–7, 32, 88, 99, 102, 295–96n4
Duke, David, 265
Dunham, Katherine, 116
Dutch colonizers, 43, 122
Dutch East India Company (DEIC), 28
Dutton, Peter, 265
Dylan, Bob, 168

East Indies, 28
Ecuador, cimarronaje (slave uprisings) in, 76
Edison, Tomás Wayne, 315n71

INDEX

Ejército Zapatista de Liberación Nacional (Zapatista Army of National Liberation, EZLN), 18–19, 231, 238–39. *See also* Zapatista Movement
Ellison, Ralph, 22, 203–4
empathy, conceptual framework of, 118
the End of the world, 4
Engerman, Stanley, 287n158
Enlightenment, 32–33, 152
environmental racism, 16, 321n103
epistemology: colorblindness as, 52–53; of disavowal, 49, 95, 111, 150; racist, 35–36; white, 23, 137
equality, discourses of, 32–33
Erasmus, Zimitri, 152; "Apartheid Race Categories: Daring to Question Their Continued Use," 151–52; "Confronting the Categories: Equitable Admissions without Apartheid Race Classification," 152
Erdrich, Louise, *Tracks*, 237
Escobar, Federico, 195–96; anti-Black racism and, 196; "Nieblas" (Mists), 195–96
ESCUDO CUBENA (Cubena Shield), 200–201, 216
Esteva-Fabregat, Claudio, 124
ethnicity, 48, 150
ethnography, 74, 75
eugenics, 9, 37–38, 44–46, 57–58, 71, 124–25, 282n61; in Latin America, 88, 91, 100–101; Ortiz and, 100–101; racial purity and, 59; in United States, 92
Euripides, *Medea*, 245, 320–21n100
Eurocentric humanism, Blackness and, 286–87n155
Euromodernity, 217
Europe, 21, 45, 52, 68, 80, 86, 101, 192, 205–6, 225, 263. *See also* European Union; *specific countries*
European immigration, to Latin America, 84–85
European imperialism, legitimized by academic disciplines, 36–37
European racialism, roots of, 286n147

European Union, 265
exception clause, 16
Eze, Emmanuel, 165

Fanon, Frantz, 15, 23, 30, 33, 51, 214, 217, 265, 278–81n50, 281n56; *Black Skin, White Masks*, 195; "Racism and Culture," 1, 13–14; "West Indians and Africans," 195; *The Wretched of the Earth*, 205, 261
Farage, Nigel, 80
Farley, Anthony, 15
farm murders, as white discourse, 265
favelas, 16, 211
Federal University of Rio de Janeiro, Institute of Philosophy and Social Sciences, 134
feminism, Black, 222–23; Chicana, 49, 222–23, 257–58, 318n33, 320n97; indigenism and, 257 (*see also* Chicana feminism); white, 7, 49, 222–23; women of color feminism, 49
Ferdinand of Spain, 38–39
Ferguson, Missouri, 2–3, 18
Ferguson, Roderick, 193–94
Fernandes, Luis, 123
Fernández, Carlos, "La Raza and the Melting Pot: A Comparative Look at Multiethnicity," 82
Fernandez, Ronald, 297–99n10
fiction, theory and, 50
Fields, Barbara J., 14, 124
Fields, Karen E., 14, 124
First Congress of the Black Panamanian, 57
Floyd, George, 3–4, 21
Fogel, Robert, 287n158
formal-race unconnectedness, 140
formerly enslaved people, 299n30
Forrest Gump, 234, 237, 241
Forum of Black Journalists, 142
Foucault, Michel, 5, 276n21
Fourteenth Amendment, equal protection clause, 136
France, 4, 78, 80
freedom, discourses of, 32–33

374 INDEX

free-market ideology, 18–19, 156–57.
 See also capitalism
Freyre, Gilberto, 9, 46, 87–88, 90,
 113, 124; anti-Blackness in,
 120–22; *Casa-grande e senzala:*
 formação da família brasileira sob
 o regime da economia patriarcal
 (*The Masters and the Slaves:*
 A Study in the Development of
 Brazilian Civilization), 87, 113,
 115, 145; colonialism and, 115,
 122–23; displacement of racism
 by, 117–18; epistemology of
 disavowal and, 126; Kamel and,
 145–46; misreadings of, 123;
 on racial discrimination, 116;
 reception of, 123; "Report on
 the Most Important and Most
 Effective Methods for Eliminating
 Racial Conflicts, Tensions, and
 Discriminatory Practices Employed
 with Positive Results in Countries
 in Different Geographical Regions,
 in Particular Countries Where
 Conditions Approximate Most
 Closely Those of the Union of
 South Africa," 46, 87, 89, 112–23,
 124; support for colonialism, 115
Fry, Peter, *A persistência da raça: ensaios*
 antropológicos sobre o Brasil e a
 África austral (The Persistence of
 Race: Anthropological Essays on
 Brazil and Southern Africa), 146–47
fungibility, 34
future of whiteness thesis, 13

Gage, Thomas, 77
Gallers, Anita, 213
García Canclini, Néstor, 125
Garuba, Harry, 137
Garvey, John, 168
Garvey, Marcus, 66, 102, 202
Gauteng, 17
gay rights discourses, 247–48
gender, 48, 223. *See also* feminism
gender-based violence, 223
genocide, 27, 45–46; mestizaje and,
 45–46, 70–71, 81–126; silencing
 of, 68

Genova, Italy, 21
Gilliam, Angela, 81
Gilmore, Ruth Wilson, 15–16
Gilroy, Paul, 125–26, 190, 278–81n50,
 281n56
Ginsberg, Morris, 115
Goffman, Alice, *On the Run: Fugitive*
 Life in an American City, 74, 75
gold, 77, 78
Gold Roll (Panama Canal Zone), 78
Gómez de Avellaneda, Gertrudis,
 312–13n1
Gordon, Lewis R., 23, 126, 165, 217
Gotanda, Neil, 140
Graham v. Connor, 10
Gramsci, Antonio, 278–81n50
Greaves, Lester León, 197–98
Greece, 295n101
Griffith, D. W., 58
Group Areas Act, 155
Guidotti-Hérnandez, Nicole, 322n139
Guillén, Nicolás, 190, 203, 208
Gutiérrez, Eulalio, 91
Gutiérrez-Jones, Carl, 170, 237

Haggerty, Daniel, "White Shame:
 Responsibility and Moral
 Emotions," 180–81
Haiti, 40, 44, 76
Haitian Revolution, 40, 44
Haitians, 112
Halley, Janet, 247
Hamilton, Charles, 141; *Black Power:*
 The Politics of Liberation, 118
Harlan, John Marshall, 139
Harney, Stefano, 3, 132
Harris, Cheryl, 29, 182
Harris, Kamala, 267
Hartman, Saidiya, 16, 34, 193, 205;
 Scenes of Subjection, 193
Hawai'i, Polynesians in, 92
Hellwig, David, 295–96n4
Hernández, Gaspar Octavio, 195; "El
 culto del idioma" (The Cult of
 Language), 197; cult of whiteness
 and, 196–97; "Ergo Sum," 197
Herrera, Juan Felipe, *Mayan Drifter:*
 Chicano Poet in the Lowlands of
 America, 232–33, 235

INDEX

heteropatriarchy, 194, 218, 222, 245;
as antithetical to Black liberation,
48; of the Chicano Movement,
226; critique of heteropatriarchy
in Chicana literature, 49, 226–
27, 249; Cubena and, 190;
heteropatriarchal homogeneity,
193; heteropatriarchal ideologies,
219; mobilization of race to
critique heteropatriarchy, 230;
Wright and, 194
heterosexuality, Blackness and, 48
higher education, 135, 138. *See also*
education; universities
Hispaniola, 38–39
history, manipulation of, 155
Hitler, Adolf, 62, 210, 211
Hoeg, Jerry, 100
Holborn, Lucy, 309n125
Holland, 28
Holocaust denial, 160
homophobia, 239–40, 247
homosexuality, 239–40, 258–59
Hooker, Juliet, 88
hooks, bell, 199–200
Hosang, Daniel Martinez, 32
Hugo, Victor, 217
Huitzilopochtli, 246
the Human, category of, 30, 35, 111,
116, 118, 152–53, 286–87n155
the human, in Chicana literature,
251–52
humanism, 7, 11, 48, 152–53, 286–
87n155, 308n88
humanities, 10, 132
Humanness, anti-Black violence and, 30
hybridity, 84, 86, 125, 145, 147–49;
anti-Blackness and, 125; anti-
Indigeneity and, 125; racism and,
147–49; romanticization of, 126;
white supremacy and, 84, 148. *See
also* mestizaje

ideology, definition of, 278n43
idleness, 43
Ignatiev, Noel, 168
ignorance. *See* white ignorance
immigrants: demonization of, 262,
263–64; exploitation of, 264–65;

Latinx, 262, 266, 297–99n10;
racialized, 59; undocumented,
249–51, 259, 262–63
immigration, 57–58; anti-Blackness
and, 264; European immigration
to Latin America, 84–85; mestizaje
and, 297–99n10; in United States,
322n2
imperialism, 28–29, 207–8; disguised
as civilization and Christianization,
26, 42; legitimized by academic
disciplines, 36–37. *See also* US
imperialism
impurity, 126. *See also* miscegenation
Inca, 94
incarceration, 15; in Brazil, 85; in
Cuba, 19; labor exploitation and,
16; mass, 16, 266; Ortiz advocating
for, 104; slavery and, 282n75
India, 93
indianismo, 318n36
Indian South Africans, 151
indigeneity: affirmation of, 222;
Afrikaners' claims to, 84; Chicana
literature and, 257 (*see also*
Chicana indigenist imaginaries);
politics of, 257; in Vasconcelos,
91
indigenism(o), 97, 222, 251, 257,
318n36
Indigenous history, 205
Indigenous identity, 225–26, 248–49,
255–56
Indigenous knowledge, 252
Indigenous mythology, 205, 225–26.
See also specific mythologies
the Indigenous Other, 49, 229, 257
Indigenous people, 230–41; banning
of enslavement of, 42; of Cape
of Good Hope, 28; Chicano
indigenism(o) and, 227–30
(*see also* Chicana indigenism);
Chicanxs and, 251–52, 322n139;
displacement of, 222; European
violence during conquest and, 26–
27; genocide of, 26–27, 77, 96,
256, 257; loss of sovereignty and,
256; in Mexico, 18–19, 91–98; of
Mexico vs. United States, 93–94;

INDEX

Indigenous people (*continued*)
oppression of, 258; purported
extinction of, 93–94; represented
in Chicana literature, 229–30;
romanticization of, 93–94, 226;
US violence against, 27. *See also
specific groups*
Indigenous resistance, 50, 87, 94, 98
Indigenous subjectivity: appropriation
of, 93–94, 226, 252, 257, 258;
Chicana collective memory and,
252
Indigenous traditions, 251–52
Individual, white appropriation of
category of, 35–36
individualism, liberal humanism and,
152–53
individual racism, structural racism
and, 164, 216, 218–19
inequality: attributed to class rather
than race, 156–58; interracial
vs. intraracial, 157; in Panama
Canal Zone, 78–79; racism and,
308–9n103; in South African
universities, 130–31. *See also* racial
inequality
inhumanity, language used to justify,
33–34
injustice, 171–72, 178–79
Institute of Race Relations (IRR), 158–
59, 309n125
Institute of Statistics (INEGI)
(Mexico), 285n116
institutional racism, 47–48, 118–
19, 154, 166, 182, 183–84, 186,
191–92
Instituto Nacional Indigenista (INI),
97, 98
integration, 98, 105, 118, 136;
artificial integration, 105, 110;
national integration, 105, 110; real
integration,105; self-determination
and, 110; voluntary integration
program, 136
Interlandi, Telesio, 62
International Monetary Fund, 24
Interracial/Intercultural Pride (I-Pride),
83
interracial organizing, control of, 45

intersectionality, 49; Chicana feminism
and, 257–58; racial subordination
and, 222; theory of, 223
intraracial inequality, in South Africa,
149, 157
Islamic extremists, 263
Italy, 8, 20–21, 295n101; anti-
Blackness in, 264; anti-Black
violence in, 4, 20; demonization of
immigrants in, 263–64; fascism in,
21, 62; racial inequality in, 264–
65; right-wing politicians in, 80;
Ortiz ambassador in, 104

Jackson, George, 261; *Blood in My Eye*,
261, 266
Jackson, Richard, 217
Jackson, Shirley, 312–13n1
Jackson, Zakiyyah Iman, 81, 84, 125,
286–87n155
Jaén, Justo, 1–2, 3, 4, 6, 61, 79–80,
275n1
Jamaican immigrants, 65, 112, 190.
See also West Indian immigrants
James, C. L. R., 33, 99; *The Black
Jacobins*, 27–28
Jameson, Fredric, 278n43
JanMohamed, Abdul R., 44, 74, 213
Jansen, Jonathan, 138
Jan Smuts student residence, 130, 305n3
Jefferson, Thomas, 33
Jefferson County, Kentucky, 47, 133,
136, 138, 139–40
Jesuits, 287n158
Jews, 25, 28, 51, 317
Jim Crow, 8, 16
João IV, 84
Johannesburg Stock Exchange, 157
Johnson, Lyndon B., 135
Jolly, Rosemary, 151; "Rehearsals
of Liberation: Contemporary
Postcolonial Discourse and the
New South Africa," 149–51
Jones, Gayl, *Corregidora*, 295–96n4
Jones, Ward, 167
Jooste, Franz, 142
Jordan, David Starr, 57
journalism, colorblindness in, 134
Journal of Social Philosophy, 166

INDEX

Kamel, Ali, 153; anti-Blackness in, 145;
Freyre and, 145–46; *Não somos
racistas: uma reação aos que querem
nos transformar numa nação bicolor*
(We Are Not Racist: A Reaction to
Those Who Want to Transform Us
into a Bicolor Nation), 47, 133–34,
144–47, 153, 157–58
Kant, Immanuel, 33, 36, 288n177
Katopodis, Katy, 142
Katz, Judith, 168
Kelley, Robin D. G., 75, 156
Kennedy, Anthony, 147
Khoena, 28, 39–42, 43–44, 76, 266,
286n142
Khoe-San, 28, 33–34, 286n142
Khoi, 286n142
Khoikhoi, 286n142
Kim, Claire Jean, 69, 276–77n22
King, Martin Luther, Jr., 73, 261;
*Where Do We Go from Here: Chaos
or Community?*, 266
King, Tiffany Lethabo, 43
kitchenettes, 92
Kommandokorps, 142
Krauze, Enrique, 123–24; *La historia
cuenta*, 68
Ku Klux Klan, 91, 207, 209, 210

La Barre, 76
labor: Black, 50, 65–66, 158, 163, 206,
264–65, 292–93n34; exploitation
of, 16, 158, 264–65; incarcerated,
16; race and, 29
labor movement, Panamanian, 50,
65–66
Lacan, Jacques, 23
Lacandón people, 231–32, 237–38
Lacerda, João Batista de, 58, 71
Lafont, Anne, 29
Lahaye Guerra, Rosa María de, 99
laissez-faire racism, 15, 282n68
La Llorona, 245, 252–53, 320–21n100
land redistribution, 129–60, 177–78,
265
land theft, 29
Larsen, Nella, *Passing*, 295–96n4
Latin America: Black resistance in, 76;
cimarrón revolts (slave uprisings)

in, 50; eugenics in, 88; European
immigration to, 84; mestizo elites
in, 84–85; mixed-race standard
in, 92; modernization in, 84–85;
multiculturalism in, 86–87; racial
genocide in, 68; racial history of,
46; racial purity in, 92–93; racism
in, 68, 92–93, 123–24, 190, 207–
11, 208; racist violence in, 68, 208;
repression of Black and Indigenous
communities and practices in, 85;
romanticization of race relations
in, 81–82; segregation in, 92–93;
US imperialism in, 60–61; white
elites in, 84–85; white intellectuals
in, 84–126; whiteness in, 84–85;
whitening policies in, 84–86; white
people in, 207–11. *See also specific
countries*
Latin Americanization thesis, 13
Latinx immigrants, 262, 266,
297–99n10
Latinx people, targeting of, 264–65
Latorre, Guisela, 222
law, 47; as colorblind tool, 31, 138–39;
as instrument of ontologization,
30–31; reproduction of white
power and, 30–31, 132–33, 135;
as technology of white supremacy,
30–31. *See also* colorblind
jurisprudence
laziness: stereotype of, 43–44. *See also*
idleness
Leach, Colin Wayne, 14
Lega Nord (Northern League), 263–64
legitimacy, anxiety over one's, 258
Lei Arinos, 117
Le Pen, Marie, 80
Lesbian Plenary Session, 1988
National Women's Studies
Association conference, 258–59
Levi-Strauss, Claude, 115
Lewis, Lancelot, 294n84
LGBTQ people, 193, 247–48. *See also*
homosexuality; white gay rights
discourses; *specific groups*
liberal humanism, 7, 11, 48, 152–53,
308n88
liberal individualism, 48, 189–219

378

liberalism, 59–60, 163–64, 184, 186, 192, 193; anti-Blackness and, 161–86; dangers of, 164
liberals, 163–64, 184, 186; discursive practices, 164; white supremacy and, 47, 166
Libya, 265
lies, 38; institutionalization of, 8
life expectancy, discrepancy in, 25–26
like-race comparisons, 247
Limón, Graciela, 11; anxiety about Chicana authenticity in Indigenous spaces, 258; appropriation of Blackness and, 258–59; collapse of Chicana and Indigenous subjectivities in, 258–59; *Erased Faces*, 48–49, 230–41, 257, 258, 318n33; homosexuality in, 240; reproduction of colonial images of Indigenous peoples in, 236; strategic Blackness and, 234–35; white saviorism and, 237–38
Limón, José, 317n19
linear time, 12
Linnaeus, Carolus, *Systema Naturae*, 29
Lipsitz, George, 52, 158, 172
literacy tests, 16
literary scholarship: British, 288n194; conventions of, 50; racial discourses and, 50, 278n41
Lizardi, José Joaquín Férnandez, 312–13n1
Lombroso, Cesare, 104; *L'uomo bianco e l'uomo di colore: Letture sull'origine e le varietà delle razze umane* (The White Man and the Man of Color: Lectures on the Origins and Varieties of the Human Races, 1871), 37–38, 44, 107, 289–90n200; *L'uomo delinquente studiato in rapporto alla antropologia, alla medicina legale ed alle discipline carcerarie* (*Criminal Man*, 1876), 38
Lomelí, Francisco A., 226
the long emancipation, 65
Lonmin Public Limited Company, 17
López-Calvo, Ignacio, 318n33

Lorde, Audre, 223; "The Master's Tools Will Never Dismantle the Master's House," 7, 11; "The Uses of Anger: Women Responding to Racism," 180
Lott, Eric, 168
Louisiana, 139
Lowe, Lisa, 99, 192
loyalty, racist myth of, 75–76
Lugones, María, 165
Lund, Joshua, 100, 123
Lusotropicalism, 113
lynching, 16

Mahumapelo, Supra, 17
Makhanda, South Africa, 130
Malan, Rian, 169
Malcolm X, 15, 25, 141–42
Malinowski, Bronislaw, 111–12
Mamdani, Mahmood, *Citizen and Subject*, 150
Manichean allegory, 74, 75, 213
Manzano, Juan Francisco, *Autobiografía de un esclavo* (*Autobiography of a Slave*), 195
Marcos, Subcomandante, "Closing Remarks at the First Intercontinental *Encuentro* for Humanity and against Neoliberalism," 238–39
Maré, Gerhard, *Declassified*, 146–47, 153, 154, 157, 158, 160
Mariátegui, José Carlos, 318n36
Marikana massacre, 17
the mark of the plural, 35, 72
maroons, 122
Marriott, David, 28, 34–35
Martínez, Iván Flores, 285n116
Marxism, 193
Mashaba, Herman, 80
mass deportation, 266
the master, 1, 6, 7, 11–12, 108, 113, 222, 299n30; as equivalent of Human, 118; colonial masters, 122; "The Master's Tools Will Never Dismantle the Master's House," 7, 11; white women and, 7. *See also* mistress
Maya, 94, 98, 205, 225, 231, 246, 257, 321–22n124

INDEX 379

Maya languages, 98
Maya mythology, 257
Mbeki, Thabo, 147
McCullough, David, 292–93n34
McKaiser, Eusebius, 166, 167
McNee, Malcolm, 123
Medea, 244–45, 252–53, 256, 320–21n100
the media, 21, 47, 130, 132, 134, 142, 147
medicine, and biological understandings of race, 281n61
Melamed, Jodi, 59–60, 278n41
Memmi, Albert, 72; *The Colonizer and the Colonized*, 34–35
mental slavery, 201, 216–17
merit, 153, 263
meritocracies, 153
Mesoamerican civilization, 205–6
Mesoamerican mythology, 225, 227. *See also specific mythologies*
mestiçagem, 9, 86, 87, 89, 112–23, 295–96n4; disavowal of racism and, 147; as efficient method of racial control, 119–23. *See also* mestizaje
mestiza identity, embrace of, 222
mestizaje, 45–46, 81–126, 222; Anzaldúa on, 228–29; assimilation and, 92; Blackness and, 224–25, 235; in Brazil (*see* mestiçagem); in Cuba, 87; as effective method of whitening, 86; as eugenic solution, 9, 92, 124; genocide and, 45–46, 70–71, 81–126; idealization of, 124; immigration and, 297–99n10; as means of modernizing Indigenous people, 90–91; in Mexico, 18–19, 87, 93–94; modernization and, 94–95; as racial degeneration, 86; racial harmony and, 95; as racial technology, 72; racist violence and, 208; romanticization of, 46, 81–82, 95, 126; Spanish colonizers and, 92–93, 96; state-sponsored, 257; as state-sponsored ideology, 93–94; as tool of "whitening," 46; transculturation

and, 108, 111; white deployment of, 72; white supremacy and, 89–90; white USAmericans and, 90–98
mestizos: mestizo elites, 84–85; mestizo futurisms, 88; mestizo intellectuals, 85, 86; mestizo Panamanians, 1–2
method, note on, 49–53
Mexican Americans, 297–99n10; Indigenous roots and, 225–26; Spanish heritage and, 225
Mexican-American War, 223–24
Mexican indigenismo, Blackness and, 224–25
Mexican Instituto Nacional Indigenista (INI), 232
Mexican nationalism, Aztec mythology and, 253
Mexican Revolution, 85
Mexico, 6, 8, 50, 322n139; anti-Black violence in, 4; assimilation policies in, 98; cimarronaje (slave uprisings) in, 76; European immigration to, 84; indigenismo in, 97; Indigenous people in, 18–19, 91–98; Indigenous resistance in, 98 (*see also* Zapatista Movement); mestizaje in, 18, 87, 93–94; multiculturalism in, 97; racial hierarchy in, 95; racial inequality in, 24; state-sponsored aid to Indigenous populations in, 97–98; United States and, 223–24; white intellectuals in, 45–46; Yanga rebellion in, 19
Meyer, Deon, *The Woman in the Blue Cloak*, 234
Middle Passage, 27
migrants, 21. *See also* immigrants
Miller-Young, Mireille, 233
Millin, Sarah Gertrude, *White Africans Are Also People*, 33–34
Mills, Charles, 22, 23, 165, 167, 192, 213
minstrel shows, in United States, 68
the mistress, 113, 299; as equivalent to the master, 7
miscegenation, 58, 70, 108, 291n6

380   INDEX

miscegenation ideology, anti-African bias of, 83

Mngxitama, Andile, 152, 212–13, 308n88; "End to Whiteness as a Black Issue," 184

modernity: colonial modernity 5, 7; liberal-capitalist modernity, 60; the mestizo as embodiment of, 94; Western modernity, 12. *See also* Euromodernity

modernization, in Latin America, 84–85, 94–95

Monroe, James, 292n17

Monroe Doctrine, 292n17

Montaigne, Michel de, 257

Moore, Carlos, 19; *Pichón*, 191

Moraga, Cherríe, 11, 223; anti-Blackness and, 249; anxiety about Chicana authenticity in Indigenous spaces, 258; Blackness and, 244–45, 249, 258–59. *See also* Moraga, Cherríe, works of

Moraga, Cherríe, works of: collapse of Chicana and Indigenous subjectivities in, 258–59; exclusion of Black people and Native Americans from Chicanx community, 256–57; "La Güera," 219; *The Hungry Woman: A Mexican Medea*, 48–49, 229–30, 241–59, 257, 258, 320–21n100, 320n97; Indigenous identity and, 241–59, 255–56; Indigenous traditions and, 251–52; *The Last Generation*, 248; *Loving in the War Years*, 248; pastiche aesthetics of Indigenous Chicanx identity in, 255–56; "Pesadilla," 248; privileging of nationalist Chicanx identity by, 256–57; "Queer Aztlán: The Reformation of the Chicano Tribe," 226–27; racial essentialism in, 254–55; sexual politics in, 247, 249–50; subordination of Indigenous characters in, 242–43; *This Bridge Called My Back*, 248; *A Xicana Codex of Changing Consciousness*, 252

morenos, 294n66

Morrison, Toni, 32, 50, 75, 214; *Playing in the Dark*, 227, 252, 286–87n155

Moten, Fred, 3, 35, 132, 282n75

Moura, Clovis, 84

Movimento Negro (Black Movement), 141, 143–47

Moya, Paula, 10–11

Mozambique, 114, 116

Mudimbe, V. Y., 315n50

mulatto escape hatch, 296n6

multiculturalism, 229; colorblindness and, 149–50; hegemonic, 49; in Latin America, 86–87, 97; in Mexico, 97

multiracial identity: appropriation of, 83; legal recognition of, 83; politicization of, 83

multiracialism, 83

Murakawa, Naomi, 12

Museo di Antropologia Criminale Cesare Lombroso (Cesare Lombroso Museum of Criminal Anthropology) at the University of Torino, 104

Museum of Natural History, New York City, 251–52

Muslim travel ban, 263

Mussolini, Benito, 62

mutuality of harm hypothesis, 170

mythic discourses: racial regimes and, 6, 9, 34–35. *See also specific mythologies*

myth of time as racial healer, 26. *See also* colorblind time

mythohistorical interventions, 225

Nascimento, Abdias, 81, 83, 114, 122, 144, 208

Nascimento, Elisa Larkin, 141

National Chicano Youth Liberation Conference, Denver Colorado, 224

National Conference on Race Betterment, 45, 57–58

National Day of Action against Racism and Student Debt, 135

national identity, Panamanian history and, 203

INDEX   381

nationalist rhetoric, 89, 208, 212–13, 263
nationality, 48
national liberation movements, 89
National Party (NP), 305n8
National Press of Panama, 66
national unity, discourse of, 212–13
nation building, 46, 57–80, 63–64, 205–6; colorblindness as technology of, 63–64
Native Americans, 94, 254, 256–57. *See also specific groups*
Nattrass, Nicoli, *Class, Race, and Inequality in South Africa*, 156–57
negrismo, 194, 312–13n1
Negritud, 48, 189–90, 194, 195, 312–13n1
Negritude, 190
"the Negro," 29–30, 42, 259
Negro World, 66
neocolonialism, 24, 80
neocolonial organizations, 24
neofascism, 262, 266
neoliberalism, 18–19, 308–9n103
neo-racism, 15, 282n68
neutrality, 37–38. *See also* objectivity
New Mexico, 224
New Racial Domain, 15, 282n68
new racism, 14, 15, 44, 262, 278–81n50, 281n56, 282n68
Newton, Huey P., 5
New Zealand, 4, 8
Niemand, Bernoldus, "Reggae Vibes Is Cool," 168
Nieuhof, Johan, 43
nonracialism, 17, 154. *See also* colorblindness
Norman Wait Harris Foundation, University of Chicago, 88
North American Free Trade Agreement (NAFTA), 18–19
Nova Friburgo, Brazil, 84
Nuttall, Sarah, 125, 149, 307n67; *Entanglement: Literary and Cultural Reflections on Post-Apartheid*, 147–49

Obama, Barack, 35, 210, 261–62, 266
Obasogie, Osagie K., 51

objectivity, 37–38, 104–5, 110
Olguín, B. V., 322n139
Olmecs, 205
Omi, Michael, 12–13
ontological difference, disavowal of, 31
Operation Just Cause, 20
oppression, specificity of, 223
Ortiz, Fernando, 46, 85, 86, 87–89, 90, 123, 124; anti-Blackness in, 98–112; *Contrapunteo cubano del tabaco y del azúcar* (*Cuban Counterpoint: Tobacco and Sugar*), 87, 99, 101, 111–12; epistemology of disavowal and, 111, 126; eugenics and, 100–102; *Hampa afro-cubana: Los negros brujos* (Afro-Cuban Underworld: The Black Sorcerers), 99, 103, 104, 105, 106–8; impact of, 104; Lombroso and, 104; misreadings of, 99–100; "Por la integración cubana de blancos y negros" (For the Cuban Integration of Whites and Blacks, translated as "The Relations between Blacks and Whites in Cuba"), 46, 87, 89, 98–112; racial hierarchy and, 110–11; reception of, 99–100; scientific discourse and, 104–5. *See also* transculturation
the Other, 28; in Chicana literature, 48–49, 221–59 (*see also* the Indigenous Other); denigration of, 69; fear of, 68–69; racialization of, 263; scapegoating of, 63–64
Outlaw, Lucius, 165
outsider status, acknowledgment of, 258
Oventic, Chiapas, 238

Page, Thomas Nelson, 68, 70
palenques, 76, 294n84
Palés Matos, Luis, 190
Palmer, Tyrone, 174
Palthey, George, 89
Pan-Africanism, 120–22
Panama, 6, 8, 25, 45, 48, 122; anti-Blackness in, 45, 190; Blackness in, 45, 58–80, 190; cimarronaje

382 INDEX

Panama (*continued*)
(slave uprisings) in, 76; divide-and-conquer strategy in, 191; erasure of Black people's contribution to, 77; institutionalized racism in, 191–92; Law 6, 66; Law 13, 66; romanticization of race relations in, 19–20; slavery in, 77; United States and, 20, 45, 61, 191, 197–98, 292n17; West Indian immigrants in, 1–2, 48, 58–80, 264; whiteness in, 190; white supremacy in, 45, 190
Panama Canal: completion of, 57–58; construction of, 45, 64–65, 78, 292–93n34; Jamaican immigrants who built, 190; romanticization of construction of, 64–65
Panama Canal Zone, 2, 45, 191, 197–98; Black workforce in, 64–65, 78, 292–93n34; inequality in, 78–79; Jamaican workers in, 65; living conditions in, 78; racism in, 198; segregation in, 78–79, 198; US control of, 61; US imperialism and, 190–91
Panamanian history, national identity and, 203
Panamanian labor movement, 50, 65–66
Panamanian literature, 48; location of Blackness in, 194–99; Negritud and, 190
Panamanian national and racial imaginary, Blackness and, 203
Panamanian nationalism, 190
Panamanian poets of African descent, 194–95
Panamanians of West Indian descent, stripped of citizenship, 66
Panama-Pacific International Exposition, 45, 57–58, 65
Panama provinces, Panama, 69–70
Panama Railroad, 78, 191
pan-indigenism, 246–47
Paredes Arosemena, Ana, 60
Parents Involved in Community Schools v. Seattle School District No.1, 133,

136, 138, 139–40, 144, 147, 153, 154, 170
Partido dos Trabalhadores (Workers' Party), 134
Partido Independiente de Color (PIC), 85
Partido Revolucionario Institucional (PRI), 19, 97
pastiche aesthetics, 227–29, 255–56
pathologizing discourse, 44, 74, 75
Paton, Alan, 47, 109, 161–62, 185; "Black Consciousness," 161–63, 164; *Cry, the Beloved Country*, 162; defense of apartheid, 162–63
patriarchy, 7, 193–94, 222, 227, 249
Penha, Roberto, 18
people with disabilities, affirmative action and, 140
Pérez, Emma, 278n44
Pérez-Torres, Rafael, 100, 126, 225
personhood, Christianity and, 42
Pesquisa Nacional por Amostra de Domicílios (National Household Sample Survey), 143
pessimism, 50. *See also* Afropessimism
Petta, Gianluca, 20
Pezão, Luiz, 18
Philippines, 95
philosophy of race, 47, 165, 166
Pike, Ruth, 76
Pimentel, Rodolfo Pérez, 63
Pinto, L. A. Costa, 115
El Plan Espiritual de Aztlán (The Spiritual Plan of Aztlán), 224–25, 244, 254–55
Plessy, Homer, 139
Plessy v. Ferguson, 139
police, 1–4, 16. *See also* police violence
police violence: anti-Black, 1–4; arguments used to absolve officers, 4–5; in Brazil, 18; protests against, 266; in United States, 3–4, 10, 276n14
political consent, manufacturing of, 262
Polynesians, in Hawai'i, 92
Portugal, 27, 28

INDEX

Portuguese colonizers, 27, 113–14; idealization of, 115–16, 120, 122; resistance to, 122
Posel, Deborah, 158
positional superiority, 73, 74
post-apartheid scholarship, racial classification and, 137–38
postcolonial discourse, 149–50
postcolonial fiction, 192–93
postcolonial theory, 49
postmodern racism, 15, 282n68
postrace, 15, 282n68
post-racial racism, 15, 282n68
post-racialism, 15, 282n68
post-racial liberalism, 15, 282n68
power, 276–77n22; camouflage and, 5; colorblindness as tool of, 262; contingent on disguise for its reproduction, 5; racial, 5, 137–60, 262, 276–77n22; reading, 137–60; reversal of, 169–70. *See also* Black empowerment; colonial power(s); racial power; white power
Pratt, Mary Louis, 100
Primer Congreso del Negro Panameño (First Congress of the Black Panamanian), 79
Pringle, Helen, 253
progress, 12, 119
projection, 38
property, race and, 29
public schools, desegregation and, 136, 138, 139–40
Puerto Rico, Negritud in, 48

queer Chicanas, 230
Quilombo, 144
Quilombo dos Palmares, 122
Quintero, Luis, 206

race, 157–58; class and, 29; disavowal of, 159–60; European invention of, 9, 28–29; genetic understandings of, 124–25; labor and, 29; philosophy of, 47, 165, 166; property and, 29; as relational, 259 (*see also* relationality); sexuality and, 247–48; silencing

of, 46–47, 308–9n103; skin color and, 28–29, 51, 285n116; as social construction, 12–13; structured by racist disavowal, 28; suppressed as category of analysis, 160; understood as metaphor, 10. *See also* racial classification; racism
race after race, 15, 282n68
raceblindness, 51
race consciousness, centrality of, 23
race science, 124–25. *See also* scientific racism
racial amalgamation policies, 92
racial binarism, white attack on, 143–44
racial biologization, 15, 279n50; 282n68
racial break, theory of, 59–60, 280n50
racial capitalism, 29
racial classification, 51, 81–82, 143–47; apartheid and, 155; attacks on, 138, 140, 142–45; post-apartheid scholarship and, 137–38; for the purpose of redress, 143–44
racial degeneration, mestizaje as, 86
racial democracy, 8, 17–18, 295–96n4; invocation of, 67, 68; myth of, 76, 114
racial demographics, shift in, 13
racial dictatorships, 12, 59
racial difference: acknowledgment of portrayed as reactionary, 149–51; transformed into moral and metaphysical difference, 44
racial disavowal: in Chicana literature, 230, 234, 257; contestation of, 18, 207–11; in Freyre, 116; white discourse and, 6, 257; white scholarship and, 23, 160. *See also* colorblindness
racial discourses, literary scholarship and, 278n41
racial discrimination. *See* racism
racial fluidity, 82, 296n6
racial formation, theory of, 12–13
racial harmony, 20, 95
racial hegemony, 15, 280n50, 282n68

384 INDEX

racial hierarchy: Black people and, 248, 259; in Brazil, 82; Cubena and, 214; disavowal of, 144; in Mexico, 95; Ortiz and, 110–11; in Philippines, 95; in Panama, 67; Vasconcelos and, 91, 96–97. *See also* racism; white supremacy
racial hybridity. *See* hybridity
racial identity, social status and, 51
racial inequality, 10, 24–25, 47, 89, 133, 137–38, 152, 157, 182; in Brazil, 24, 47, 133, 284n114; Chicana literature and, 235; as contingent on ongoing exploitation, 156; in Cuba, 25; global, 24; in higher education, 131; in Italy, 264–65; in Mexico, 24–25, 282n90, 285n116; monitoring of, 145; multiracial politics and, 83; in Panama, 25; in the school system, 135; silencing and disavowal of, 154, 157, 159, 160; in South Africa, 24, 47, 159, 284n111; at Stellenbosch, 39; and transformation, 159; in United States, 24, 47
racial liberalism, 45, 59, 192
racialization, 28–29, 44, 63–64, 69, 263
racialized anti-immigrant propaganda, populist deployment of, 63–64, 69
racialized knowledge, vs. white ignorance, 159–60
racialized xenophobia: colorblind language and, 263; as nation-building tool, 263
racial meanings, mutability of, 15
racial mixture: British colonizers and, 93; as evidence of, 145; ideologies of, 8–9, 46, 86. *See also* mestizaje
racial order, shifts in, 14–15
racial positionality, 252, 259
racial power, 276–77n22; colorblindness as tool of, 262; contingent on disguise for its reproduction, 5; reading, 137–60
racial privacy, 176–77
racial production, modes of, 38

racial progress, notions of, 25
racial purity, 92, 126; British colonizers and, 93; eugenics and, 59; ideologies of, 8–9, 46, 59, 86; in Latin America, 92–93
racial quotas: in Brazil, 153; in universities, 143–44. *See also* affirmative action
racial redress and redistribution, demands for, 132–33
racial regimes: historical contingency of, 6; hostility of, 6; modes of operation, 6; mythic discourses and, 6, 9, 34–35; operating in secrecy, 6
racial subordination, intersectionality and, 49, 222, 239
racial systems, Catholic/Portuguese vs. Protestant Anglo, 119
racism, 116, 154–55; academia and, 47; affective responses to, 180–82; benefitting white people, 24; in Brazil, 81–82; camouflage of, 5–6, 14, 15; colorblind, 6, 15, 44 (*see also* colorblind discourse; colorblindness); constancy of, 14–15; cosmetic change of, 5; cultural, 13–14, 15, 44; culturalist, 15, 282n68; definition of, 15–16, 117, 118; depicted as irrational, 210–11; depicted as unconscious, 23; differentialist, 15, 282n68; disavowal of, 2, 5–8, 12, 21–24, 28, 80, 116, 132–33, 147, 153–55, 159–60, 207–11, 266–67; disguise of, 5; displacement of, 117–18; framed as moral dilemma, 182; global dimensions of, 50; as great white unifier, 64; history of, 13; homophobia and, 239–40, 247; hybridity and, 147–49; individualized, 182, 183–84; inequality and, 308–9n103; institutionalized, 47–48, 118–19, 154, 166, 182, 183–84, 186, 191–92; justified by colorblind tools, 37–38; in Latin America, 81–82, 123–24, 190, 198, 207–11 (*see also specific countries*); liberalism

INDEX

385

and, 192; as moral dilemma, 166; new, 12, 14; in Panama Canal Zone, 198; permanence of, 267; proposed post–World War II shift from biological to cultural, 13–14; relational dimensions of, 257–58 (*see also* relationality); reproduction of, 5, 32, 147; reverse, 140–42, 169–70; scholarship on, 12; scientific, 29, 44, 70, 74, 95, 124–25; sex discrimination and, 223; silencing of, 24, 50, 123–24, 147, 170; social science research and, 36–37; structural, 5, 47–48, 117–18, 153, 164, 216, 218–19; today vs. in the past, 12; white antiracism and, 161–86; white investment in, 133; whiteness and, 165; white people's collective responsibility for, 175–76; white scholarship and, 47
racism 2.0, 15, 282n68
racism without races, 15, 282n68
racism without racism, 15, 282n68
racism without racists, 15, 282n68
racist epistemology, 35–36
racist ideologies, Latin American vs. Euro-American, 71–72
racist infrastructure, sustainment of, 48
racist projections, as colorblind tool, 34
racist propaganda, divide-and-conquer strategy and, 64, 69, 191
racist stereotypes. *See* stereotypes, racist
racist violence: in Latin America, 208; mestizaje and, 208; in United States, 207, 209. *See also* police violence
Rama, Ángel, 99–100
Ramaphosa, Cyril, 17, 265
Rampolokeng, Lesego, "Rapmaster," 11
rape, 27, 108, 113–14, 214
Raven-Hart, R., 43
"La Raza" (The Race), 224
"La Raza de Bronce" (The Bronze Race), 224
Reaja ou Será Morto! (React or You Will Die!), 18

Rechy, John, *The Miraculous Day of Amalia Gómez*, 237
Reconciliation, Healing, and Renewal program, 17
Reconstruction, 16, 193
Reconstruction Amendments, 193
Reddy, Chandan, 247–48
redistribution, 129–60, 177–78, 265
redress, 152. *See also* redistribution; reparations
reform: racism infrastructure reproduced through, 15; white supremacy reproduced through, 267
refugees, 20–21, 250, 263–64
Regents of University of California v. Bakke, 135
relationality, 277n34; between Black poverty and white wealth, 171; relational study of racism, 8
reparations, 17, 178–79
reservations, 27, 163, 226, 247
resistance, 7, 9, 15, 50, 76, 258. *See also* Black resistance; Indigenous resistance
"reverse racism," 140–42, 169–70
Rhodes, Cecil John, 130, 184
Rhodes Must Fall Movement, 50, 130
Rhodes University, 130, 131, 305nn2–3
Riebeeck, Johan van, 28
right of conquest, 26
right of discovery, 26
right to self-defense, 142
Rio de Janeiro, Brazil, 18, 85
Ritter, Jorge E., 57, 79
Rivera-Barnes, Beatriz, 99
Roberts, Neil, 76
Robinson, Cedric J., 5–6, 9, 29–30, 49, 99, 286n147
Rodney, Annabelle, 197
Rodney, Walter, 99
Rodrigues, Wesley, 18
Rodriguez, Gregory, 297–99n10
Rodriguez, Richard, *Brown: The Last Discovery of America*, 124
Roman Catholic Church: hypocrisy of, 30, 287n158; slavery and, 287n158

386

Rosaldo, Renato, 89
Rousseau, Jean-Jacques, 257
Rousseff, Dilma, 134

Said, Edward, 10, 73, 74; *Culture and Imperialism*, 152; *Humanism and Democratic Criticism*, 152
Saldaña-Portillo, María Josefina, 91, 228–29
Salvador de Bahia, Brazil, 18
Salvini, Matteo, 80
San, 28
Sánchez, Ricardo, 226
San Cono, Sicily, 20–21
Sandoval, Chela, 223
San Michele di Ganzaria, Sicily, 20
Santa María la Antigua, 76
Santo Domingo, 28, 76
São Paulo, Brazil, 17
Saucier, Khalil, 117–18
scapegoating, of the Other, 63–64
science, 37–38; scientific discourse, 104–5, 110; scientific ethnopornography, 253; scientific knowledge, 38
scientific racism, 29, 44, 70, 74, 95, 124–25
Scott, Darieck, 214
Seattle, Washington, 47, 133, 136, 138, 139–40, 144
Second (Inter)National March Against the Genocide of Black People, 18
Second Sex Conference, 1979, 7, 223
Seekings, Jeremy, 154–56, 308–9n103; *Class, Race, and Inequality in South Africa*, 156–57; "The Continuing Salience of Race: Discrimination and Diversity in South Africa," 154; *Race, Discrimination and Diversity in South Africa*, 154–55
segregation, 29; in Brazil, 114–15; in Latin America, 92–93; in Panama Canal Zone, 78–79, 198; in South Africa, 150, 155, 163; in United States, 91–92
Seigel, Micol, 276n14
self-determination, 109–10, 239
Senghor, Léopold Sédar, 190
separate development policy, 163

settler colonies, 29, 130–33
Severo, Davide, 20
Severo, Giacomo, 20
sex discrimination, racial discrimination and, 223
Sexton, Jared, 30, 86, 225, 256–57
sexuality, 48; race and, 247–48
sexual violence, 113–14
Shabazz, Rashad, 92
Shakur, Assata, 164
Shange, Savannah, 11
Sharpe, Christina, 20, 21, 299n30; "Learning to Live Without Black Familia: Cherríe Moraga's Nationalist Articulations," 248–49
Sharpeville massacre, 17
Shohat, Ella, 288n188
Silver Roll (Panama Canal Zone), 78
silver workers, 295n101
skin color, 28–29, 296n6; hierarchization of, 28–29; race and, 28–29, 51, 285n116
Slasha, Unathi, 129
the slave: as commodity, 34; fungibility of, 34; relegated to the position of the unthought, 225, 256
slave agency, disavowal of, 76
slave insurrections, 28
slaveowners, female, 303n153
slave patrol, 16
slavery, 14, 26–28, 34, 199–200, 207–8; abolition of, 30, 42, 76, 77, 267; afterlife of, 16, 25; Blackness and, 27; Black resistance to, 27; in Brazil, 27, 113–15, 116, 303n153; called "apprenticeship," 40–42; in Cape Colony, 40–42, 43–44; colonialism and, 30, 277n28; concealed through colorblind rhetoric, 32; in Cuba, 108; Enlightenment and, 32–33; euphemisms for, 67; incarceration and, 282n75; Mexican and Mexican American complicity with, 258; in Panama, 77; reinscribed through Thirteenth Amendment, 16; Roman Catholic Church and, 287n158; twenty-first century, 265; underwritten by lies, 33–34; in US

INDEX

387

Constitution, 31–32; violence and, 122–23; white women and, 114
Slavs, 28
Smith, Carlos, 79
social control, through racist stereotypes, 34–35; 288n188
social justice, 178–79
social sciences, 36–37, 132
social status, racial identity and, 51
Sociedad de Estudios Afrocubanos (Society for Afro-Cuban Studies), 102
Soudien, Crain, 152, 159; "The Modern Construction of Race: Whither Social Constructionism," 151; "The Modern Seduction of Race," 152
South Africa, 6, 8, 16, 25, 47, 80, 89, 115, 129–30, 159; affirmative action in, 130–32, 135, 152, 154–55, 158–59; anti-Black violence in, 4; apartheid in, 8, 46, 112–23; 117, 156, 310n8; ban on Black-only organizations, 142; Black liberation movements in, 50, 141, 151–52, 162, 184–85 (see also Black Consciousness Movement); Black middle class in, 149; colonialism in, 156; Constitution of, 26; critical whiteness studies in, 47; ethnic differentiation in, 150; injustice in, 171–72, 178–79; institutionalization of colorblindness in post-apartheid, 142; intraracial inequality in, 149; land redistribution in, 177–78, 265; mestizaje and, 119–23; myth of assailed white race in, 265; neoapartheid in, 17; post-apartheid, 17; racial hybridity in, 84, 147–49; racial inequality in, 24, 47; reparations in, 17; Rhodes Must Fall Movement in, 50; segregation in, 150, 155, 163; separate development policy in, 163; student protests in, 47; unemployment in, 155–56; universities in, 130–33; white dominance in, 149; white minority in, 13; whiteness in,

167–86; white-only paramilitary camps in, 142; white supremacist organizations in, 142–43
South African Defence Force, 142
South African Human Rights Commission, 130–31, 142
South African Journal of Philosophy, 167
South African press, 166
South African Students' Organisation (SASO), 162, 176–77
sovereignty: abolition and, 30; loss of, 256
Soviet Union, 117
Soweto, South Africa, uprising in, 129–30, 202
Spain, 28, 61, 93, 295n101
Spanish colonizers, 38–39, 95, 116; mestizaje and, 92–93, 96
Spillers, Hortense J., 1, 10, 33, 83, 248
Spitale, Antonino, 20
Stam, Robert, 288n188
Stanfield, John H., 305n10
state-sanctioned violence, 4, 15–16, 17; protests against, 266. See also police violence
stereotypes, racist, 38, 75, 172–73, 213–14, 288n188; of laziness, 43–44; as tools of social control, 34–35
Stevens, Paul, 153
Stowe, Harriet Beecher, Uncle Tom's Cabin, 68
Strongman, Roberto, 214
structural racism: attributed to individuals, 117–18; disavowal of, 153; individual racism and, 164, 216, 218–19; institutionalization of, 47–48 (see also institutional racism); reproduction of, 5; silencing of, 5, 47
subalternity, 235
subject, self-regulating, 193, 218–19
subjugation, 199–200
Sullivan, Louis R., 92
Sullivan, Shannon, 171; Good White People: The Problem with Middle-Class White Anti-Racism, 181, 182; Revealing Whiteness: The Unconscious Habits of Racial Privilege, 173, 174

388 INDEX

Sun Dance, 254, 256
suppression, 38
swart gevaar (Black peril) propaganda, 265
sweat lodge, 242–43, 256
symbolic racism, 15, 282n68

Tabensky, Pedro, 173, 184; "The Oppressor's Pathology," 170–71
Taguieff, Pierre-André, 278–81n50, 281n56
Taino people, 38–39, 243
Teixeira, Aloísio, 134
Temer, Michel, 134
temporality, 12
Texas, 224
theory, fiction and, 50
Thirteenth Amendment, 16
Thomas, Clarence, 154
three-fifths clause, 31–32
Tlali, Miriam, *Between Two Worlds*, 26
Torrijos-Carter Treaties, 191
townships, 16, 129
transculturation, 46, 98–112, 125, 126; assimilation and, 89; Blackness and, 101; five phases of transculturation process, 101–2, 105–10; mestizaje and, 108, 111; misinterpretations of, 89; romanticization of, 126; whiteness and, 111. *See also* Ortiz, Fernando
transformation in South Africa, 159
transgender people, 248
Treaty of Guadalupe Hidalgo, 223–24
Trump, Donald, 265, 266; 2016 electoral campaign, 262–63; election of, 261–62; Executive Order 13763, 263
Trump, Ivanka, 262–63
Trump Management Corporation, 263
Truter, J. A., 40–42
truth, 104–5, 110
Truth and Reconciliation Commission (TRC), 17
Ture, Kwame, 141, 164; *Black Power: The Politics of Liberation*, 118
TV Globo, 134
Tzeltal language, 98

Tzotzil language, 98
Tzotzil people, 18–19

unemployment in South Africa, 155–56
UNESCO, 115, 117, 118, 124
unified female subject, 223
United Fruit Company, 78
United Kingdom, anti-Black violence in, 4
United Nations, 89, 90. *See also* United Nations Commission of the Racial Situation in the Union of South Africa (UNCORS)
United Nations Commission of the Racial Situation in the Union of South Africa (UNCORS), 46, 87, 89, 112–23, 115, 122
United States, 6, 8, 16; affirmative action in, 133, 135; anti-Black violence in, 4; Black college enrollment in, 135; Black liberation movements in, 141 (*see also specific movements*); Chicano Movement in, 50; Chicanx oppression in, 223–24; critical whiteness studies in, 47; demographics in, 13; demonization of, 207, 208; desegregation in, 135, 138, 144, 170; eugenics in, 92; higher education in, 132, 135; immigration in, 322n2; Jim Crow in, 8; Latinx college enrollment in, 135; Latinx immigrants in, 297–99n10; Mexico and, 223–24; minstrel shows in, 68; move from biracial to triracial system in, 13; one-race standard in, 92; Panama and, 45, 61; police violence in, 3–4, 10, 276n14; race relations in, 209–10; racial fluidity in, 296n6; racial inequality in, 24, 47; racist violence in, 207, 209; segregation in, 91–92; undocumented immigrants in, 262–63, 322n2; violence against Indigenous people, 27; whiteness on plantations in, 64; youth of color in, 135
universalism, 152

INDEX

Universal Negro Improvement Association (UNIA), 66
Universal Races Congress, 58
universities: in Brazil, 132, 133, 143–44; colonial power and, 132; racial inequality at, 130–32; racial quotas in, 143–44 (*see also* affirmative action); in South Africa, 130–32, 133; in United States, 132, 135; white supremacist violence and, 130–32. *See also* academia; *specific universities*
University Currently Known as Rhodes (UCKAR), 131. *See also* Rhodes University
University of Cape Town, 130, 137, 159, 184
University of Chicago, 9, 88, 90, 92
University of KwaZulu-Natal, 137
University of Oxford, 167
University of São Paulo, 153
University of Torino, 104
University of the Witwatersrand in Johannesburg, "Revisiting Apartheid's Race Categories," 137. *See also* Wits University
"urban renewal," in Rio de Janeiro, Brazil, 85
US Census, multiracial identity in, 83
US Congress, 31
US Constitution, 139; colorblindness and, 31; Reconstruction Amendments, 193; right to self-defense and, 142; slavery in, 31–32; Thirteenth Amendment, 16
US Declaration of Independence, 33
US government, persecution of Black and Indigenous revolutionaries by, 16–17
US imperialism, 45, 244; Alfaro's complicity with, 60–61, 73; in Latin America, 60–61; Panama and, 197–98, 292n17; Panama Canal Zone and, 190–91
US imperialists, 2, 45
US literary imaginaries, Africanist presence in, 227
US multiculturalism, 222, 229. *See also* multiculturalism

US philosophy of race, 165
US presidency, 31
US Supreme Court, 31; desegregation and, 135–36, 138, 139–40, 170; *Parents Involved in Community Schools v. Seattle School District No.1*, 47, 133, 136, 138, 139–40, 144, 147, 153, 154, 170; *Plessy v. Ferguson*, 139; *Regents of University of California v. Bakke*, 135
US terrorism, 263

Van der Riet, Rijno Johannes, 39, 40–44, 76, 266
Vasconcelos, José, 9, 46, 87–88, 90, 119, 120, 122–24, 222; background of, 91; epistemology of disavowal and, 126; impact of, 97–98; investment in "desaparacer el negro" (disappearing the Negro), 91; on resolution of "Indian problem," 95–96. *See also* Vasconcelos, José, works of
Vasconcelos, José, works of: anti-Blackness in, 95, 96; Blackness in, 91, 95, 96; elision of Afro-Mexicans by, 96; epistemology of disavowal and, 95; indigeneity in, 91; misreadings of, 88; "The Race Problem in Latin America," 46, 87, 88, 90–98; racial hierarchy in, 91, 96–97; *La raza cósmica* (*The Cosmic Race*), 58, 70, 87, 90, 91, 224; romanticization of Mexico's Indigenous people by, 93–94; whiteness in, 91, 95; white supremacy in, 95
Venezuela: cimarronaje (slave uprisings) in, 76; European immigration to, 84
Verwoerd, Hendrick, 310n8
Vice, Samantha, 166, 175–76; "How Do I Live in This Strange Place?," 47–48, 165, 166–86, 310n17; *Mail & Guardian* column, 167; silencing of land redistribution question, 177–78; "Why My Opinions on Whiteness Touched a Nerve," 167
Villaverde, Cirilio, 312–13n1

390 INDEX

violence: anti-Black violence, 1–3, 4, 15–16, 17, 30; mystification of, 122–23; police violence, 1–5, 10, 18, 266, 276n14; racist violence, 207, 208, 209 (*see also* police violence); sexual violence, 113–14; slavery and, 122–23; state-sanctioned violence, 4, 15–16, 17, 266 (*see also* police violence); white supremacist violence, 130–32, 148, 240; white violence, 1–3, 130–32, 148, 240, 265. *See also* police violence; racist violence
Vittoria, Stephen, 43
Voltaire (François Marie Arouet), 33
vulgar racism, 14

Wade, Peter, 207
Walcott, Rinaldo, 30, 65, 67
Warren, Calvin, 25; *Ontological Terror*, 30–31
Washington, Booker T., 73
Watson, Sonja Stephenson, 198
Westerman, George, 216
Western modernity, historical temporality in, 12
West Indian immigrants, 50, 58–80; assimilation of, 70–72; demonization of, 1–2, 68–69, 72–73, 75–76, 80, 190–91; in Panama, 48, 58–80, 264; in Panamanian labor movement, 65–66
West Indianness, Blackness and, 193
West Indian Panamanian identity, 190–91
West Indian Panamanians, 79, 191–92; Afro-Panamanians and, 72, 191, 211–19; Cubena and, 191
West Indians, 45; usage of term, 275n1
white abolitionists, 185–86
white academic knowledge, white racial consciousness and, 166
white antiracism: impossibility of, 48; perils of, 47–48, 161–86; white racism and, 161–86. *See also* antiracism
white anxiety: about Black empowerment, 185; Black resistance and, 119; of losing

privileges, 262; in South Africa, 150; used as justification for police violence, 10
white backlash, 261, 266
white dominance, 9; in Brazil, 296n6; liberal humanism and, 308n88; modes of, 5; racial fluidity and, 296n6; silencing of, 308–9n103; in South Africa, 149
white elites, in Latin America, 84–85
white epistemology, 23, 137
white feminism, 7, 49, 222–23
white freedom, black bondage and, 32–33
white gay rights discourses, 247–48
white guilt, 47, 165–66, 180–82
white habits, 47, 165–66
white ignorance, 22; claim of, 7; epistemology of, 22; vs. racialized knowledge, 159–60; as tactic of domination, 23–24; theory of, 22–23; white epistemology and, 23; white performance of, 23–24
white injury, 308n102; Katopodis and, 142; Ortiz and, 102; as transnational discourse, 154; Vice and, 170
white intellectuals, 68; in Brazil, 45–46; in Cuba, 45–46; in Latin America, 45–46, 84–126 (*see also* white elites); in Mexico, 45–46
white knowledge, 23–24, 137, 177. *See also* white epistemology
white Latin Americans: elites, 84–85; intellectuals, 45–46, 84–126; mestizaje and, 90–98; strategy of confining racism to the United States and Europe, 68, 208. *See also specific countries*
white methods, 69; definition of, 36
white mobilization, against desegregation and redistribution, 129–60
white nationalism, 45, 48, 191
whiteness, 308n88; academia and, 47; Christianity and, 42; in Cubena, 213, 218–19; enforced homogenization and, 35; essentialization of, 179; future of

INDEX 391

whiteness thesis, 13; homosexuality and, 259; investment in, 22, 97; in Latin America, 84–85; lies mobilized for protection of, 8; modernization and, 84–85; normativity of, 136; in Panama, 190; philosophical scholarship on, 165–66; preservation of, 120; as a property in itself, 29, 182; racism and, 165; rehabilitating, 166–86; in South Africa, 167–86; technologies of, 35; transculturation, theory of and, 111; on US plantations, 64; in Vasconcelos, 91; white scholarship and, 47

whiteness studies, 170–71

whitening policies, 84–86, 89

white Panamanians, 61–62, 190–91

white people, 4, 5, 7, 32, 114, 140, 207–11; antiracism and, 47–48, 161–86; disavowal of racism and, 2, 5–8, 12, 21–24, 28, 80, 116, 132–33, 147, 153–55, 159–60, 207–11, 266–67; anxieties of, 10, 119, 150, 185, 262; mestizaje and, 90–98. *See also specific countries*; *specific groups*

white power, 32; Black resistance to, 164; preserved through white victimization, 170; reproduction of, 132–33, 135

white privilege, 47, 145, 151, 165–66, 175–76, 179–80, 259; consciousness of, 137; desire to protect, 137; disavowal of, 84, 155, 156; global, 24–25; protection of, 265; in South Africa, 150; white anxiety about losing, 262

white racial consciousness, 24, 166

white savior, 105, 237, 319n69; in *Erased Faces*, 237; white savior narratives, 236; white saviorism, 229

white shame, 47, 165–66, 180–82

white supremacist organizations, in South Africa, 142–43

white supremacist violence, 240; racial hybridity and, 148; universities and, 130–32

white supremacy, 6–7, 30, 38, 39–40, 142, 166, 210–11; across ideological and national boundaries, 8–9; Christianity invoked in support of, 42; discourse of, 44; institutionalization of, 118–19; law as technology of, 30–31; legitimized by academic disciplines, 36–37; mestizaje and, 89–90; in Panama, 45, 190; as political system, 210–11, 213; racial hybridity and, 84; reproduced through reform, 267; in South Africa, 150–51; as totalitarian system, 176; transnational discourse of, 45; universalization of, 67; in Vasconcelos, 95; white investment in, 90; white liberals and, 47, 166; white people's investment in maintaining, 48; white women as central agents of, 7. *See also* white supremacist violence

white terrorists, 263

white USAmericans, 32; mestizaje and, 90–98

white victimization, 170–71, 265

white violence, 1–3, 130–32, 148, 240, 265

white wealth, Black poverty and, 171–72

white women: affirmative action and, 140; as central agents of white supremacy, 7; claim of ignorance and, 7; reproduction of racist and sexist structures of domination by, 7; slavery and, 114, 303n153

Wiegman, Robyn, 170, 234

Wilderson, Frank B., 1–4, 11, 26, 47–48, 79, 118, 152, 161

Williams, Henry Smith, 57–58

Wilson, Carlos Guillermo, 200. *See also* Cubena (Carlos Guillermo Wilson)

Wilson, Darren, 2–3, 10

Wilson, Ricardo, 283n90

Winant, Howard, 12–13, 59–60, 278–81n50

Wirth, Rex, 124–25

Wits University, 137, 167. *See also* University of the Witwatersrand
women of color feminism, 49
World Bank, 24
World War II, 12, 60, 262, 280
Wright, Michelle M., 193
Wright, Richard, 194
Wynter, Sylvia, 42, 99, 116

xenophobia, racialized, 263

Yanga, 206, 283n90
Yanga rebellion, 19
Yaqui, 254, 255, 256

Yaqui Indian War, 254
Yelvington, Kevin, 99
Young, David, 14
youth of color, in United States, 135

Zangwill, Israel, 297–99n10
Zapatista Movement, 18–19, 50, 94, 98, 229, 230–41, 246–47, 318n33
Zizumbo-Colunga, Daniel, 285n116
Zonians, 65, 78
Zuberi, Tukufu, 36, 51, 69, 155
Zuma, Jacob, 309n125
Zumoff, Jacob, 65